The Practical Guide to Making Salami

Stanley Marianski, Adam Marianski

Bookmagic, LLC.
Largo, Florida.

The Practical Guide to Making Salami
Stanley Marianski, Adam Marianski

ISBN: 978-0-9904586-9-2

Bookmagic, LLC.
http://www.bookmagic.com

Printed in the United States of America.

Table of Contents

Introduction

The Practical Guide to Making Salami is a companion book to *The Art of Making Fermented Sausages,* published in 2008. Since then, more information has become available; safety standards have been updated and tightened, new cultures have appeared, and getting supplies and newer equipment online has become more accessible. The most relevant theory has been transferred from *The Art of Making Fermented Sausages.* Still, *The Practical Guide to Making Salami* includes plenty of new materials such as fermented spreadable sausages, acidified sausages, or combining acidulants with natural fermentation. The recipes section has been expanded and includes 264 selected recipes from different countries.

The book consists of two parts:

Part I - provides in-depth insights into crucial topics such as acidity, water activity, humidity, fermentation, working with bacteria, selecting cultures, using predictor tools, and shelf-stability. This section is particularly relevant for those in the meat production industry and is a go-to reference for any questions. It also covers proper manufacturing practices, government standards and regulations, and safety measures.

Part II - covers general aspects of sausage making, such as meat selection, comminuting, mixing and stuffing, smoking, drying and cooking, and storing. Practical advice and tips are provided, and 264 detailed recipes are included so the reader can immediately produce sausages.

As in the previous book, special attention was given to proper manufacturing practices so that meat safety is never jeopardized and the end product is safe even when produced at home. By studying the book, the reader should acquire enough knowledge to design and produce any fermented sausage without searching for a "magical recipe" online. Besides having great satisfaction in creating his recipes, he should be able to distinguish a good recipe from an amateurish one easily. He should be in total command of the process, able to decide the taste, flavor, and aroma of the sausage he wants to make, and most importantly, he will know that his product conforms to the official government requirements and is safe to consume.

Stanley Marianski

June 2024.

Disclaimer

The Practical Guide to Making Salami is not a book for someone who has never made a sausage and wants to learn the skill. Fermented sausages must be produced at low temperatures; otherwise, bacteria growth will escalate. Some hobbyists may perform these operations at higher kitchen temperatures, and under such conditions, this is not the right place to learn the trade.

This does not mean that fermented sausages cannot be made at home. We have been making salami for thousands of years, and the slow-fermented products made the traditional way still taste better than anything made with expensive microprocessor-controlled equipment. To make great fermented sausages, you need to:

> *learn the underlying technology behind fermentation and understand the process. Familiarize yourself with basic microbiology concepts and learn how to control bacteria. Read the chapter on safety hurdles and follow these rules to the letter.*

The use of starter cultures combined with good manufacturing practices will make production of fermented sausages at home safe and enjoyable. The information and recommendations contained in the book are presented in good faith and are believed to be accurate.

Great Sausage Making

PART I

Working with Bacteria Together

Chapter 1

New Concepts of Vital Importance

This important chapter introduces new concepts which are of crucial importance when making fermented sausages. They are seldom mentioned during manufacturing of common sausages however, they need to be understood, otherwise one might get confused and discouraged later seeing unfamiliar words.

Acidity

Bacteria hate acidity and this fact plays an important role in the production and stabilization of fermented sausages. Increasing acidity of meat has become main hurdle against pathogenic bacteria in sausage making, hence understanding of how to use and control it is crucial for producing microbiologically stable products. Acidic and alkaline (or "basic") are two extremes that describe substances, usually liquids or chemicals, just like hot and cold are two extremes that describe temperature.

The pH Scale

The pH scale measures how acidic or alkaline a substance is. The scale ranges from 0 to 14. A pH of 7 corresponds to pure water and is neutral. A pH less than 7 is acidic, and a pH greater than 7 is basic (alkaline).

The pH value of 4.6 is the division between high acid foods and low acid foods.

Given that bacteria hate acidity, acidic foods having pH below 4.6 do not require as severe heat treatment as the ones with pH 4.6 or above. Red meats, seafood, poultry, milk, and all fresh vegetables are low acid foods and need additional attention when being processed. This is why low acid foods cannot be processed at 212° F (100° C) in an open water bath canner, but must be processed at 240-250° F (116-121° C) in a *pressure* canner.

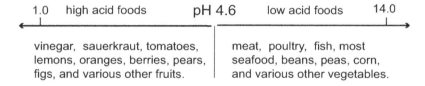

1.0 high acid foods	pH 4.6 low acid foods 14.0
vinegar, sauerkraut, tomatoes, lemons, oranges, berries, pears, figs, and various other fruits.	meat, poultry, fish, most seafood, beans, peas, corn, and various other vegetables.

Fig. 1.1 pH 4.6 separates low acid foods from high acid ones.

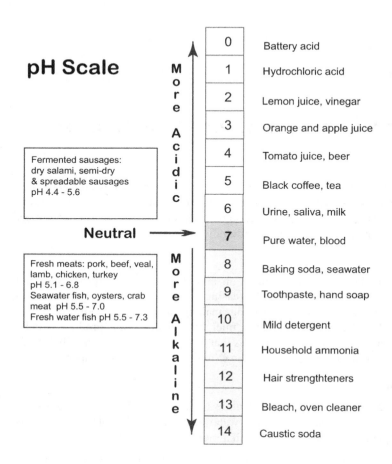

Fig. 1.2 pH scale.

pH is a logarithmic scale; this means that a small difference in pH, a pH of 4 is ten times more acidic than a pH of 5, a pH of 9 is ten times more alkaline (or "basic") than a pH of 8. A substance with a pH 1.0 is 1000 times more acidic than a substance with a pH 4.0. If freshly minced meat has an initial pH of 5.7 and the resulting semi-dry sausage displays a pH of 4.7, the finished sausage is 10 times more acidic, and its taste is tangy/sourly.

The pH, a measure of acidity, plays a very important role in the manufacture of dry-cured, naturally fermented, or acidified products as it affects processes such as food safety, color, sliceability, drying, and even flavor. The lower the pH value, the more acidic the food, and vice versa. Acidity may be natural, as in most fruits, for example, lemon, or added, as in pickled food. Bacteria will not grow when the pH is below the minimum or above the maximum limit for a particular bacteria strain. All bacteria have their own preferred acidity level for growth, generally around neutral pH (7.0). As the pH of foods can be adjusted, this procedure becomes a potent weapon for the control of bacteria. The thermal resistance of microorganisms decreases as the pH of their medium is lowered.

pH of foods varies from pH 2.0 to pH 8.0 and their microbiological safety is controlled by the fact that most bacteria, will not grow below pH 4.6.

Fresh Meats and Finished Sausages	
Name	pH
Raw meat	5.6 - 6.8
Pork, beef, sheep, horse, wild game	5.6 - 5.9
Lamb, goat	6.0 - 6.8
Poultry	5.6 - 6.4
Fish	6.2
Dry Salami	5.3 - 5.6
Semi-Dry Sausages	4.6 - 5.3

Adjusting pH

Adding alkaline substances to acidic ones would decrease acidity as pH will shift lower; for example, adding water (pH 7.0) to fresh meat (pH 5.7) will shift pH to 5.8 - 6.0, depending on the amount added. However, this should be avoided as it creates favorable conditions for microorganisms to grow. Meat that we buy in a supermarket has already been "aged" (rested) in coolers from hours to days, depending on the animal, and its pH is usually around pH 5.6 - pH 5.8. at least for pork and beef. Combining pork and beef or even selecting different cuts from the same animal will produce a sausage mass of a certain pH, and the pH meat tester will display the result. As most official safety standards are based on increasing acidity to pH 5.3 and lower, we need to introduce procedures that will do just that.

The acidity in meat can be *increased* by:

• Fermenting meat naturally or with starter cultures. Generally, more sugar is added to meat as food for lactic acid bacteria so they can produce more acid.

• Adding acidulants such as Gdl (glucono-delta-lactone) or citric acid. Acidulants, upon contact with moisture in the meat, start the production of acid through a chemical reaction.

• Adding any substance that is more acidic than the meat, for example, lemon juice, vinegar, soy sauce, or dry wine.

pH and Meat

Bacteria prefer meats with a pH of 6.0 - 7.0, which falls near the neutral point of the pH scale. *As the meat's acidity increases, the growth of bacteria becomes severely restricted.* A pH drop is accomplished by lactic acid bacteria, which consume sugar and increase the meat's acidity by producing lactic acid. Foods with a low pH value (high acidity) develop resistance against microbiological spoilage. Pickles, sauerkraut, eggs, pig feet, and anything submerged in vinegar will have a long shelf life. Even ordinary meat jelly (head cheese) will last longer if some vinegar is added, and this type of head cheese is known as "souse." When buying meat marinade, look at the list of ingredients. The list invariably includes items like vinegar, dry wine, soy sauce, lemon juice, and other ingredients that are acidic or salty by nature. Although those ingredients are added mainly to tenderize meat by unwinding the protein structure, they also inhibit the growth of bacteria. A sausage can be made safe by acidity alone if its pH is 4.6 or lower, but its flavor will suffer and be very sour. To avoid this, sausages may be fermented to a higher pH but must be dried or cooked for safety reasons.

pH meter

The Hanna Instruments HI 99163 Meat pH Meter is simple to use with only two buttons. The replaceable penetration blade allows the user to measure not only the surface, but also the internal pH of the meat. The unit is very accurate and the reading is obtained within seconds.

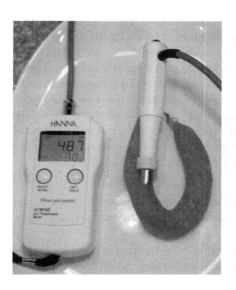 

Photo 1.1 and **Photo 1.2** HI 99163 Portable Meat pH Meter.

Photo and information courtesy Hanna Instruments, http://www.hannainst.com

pH Test Strips

Another simpler method for measuring pH is to use disposable testing strips made by Micro Essential Laboratory, Inc., which are available online.

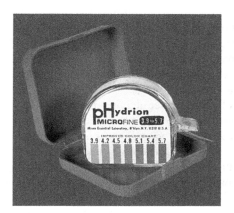

Photo 1.3 pH testing strips
pH range: 3.9 - 5.7.

Photo 1.4 pH testing strips
pH range: 4.9 - 6.9.

These two strips will cover the entire range of pH values of fresh materials (meats and fats) and finished sausages. Mix 1 part finely chopped meat and 2 parts distilled water, tear off a strip of pH paper, dip into the test solution, and match immediately to the color chart. No technical training is necessary. The results may be less accurate than those obtained with a pH meter, but the strips are inexpensive. Pet stores that sell aquarium fish carry such strips, too.

Aw (Water Activity)

All microorganisms need water to live. When enough water is removed, they stop growing and die. This statement explains the science of drying foods.

Water exists in meat as:

- Bound (restricted or immobilized water) - structurally associated with meat proteins, membranes, and connective tissues. This water (3-5% of the total) can only be removed by high heat and *is not available* for microbial activities.
- Free or bulk water - held only by weak forces such as capillary action. This free water *is available* for microorganisms for growth.

Water activity (Aw) indicates how tightly water is "bound" inside a product. It does not say how much water is there, but how much water is available to support the growth of bacteria, yeasts, or molds. Below certain Aw levels, microbes cannot grow. United States Department of Agriculture guidelines state that: *"A potentially hazardous food does not include . . . a food with a water activity value of 0.85 or less."*

The amount of water available in a food depends on the total concentration of all dissolved substances in the product because they bind water. Thus, if ingredients such as salt, sugar, starch, flour, soy protein, non-fat dry milk are added to food, *they compete with the bacteria for available water.*

Lower water activity inhibits the growth of spoilage and pathogenic bacteria, which is essential during the first production phase. The amount of free water and water activity can be lowered by changing the proportion of lean meat (75% of water) to fat (15% of water). The addition of more fat delivers less water to the sausage, which lowers Aw. As the sausage goes through different processing stages, it will keep on losing moisture, so its Aw will also be lower.

A simple scale is used to classify foods by their water activity, and it starts at 0 (bone dry) and ends at 1 (pure water). Freshly minced meat has a very high water activity level of around 0.99, meaning that 99% of all water in meat is unbound and available since it is a breeding ground for bacteria. A meat product having Aw 0.85 indicates that only 85% of water is available for bacteria and is usually considered shelf stable as it would not support the growth of pathogenic microorganisms.

Adding salt w/wo sugar to minced meat immediately "binds" some of this free water and lowers the amount of available water to bacteria, which inhibits their growth. Depending on the amount, adding salt to meat drops this value immediately to 0.96-0.97. Sugar preserves foods such as candies and jellies by drawing moisture out from the food's cells, leaving less moisture for bacteria to function and grow. By binding this moisture, sugar also lowers Aw water activity. However, sugar is added to meat in smaller amounts, so it is less effective than salt.

Water activity (Aw) of some foods	
Pure water	1.00
Fresh meat	0.95 - 1.00
Cured meat	0.87 - 0.95
Fresh fish	0.99
Bread	0.97
Aged cheese	0.85
Jams & jellies	0.80
Plum pudding	0.80
Dried fruits	0.60
Biscuits	0.30
Milk powder	0.20
Instant coffee	0.20
Bone dry	0.00
Sugar	0.10

From www.clemson.edu: Water activity is a good predictor of food safety and how long a food product will last on the shelf. Foods with higher moisture content might be expected to have higher water activity than dry foods, but the expectation is not necessarily correct. Products with the same water content may have very different water activities. For example, salami and cooked beef have similar total moisture (approximately 60%). However, salami's water activity is 0.82, and cooked beef is about 0.91. This implies that in salami, only 82% of water is available to bacteria, in contrast to 91% in cooked beef. Therefore, salami can be kept for weeks at room temperature, but cooked beef will spoil after a few days.

Well, this is where the concept of water activity becomes useful. Although adding salt to meat does not force water to evaporate, it does something similar: it immobilizes free water and prevents bacteria from using it. The same happens when we freeze meat, though, we never think of it. Frozen water takes the shape of solid ice crystals and is no longer free. Adding more salt immobilizes more water; however, adding too much salt will make the product unpalatable and may inhibit the growth of lactic acid bacteria. The table shows that except *Staphylococcus aureus*, the growth of other microorganisms is severely restricted below Aw 0.92. This is why drying is such an effective method of preventing bacteria growth and preserving foods in general.

Microorganisms That Grow at or above this Aw	
Molds	0.80
Staphylococcus aureus	**0.85**
Yeasts	0.85
Listeria	0.92
Salmonella	0.91
Cl. perfringens	0.95
Cl.botulinum	0.91
E.coli	0.95
Campylobacter	0.98

Lowering Aw

Fresh blocks of meat contain 75-80% moisture, and its water activity is Aw 0.99, out of a maximum of Aw 1.00 for pure water. Adding salt to ground meat lowers Aw immediately; the amount of drop depends on the salt level. Adding 2.5 - 3% salt to the fresh sausage mixture lowers the initial Aw 0.99 to 0.96 - 0.95, depending on the fat content in the formulation, given that fat contains less moisture than lean. During the following processing steps (fermentation, drying, cooking, drying), there will be an additional Aw drop due to the removal of water.

Sausages can lose 10-40% of moisture during smoking, depending on whether they are hot or cold smoked. Removing (lowering Aw) inhibits or delays the growth of undesired spoilage and dangerous bacteria, which is very important in the initial stage of processing when lactic acid bacteria are still in the lag phase and do not produce acidity.

Aw of some meat products	Aw
Fresh unprocessed meat	0.99
Beef, raw	0.99
Fish, fresh	0.99
Minced pork/beef, 2.5-3%	0.96-0.95
Fresh sausage	0.98
Liverwurst	0.96
Cooked sausages	0.97-0.96
Salami dry sausage	≤ 0.89
Salami dry - Hungarian	0.84

Fast Aw Drop

If dropping Aw is an effective safety hurdle, why not drop it as fast as possible? Well, we could add more substances that will bind water, such as non-fat milk powder, starch, flower, or gums (hydrocolloids). However, that will prevent lactic acid and flavor-forming bacteria from working, given that they need some moisture to stay alive. We won't be able to make a naturally fermented sausage.

Relationship between Water Content and Water Activity

Water content on its own is not enough information to determine food safety or predict product shelf life. The relationship between water content and water activity is complex and related to the relative humidity of the food and its water content. This relationship must be determined for each specific food item.

Generally, foods with higher water content will have a higher water activity than dry foods. Most food has a water activity greater than 0.95 which supports the growth of bacteria, yeast and mold.

Meat Product	Aw	% Water
Beef, raw	0.99	73
Beef, cooked	0.91	62
Chicken, raw	0.99	69
Chicken, cooked	0.91	62
Salami, beef	0.82	60
Beef jerky	<0.80	23

Estimating Aw

All factors such as pH, Aw, water moisture and weight loss decrease in time, only salt content increases proportionally as there is less moisture, but it must be noted that the amount of salt is the same as the amount that was introduced during at the beginning of the process.

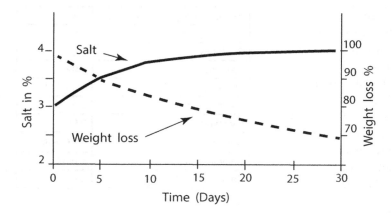

Fig. 1.3 Relationship between salt and loss of weight. Loss of moisture and Aw drop curves will look similar to the loss of weight curve.

Aw cannot be estimated accurately without a meter; it would be a guessing game. For example, the initial Aw of fresh pork or beef may be Aw 0.99, but the moment salt is added, the Aw can drop to 0.97 or 0.96. Generally, Aw follows the moisture curve, but the relationship is not linear. Although both water activity and moisture drop lower in time, they take different paths.

Generally, it is accepted that salami reaches Aw of 0,89 when it loses around 30% of its original weight. To be shelf-stable by drying alone its Aw should drop to 0.85 which corresponds to about 40-45% loss of its original weight. In semi-dry sausages decreasing Aw plays secondary role given that the safety of the sausage is obtained by a low pH which is followed by additional drying or cooking.

Water Activity Meter

Measuring water activity involves more than reading pH drops and requires more expensive equipment. However, it is a must-have for commercial producers, whom meat inspectors continuously monitor. Decagon Devices Inc., presently known as Meter Group, produces Aqualab instruments, which are the fastest, most precise water activity meters available.

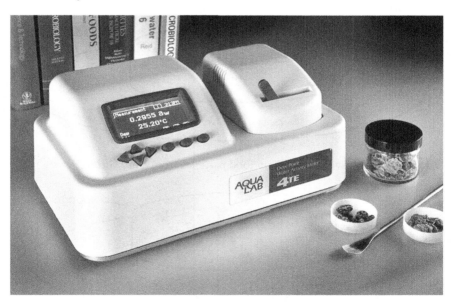

Photo 1.5 AquaLab 4TE benchtop water activity meter is a lab-grade, bench-top instrument that has an accuracy of ±0.003 aw.

Photo courtesy: Meter Group, Pullman, WA, USA.

Given that all professional literature and the food industry use Aw for manufacturing dry foods, sausages, and jerky, Aw is continuously mentioned throughout this book, and understanding it is essential.

It is unlikely that a hobbyist would use an Aw meter, but he will, instead, weigh the sausage to see how much it has lost of its original weight. This simple method has been used for centuries. When the price of the testers drops, they will become as popular as pH testers.

Drying Food

In order to remain alive, the microorganisms need nutrients and moisture. When water is eliminated, bacteria cannot eat, so they will not grow and eventually die. This is the theory of preserving food by drying.

How do Bacteria Eat?

They do not have mouths, so they have to absorb food differently. They have to dissolve food in water first before the food can be absorbed. Bacteria are like a sponge; they absorb food through the wall, *but the food must be in the form of a solution.* Imagine some sugar, flour, or bread crumbs spilled on the table. Place a dry sponge on top of them, and you will see that the sponge will not pick up any of the ingredients. Pour some water over the ingredients and repeat the sponge procedure. The sponge will absorb the solution without any difficulty.

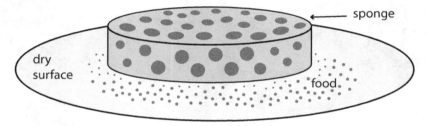

Fig. 1.4 Sponge will not pick up food particles from a dry surface.

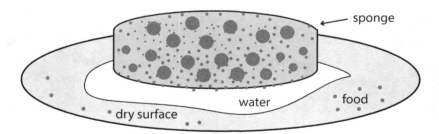

Fig. 1.5 Sponge easily picks up food particles that dissolved in water.

Drying is affected by:

• Humidity - higher humidity, slower drying.
• Temperature - higher temperature, faster drying.
• Air flow - faster air flow, faster drying.

Drying Sausages

Drying starts from the moment a sausage is stuffed in a permeable casing and continues through fermentation, smoking, baking, ripening, drying, and storage until the sausage is consumed. Removing water content by drying a sausage is a slow process, depending on diameter; slow-fermented sausages require three months or more to be declared safe for consumption. As the process proceeds, water starts to evaporate, making meat stronger against spoilage and pathogenic bacteria. There eventually comes a point when there are no bacteria present, and the meat is microbiologically stable, provided it is stored at low temperatures and at low humidity levels. If the temperature and humidity go up, new bacteria will establish a colony on the surface, and mold may appear.

Sausages dry from inside out. For a correct drying process, there must be a balance between moisture diffusion towards the surface and moisture evaporation from the surface. If diffusion is faster than evaporation, moisture will accumulate on the surface of the sausage, causing it to be slimy. Yeasts and molds will soon follow. If evaporation is faster than diffusion, the outside surface area of the sausage will dry out and harden and will act as a barrier to subsequent moisture removal. As a result, moisture will be trapped inside of the sausage, creating favorable conditions for the growth of spoilage and pathogenic bacteria.

Controlled drying is a crucial procedure when making dry-cured or slow-fermented sausages, as their safety depends on the removal of moisture. It would be nice to dry a sausage quickly and be done without worrying about pH, weight loss, and other details. Well, there are basically two reasons:

1. The outside layer of the sausage must not be hardened as it may prevent the removal of the remaining moisture. It may inhibit action of the curing bacteria and the outside layer of the sausage may develop a gray ring that may be visible when slicing the sausage.

2. Bacteria naturally found in meat and/or introduced starter cultures need moisture to grow. They have to go through the so-called "lag phase" first. Only then can they metabolize sugar and produce lactic acid. Once a desired pH drop is reached, more moisture can be removed. For example, bacteria responsible for curing and flavor development are concentrated close to the surface where they easily find oxygen. They are sensitive to changing water activity levels so very fast drying can prematurely dry out the surface of the sausage.

The moisture removed from the surface is replaced by the moisture coming from the inside of the sausage.

Fig. 1.6 Balanced moisture removal: *diffusion rate = evaporation rate*

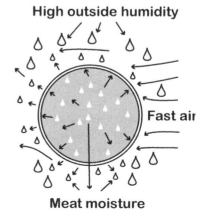

High outside humidity

Fast air

Meat moisture

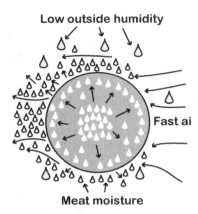

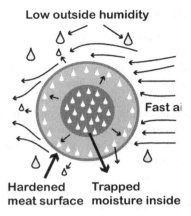

Fig. 1.7 Fast moisture removal. The moisture traveling towards the surface cannot keep up with the moisture escaping the surface. The sausage becomes dry on the outside and moist inside.

Fig. 1.8 Trapped moisture - the effect of fast drying. The surface is dry, and there is a visible grayish ring on a sliced sausage. The inside moisture may be permanently trapped, and bacteria may spoil the sausage.

Fig. 1.9 Finely minced sausage. In a fine grind, the particles are very small, and moisture has to overcome more surface area on its way to the surface. Its path is longer. The airspeed can be slower. This problem is magnified in large-diameter sausages, which should be dried at a slower pace.

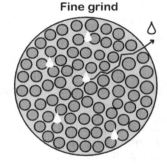

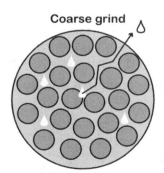

Fig. 1.10 Coarse minced sausage. In coarse ground meat, the moisture has more free room and a shorter distance to the surface.

A medium-diameter sausage might experience 1.0-1.5% weight loss per day when in a fermenting room. The same sausage should lose about 0.5-0.7% of its weight per day when in a drying chamber.

There is more moisture to remove from a leaner sausage given that meat contains about 75% of water and fat only ~15%. Thus a fatty sausage requires less time to dry out.

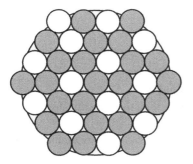

Fig. 1.11 Meat and fat particles of the same size are cut through the same grinder plate.

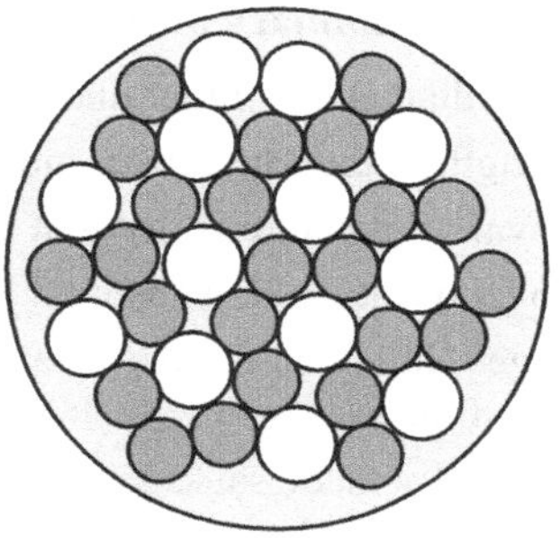

Fig. 1.12 Sausage lost 30% of its original weight. Meat particles lose most of the water, and fat loses less. This is why the fat stands out more.

For the perfect drying, the humidity of the drying room should be 5% lower than the water activity (Aw) within the sausage. This requires water activity measurements and computer operated drying chambers where parameters such as temperature, humidity and air speed are continuously monitored and readjusted. This relationship remains constant and every time the water level drops, the humidity is lowered accordingly.

Air Speed

A continuous movement of air is needed to remove moisture from the sausage. Air speed is a factor that helps remove moisture and stale air, and of course, it influences drying. It can be compared to the air-blower that blows away leaves on the street; however, in our case, it blows the moisture away from the surface of the sausage. Sausages will dry faster at higher temperatures; however, blowing air will remove moisture at very low temperatures, too. The best examples are Eskimos, who dry fish or seal meat in the Arctic, and Norwegians, who dry cod at freezing temperatures. People in northern countries hang laundry outside in winter, and it will dry, developing a pleasant smell and aroma.

The speed of drying sausages does not remain constant, but changes throughout the process: it is fastest during the beginning of fermentation, then it slows down to a trickle. The surface of the freshly stuffed sausage contains a lot of moisture which must be continuously removed otherwise slime and mold will appear.

If the sausages are soaking wet during fermentation, the humidity should be lowered. At the beginning of fermentation, the fastest air speed is applied at about 0.8 - 1.0 m/sec. The speed of 3.6 km/h (2.2 mile/hour) corresponds to the speed of 1 meter/second which is basically a walking speed. Ideally, the amount of removed moisture should equal the amount of moisture moving to the surface.

Drying Sausages - Summary of Important Issues

- Sausage diameter - bigger diameter, slower drying.
- The length of the sausage has no influence on drying time.
- Removal of moisture is faster at higher temperature.
- Removal of moisture is faster at lower humidity.
- Sausages should be dried at a rate not higher than the moisture-losing ability of the sausage.
- Traditionally made sausages have a pH of about 5.3 and Aw of about 0.88 at the end of the drying process.
- Overloading the drying chamber can impede the air movement.
- Air speed - higher air speed, faster drying. The average air speed varies between 0.5 and 0.1 m/sec.
- Casing type (pore size) - bigger pores, faster drying.
- Amount of fat - more fat in sausage, faster drying.
- Meat particle size - bigger size, faster drying.
- In general, when pH drops rapidly the sausage dries faster.
- Molds will develop more quickly if there is no air draft at all.
- If the outside of the sausage becomes greasy, it should be wiped off with a warm cloth otherwise it may inhibit drying.
- The speed of 3.6 km/h (2.2 mile/hour) corresponds to the speed of 1 meter/second which is basically a walking speed. The air speed of 0.5 m/sec (1.8 miles/per hour) corresponds to a slow walk.
- Often air speed is given in air changes per minute. Typical values for *fermentation* rooms are 4-6 air changes per minute, and less than two air changes per minute for *drying* chambers.
- Depending on the process, diameter of a casing and the content of fat, fermented sausages lose from 5-40% of their original weight.
- Once the meat is stuffed into the casings the sausage will start drying regardless of what processing steps will follow.
- Case hardening. In slow-fermented sausages, the fermentation is performed at high humidity (92-95%) to prevent case hardening. If the humidity were low and the air speed fast, the moisture would evaporate from the surface so fast that the moisture from the inside of the sausage would not make it to the surface in time. The surface of the casing will harden, creating a barrier to the subsequent drying process. The sausage may never dry out, and the product will spoil. As the sausage enters the drying stage, less moisture remains inside, and the humidity and air speed are lowered. After about a week, the airspeed is only about 0.5 m/sec, and after another week, it drops to 0.1 m/sec (4 inches/sec). It will stay below this value for the duration of the drying.

Humidity Control

Humidity, or better said, "relative humidity," defines how much water is present in the air at a particular temperature. The air always contains some water vapor: we may not see it, but it is there, and it has a certain mass. The higher the temperature, the more water can be held by air and vice versa. Humidity changes throughout the day and is dependent upon temperature. When the temperature goes up, the humidity goes down, and vice versa. This means that there is higher humidity in the air at night when temperatures are lower. When the clouds come in and it starts to drizzle, the humidity goes up immediately. There is more humidity in areas containing lakes, rivers, or being close to the seashore than in arid areas such as deserts or mountains with less water and subsequently less humidity.

As seen on the graph, there was a steep rise in humidity levels (60% → 90%) when the temperature dropped from 70° F/21° C (6 PM) to 62° F/17° C (11 PM). This high humidity continued until 7 AM. There was a big drop in humidity levels from 90% → 36%, when the temperature increased from 60° F/16° C at 7 AM to 77° F/25° C at 12 PM-noon. At 7 AM there was so much humidity that there was a fog in the area which completely disappeared one hour later.

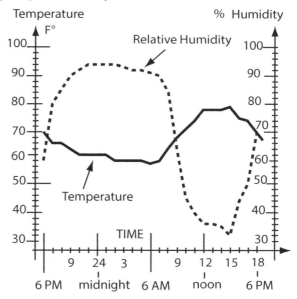

Fig. 1.13 Humidity and temperature changes recorded in Florida on November 10/11, 2006.

Photo 1.6 - 7 AM, fog, 90% humidity.

Photo 1.7 - 8 AM, clear, 84% humidity.

This humidity behavior can be used to our advantage when a large drying chamber or smokehouse is outside. The amount of moisture in the air is fixed for at least some time, but raising the temperature lowers the relative humidity. As you cannot change the physical location of the drying chamber, you have to learn how to improvise a little:

- There are portable devices (humidifiers and dehumidifiers) that can be placed inside the drying chamber. They are inexpensive and have a thermostat that allows automatic humidity control.
- In smaller chambers, such as an old refrigerator box, the most straightforward humidifier is a bowl filled with water that is placed inside. The larger the surface area of the dish, the more evaporation will take place.
- Sausages can be sprayed or immersed briefly in water to increase humidity.
- Humidity testers are inexpensive, and there is no excuse for not having one.
- In home freezer or refrigerator, humidity varies between 40-50%.

For controlled drying humidity should lag the sausage Aw from 0.2 to 0.5 units, 0.3 being the average. *Example:* sausage Aw 0.95, humidity 92%, Sausage Aw 0.92, humidity 89%. sausage Aw 0.89, humidity 0.86.

If a cold sausage is taken out from the refrigerator and placed in a warmer area, there will be a condensation water on its surface. This phenomenon is known as "the dew point" and dew point tables are available online. The condensation can be corrected by:

- Lowering the temperature in the room *OR*
- Reducing the humidity in the room and not changing the temperature.

Ripening - Maturing - Aging - Drying

Different sources use these terms to describe a part of the "drying" stage, which can last from days to many months. During this period, the sausage loses moisture and undergoes many changes due to ongoing reactions with protein and fats. Those periods follow fermentation and are called ripening, maturing, or aging, but they are just a part of the drying process. During those processes, many natural reactions occur inside the sausage, determining its color, texture, taste, flavor, and aroma.

Room Temperature

It is often mentioned that a sausage should rest or be stored at "room temperature." This term refers to European room temperatures, which in most countries do not exceed 64° F (18° C) for most of the year. It is hard to find an air conditioning unit in North European countries. On the other hand, in Southern USA, room temperature implies a temperature of ~ 75° F (24° C) with air conditioning on, which is too hot for meat storing.

Chapter 2

The Magic Behind Fermented Sausages - *It's All About Bacteria*

Understanding Bacteria

Learn how to work with and how to control bacteria. After all, they, not you, make the sausage; you are just the driver. Making fermented sausages combines the art of the sausage maker and unseen magic performed by bacteria. The friendly bacteria work with a sausage maker, but the dangerous ones are trying to wreak havoc. Using his knowledge, the sausage maker monitors temperature and humidity, allowing him to control reactions inside the sausage. This game is played for a while, and a high-quality product is created at the end.

We have been making dry sausages for centuries, but only recently we have come to understand the inner Whys and Hows of the fermentation process. Let's make something clear: it is impossible to eliminate bacteria, life on the planet will come to a halt. Although they are everywhere: on the floor, on walls, in the air, on our hands, there is no reason to be afraid since, once we understand their behavior, we can create conditions that will:

- Inhibit spoilage and dangerous bacteria.
- Take a good care of friendly bacteria so they can prosper and work for us.

Microorganisms

All microorganisms can be divided into the following groups:

- Bacteria
- Yeasts
- Molds

They all share one thing in common: they want to live and given the proper conditions they will start multiplying. They don't grow bigger, they just divide and divide until there is nothing for them to eat, or until conditions become so unfavorable that they stop multiplying and die.

Fig. 2.1 Bacterial growth. A bacterial cell enlarges in size, then a wall separates the cell into two new cells exactly alike.

All bacteria need moisture, nutrients, and warm temperatures to grow. Keeping them at low temperatures does not kill them but slows them from multiplying. Once when the conditions are favorable again, they awaken and start growing again. Most bacteria need oxygen (aerobic), others thrive without it (anaerobic).

Meat contains about 75% of water and this moisture is the main reason it spoils. It is a community pool and if the weather is warm, all bacteria types go swimming. Given favorable conditions they can double up in numbers every 20 minutes. Their number will also grow in a refrigerator, albeit at a reduced pace, but they can double up in 12 hours. Only deep freezing stops bacteria from contaminating meat, however, even then they don't die, but only go to sleep. With the raise of temperature the conditions for bacteria growth become favorable again and they wake up and grow again. At room temperatures bacteria will grow anywhere they can access nutrients and water.

Restricting Bacteria Growth

Bacteria are walking their way into the meat from the outside. Most of them need oxygen to survive and there is a lot of air between particles of minced meat. Meat that is finely comminuted is at higher risk due to its large surface area, which is why ground meat has the shortest life. We all know meat at room temperature will spoil, so we store it in a refrigerator/freezer. Yet fermented dry or air dried sausages are made of raw meat and are neither cooked nor refrigerated. What makes them safe? Well, it is our job to provide safety by restricting growth of undesirable bacteria.

Bacteria growth can be restricted by:

- Limiting exposure time.
- Working at low temperature.
- Increasing acidity.
- Removing moisture.
- Increasing amount of salt.

Bacteria Growth in Time

Under the correct conditions, bacteria reproduce rapidly, and populations can grow very large. *Temperature and exposure time are the factors that affect bacterial growth the most.* Looking at the table it becomes very clear what happens to a piece of meat left on the kitchen table on a beautiful and hot summer day.

Bacteria Growth With Temperature

Most of them love temperatures that revolve around the temperature of our body, 98.6° F (37° C). Holding products at temperatures higher than 130° F (54° C) restricts their growth. Increasing temperatures over 140° F (60° C) will start killing them. All bacteria hate cold, and around 32° F (0° C), they become lethargic and will become dormant when the temperature drops lower.

It can be seen on the right that at 32° F (0° C) bacteria need as much as 38 hours to divide in two. That also means that if a piece of meat had a certain amount of bacteria on its surface, after 38 hours of lying in a refrigerator the amount of bacteria would double. If we move this meat from the refrigerator to a room having a temperature of 80° F (26.5° C), the bacteria will divide every hour (12 times faster). They will divide at 90° F (32° C) every 30 minutes.

Number of bacteria	Elapsed time
10	0
20	20 minutes
40	40 minutes
80	1 hour
160	1 hour 20 min
320	1 hour 40 min
640	2 hours
1280	2 hours 20 min
2560	2 hours 40 min
5120	3 hours
10,240	3 hours 20 min
20,480	3 hours 40 min
40,960	4 hours
81,920	4 hours 20 min
163,840	4 hours 40 min
327,680	5 hours
655,360	5 hours 20 min
1,310,720	5 hours 40 min
2,621,440	6 hours

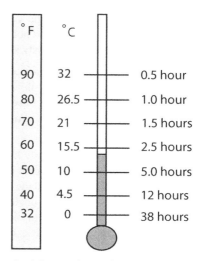

Fig. 2.2 Bacteria growth with temperature.

Data courtesy College of Agriculture, Auburn University, Alabama.

The above drawing (Fig. 2.2) shows the time required for one bacteria cell to become two at different storage temperatures. Once the temperature reaches 50° F (10° C), bacteria will double up twice as fast every time we raise the temperature by about 10° F.

From the above examples, we can draw a logical conclusion: if we want to process meats, we should perform these tasks at temperatures not higher than 50° F (10° C). And those are the temperatures present in meat processing plants. You might say that lowering the room's temperature will still be better. Of course it will, but people working in such conditions for 8 hours daily will find it very uncomfortable. Keep in mind that meat is processed at 50° F (10° C) for a short time and then goes back into a cooler. Bacteria growth data in the above tables hold for optimal conditions: no salt or nitrite and ample moisture supply. Once we introduce unfavorable conditions to bacteria (salt, nitrite, acidity), their growth will be inhibited.

Below 45° F (7° C), bacteria grow slowly, and at temperatures above 140° F (60° C), they start to die. In the so-called "danger zone" between 40 ° F (4-60° C), bacteria grow very well. For instance, the infamous *E. coli* grows best at 98° F (37° C) and toxin producing *Staphylococcus aureus* at 86-98° F (30-37° C).

Bacteria Types

Bacteria which are of interest to us can be classified as:
- Food spoilage bacteria.
- Dangerous (pathogenic) bacteria.
- Beneficial bacteria - lactic acid producers, color and flavor forming.

How Do Bacteria Spoil Food?

Spoilage bacteria are abundant everywhere, and like all living creatures, they must eat. They break down meat proteins and fats, deteriorating food and causing unpleasant odors, tastes, and textures. They excrete the waste, which accounts for the unpleasant smell. Fruits and vegetables get mushy or slimy, and meat develops a bad odor. Most people would not eat spoiled food; however, even if they did, they probably would not get seriously sick.

Bacteria such as *Pseudomonas spp.* or *Brochotrix thermosphacta* cause slime, discoloration, and odors but do not produce toxins. Different spoilage bacteria reproduce at specific temperatures. Some can grow at low temperatures in the refrigerator or freezer. Others grow well at room temperature and in the "Danger Zone" 40-140° F (4-60° C).

Most spoilage bacteria are easily killed when exposed to boiling water 212° F (100° C), however, their growth in meat is easily prevented by adding 2-3% of salt. Under the favorable conditions, spoilage bacteria reproduce rapidly and their populations can grow very large. Spoilage bacteria love moisture and stop growing at Aw < 0.97. They also need oxygen. That implies that they first attack the meat's surface, placing minced meat at the greatest risk. If left at warm temperature, a fully cooked piece of meat will spoil again, as new bacteria will jump on its surface and start growing.

Pathogenic Bacteria

It is commonly believed that the presence of bacteria creates immense danger to us, however, only a small percentage of bacteria can do that. Most of us with a healthy immune system can fight them off. Pathogenic bacteria cause illness. They grow rapidly in the "Danger Zone" and do not generally affect food taste, smell, or appearance. Food left too long at warm temperatures could be dangerous to eat, but smell and look just fine. *Clostridium botulinum, Bacillus cereus* or *Staphylococcus aureus* can produce and infect food with toxin which are not easily destroyed by cooking. Others like *Salmonella* or *Escherichia coli* will find the way with infected meat into our intestines and pose a serious danger if present in sufficient numbers. Pathogenic bacteria hate cold and lie dormant at low temperatures waiting for an opportunity to jump into action when the conditions get warmer again. Most pathogenic bacteria, including *Salmonella, E.coli 0157:H7, Listeria monocytogenes,* and *Campylobacter*, can be easily destroyed using a mild cooking. Maintaining a minimum temperature within 130-165° F (54-74° C) for a specific time will kill them.

Control of Microbiological Hazards Associated with Fermented Sausages

Staphylococcus aureus - This bacteria, often called "staph", is present in many healthy individuals' nose, throat, skin and hair. Contamination is most often caused by human contact with raw and cooked foods and can be controlled by hand sanitation and disposable gloves. It tolerates salt up to 10% and can function at low moisture level down to Aw 0.85. Without oxygen it will not grow below Aw 0.90. Slow growing at low temperatures, but at 60° F (15.6° C) starts growing rapidly and may produce toxin. A rapid acidity drop to pH <5.3 slows S. aureus growth.

Clostridium botulinum - the most deadly pathogen of them all. The toxin it produce attacks the body's nerves and causes difficulty breathing, muscle paralysis, and even death. Grows best without oxygen and it can grow in most low-acid foods such as on the surfaces of fruits and vegetables and in seafood. Addition of sodium nitrite is the most effective hurdle.

Clostridium perfringens - can grow without oxygen and is normally found in the intestines of humans and animals. When ingested in sufficient numbers, it is also a common cause of food poisoning. This commonly occurs when cooked food contaminated with the bacteria is left out, which allows the rapid multiplication of *C. perfringens*. Illness results from toxin production in the intestines. Common food sources include meat and poultry dishes, soups, and sauces.

Salmonella - Salmonella is carried in the intestinal tracts of sheep, cattle, swine and poultry. *Salmonella* grows very slow below 50° F (10° C). It can grow with or without oxygen at temperatures from 40-117° F (5-47° C). It does not grow above 130° F (54° C) and at low pH levels. *Salmonella* is heat-sensitive and cooking meat at (150-165° F (65-74° C) will rapidly destroy it.

E. coli 0157:H7 - resides in the intestinal tracts of animals, especially cattle, and can be shed in feces. During the slaughter, the bacteria can contaminate the carcass. *E.coli 0157:H7* is a strain of E. coli hardy pathogen that can survive refrigerator and freezer storage. It survives the acidic environment well down to pH 4.0. The procedures used to destroy *E.coli 0157:H7* include a combination of pH, Aw, and temperature controls. It multiplies very slowly at refrigerator temperatures. Since 1994, it has been linked to many pork recalls, most likely through cross-contamination. A thorough cooking is the most reliable method to destroy this pathogen.

STEC - Shiga toxin - *E. coli* strains that can cause severe illnesses in humans by producing toxins that can damage the lining of the intestines and kidneys.

Listeria monocytogenes - present in soil, vegetation, and water and can be carried by humans and animals. It can be found at every level of the meat processing chain and in various meat products. *Listeria monocytogenes* can grow with or without oxygen, survive dry conditions, and are salt-tolerant. *Listeria* has a wide temperature growth range from 36-112° F (2-44° C). At 39° F (4° C), it can double in numbers every 1.5 days. In fermented sausages, *L. monocytogenes* is controlled through a combination of low pH, high salt levels, drying process, protective cultures like SafePro® B-LC, and varying degrees of heat processing.

Trichinella spiralis - the disease is caused by the ingestion of undercooked meat containing parasite-encysted larvae. *T. spiralis* is a parasite (roundworm) found in free-range roaming pigs, rodents, and wild carnivore animals such as bears, moose, and wild boars. Many mild cases of *trichinosis* are never specifically diagnosed because they are assumed to be the flu or other common illnesses. If the infection is heavy, people may have trouble coordinating their movements and have heart and breathing problems. For mild to moderate infections, most symptoms go away within a few months.

Toxoplasma gondii - eating undercooked, contaminated meat (especially pork, lamb, and venison) or shellfish (for example, oysters, clams, or mussels). *T. gondii* is a parasite found worldwide and can persist in the bodies of humans and animals for long periods, even for a lifetime. A healthy person's immune system usually keeps the parasite from causing illness. However, pregnant women and individuals with compromised immune systems should be cautious; for them, a Toxoplasma infection could cause serious health problems.

Beneficial Bacteria

- Without beneficial bacteria, it will not be possible to make fermented sausages. Today, beneficial bacteria are commonly added to the meat as starter cultures. There are two classes of beneficial (friendly) bacteria:

- Lactic acid producing bacteria - *Lactobacillus*, *Pediococcus*.

- Color and flavor forming bacteria - *Micrococcus* (also known as *Kocuria*) and *Staphylococcus*.

Lactic Acid Bacteria

Lactic acid bacteria are ubiquitous and come from the environment in the broad sense. They are always present in meat. However, their initial number may need to be more significant to trigger meaningful fermentation; moreover, if the sugars are low, insufficient acidity will be generated to fight undesirable bacteria. Therefore, it is advisable to add sugars and use starter cultures. These are highly competitive microorganisms and can grow with or without air. Their diet is a simple one; all they eat is sugar. The lactic acid bacteria belong to two main groups:

- Homofermenters - produce mainly lactic acid.
- Heterofermenters - produce lactic acid, ethyl alcohol, acetic acid and carbon dioxide.

The most useful lactic acid bacteria families are:

- **Lactobacillus**: *(Lb.sakei, Lb.plantarum, Lb.farcimis, Lb.curvatus).*
- **Pediococcus**: (*Pediococcus pentosaceus, Pediococcus acidilactici*).

Lactic acid bacteria can grow from 41-113° F (5-45°C) and tolerate acidic conditions well, with most strains growing down to pH 3.5. They resist small changes in water activity, but their action slows down at Aw $\leq$ 0.95. This means that fast-fermented sausages must not lose moisture too fast. Otherwise, the fermentation will become slower, given that lactic acid bacteria need moisture. Lactic acid bacteria exhibit a higher salt tolerance than spoilage or pathogenic bacteria, but not as high as color and flavor-forming *Staphylococcus spp.*

The initial counts of lactic acid bacteria in raw meat mixes are around 10^3 - 10^4 cells/g. During fermentation, those numbers increase to 10^6 - 10^7 cells/g. Lactic acid bacteria produce mainly lactic acid contribute little to the development of flavor, although *Pediococcus spp.* possess some proteolytic ability (breaking down meat proteins) and *Pediococcus acidilactici* offers some protection against *Listeria monocytogenes.* Not all lactic acid bacteria in meat are desirable, as wild strains may create undesirable results such as gas production, unacceptable souring, and off-flavors and odors. That is why starter cultures are so effective: They contain only carefully selected and grown bacteria under laboratory conditions.

Color and Flavor Forming Bacteria

Bacteria strains such as *Staphylococcus carnosus, Staphylococcus xylosus,* and *Kocuria (formerly Microccocus)* belong to the *Micrococcaceae* family and are known to be the main mechanisms of producing nitrite from nitrate during the curing process. They are not directly involved in the fermentation process. However, these bacteria are responsible for the sausage's color, taste, and flavor. Without these bacteria, developing a cheesy flavor in traditional salami would not have been possible. *Micrococci* come from the skin of animals, need oxygen to multiply and are not slowed down by the amount of salt added to salami; they develop immediately and intensively, consuming all the oxygen they can find in the mix.

Staphylococcus and *Kocuria do not perform well at high acidity levels (pH < 5.4),* so their performance in fast-fermented sausages is severely restricted. Their activity is limited to the first hours and, although very short, has a great importance; hydrolyzing fats and producing flavoring compounds contribute to the product's maturation.

Color and flavor-forming bacteria grow very slowly and are needed to produce quality slow-fermented sausages made with nitrate or nitrite/nitrate. Even so, the number of *Staphylococcus* might be pretty small by the time the sausage enters the ripening stage. To ensure the flavor development of these bacteria in the late ripening/drying stage, a sufficient number of bacteria (10^6 - 10^7 /g of meat) in a form of starter cultures should be added. They might not grow much in the late ripening stage, but they will still react with the meat due to their large number.

Since *Staphylococcus* and *Micrococcaceae* species are aerobic (need oxygen to survive), they are concentrated close to the surface of the sausage, where they quickly find oxygen. Hence, there is little growth in the core, a fact to remember when making a large-diameter sausage. They are sensitive to changing water activity levels, and fast drying at low humidity levels will prematurely dry out the surface of the sausage. A gray surface ring is a typical example. Like other bacteria, they need moisture to grow; the dry surface area will affect their growth.

The direct introduction of nitrite (Cure #1) to sausage mince guarantees the characteristic pink color. Although nitrite reacts with myoglobin immediately, it also rapidly dissipates in meat as part of it reacts with proteins and fat.

In slow-fermented sausages that use nitrate alone, *Micrococcus* curing bacteria are needed to force nitrate into releasing nitrite, which will start curing meat. Adding nitrate along with nitrite (Cure #2) guarantees a longer supply of nitrite, which is "extracted" from nitrate by color-forming bacteria. For this reason, nitrite and nitrate are added together (Cure #2) to slow-fermented products.

As a rule, *Staphylococcus spp.* are preferred to *Micrococcus spp.* as they require less oxygen. This allows *Staphylococcus spp.* to be active inside the sausage, whereas *Micrococcus spp.*, being aerobic (needing oxygen), is more active in the surface area. In addition to possessing nitrate reductase (a protein releasing nitrite from nitrate), they produce the enzyme catalase (a protein), which protects the sausage against oxygen activity and delays the rancidity of fats.

Staphylococcus is the main factor that develops flavor and aroma in traditionally made slow-fermented sausages. In addition to their nitrate-to-nitrite-reducing capabilities, these bacteria contribute to flavor development by:

- Proteolysis-break down of proteins into free amino acids.
- Lipolysis-break down of fats into free fatty acids.
- Catalase activity - ability to bind oxygen and to convert undesired hydrogen peroxide (H_2O_2) to water and molecular oxygen.

Yeasts

Yeast and molds grow much slower than bacteria, developing later in drying. They metabolize some of the lactic acid created during the fermentation stage, thus increasing pH (lowering acidity) which improves flavor in a slow-fermented product making it more mellow. They don't seem to be affected by a pH drop in the fermentation stage and will grow at 46-78° F (8-25° C) as long as a chamber has high humidity. They are less sensitive to increased salt levels than lactic acid bacteria. Yeasts need little oxygen to survive, and live on the surface or just below the surface of the sausage.

The preferred yeasts are: *Debaromyces hansenii, Candida formata* as they exhibit a high salt tolerance. *D. hansenii* decomposes peroxides and consumes lactic and acetic acids in fermented sausages. As a result, pH increases and the meat is less acidic, contributing to the milder flavor. In addition *D. hansenii* produces ammonia, which is alkaline (pH 11.5) and changes the balance of pH forcing it higher (less acidic). *D. hansenii,* similarly to *Staphylococcus spp.*, can break down meat proteins (proteolysis) and fats (lipolysis), contributing to flavor development.

Molds

Molds are aerobic (need oxygen) and will grow on the surface of the sausage only. They tolerate low temperatures and high amounts of salt quite well. Vacuum-packed products do not develop molds. On fermented European sausages, the development of mold is often seen as a desired feature as it contributes to the milder flavor of the sausage. If mold appears during processing, it can be scrubbed off with a stiff brush or wiped off with vinegar or oil. Dry white mold is generally considered a good mold because it can prevent "bad mold," usually green or black, from growing. The positive characteristics of molds are numerous:

- They help to moderate drying by preventing oxygen from reaching the inside of the sausage, which prevents loss of color and delays rancidity.
- They can metabolize some of the lactic acid, which causes an increase in pH (lower acidity) and contributes to a mellower flavor.
- They contribute to more uniform drying with less chance for case hardening.
- *P. nalgiovense* mold enhances flavor formation by promoting lipolytic (fat breakdown) and proteolytic (protein breakdown) activities.

Stay away from wild molds, even if they are white or slightly yellowish, as they are of unknown composition.

Toxins

Toxins of most concern are produced by *Clostridium botulinum, Clostridium perfringens,* and *Staphylococcus aureus.* All are the result of the growth of bacteria in foods that have been mishandled. Proper cooking, fermentation, cooling, and storage of food can prevent the growth of these bacteria and more importantly, the production of their toxins.

Clostridium botulinum is the deadliest bacteria, and it is spore-forming. When these bacteria feel threatened, they envelop themselves into protective shells to defend themselves. Under normal conditions, *C. botulinum* does not become spores. Spores have thick walls. They can resist high temperatures, humidity, and other environmental conditions. Spores can only be killed by boiling them in water for 5 hours or heating them in a pressure canner at 240 F (116° C) for 2 minutes. Once bacteria become spores, they enter a dormant stage, during which they exhibit minimal metabolism and respiration, which allows them to survive for years through periods of unfavorable conditions. Once the spores find favorable conditions again, they wake up (germinate), leave the shell, and become a new, even stronger bacteria that produce a deadly toxin. Although botulinum spores are heat-resistant, the toxin produced by bacteria growing out of the spores is destroyed by boiling at 212° F (100° C) for 5 minutes.

Fig. 2.1 Botulinum spore.

Clostridium perfringens is a spore-forming bacteria that may survive cooking. However, it returns to its vegetative state and multiplies when the meat is warm again. Then, when the meat is consumed, the organism produces an enterotoxin in the digestive system and causes diarrheal illness.

Staphylococcus aureus produces a toxin but does not form spores. Although the organism itself is easily destroyed by heating, the toxin is quite resistant to heat.

Chapter 3

Fermentation and Acidification

Fermentation Step by Step

In simple terms, meat fermentation is the spoilage of meat by bacteria. Leaving meat at room temperature to itself will result in spoilage, but if the process is properly controlled, the result is a quality fermented product. Meat fermentation always involves lactic bacteria, which are naturally present in meat or added as starter cultures. These bacteria feed on a small amount of sugar (glycogen), which is always present in meat. However, more sugar is usually added to generate more acidity, which prevents the growth of spoilage and pathogenic bacteria.

When a sausage is stuffed, salt and nitrite are the only barrier that protects the meat from spoiling. Fresh meat always contains some bacteria, and they will grow over time. Initially, there was fierce competition among different groups of bacteria for food. Still, beneficial bacteria slowly but steadily gained the upper hand in this fight by eliminating spoilage and pathogenic types. "Survival of the fittest" at its best. The reason that beneficial bacteria get the upper hand in this war is that they are:

- Stronger competitors. They become even stronger when the starter culture introduces millions of beneficial bacteria into the mix.

- Better tolerate exposure to salt, nitrite, and decreased water levels than undesirable bacteria types.

When a sausage is introduced into a fermentation chamber, the bacteria hold all cards in their favor:

- Warm temperature - right inside of the danger zone.
- Moisture - meat contains 75% water.
- Food - a lot of nutrients, including a small amount of sugar.
- Oxygen - present in air.

Adding salt, nitrite, and starter cultures creates favorable fermentation conditions. However, spoilage and dangerous bacteria such as *Listeria, Salmonella, Staphylococcus aureus,* and *E. coli 0:157:H7* can still grow, although slower. Sodium nitrite (Cure # 1) inhibits pathogenic spore-forming *Clostridium botulinum.* When a sausage enters a warm fermentation chamber, all bacteria types spring into action and start to multiply, but they react to the new environment differently:

- **Food spoilage bacteria.** Adding salt to the raw sausage mixture immediately reduces the water activity to Aw 0.96-0.97, and all types of bacteria start rapidly consuming oxygen. Food spoilage bacteria *(Pseudomonas)* need oxygen and begin to choke as there is little air inside the sausage. In addition, *Micrococcus spp.* (species) being oxygen-hungry consumes plenty of oxygen. The salt, nitrite, and decreasing moisture further inhibit their growth, and the degradation of amino acids eliminates their ability to cause off-odors typical in spoiled meats. Once lactic acid bacteria start to produce lactic acid, the increased acidity inhibits spoilage bacteria even more.

- **Lactic acid bacteria** *(Lactobacillus* and *Pediococcus)* are initially less numerous than *micrococcus* and capable of developing without oxygen, so they jump into action next. These bacteria ferment the sugars in the mix (a part of which has been consumed by *micrococci*). They tolerate salt well and function well at slightly reduced water levels. As they grow in numbers, they eat more sugar and produce more lactic acid, which creates a barrier against undesirable bacteria types. Lactic acid bacteria strains *(Pediococcus acidilactici, Lactobacillus curvatus)* can produce bacteriocins hostile towards wild lactic bacteria strains and pathogenic *Listeria monocytogenes*.

- **Color and flavor forming bacteria** (*Micrococcus* and *Staphylococcus*) tolerate increased salt levels very well, but they grow slowly. They can grow in the presence of oxygen or without it. They are sensitive to acidity, and at pH below 5.5, they become less effective in developing the flavor of fast-fermented sausages. They need not days but months of time to break meat proteins and fats in order to produce all those aroma-releasing enzymes. In fast-fermented sausages, a drop of pH 5.0 can be achieved in just 12 hours, giving them little chance to perform.

- **Pathogenic bacteria** (dangerous) are kept in check primarily by salt and nitrite. Once lactic acid bacteria produce lactic acid, this increasing acidity inhibits pathogenic bacteria, especially *Staphylococcus aureus*, which is very sensitive to acidity. However, it functions very well at low moisture levels.

In traditionally made slow-fermented dry sausages, the natural fermentation occurs only when there is enough lactic bacteria in the meat. To increase their number, a 2-3 days long curing step was performed, which allowed lactic acid bacteria to grow. Unfortunately, spoilage and pathogenic bacteria were also growing, although much slower, due to the effects of salt and nitrate.

Curing is not practiced today, given that adding cultures introduces huge numbers of lactic bacteria, which guarantees healthy and strong fermentation. These armies of beneficial bacteria start competing for food with other undesirable bacteria types, decreasing their chances for growth and survival.

The fermentation process is influenced by:

- Temperature - the most important factor which influences the speed of fermentation.
- Type of sausage desired and the starter culture chosen. The time can be from 12 hours to 3 days or more.
- Sugar amount and type - this determines the amount of acidity (pH drop)
- pH lowering acidulants such as Gdl or citric acid (if added).
- Meat selection - pork, beef, chicken, or even different cuts from the same animal have a different initial pH, which affects the time needed to reach the desired pH.

When a cold stuffed sausage is placed in a warm fermentation chamber, lactic acid bacteria that were frozen in starter culture suddenly wake up and enter the "waiting" stage, which is known as the lag phase. They sit, they look around, they slowly start consuming sugars, and they get comfortable and ready for the action. At this period, the sausage is at the highest risk as other bacteria types will try to grow as well. The only protection is that nitrite and salt were added to the mix. Then, all types of bacteria go on a rampage and start to multiply.

The speed at which they will keep growing (not in size but in number) depends on the temperature. The amount of acid they will produce depends on the type and total sugar added.

In general, faster fermentation results in a lower pH even if the same amount of sugar is added. According to Chr. Hansen, a 5° C increase in temperature, if close to the optimum growth temperature for the specific lactic acid bacteria, doubles the rate of lactic acid formation.

The End of Fermentation

It is difficult to predict the time when the fermentation ends, and the drying begins without performing pH acidity tests, as both processes are closely related and run together simultaneously. *The sausage pH, not the time,* is the factor that determines when the fermentation is completed.

We may assume the fermentation stage ends when the lowest pH reading is indicated. The question is even more complicated to answer in the case of slow-fermented products, which are made with little sugar, resulting in a slow and small pH drop. Once the fermentation starts, it will continue until:

- No more sugar is available to lactic acid bacteria.
- There is not enough free water (Aw < 0.95) available. This can happen when a sausage dries rapidly in low humidity or air speed is too fast.
- Temperature is lowered below 53° F (12° C), or the product is heated above 120° F (50° C).
- There is so much acidity (~ pH 4.5) that lactic bacteria stop working.

There are two types of fermentation:

- Slow fermentation.
- Fast fermentation.

Traditional Slow Fermenting Process

The production of traditionally fermented sausages is possible because of:

- Naturally present bacteria inside of the meat.
- Bacteria residing on the premises and equipment, including our body.

Without laboratory testing, it is impossible to predict the number of lactic acid bacteria present in meat. This is why chopped meat was often cured for 48 hours with salt, nitrite, and sugar in a cooler in the hope that the lactic acid bacteria would grow in number.

In traditionally made sausages, the total drop of pH and resulting acidity will be small, around pH 5.3 or higher, given that a small amount of sugar is added. Even if no sugar is introduced, some fermentation will still take place as meat contains a small amount of sugar (glycogen), generally around 0.3%. For safety reasons, slow-fermented sausages are made with 3% or more salt. Lactic acid, color, and flavor-forming bacteria grow quite well at slightly elevated salt levels, but spoilage and pathogenic bacteria find a salty environment increasingly hostile.

If you look at the Fig. 3.1 drawing on the next page, you will see that as lactic, curing, and flavor bacteria grow, the number of spoilage and pathogenic bacteria decreases. As lactic acid bacteria consume sugar, they produce acidity, which makes meat more resilient to undesirable bacteria. It is best to create plenty of acidity to guard meat against spoilage as soon as possible. Well, this is often done. However, it introduces a sour flavor that not everybody likes.

Curing and color and flavor-forming bacteria *(Micrococcus and Staphylococcus)* are responsible for the development of flavor, which they accomplish by breaking down meat proteins and fats. They are salt tolerant. However, they do not tolerate acidity well. Once acidity reaches pH 5.4-5.5, the curing and flavor bacteria become less effective and will stop working when acidity increases to pH 5.0. It is in our interest to delay an increase in acidity for as long as possible so that flavor-producing bacteria will keep on working.

As the growth of any bacteria is directly related to the increase in temperature, lactic acid bacteria will grow faster and produce lactic acid faster. High temperatures can increase the production of lactic acid so fast that curing and flavor bacteria can prematurely stop working. The sausage will be stable, but no more flavor development will take place. Traditionally made sausages are usually fermented at moderate temperatures, around 68° F (20° C). At these temperatures, lactic acid bacteria metabolize sugar slowly, which results in a slow increase in acidity.

Given that acidity accumulation (pH drop) is directly proportionate to the amount of introduced sugar, the amount of added sugar should not be higher than 0.5%. If less than 0.3% sugar is added, the acidity will not reach pH 5.0, and curing and flavor bacteria will work to their fullest. As the pH of the sausage drops below pH 5.3, moisture removal becomes easier. At around pH 4.8, a point is reached, called the isoelectric point, when water-holding forces become weaker and the sausage starts drying fast. Slow-fermented sausages usually do not reach the isoelectric point.

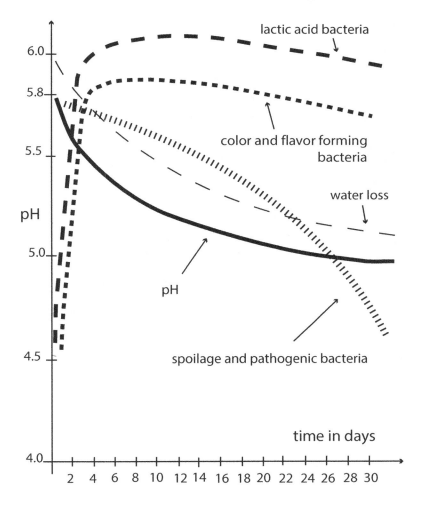

Fig. 3.1 Slow-fermented sausage without starter culture. Nitrate added, little sugar. Fermented at 64-70° F (18-20° C).

Data of Nurmi (1966)

As the process continues, less free water is available to bacteria, creating an additional hurdle against their growth. The sausage becomes much firmer. Once the supply of sugar is exhausted, the lactic acid bacteria go dormant, but curing and flavor-producing bacteria (*Micrococcus* and *Staphylococcus*) continue working as long as the acidity is not higher than pH 5.0. When the sugar supply is exhausted, lactic acid bacteria (*Lactobacillus* or *Pediococcus*) die.

Influence of Sugar on Slow Fermentation

Using starter cultures permits a better control of fermentation. The data below shows that for slow-fermented T-SPX culture being fermented at 75° F (24° C), this will occur within 48 hours (curves 1, 2, and 3).

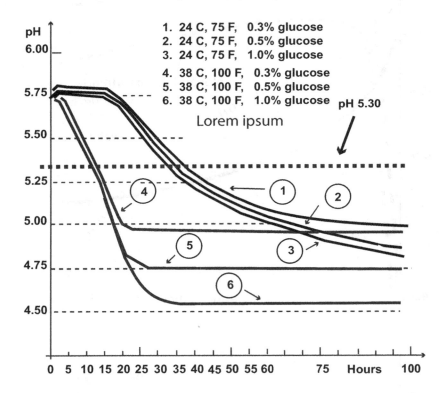

Fig. 3.2 Influence of amount of glucose on the pH-decrease induced by the traditional fermenting culture T-SPX, containing a *P. pentosaceus* bacteria strain, at two temperatures: 24° C (75° F), 38° C (100° F).

Data of Chr. Hansen

The 1,2,3 curves remain almost the same during the first 48 hours, regardless of the amount of sugar added. At 100° F (38° C), the pH drop is faster (curves 4, 5, and 6), and the sausage is stable within 24 hours of fermenting (curve 6).

When making a traditional fermented sausage, the pH values *should not fall below* 4.8-5.0 as this will inhibit the action of color and flavor forming bacteria which are sensitive to acidity. To meet this requirement when applying T-SPX culture shown in the graph above, fermentation temperatures must be kept in the 64-75° F (18-24° C) range and only a small amount of glucose should be added (0.2-0.3%).

Influence of Temperature on Slow Fermentation

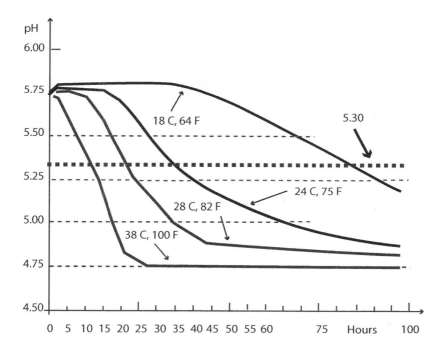

Fig. 3.3 Influence of fermentation temperature on the pH-decrease induced by the traditional fermenting culture T-SPX, containing a *P. pentosaceus* bacteria strain. Sausage mince contains 0.5% glucose.

Data of Chr. Hansen

The above figure shows the culture profile for the pH decrease of the T-SPX Chr. Hansen culture contains traditional and fast fermenting *P. pentosaceus* strain with an optimum growth temperature of around 95° F (35° C). However, the culture can be applied at lower temperatures, where it will ferment slower, although ***below*** 64° F (18°C), T-SPX does nothing.

The amount of added sugar will determine the pH drop. The graph's data shows the importance of temperature in fermentation. Cultures containing different bacteria strains have different optimum growth temperatures, but the general profile will look like the above graphs.

Fast Fermentation

These are economically produced sausages that end up in local supermarkets or as pizza toppings. They are characterized by a fast drop in pH that increases the acidity to such a level that a sausage can be made within 7 days and be microbiologically stable. Its tangy flavor is already set and will not be improved with additional drying, as flavor-forming bacteria cannot tolerate such high acidity levels. A few days of drying will add to the overall safety of the sausage, but there is no need for long-term drying as it will only decrease the weight of the sausage.

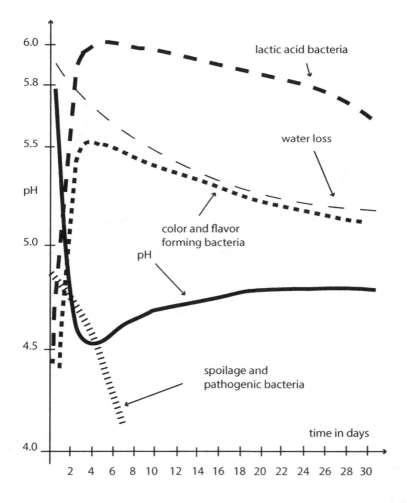

Fig 3.4 Fast-fermented sausage without starter cultures. Nitrite added plus a large amount of sugar. Fermented at 75° F (24° C).   *Data of Reuter at al. (1968)*

Influence of Sugar on Fast Fermentation

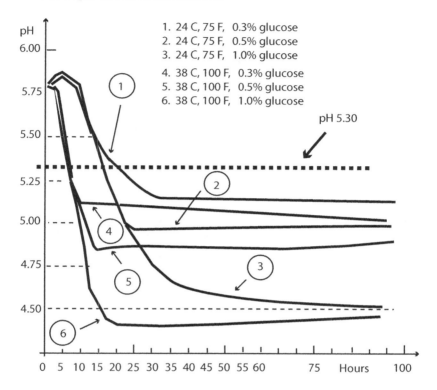

1. 24 C, 75 F, 0.3% glucose
2. 24 C, 75 F, 0.5% glucose
3. 24 C, 75 F, 1.0% glucose
4. 38 C, 100 F, 0.3% glucose
5. 38 C, 100 F, 0.5% glucose
6. 38 C, 100 F, 1.0% glucose

Fig. 3.5 Influence of amount of glucose on the pH-decrease induced by the fast fermenting culture F-1, containing a *P. pentosaceus* bacteria strain, at two temperatures: 75° F (24° C) and 100° F (38° C).   *Data of Chr. Hansen.*

In the above graph it can be seen that F-1 fast-fermenting culture at 100° F (38° C) temperature will drop pH to <5.3 within 12 hours (curves 4, 5 and 6) what will eliminate danger from toxin producing *Staphylococcus aureus*. At 75° F (24° C) pH drop to 5.3 will be obtained within 24 hours (curves 1, 2 and 3).

A fast-fermented sausage can be made in a short time by adding:
- A large amount (0.7-1%) of fast fermenting sugar (dextrose).
- A fast fermenting starter cultures which allow to undertake the fermentation process at temperatures as high as 104° F (40° C).

The smoke can be applied at the end of fermentation. Fast-fermented sausages are generally partially or fully cooked.

Influence of Temperature on Fast Fermentation

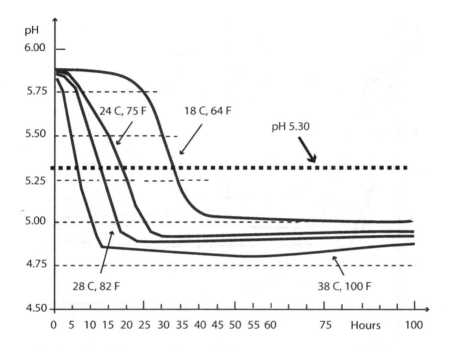

Fig. 3.6 Influence of fermentation temperature on the pH-decrease induced by the fast fermenting culture F-1, containing a *P. pentosaceus* bacteria strain. Sausage mince contains 0.5% glucose.

Data of Chr. Hansen

With starter cultures, the fermentation temperature should lie within the optimal temperature range for a particular culture. Given that at higher temperatures, the speed of fermentation is faster, the fermentation process will be shorter. It is accepted that starter cultures can decrease the fermentation time by 15 to 20% compared to natural fermentation. The temperature of the fermentation will be influenced by the selection of a starter culture, but the type and the amount of sugar added will decide the number of hours that are needed to reach the desired pH. Those decisions should conform to and be within the limits of degree-hours tables to prevent the growth of pathogenic bacteria (see Chapter 6).

Chapter 4

Starter Cultures

A recipe can be downloaded from the Internet, and one may produce quality salami at home with some luck. However, the next time, the sausage may turn out completely different, even if the same ingredients were included. Starter cultures solve the problem. They significantly increase the chances of making a successful product and provide a safety hurdle against the growth of undesirable bacteria. They are inexpensive and easy to use, and there is no excuse for not using them.

In many parts of the world, cultures may be hard to obtain, so the traditional methods of natural fermentation are still used. However, in Western countries, these techniques are being replaced by the application of commercially grown starter cultures. Americans started experimenting with bacteria to produce sausages faster and cheaper in the 1930s. In 1940, the first US patent, # 2,225,783, was granted to Jensen & Paddock for their research on *Lactobacilli* bacteria in making fermented sausages. Although the theory was solid, it took a lot of work to produce *Lactobacilli* starter culture commercially, as there were problems with freezing bacteria and reactivating them later. More research was done, and *Pediococcus cerevisiae* was discovered that could survive freezing and drying techniques. Thus, the practice of adding starter cultures to sausages was first born in the USA. *Pediococcus* cultures performed best at high temperatures, and manufacturers have embraced this technology. As a result, sausages were made faster and at reduced costs.

In Europe, where the tradition of making fermented sausages dates back thousands of years, sausages were always fermented at much lower temperatures, which led to a much milder flavor. For that reason, American fast-acting starter cultures were not really embraced. These cultures produced lactic acid so fast that this sudden increase of acidity prevented color and flavor-forming bacteria from reacting with meat. As a result, there was no development of the expected and well-liked flavor. The first European culture produced in the 1950s was curing cultures aimed at color and flavor development.

The first lactic acid bacteria of practical and universal use was an isolated bacteria from a fermented sausage in 1966 by Nurmi. It was called *Lactobacillus plantarum* and could be used at moderate temperatures, 68-72° F (20-22° C). It is still in use today. Then, in 1970, researchers combined lactic acid and curing bacteria to form multi-strain cultures. Those cultures, in addition to fermenting meat, can speed up the development of color and flavor and fight off other undesirable bacteria.

Bacteria residing in meat are hetero-fermentative, meaning many bacteria strains have unknown numbers and quality. Being of wild variety, they can produce unexpected results by producing lactic acid and creating many different reactions that can produce unpleasant odors and affect the entire process. Hence, naturally fermented sausage can be an excellent or poor product. Starter cultures are homo-fermentative and produce lactic acid only, although some strains will develop mold or a more robust color. One gram of culture introduces up to 10 million bacterial cells, which assures microbial dominance over other undesirable microorganisms that might be present. Those other microorganisms might be wild lactic acid bacteria naturally present in meat or pathogenic bacteria that must be eliminated.

The commercial starter cultures are produced by isolating the desired bacteria strains that are naturally found in meat products. Next, by purifying and then growing them under controlled laboratory conditions, the desired characteristics are obtained. Then, they are concentrated and preserved by freezing or drying.

Today, the commonly available starter cultures help us produce fermented sausages of many types, such as slow or fast-fermented, dry or semi-dry, sliceable or spreadable, with mold or without. Choosing a type of sausage to make decides the starter culture and establishes the parameters of the fermentation process, as different cultures prefer different fermentation temperatures.

Why Use Cultures

The advantages of starter cultures are numerous:

- They are of known number and quality. There is no guessing as to whether there is enough bacteria inside the meat to start fermentation, or whether a strong curing color will be obtained.
- Cultures are optimized for different temperature ranges that allow production of slow, medium or fast-fermented products.
- Starter cultures decrease fermentation time.
- A product of constant quality can be produced year round as long as proper natural conditions or fermenting/drying chambers are available.
- They provide safety by competing for food with undesirable bacteria thus inhibiting their growth.

Culture Types

Cultures can be classified into the following groups:

- Lactic acid producing cultures.
- Color and flavor forming cultures.
- Surface coverage cultures (yeasts and molds).
- Bio-protective cultures (producing bacteriocins). You may think of bacteriocins as some kind of antibiotics which kill unwanted bacteria.

Chr. Hansen Starter Cultures

There are many manufacturers of starter cultures in Europe and the USA. We list products made by the Danish manufacturer Chr. Hansen, as their products demonstrate superior quality and are easily obtained from American distributors of sausage-making equipment and supplies. Even more, the company offers wonderful technical support, and we are deeply indebted to them for the detailed specifications of their products.

Acidifying Cultures

Lactobacillus - all *Lactobacillus* bacteria strains used in starter cultures are homo-fermentative (producing a fermentation resulting wholly or principally in a single end product), which grow best at low oxygen levels, and their main fermentation product from sugar is lactic acid. On the contrary, endogenous (naturally occurring) *Lactobacillus* bacteria found in meats are hetero-fermentative (producing fermentation resulting in a number of end products) and, in addition to lactic acid, will also produce volatile acids and carbon dioxide. Those byproducts react with meat and achieving a constant quality product is hindered.

Culture	*L. pentosus*	*L. sakei*	*L. plantarum*	*L. curvatus*
Opt. growth temp.°C/°F	35/95	30/86	30/86	30 or 37°/ 86 or 99°
Salt limit (% salt in water)	9	9	13	**10**
Fermentable sugars:				
Glucose (dextrose)	+	+	+	Strain dependent, please refer to product sheets
Fructose	+	+	+	
Maltose	+	-	+	
Lactose	+	-	+	
Saccharose (sucrose)	+	-	+	
Starch	-	-	-	

Pediococcus - *Pediococcus* species used in starter cultures are homo-fermentative (producing a fermentation resulting wholly or principally in a single end product) which grow best at low oxygen levels. Compared to *Lactobacillus* strains the *Pediococcus* strains in general grow at higher temperatures and have a broader sugar fermentation pattern.

Culture	*P. pentosaceus*	*P. acidilactici*
Opt. growth temp.°C/°F	35/95	40/104
Salt limit (% salt in water)	7	10
Fermentable sugars:		
Glucose (dextrose)	+	+
Fructose	+	+
Maltose	+	+
Lactose	(+)	(+)
Saccharose (sucrose)	+	(+)
Starch	-	-
+ property present, (+) property depending on strain		

Color and Flavor Forming Cultures

Staphylococcus - the *Micrococcaceae* species most often encountered in the largest numbers in indigenous fermented sausages are different species of *Staphylococcus*, more specifically *S. xylosus, S. saprophyticus* and occasionally *S. carnosus*. *Staphylococcus* species are thus clearly dominant compared to the *Kocuria* species sometimes offered, due to their higher salt tolerance and lower oxygen requirements.

Culture	S. carnosus	S. xylosus	Micrococcaceae spp.
Opt. growth temp.°C/°F	30/86	30/86	30/86
Salt limit (% salt in water)	16	15	16
Fermentable sugars:			
Glucose (dextrose)	+	+	+
Fructose	+	+	+
Maltose	-	+	-
Lactose	+	+	+
Saccharose (sucrose)	-	+	-
Starch	-	-	-

Staphylococcus are oxygen hungry during growth and may find insufficient air inside firmly stuffed sausage, limiting their growth to the surface areas only. However, they are capable of using Nitrate (in Cure #2) as an electron acceptor *instead of oxygen* during respiration, which will promote their survival. Otherwise *Staphylococcus* inoculated into the mince will only grow little or not at all during ripening, and mostly in the outer parts. As long as sufficient number of bacteria (10^6-10^7 cfu/g) are introduced to the sausage mince, they will produce flavors even though they might not significantly grow in numbers. It is important, though, to restrict the rate of lactic acid formation because their survival is sensitive to low pH.

Yeasts - are often associated with indigenous fermented sausages, but species from the genus *Debaryomyces,* particularly *Debaryomyces hansenii,* predominate due to their high salt tolerance. *D. hansenii* does not reduce nitrate but decomposes peroxides (known for sulphuric-type off flavor) and consumes both lactic and acetic acids in the sausage, thereby increasing pH during the ripening period, which removes some of the sour taste. Additionally, *D. hansenii* produces ammonia (pH 11.5), which also increases sausage pH and possesses lipolytic (fat breakdown) and proteolytic (protein breakdown) activities of importance to flavor development. *D. hansenii* only *grows near the surface* of the ripening sausages. It needs oxygen for growth.

Molds - the predominant molds isolated from spontaneous colonized dried sausages are different *Penicillium species*, but *Scopulariopsis, Aspergillus* and other fungi may also be present. *Mold spores are present in the house-flora and in humid conditions will settle on the surface of the sausage.*

Chr. Hansen offers different strains of *Penicillium nalgiovense*, giving the sausage surface a whitish-grayish appearance. As with yeasts, *molds oxidize lactic acid and other acids and produce ammonia* (pH 11.5), thereby increasing pH and removing some of the sourness, *contributing to a more mellow flavor of traditional dry sausages.* Since molds form a coating over the surface, use oxygen, and produce catalase, they reduce chemical lipid oxidation and rancidity. Additionally, *P. nalgiovense* affects flavor formation due to diverse metabolic activities such as lipolytic and proteolytic activity. In addition to *Penicillium species*, yeast strains are also used for surface treatment of South European-style dried sausages.

Protective Cultures

Despite good manufacturing practices and safety hurdles, there is a risk that certain pathogenic bacteria may survive the production, the most likely reason being an unusually high initial count of pathogenic bacteria in the raw materials. In addition to being powerful competitors for nutrients against pathogenic and spoilage bacteria, lactic acid bacteria are known to produce compounds named "bacteriocins," which can act against other microorganisms. *Pediococcus acidilactici* and *Lactobacillus curvatus* produce *pediocin* and *curvacin*, respectively, that destroy the cell membrane of *Listeria monocytogenes* and reduce their numbers.

4.3 Guidelines for Choosing Chr. Hansen Starter Cultures

4.3.1 Starter cultures for traditional fermented sausages - in the production of traditional-style sausages, the fermentation profile must have a short lag phase in order to ensure the growth of the added starter culture at the expense of the unwanted bacteria. The acidification profile must be rather flat and not go below pH 4.8-5.0 at any time. This will ensure that *Staphylococci* maintain their activity over a longer period of time, foremost, their nitrate reductase and flavor-forming activities. The cultures listed below are specifically selected for traditional fermentation profiles applying fermentation temperatures not higher than 75° F (24° C).

Culture	Bacteria included	Characteristics
Bactoferm® T-SC-150	*Lactobacillus sakei* *Staphylococcus carnosus*	Gives a product flavor which is very typical for German salami such as Westphalia salami type. The acidification leads to a clear lactic acid taste. The used *Lactobacillus sakei* has a very good growth potential and is able to suppress the growth of a lot of indigenous bacteria. The used *Staphylococcus carnosus* gives good color stability and a mild aroma. Attention: This *Lactobacillus sakei* is sucrose negative.
Bactoferm® TRADI-302	*Lactobacillus sakei* *Staphylococcus xylosus* *Staphylococcus carnosus*	Same features as T-SC-150, but the combination of the two *Staphylococci* leads to a more intensive color formation and a slight milder aroma.

Bactoferm® SM-182	*Lactobacillus sakei* *Staphylococcus xylosus* *Debaryomyces hansenii*	Same features as T-SC-150, but the yeast *Debaryomyces hansenii* on top gives a more "Mediterranean" flavor.
Bactoferm® T-SPX	*Pediococcus pentosaceus* *Staphylococcus xylosus*	Aromatic culture with mild acidification. The high concentration of *Pediococus pentosaceus* gives a controlled and moderate pH drop. The acidification gives a mild lactic acid taste. *Staphylococcus xylosus* gives good color formation and stability. Furthermore *Staphylococcus xylosus* gives a very round and mild flavor which is very typical for South European salami types such as Milano.
BactoFlavor® BFL-T03	*Pediococcus pentosaceus* *Staphylococcus carnosus ssp.*	Same features as T-SPX, but the new developed *Staphylococcus carnosus ssp.* Gives a milder and more "Mediterranean" flavor.
Bactoferm® SM-181	*Lactobacillus sakei* *Staphylococcus xylosus*	The sucrose positive *Lactobacillus sakei* gives a moderate pH-drop. This *Lactobacillus sakei* has a very good growth potential and is able to suppress the growth of a lot of indigenous bacteria. The used *Staphylococcus xylosus* gives good color formation and stability. The very high number of *Staphylococcus xylosus* leads to a very round and mild "Mediterranean" flavor.

4.3.2 Starter cultures for fast-fermented sausages

In producing North European and US-style sausages, the fermentation profile must have a very short lag phase to rapidly onset fermentation and exhibit a fast drop in pH to below 5.3 within 30 hours at minimum. This ensures an efficient inhibition of unwanted bacteria and an early onset of fast drying. Total production time is typically less than 2 weeks.

Staphylococci and *Micrococcaceae spp.* are not added to all cultures, so to enhance color formation *Staphylococci* or *Micrococcaceae spp.* must be added on the side. This may be unnecessary in the US-style process (fermentation temperatures 35–45°C/100–115°F, very fast pH-drop, very low final pH < 4.8) since *Staphylococci* generally do not survive the fast pH lowering. In some instances, however, adding *Staphylococci* or *Micrococcaceae spp.* has proven beneficial for color stability in the US-style process for meat snack sticks. *The Pediococcus* in F-1 and BFL-F02 have lower salt tolerance than the other fast fermenting strains and are, therefore, not recommended for sausages with very high salt-in-water levels (>6%) and high -fat contents.

Culture	Bacteria included	Characteristics
F-SC-111	*Lactobacillus sakei* *Staphylococcus carnosus*	Same features as T-SC-150, but faster in pH drop by different amount and production treatment of the applied *Lactobacillus sakei*. (Faster version of T-SC-150). Fast culture targeted for fermentation temperatures 70-90° F (22-32° C).
F-1	*Pediococcus pentosaceus* *Staphylococcus xylosus*	Same features as T-SPX, but faster in pH drop by different amount and production treatment of the applied *Pediococcus pentosaceus*. (Faster version of T-SPX). Fast culture targeted for fermentation temperatures 70-90° F (22-32° C).
BactoFlavor® BFL-F02	*Pediococcus pentosaceus* *Staph.carnosus ssp.*	This is the fast version of BFL-T03. Acidification features as mentioned under F-1.
BactoFlavor® BFL-F04	*Lactobacillus sakei* *Staphylococcus carnosus.* *Staphylococcus carnosus ssp.*	The sucrose positive *Lactobacillus sakei* shows a very good growth potential and is able to suppress the growth of a lot of indigenous bacteria. The combination of the two new developed *Staphylococci* gives a very good color formation and a more intensive, but mild aroma development. The special combination of the strains shows a fast pH drop and leads to a firm texture.
BactoFlavor® Flora Italia	*Lactobacillus sakei* *Staphylococcus carnosus.* *Staphylococcus carnosus ssp.*	The sucrose positive *Lactobacillus sakei* shows a very good growth potential and is able to suppress the growth of a lot of indigenous bacteria. Despite the very fast pH drop it gives a very mild Mediterranean flavor like a traditional sausage. The combination of the two new developed *Staphylococci* gives a very good color formation and a more intensive, but mild aroma development.
Bactoferm® SM-194	*Pediococcus pentosaceus* *Lactobacillus sakei* *Staphylococcus xylosus* *Staphylococcus carnosus* *Debaromyces hansenii*	Multi application culture that combines all positive features of the different strains. *Lactobacillus sakei* with very good growth potential and the ability to suppress the growth of a lot of indigenous bacteria. *Pediococcus pentosaceus* by its mild lactic acid taste and the accelerated pH drop at higher temperatures. The combination of two different *Staphylococci* for more intensive color formation and mild aroma development. And the yeast *Debaromyces hansenii* on top to obtain a more "Mediterranean" flavor.
Bactoferm® LHP DRY	*Pediococcus acidilactici* *Pediococcus pentosaceus*	Extra fast cultures targeted for fermentation temperatures 80-100° F (26-38° C)
Bactoferm® CSB (pellets)	*Pediococcus acidilactici* *Micrococcaceae ssp.*	Extra fast cultures targeted for fermentation temperatures 86-113° F (30-45° C).
HPS (pellets)	*Pediococcus acidilactici*	Very fast cultures targeted for fermentation temperatures 90-113° F (32-45° C).

4.3.3 Starter cultures for enhancing flavor and nitrate reduction

Sausages fermented with a chemical acidifier such as Gdl or encapsulated acid instead of lactic acid bacteria, generally require *Staphylococci* or *Micrococcaceae spp.* to obtain an acceptable flavor and color. Those single strain cultures are recommended in all sausage products in need of extra flavor or nitrate reductase activity. *S. carnosus* is more salt tolerant than *S. xylosus* and convey a more intense flavor in fast-fermented products.

Culture	Bacteria included	Characteristics
Bactoferm® CS-300	*Staph. carnosus ssp. Staphylococcus carnosus*	The combination of the two different *Staphylococci* leads to intensive color formation and color stability. Furthermore it gives a mild and round aroma. The high concentration of both *Staphylococci* gives high nitrate reductase activity.
Bactoferm® S-B-61	*Staphylococcus carnosus*	For a good color formation and color stability and additional flavor development.
Bactoferm® S-SX	*Staphylococcus xylosus*	For a good color formation and color stability and additional flavor development. Especially suitable in case of too much and undesired acidification taste.

4.3.4 Starter cultures for surface coverage

Mold present on traditional sausages prevents mycotoxin formation by wild molds. It allows for uniform drying and contributes positively towards flavor.

Culture	Bacteria included	Characteristics
Bactoferm® Mold 600	*Penicillium nalgiovense*	Fast growing and strong suppression of wild flora. Dense, medium fluffy and uniform coverage. Traditional white coverage. Pronounced mushroom flavor.
Bactoferm® Mold 800	*Penicillium candidum Penicillium nalgiovense*	Fast growing and strong suppression of wild flora. Dense, medium to very fluffy coverage. Generates a fresh camembert aroma/strong mushroom flavor and a typical scent of moss. Good growth potential in dry and unstable conditions.

4.3.5 Starter cultures for bio-protection

Listeria monocytogenes contamination of meat products appears to be an increasing problem. Chr. Hansen has developed several cultures for fresh, cooked, and cured meat products to lower the general level and/ or reduce surface contamination. For example, F-LC for fermented sausages is a patented culture blend capable of acidification and preventing *Listeria* growth, and it operates in a wide temperature range.

A low fermentation temperature < 77° F (< 25° C) results in a traditional acidification profile, whereas high fermentation temperature 95-113° F (35-45° C) gives a US-style product.

Culture	Bacteria included	Characteristics
SafePro® B-LC-20	*Pediococcus acililactici*	Adjunct culture for prevention of *Listeria* for use on top of existing starter cultures.
SafePro® B-LC-35	*Pediococcus acililactici* *Lactobacillus curvatus* *Staphylococcus xylosus*	*Pediococcus acililactici* and *Lactobacillus curvatus* give a slow, but controlled pH drop with a mild acidification flavor. The used *Staphylococcus xylosus* gives a good color formation and stability and mild flavor.
SafePro® B-LC-007	*Pediococcus acidilactici* *Pediococcus pentosaceus* *Lactobacillus sakei* *Staphylococcus xylosus* *Staphylococcus carnosus* *Debaromyces hansenii*	Same features as SM-194, but with additional strong antagonistic properties against *Listeria monocytogenes*.
SafePro® B-FLC-55	*Pediococcus acidilactici* *Lactobacillus sakei* *Staphylococcus carnosus*	Same features as F-SC-111, but with additional strong antagonistic properties against *Listeria monocytogenes*.
SafePro® Flora Italia LC	*Pediococcus acidilactici* *Lactobacillus sakei* *Staphylococcus carnosus* *Staphylococcus carnosus ssp.*	Same features as Flora Italia, but with additional strong antagonistic properties against *Listeria monocytogenes*.

Note: for more detailed product information, please visit www.chr-hansen.com or contact meat@chr-hansen.com or your local representative.

For a hobbyist, many cultures are available on the Internet or from distributors of sausage-making equipment and supplies.

4.4 How to choose the correct culture

In order to choose the correct culture the following advice may be used as general guidelines:

1. What style of sausage is produced?
   - Traditional South and North European: choose cultures in **Traditional fermented sausages** in paragraph 4.3.1.
   - North European fast fermented: choose **Fast fermented cultures** in paragraph 4.3.2.
   - US style: choose the *extra fast* and *very fast* cultures in **Fast fermented cultures** in paragraph 4.3.2.

2. A very short on-set of fermentation is needed.
   - Choose a frozen culture instead of a freeze-dried culture.
   - Increase the amount of culture.

3. The salt-in-water percentage in the fresh mince is:
   - > 6% : avoid F-1, LHP, BFL-202, BFL-T03 and T-SPX.

The above statement applies to products containing a large amount of salt.

4. The type of sugar is:
   - Glucose: all cultures will ferment.
   - Sucrose: avoid TRADI-302, T-SC-150, BFL-FO5 and F-SC-111.

5. Nitrate is added as a color forming agent to the mince.
   - Choose cultures in **Traditional fermented sausages** in paragraph 4.3.1. and **Fast fermented sausages** in paragraph 4.3.2 and adjust the process correspondingly to traditional/slow fermentation.
   - Add extra *Staphylococci* or *Micrococcaceae spp.* from **Starter cultures for flavor enhancemnet** in paragraph 4.3.3 to enhance nitrate reductase activity.

6. A product with an intense flavor.
   - Choose traditional technology and cultures from **Traditional fermented sausages** in paragraph 4.3.1.
   - Add extra *Staphylococci* or *Micrococcaceae* spp. from **Starter cultures for flavor enhancemnet** in paragraph 4.3.3. to enhance flavor formation.

4.5 Lag Phase

Before culture can react with meat, it must go through what is known as the "lag phase." It has been in a deep freeze of sleep and now must wake up and recover. It can be compared to a patient recovering from the effect of anesthesia. He needs some time to shake off the effects of his induced sleep and be himself again. During the lag phase, there is little fermentation taking place; lactic acid bacteria just get comfortable and start growing in numbers. Mixing freeze-dried cultures with chlorine-free cold water for 15-30 minutes before use helps them to "wake up" and to react with meat and sugar faster when introduced into the meat.

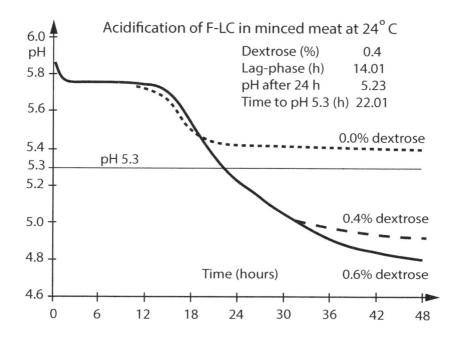

Fig. 4.1 Acidification of Bactoferm™ F-LC in a minced meat at 24° C (75° F).

As can be seen on the graph, the lag phase of F-LC culture at 75° F (24° C) is about 14 hours. The lag phase is when bacteria need to shake off the effects of freezing and grow in numbers to start producing a significant amount of lactic acid. This time can be faster or slower for a culture, depending on the temperature, which regulates bacteria activity. There was a slight increase in acidity (around pH 5.4; see 0.0% dextrose curve) even though dextrose was not added due to glycogen (sugar) in meat. 0.4% and 0.6% dextrose curves have the same slope of pH drop for the first 32 hours, and they both reach pH 5.3 in 22 hours. After 32 hours 0.4% dextrose curve becomes flat as there is no more sugar to support fermentation. It can be seen on the graph in Fig. 4.3 that at 98° F (37° C), LHP culture needs only 6 hours to start a full production of lactic acid. The fermentation process ends in 12-18 hours. Of course, at 80° F (27° C), its lag phase will be longer and the pH curve flatter. At 80° F (27° C), it may take 36 hours to develop the same pH drop as it did at 98° F (37° C) in 18 hours.

Cultures come in two forms: frozen cultures and deep freeze-dried cultures. The latter type needs more time to shake off the effects of the lag phase, a fact that may be of importance for a commercial plant but hardly for a hobbyist. Fermentation is usually more rapid when using frozen cultures (~6-hour lag phase) compared to deep freeze-dried cultures (~12-hour lag phase). All cultures sold online are deep-freeze-dried types, and it is doubtful that a hobbyist could obtain frozen-type cultures unless he comes up with a large order.

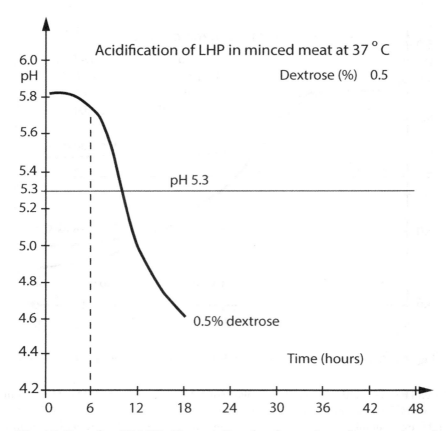

Fig. 4.2 Bactoferm™ LHP pH curve. *Very fast-fermenting cultures go through a much shorter lag phase,* from 30 minutes to a few hours, as they are fermented at higher temperatures.

After the culture is mixed with cold meat, stuffed, and transferred to a warm fermentation chamber, the temperature of the cold sausage will slowly start rising, what is known as "warm-up" time. During that time, the culture is still sluggish, but at around 50-53° F (10-12° C), it will start production of lactic acid. The lag phase can be shortened by:

- Using frozen culture instead of a freeze-dried culture.
- Increasing the amount of culture.
- Increasing the temperature.

Increasing the dosage of the culture introduces more bacteria into sausage mince. They will compete for moisture and nutrients with each other and grow slower. However, the fact remains that a larger number of bacteria will start fermenting more sugar, and a faster pH drop will be obtained. Given that it inhibits the growth of pathogenic bacteria, the lag phase should be as short as possible.

When freeze-dried cultures are used, it is recommended that they be dispersed in water. There are about 10 million bacteria in one gram of culture. Adding 25 grams of powdered culture to 200 kg (440 lbs) of meat makes uniform distribution quite challenging. Therefore, it is advisable, especially at home conditions, to mix 1/2 teaspoon of culture in 1/8 - 1/4 cup (30 - 60 ml) of chlorine-free water and then pour it down over 1 kg (2.2 lb) of minced meat.

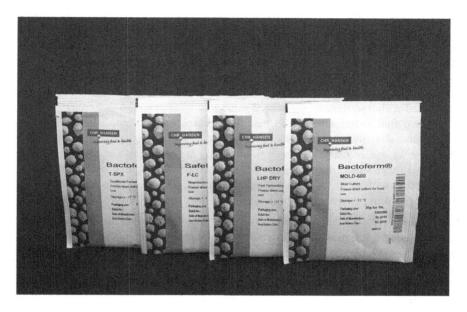

Photo 4.1 The Chr-Hansen cultures T-SPX, F-LC, LHP and Mold 600.

Technical information sheets provide the recommended temperatures for fermentation; however, bacteria will also ferment at lower temperatures, just more slowly. For example, T-SPX is listed at 78-100° F (26-38° C), the optimum being 90° F (32° C). T-SPX will ferment as well at 68-75° F (20-24° C), which is not uncommon for "European" style sausages, and 48 hours or more is not atypical.

Taking into consideration that fermented sausages have been made for thousands of years, the starter culture technology is very young indeed. Meat inspectors like them as they increase the safety of products. Manufacturers like them because they allow the making of sausages much faster and with predictable quality. Home sausage makers should love them as starter cultures make making fermented sausages at home practical, easy, safe, and of predictable quality. As some sausages, notably slow-fermented ones, take many weeks or even months to produce, it is a great loss to waste so much time and investment due to insufficient know-how or one's negligence.

Note: a number of starter cultures include *Staphylococci* strains which may be confusing as *Staphylococcus aureus* is a dangerous toxin-producing bacteria. As an example, *Staphylosossus xylosus* which is a flavor forming culture, belongs to *Staphylococci spp.* bacteria family, however, *in a culture, it is a harmless bacteria strain.*

Be aware that some cultures contain bacteria that do not ferment sugar or lactose, such as *Lactobacillus sakei*, so you need to use dextrose/glucose, which all bacteria are able to metabolize. This fact can be used to your advantage by adding sugars that will not be fermented, yet they will remain in the sausage, contributing to a sweeter taste. *Staphylococcus carnosus* and *Staphylococcus xylosus* are responsible for the development of flavor, which is accomplished by breaking down meat proteins and fats. This proceeds very slowly and does not take hours but weeks. It is typically associated with traditionally fermented sausages.

Given that extremely fast-fermenting cultures can accomplish fermentation within one day, they often contain only fast-acting lactic acid producers such *Pediococcus spp.* or *Lactobacillus spp.* Including in the culture *Staphylococcus spp.* might not make much difference as these bacteria will be killed by acidity before able to react with meat. In most published sources *Micrococcus* is listed as curing and color forming bacteria, but be aware that it was renamed to *Kocuria varians.*

Let's investigate what happens when the culture is added to the cold meat mixture and the stuffed sausage is placed in a warmer fermentation chamber. As the culture is designed to work best at a certain range of temperatures, it will start producing lactic acid when the internal meat temperature corresponds to the culture's optimal range of temperatures. Every Product/Culture Info sheet has a minimum/opt/maximum temperature for culture strains, which means when they start to ferment when they are performing the best, and when they will die/be killed off.

Let's assume that we have a T-SPX culture. Inserting stuffed sausage having an internal temperature of 50-53° F (10-12° C) into the fermentation chamber at 68° F (20° C) temperature will allow lactic bacteria to multiply *but will not start fermentation yet. They have to get close to their minimum optimal temperature, which for T-SPX is 64° F (18° C),* but its ideal temperature to really start dropping pH (making acid rapidly) is 95° F (35° C).

CHR-Hansen Technical data for T-SPX Bactoferm™, *see graph, Fig. 3.3 in Chapter 3.*

Culture	T-SPX	
Bacteria strain composition	*Staphylococcus xylosus*	*Pediococcus pentosaceus*
Growth temperature Optimum/maximum/minimum	30°C / 40°C / 10°C (86°F / 104°F / 50°F)	35°C / 48°C / 15°C (95°F / 118°F / 59°F)

Chapter 5

Additives and Ingredients

Additives are ingredients added during the manufacture of food to modify the characteristics of the primary material, in this case, the meat. In-home production, their use is limited to just a few; however, commercial producers apply a wide variety of ingredients to increase the product's shelf life and preserve its look and color.

The Importance of Salt

When adding salt to fermented sausages, try to think of salt not as a flavoring ingredient but as a barrier against undesirable bacteria. Almost all regular sausage recipes (fresh, smoked, cooked) contain 1.5-2% salt, which is added to obtain good flavor and binding. These amounts are not high enough to provide safety against bacteria in uncooked fermented products, and more salt is needed. This salt, combined with sodium nitrite (Cure #1), is our first line of defense against undesirable bacteria.

Adding salt to fermented sausages		
Non-heated dry fermented sausages	3.0 - 3.3% *	30 - 33 g/kg meat
Non-heated cold smoked/dried sausages	3.0%	30 g/kg meat
Semi-dry fermented sausages	2.5%	25 g/kg meat
Spreadable fermented sausages	2.0 - 2.5%	20 - 25 g/kg meat
* Adding salt above 3.3% decreases growth of lactic acid bacteria and may lengthen fermentation.		

Sea Salt

Sea salt, made by evaporating seawater, includes traces of different minerals that were diluted in water and too heavy to evaporate. But it is still sodium chloride salt, which people on low-sodium diets try to avoid. These impurities include different minerals and chemicals such as magnesium, calcium, or nitrate. Even a small amount of nitrate applied at 10 ppm/kg to meat may be sufficient to cause a slight pinkish color; however, it is not sufficient to protect meat against bacteria.

Low Salt Diet

The salt we use for cooking is sodium chloride (NaCl), and sodium is what increases our blood pressure. For people on a low-sodium diet, the only way to reduce sodium intake is to substitute sodium chloride salt (NaCl) with potassium chloride salt (KCl). Potassium chloride does not contain sodium and is used by commercial manufacturers to make low-sodium salts. It has a bitter metallic taste, so it is mixed in varying amounts with regular sodium chloride salt. Fermented/dry and cold smoked sausages should not be made with salt substitutes as sodium chloride (regular salt) provides microbiological safety in those products.

Nitrite and Nitrate

We have been using nitrite/nitrate for centuries because they:

- Impart a characteristic cured flavor the meat.
- Offer protection against pathogenic *Clostidium botulinum*.
- Retard the development of rancidity in fats.

Curing. For any aspiring sausage maker it is necessary to understand and know how to apply Cure #1 and Cure #2. Those two cures are used worldwide, though under different names and with different proportions of nitrates and salt.

Cure #1 (also known as Instacure #1, Prague Powder #1 or Pink Cure #1) is a mixture of 6.25% *sodium nitrite* and 93.75% of salt. Because it contains sodium nitrite, it does not depend on microbial action. It can react with meat immediately and at refrigerator temperature.

Cure #2 (also known as Instacure #2, Prague Powder #2, or Pink Cure #2) is a mixture of 6.25% sodium nitrite, 4% sodium nitrate, and 89.75% salt. Cure #2 is often applied to slow-fermented products, as nitrite starts an immediate reaction with meat and nitrate guarantees a steady supply of nitrite during drying.

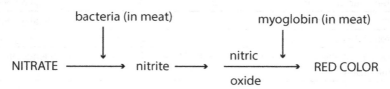

Fig. 5.1 Curing with nitrate.

In the past potassium nitrate was exclusively used because its derivative, sodium nitrite, still needed to be discovered. *Sodium Nitrate (NaNO₃) does not cure meat directly* and initially not much happens when it is added to meat. After a while, naturally present in meat *Micrococci* curing bacteria react with nitrate forcing it to release *sodium nitrite* ($NaNO_2$) to begin the curing process. The curing process may suffer if those bacteria are not present in sufficient numbers. Bacteria are sluggish at low temperatures, so meat cured with potassium nitrate is kept at 46° F (8° C).

Dry sausages made with nitrate frequently taste better than those made with the usual amount of nitrite. The amount of potassium nitrate added to raw sausage mixtures is usually between 200 and 600 mg/kg (in Germany, it is limited to 300 mg/kg).

Nitrite Amount	PPM (parts per million)	Cure #1 in grams per 1 kg of meat
USA maximum limit for sausages	156	2.5 g
Sufficient cured color	30 - 50	0.48 - 0.80 g
Good color and flavor	100	1.6 g
Protection against pathogenic bacteria	130-156	2.08 - 2.49 g
Residual nitrite left after 10 days	10 - 20	-------
Residual nitrite left after 30 days	< 10	-------
European * max limit for sausages	150	2.4 g

Sodium nitrite dissipates rapidly during fermentation, smoking, drying, and cooking; however, not all nitrite is spent on developing color; about 50% reacts with meat proteins (enzymes), creating so-called "curing flavor" during the ripening of the sausage. When the product is ready for consumption, it hardly contains any nitrite. Commercially prepared meats in the USA contain about 10 ppm of nitrite when bought in a supermarket. Cure #1 and Cure #2 include a small amount of Food and Drug Administration-approved red coloring agents that give them a slight pink color, thus eliminating any possible confusion with common salt, which is why they are sometimes called "pink "curing salts.

European Cures

What counts is not the name of the cure or where it is manufactured but how much sodium nitrite is introduced to meat. As most European cures contain salt and only 0.6% sodium nitrite, there is no danger of accidental overdose, so cures remain white and not colored. Such a low nitrite percentage in salt is self-regulating, and it is almost impossible to apply too much nitrite to meat, as the latter will taste too salty. You could replace salt with peklosól (0.6% sodium nitrite), and the nitrite limits will be preserved.

Making Sausages without Nitrite

Fermentation can be attempted with salt only, but there is a greater microbial risk if no nitrite is used, given that it strongly inhibits the growth of *Cl. botulinum* and retards the growth of salmonella. In the absence of nitrite, if the product is dried, the color of the meat will be darker, even more so if the smoke is applied to the moist surface. Additionally, fat rancidity will develop sooner, a fact to consider in dry sausages or in long-term storage.

Curing with Celery Powder

Saying "no nitrates or nitrites added, other than those which naturally occur in celery powder" is just a different way of packaging nitrite. In order to expand sales, producers came up with a variety of "natural" and "organic" processed meats employing catchy slogans such as "no synthetic preservatives" or "no nitrites added." It is hard to blame an average consumer for believing that if the label says no nitrate/nitrite was added, the product would be healthier. However, there is another sentence on the label marked with an asterisk *, which should be read as well: "no nitrites or nitrates added": *except for those naturally occurring nitrates and nitrites in celery powder.* Vegetables that contain the most nitrite are spinach, beetroot, lettuces, celery, then, in smaller amounts, cabbages, potatoes, and carrots. They acquire nitrite from fertilizers, which are added to the soil. This means that a customer eats the same nitrite, although it has been hidden in the fine print.

Why celery? - after careful studies and trials, it has been determined that celery juice was most suitable for meat products as it did not alter the finished product flavor or appearance. How much celery juice powder to add to meat is difficult to evaluate. Adding too little will not cure meat properly and may even create a safety hazard, for example, when making fermented sausages. It has been generally accepted that adding 0.2% - 0.4% celery juice powder to meat will deliver satisfactory results. Adding more will affect the flavor of the meat. Adding celery powder may be an acceptable practice for producing regular meats and sausages, but it should not be used in fermented sausages where precise amounts of sodium nitrite must be added.

Curing Accelerators

Color development with nitrite is slow as it takes place at low temperatures. Adding ascorbic acid (vitamin C), sodium ascorbate, or sodium erythorbate speeds up and enhances color development. Those additives speed up the chemical conversion of nitrite to nitric oxide, which will react with meat myoglobin to create a pink color. They also retard oxidation which slows the development of fat rancidity. They are typically added at 0.5-0.7 g per kilogram of the sausage mix.

Ascorbic acid speeds up the development of color in any sausage that contains nitrite. It is added at around 0.05% (0.5 g=500 mg=500 ppm per 1/kg of meat). Its more popular name is vitamin C, so it is available everywhere; just check how many mg of vitamin C a particular tablet contains, smash it into a powder, and apply it to minced meat. Ascorbic acid should not come in direct contact with nitrite as the reaction produces violent toxic fumes. For this reason, ascorbic acid is added at the beginning of the sausage mix, and nitrite is added with salt at the end of the mixing process.

Ascorbate and erythorbate are very similar, although ascorbate (sodium of ascorbate acid) is a bit stronger than erythorbate (salt of erythorbic acid). Ascorbate is applied at around 0.05% (0.5 g/kg of meat), while erythorbate is at around 0.6 - 0.7 g/kg of meat)

Acidulants increase the acidity of meat through chemical reactions which do not involve lactic acid bacteria. Hence, there is no bacterial fermentation and no need for sugar. They immediately react when exposed to moisture in the meat. Given that this greatly shortens the process of lowering pH, they are used in the production of less expensive semi-dry products. The acidulants are covered in detail in Chapter 10 - Acidified Sausages. The most popular acidulants are:

Gdl (glucono-delta-lactone) - used to make cottage cheese, tofu, bakery products and fermented sausages.

Citric acid - used to add an acidic taste to foods, soft drinks and wine.

Potassium sorbate is very effective in preventing the growth of mold. Sausages are either immersed into or sprayed with a solution of potassium sorbate. In the USA many processors use a 2.5% solution of potassium sorbate in water, however, at this strength the solution is effective only for a short time. Applying stronger solution at 10 -20% will prevent mold growth for up to a month.

Guar gum is a free-flowing, off-white powder produced from guar beans. Guar gum is a very potent water-thickening agent.

Mustard flour binds water well and is often added to spreadable sausages at 1.0-1.5% to extend spreadability.

Non-fat dry milk is often added to fermented sausages as it contains about 50% lactose (slow fermenting sugar). It binds water well, leaving less of it for bacteria.

Flavor enhancer. MSG (Monosodium glutamate) is produced by the fermentation of starch, sugar beets, sugar cane, or molasses. Although once typically associated with Chinese restaurants, it is now found in many common food items, particularly processed foods. MSG can be added at up to 1% (10 g/kg) to enhance the flavor of poor quality sausages made with a larger proportion of skins and connective tissue.

Soy proteins. Soy protein concentrate or isolate are generally added to regular cooked sausage at 2-3%, as they enhance protein content and can bind plenty of water, contributing to the sausage's firmness. Binding too much moisture may inhibit lactic bacteria from fermenting; however, a small amount of soy protein will lower Aw and facilitate drying.

Sugar

The term sugar is usually associated with white crystallized or powdered sugar that sits on every table. However, there are more sugars, also called carbohydrates, each with different characteristics. The variety and amount of carbohydrates (sugar) added are important because they determine the rate and extent of lactic acid formation and the composition of the sausage microflora.

If large amounts of rapidly metabolizable sugar like dextrose (glucose) are added, the pH reduction can be so rapid that desired activities of the non-lactic microflora, such as curing and flavor-forming bacteria, are suppressed. On the other hand, addition of too little carbohydrate and/or selection of a carbohydrate which is degraded very slowly (maltose, lactose) may result in growth of undesired organisms during fermentation, particularly at high ripening temperatures.

Dextrose

Dextrose, also known as glucose, is the simplest form of sugar that serves as a building block for most carbohydrates and is the preferred sugar for making fermented sausages. It is generally added at 0.5-1.0% (5 g -10 g/kg). *Only glucose can be fermented directly into lactic acid by all lactic bacteria,* which is why it is the fastest fermentable sugar. The molecular structures of other complex sugars must first be broken down into simple sugars like glucose or fructose, and then newly obtained simple sugars (glucose) can be metabolized by lactic acid bacteria. Hence, more complex sugars may ferment to a lesser extent and at a slower rate, which creates a certain delay in acid production. Thus, fermentation with sucrose is slower, and the final pH is higher than if an equal amount of dextrose was used.

Dextrose is a natural sugar refined from corn starch and is approximately 70% as sweet as sucrose (ordinary table sugar). Given that sucrose is sweeter than dextrose, the sausage should taste less acidic. As a fast pH drop is the main hurdle against bacteria growth in the initial stage of production of most fermented sausages, adding dextrose alone or in combination with other sugars is a common practice.

Estimating pH Drop When Using Dextrose

When using an acidulant such as Gdl or citric acid, the desired pH drop can be estimated relatively well. This, however, becomes difficult with complex sugars, which are only partially consumed by lactic acid bacteria. Given that glucose is almost fully metabolized by all bacteria, it is possible to create approximated guidance for attaining a pH drop using dextrose. The existing rule of thumb for estimating pH drop with acidulants can also be applied when using dextrose. Hence, adding 0.1% (1 g/kg) of dextrose will result in a 0.1 pH drop; adding 1% (10 g/kg) results in the approximate decline of 1 pH unit. The fast but moderate drop in pH provides safety against undesirable bacteria, yet it is not low enough to inhibit the growth of beneficial Staphylococcus, which is needed for color and flavor formation. In most cases, different sugars are combined. Some are metabolized by lactic bacteria to produce lactic acid, and others contribute to the development of flavor. A careful administration of different sugars may manipulate the pH drop's rate and extent.

The type and amount of added carbohydrates influence the course of lactic acid formation during sausage fermentation. With glucose, sucrose or maltose, the rate and extent of lactic acid production is higher than with lactose, starch and dextrin. By using a combination of dextrose and slowly acting sugars, a rapid but small pH decrease can be achieved at the beginning of the fermentation stage and a slower rate of pH drop can be obtained in the later stages of the fermentation. This kind of control is instrumental in producing quality traditionally fermented products which are made with nitrate.

The efficiency of different sugars used in lactic acid production.

Carbohydrate (1%)	Lactic acid produced (%)	Final pH
Glucose	**0.98**	4.08
Saccharose (Sucrose)	0.86	4.04
Maltose	0.72	4.24
Maltodextrin	0.54	4.54
Galactose	0.31	4.83
Raffinose	0.08	6.10

Lactic acid production and final pH achieved by *Lactobacillus pentosus* during growth in MRS-broth at 30° C (86° F) for 12 hours. *Data of Chr. Hansen*

The table shows that complex carbohydrates produce less acidity than dextrose.

Carbohydrates (sugars) can bind free water, which immediately drops Aw. Given that lactic acid and color and flavor-forming bacteria need some moisture, adding too many carbohydrates can negatively affect fermentation and flavor development.

Sucrose (also called saccharose) is our common table sugar. It is made from sugar cane or sugar beets, but also appears in fruit, honey, sugar maple and in many other sources. Sucrose is *the second fastest acting sugar.* It can be used in naturally fermented or chemically acidulated sausages.

Maltose - malt sugar is made from germinating cereals such as barley which is an important part of the brewing process. It's added mainly to offset a sour flavor and to lower water activity as its fermenting qualities are poor.

Lactose - also referred to as milk sugar, makes up around 2–8% of milk (by weight). Lactose ferments slower than glucose. It is composed of glucose and galactose, however, not all bacteria are able to metabolize lactose. Lactose binds water very well. Lactose milk sugar is about 20% as sweet as sugar. Only when the bond in the molecule of lactose is broken, we can feel the sweetness. Usually we don't keep milk in mouth long enough to let this bond break. When milk is warmed up it can be noticed it tastes sweeter. Non-fat dry milk contains about 52% of lactose.

Fructose is known as the fruit sugar. It is frequently derived from sugar cane, sugar beets, and corn. The primary reason that fructose is used commercially in foods and beverages, besides its low cost, is its high relative sweetness. It is the sweetest of all naturally occurring carbohydrates. In general, fructose is regarded as being 1.73 times as sweet as sucrose.

Honey - consists of 50% fructose and 44% glucose.

Raffinose - little or no sweetness, occurring in the sugar beet, cottonseed, etc., and breaking down to fructose, glucose, and galactose on hydrolysis.

Galactose - makes up half of lactose, the sugar found in milk.

Starch - ferments slow, but can be used in slow-fermented sausages.

Maltodextrin can be derived from any starch. It is usually sweet or without any flavor. Maltodextrin is popular among body builders and athletes who take it along with whey protein, as it is a simple carbohydrate that converts quickly to energy. Dextrines ferment slow and their use is recommended for slow-fermented sausages.

Table of Sweetness

Sucrose, or table sugar, is a reference point with a value of 100 when comparing the sweetness of different sweeteners. If dextrose (75) were exchanged with sugar (100) by weight, the resulting product would be only 75% as sweet.

Relative Sweetness Scale - Sucrose = 100	
Fructose	170
High Fructose Corn Syrup	120-160
Sucrose (Sugar)	**100**
Brown sugar	97
Glucose (Dextrose)	70-80
Galactose	35
Maltose	30-50
Lactose	20

For example, if we combine dextrose with maltose when making a fast-fermented sausage, dextrose will be completely consumed by lactic acid bacteria, but a part of maltose will remain unfermented adding a degree of sweetness to the sausage. Once the fermentation stops, any leftover sugar will help to offset the sourly and tangy flavor of fast-fermented semi-dry sausage.

A typical amount of dextrose added to different fermented sausages		
Sausage type	Sugar per 1 kg of meat	Notes
Traditional artisanal salt-cured dry sausages	0	The production and safety of the sausage is entirely based on removal of moisture (drying), for example Hungarian salami.
Non-heated dry-fermented sausages	0.1 - 0.3% (1 - 3 g)	These are slow fermented high quality products like Italian salami or Spanish salchichón.
Non-heated semi-dry fermented sausages	0.5 - 1.0% (5 - 10 g)	After fermenting to ≤ pH 5.3, sausages are dried to lose 20% of the original weight.
Heated semi-dry fast-fermented sausages	1.0 - 2.0% (10 - 20 g)	After fermenting to ≤ pH 5.3, sausages are cooked to 145° F (63° C) for 4 minutes.
Fermented spreadable sausages	0.1-0.3% (1 - 2 g)	non-heated, fermented, usually smoked, soft texture - spreadable, short life, refrigerated

Sugar added in %	Final pH of the sausage	The data is given for orientation only the raw meat's pH can vary and needs to be measured. In general increasing sugar levels up to 1% decreases pH proportionally. *A lower pH is obtained with increasing temperature at the same sugar level.*
0.3-0.7	higher than 5.0	
0.8-1.0	lower than 5.0	
>1.0	4.5 - 4.8	

In specific products (e.g. American pepperoni), limiting the added sugar to 0.5-0.75% results in adequate fermentation with no residual carbohydrate present after.

More About Sugar

Although most reliable sources agree that adding 0.1% (1 g/kg) of dextrose will result in a 0.1 pH drop, thus adding 1% (10 g/kg) results in the approximate decline of 1 pH unit. Nevertheless, many sausage makers claim that less sugar is needed to drop pH from its initial 5.7-5.8 value to pH 5.2-5.3. They argue that 0.3-0.4% (3 - 4 g) is all needed. This amount is usually used for making traditional dry sausages. Chr-Hansen also mentions that culture graph data demonstrate that glucose concentration as low as 0.3% is enough to reach a pH below 5.3. This implies that the relationship between dextrose and pH drop is not directly proportional; it does not follow a linear scale but rather a logarithmic salami. To make it simple, a little less dextrose will suffice, especially in non-heated salami sausages. Another possible explanation is that around 0.2-0.3% of meat's natural sugar (glycogen) is metabolized by lactic bacteria and contributes to a small pH drop. However, in semi-dry sausages, when the intent is to drop pH by the full point from 5.7-5.8 to 4.6-4.8, adding 1% (10 g) of dextrose works fine.

Phosphates

Phosphates are commonly applied in the meat industry because they can bind massive amounts of water and retard fat rancidity. Most countries permit 0.5% of phosphates (5 g per kilogram of meat). Since moisture removal is crucial in producing fermented sausages, it makes little sense to add more water by using phosphates. However, in some products like cooked salami or non-fermented cooked salami, the latter having nothing in common with salami except the name and the looks, phosphates can be applied, at least in the commercial process.

Liquid Smoke

Liquid smoke is a yellow-to-red liquid that tastes like smoke. Selected woods are burnt, and the smoke is condensed in water and concentrated for the desired strength and flavor. There are different brands of liquid smoke, so run a test to verify their potency. It is widely used in commercial products as it lowers the cost. Note that, unlike natural smoke, liquid smoke will not change the color of the casings. The main advantage of using liquid smoke is that there is no need for a smoker and no emission of smoke. A sausage can be produced in the apartment without alarming the neighbors.

Flavorings and Herbal Infusions

The main flavor component in slow-fermented sausages is the meat itself, the aromatic flavors produced by the *Staphylococcu spp.* flavor-forming bacteria. Fermentation followed by an extensive drying period provides time and proper conditions for lactic, curing, and flavor-forming bacteria to start many reactions, ultimately creating those distinctive flavors. Spices bring beautiful flavors to food but are volatile, and their flavor disappears rapidly. For this reason, they play a lesser role in slow-fermented sausages, which require months of drying.

Fast or medium-fast fermented sausages, which are produced within 1-3 weeks, do not allow bacteria to fully develop meat flavor. Adding spices helps offset some of the sour flavor present in fast-fermented products.

Besides using different combinations of sugars to influence sausage flavor, many alcoholic beverages such as rum, red wine, sherry, brandy, Cointreau, or even beer are used. Popular flavoring is honey or fruit syrup. One can make herbal infusions/ flavorings by mixing about 20% fruit or whole spices with 80% spirit (vodka, rum, red wine) and leaving it in a closed container for about 3 days. Then, about 0.4% (4 g/kg) of filtered liquid (or plain spirit) may be added to minced meat. Some popular combinations (in percent):

rum-raspberry syrup 50/50
rum-honey 50/50
rum-bay leaves 90/10
rum-garlic (chopped) 90/10
red wine-garlic (chopped) 90/10
red wine-bay leaves 90/10

Spice wine: 100 g red wine, 5 g bay leaf, 5 juniper berries, 1/2 cinnamon stick, 1/2 clove. Place all ingredients in a closed glass jar and leave for 3 days. Filter and use.

You can use any quality liqueur of your choice, such as Curacao (bitter orange), Cointreau (orange), Cherry Liqueur, Drambuie (whiskey), Allasch (Caraway), Dom Benedictine (herbs), Brandy, or Cognac. Keep in mind that most liqueurs contain sugar or honey, and both of them will contribute to lower pH. However, in fast-fermented sausages, the rate of fermentation may be so rapid that lactic acid bacteria may stop working due to low pH. As a result, excess sugars and flavorings will not be converted to acid. In slow-fermented sausage, sweet combinations will increase acidity; hence, using excess sugar, sweet liqueurs, or wines should be carefully monitored. Dry wines, rum, or brandy are better choices.

Vinegar contains about 5% of acetic acid which gives it pH 2 - 3. Adding some vinegar to the mixture will increase acidity and offer more safety against bacteria.

Herbs, Spices, Seeds

Spices are mainly added for flavor. However, they also can stimulate the growth of lactic bacteria, which promotes stronger fermentation, have an antimicrobial properties on some bacteria, and have anti-oxidant properties that retards the development of fat rancidity. Black pepper is always added to fermented sausages. Spices that contain manganese are credited with promoting fermentation, and these are nutmeg, mace, ginger, paprika, garlic, allspice, mustard, cinnamon, and pepper. Other popular spices and herbs are allspice, marjoram, thyme, rosemary, fennel, anise, cinnamon, fenugreek, cloves, mace, mustard, nutmeg, ginger, cardamom, coriander, oregano; sage is normally added at around 0.1-0.2% (1-2 g/kg). Generally, the total of all spices amounts to about 1% (10 g/kg), although some spices like garlic, paprika, and Spanish pimentón are added in different amounts depending on preference.

South European sausages are more heavily spiced than North European or American types. The most plausible explanation is that those sausages are dried longer, so larger amounts of spices are added, as spices are very volatile and lose their aroma rapidly.

Allspice. It gets its name because it has flavor similar to the combination of cinnamon, cloves and nutmeg. Allspice can be used in any meat product or sausage. Some examples: *Swedish potato sausage, bologna, hotdog, frankfurter* and *head cheese.*

Anise is the star shaped dried fruit of *Pimpinella anisum.* Its flavor resembles that of fennel and of course it is added to fresh *Italian sausage* or sausages such as *Mortadella* or *Pepperoni.*

Bay leaf is principally used in vinegar pickles in products such as pigs feet, and lamb and pork tongues.

Caraway seed is the dried fruit of caraway plant which grows in Europe and the United States. An aromatic seed, somewhat resembling the cumin seed, often added to rye bread, sauerkraut, pickles and some sausages, for example *Kabanosy.*

Cardamom is the fruit that consists of a shell containing the seeds. Cardamom seeds are used in *liver sausages* and *head cheese.*

Celery seeds are used in pork sausages.

Chili peppers - originated in Mexico and spread all over the world. They have white, yellow, red or purple to black fruits and a varying degree of hotness.

Chili powder - a combination of chili pepper, cumin, oregano and garlic

Cinnamon - is the dried bark of *Cinnamomum Casia* tree which grows in India and China. Often added to *blood sausages* and *bologna.*

Cloves means nails (clavo) in Spanish and the dried flowers resemble a nail with its sharp point. Cloves go well with *emulsified sausages, head cheese, liver* and *blood sausages.* Cloves are usually inserted into hams which are baked.

Coriander seed is the dried fruit of the cilantro herb. Used in *emulsified sausages, Polish sausages, minced hams* and *pastrami.*

Cumin seed is principally used for making curry powder. It is also added to home made chili.

Curry - is a a combination of spices usually including ground turmeric, cumin, coriander, ginger, and fresh or dried chilies.

Dill seeds or leaf is added to vinegar when making cucumber pickles. Very popular in Eastern Europe where it is added to chicken soup or boiled potatoes.

Fennel is an aromatic herb very popular in Italian sausages.

Garlic, after pepper may be considered the most popular ingredient added to sausages. It also comes in dehydrated powder which is preferred as it saves storage and eliminates chores such as peeling and chopping. If using garlic powder use about 1/3 of the weight of fresh garlic. Although the flavor of fresh or granulated garlic is basically the same, fresh garlic has a much stronger aroma which unfortunately dissipates very fast.

Ginger is used in cooked sausages (white head cheese, liver sausage).

Juniper - berries from juniper tree or bush are a spice used in a wide variety of culinary dishes and best known for the primary flavoring in gin. Usually added to wild game sausages and Hunter sausages.

Mace and Nutmeg can leave a bitter taste when more than 0.01% (1g/1 kg of meat) is added. They come from the same large tree that grows in Malaysia. Mace is the covering of the seed (nut). The hard inside nut becomes nutmeg. As a rule they are not used in fresh sausages as their aroma is easily noticeable. Mace is often used in *liver sausages, frankfurters, hot dogs* and *bologna.*

Marjoram is added to liver sausages, head cheese and many Polish sausages.

Mustard is the seed of the mustard plant which is grown all over the world. There is yellow mustard (most popular), brown mustard and black mustard seed.

Onion is added to liver sausage and other sausages. It also comes in dehydrated powder which is preferred as it saves storage and eliminates chores such as peeling and chopping.

Oregano is an aromatic herb very popular in Italian and Spanish sausages.

Paprika is of two different kinds: Hungarian which is sweet, and Spanish which is slightly pungent. Paprika is a well known colorant and will give the sausage an orange tint. It goes well with *emulsified sausages (hot dog, bologna)* or any pork sausage.

Pepper. Ground pepper is the spice that is added to all fermented sausages. It is available as whole seeds but you have to grind them. It comes in two forms: **black pepper** - unripe seeds of the plant with the skin left on, **white pepper** - ripe seeds with the skin removed. It is available as coarse grind, sometimes called butcher's grind or fine grind. A recipe will call for a particular grind but the final choice will be up to you. Some recipes will call for whole pepper corns. The dividing line is whether you want to see the pepper in your product or not. Without a doubt *black pepper is the most popular spice* added to fermented sausages.

Pepper - Cayenne. Cayenne pepper is a moderately hot chili pepper used to flavor dishes. Cayenne powder may be a blend of different types of peppers and can be extremely hot.

Pepper - Red Pepper Flakes. Red pepper flakes are quite hot and consist of dried and crushed (as opposed to ground) red chili cayenne-type peppers.

Pimentón - is Spanish paprika which is usually not smoked unless the label states otherwise. Only *Pimentón de La Vera is always smoked.* Spanish sausages such as chorizo, sobrasada and others display a unique vivid red color which is due to pimentón. Spanish pimentón is darker than paprika and has a more intense flavor. It is added to dry chorizo in large quantity, often at 2 - 3%. Depending on hotness pimentón can be mild, semi-hot or hot.

Peperoncino - these peppers have a spicy, mildly fruity taste and aroma and come from Calabria in southern Italy. They are used in Italian sausages, for example in fermented spreadable Nduja.

Quatre épices (4 spices) – a French spice combination that can vary in strength and combination of spices; however, it always contains: nutmeg, cinnamon, and cloves. The fourth ingredient can be ginger, allspice, or caraway or their combination.

Rosemary is a woody, perennial herb with fragrant, evergreen, needle-like leaves. It has a characteristic and strong aroma which goes well with roasted and barbecued meats as well as with wild game meats and sausages. Add at 0.01% (1 g/1 kg).

Sage is used in pork sausages, for example American breakfast sausage.

Savory is good with any sausage. It has a slightly minty and pungent flavor and it tastes like a combination of oregano and thyme.

Tabasco peppers are grown in Louisiana and fermented into Tabasco sauce.

Thyme is added to liver sausage, head cheese, bockwurst and other pork sausages. Thyme is similar to marjoram but stronger.

Turmeric is the rhizome or underground stem of a ginger-like plant. It is available as a ground, bright yellow fine powder. It is the principal ingredient in curry powder. Turmeric is a natural yellow colorant. It is added to Asian sausages, for example to Balinese *Urutan* dry sausage.

To avoid introducing undesirable/unknown microorganisms into the sausage, fresh herbs, peppers, onions, or garlic should be avoided. All herbs or spices are available in powdered form. Dried herbs and spices must be used within 6 months after opening and should be kept in dry conditions under cold or room temperature, as high humidity will promote the growth of molds.

When using natural spices allow 12-24 hours for releasing flavor to meat. It can apply only to very fast-fermented or fully cooked sausages.

- Dark spices such as nutmeg, caraway, cloves, and allspice can darken the color of the sausage.
- Meat plants use commercially prepared extracts that have a much stronger flavor.
- Similarly to the case of coffee beans, the advantage of grinding seeds before use is a fresher aroma.

Spices and Herbs with Beneficial Properties

Beneficial Properties of Certain Herbs and Spices			
Spice - Herb	Promoting Lactic Bacteria	Anti-oxydative (fat rancidity)	Anti-microbial
Allspice	v		
Cinnamon	v		v
Cloves			v
Coriander			v
Cumin			v
Garlic	v	v	when applied at ≥ 5%
Ginger	v		
Mace	v		
Mustard	v		v
Nutmeg	v		
Oregano			v
Paprika	v		
Pimentón	v		
Red peppers (chili)	v		
Rosemary		v	
Sage		v	
Thyme		v	v

Nuts

In recent years, fermented sausages with nuts have appeared. Given that nuts have water activities that are generally less than Aw 0.70, they are shelf-stable and may be added to different types of sausages. Adding walnuts or hazelnuts creates dry sausage with a new flavor profile. Additionally, the product looks visually pleasing when sliced.

Cheeses

Given that all cured meats and salami taste great when paired with cheese, it comes as no surprise that combining cheese with ground meat makes a great salami-cheese sausage. A yellow hard cheese cut into 3/8" (1 cm) cubes will work great. A cheese with a high melting point should be selected as most semi-dry fermented sausages are heat treated to around 145° F (63° C). There is a wider range of cheeses to choose from when making a non-heated fermented dry salami, given that there is no heat treatment involved, and the cheese will dry out along with the meat. Cheeses with a high melting point: Swiss Emmental, American Cheddar, Cabot.

Chapter 6

Safety Hurdles

Food safety is nothing else but the control of bacteria. Once one knows what bacteria like or dislike, it becomes simple and easy to produce safe products.

This important chapter which explains how to:

- Protect yourself from becoming ill or seriously sick.
- Protect your sausage from spoiling - nobody wants to take care of the sausage for a month or longer and find out that the product is non-edible. This would be a disappointment and a waste of time and money.

There is a big difference between a hobbyist maintaining food safety at home and a commercial food establishment.

Advantages of a Commercial Food Establishment

1. Commercial producers are constantly supervised by meat inspectors who work for the Food Safety and Inspection Service. Even a local deli or a restaurant is subject to unannounced visits by meat inspectors from the local Health Authority who check whether the establishment is clean and up to standards. They check how dishes and equipment are washed and sanitized, whether hot water runs at 180° F (82° C), the temperature in the refrigerator and freezer, and whether the compartment sink is connected to a grease trap; they check a wash and mop sink and how clean is the rest room for employees. They even check whether the equipment carries a National Sanitation Foundation (NSF) certificate, showing that commercial food equipment meets industry sanitation and electrical safety standards. All this is done to ensure that food is produced correctly and safe for the consumer.

2. A commercial plant uses specialized equipment that is not only expensive but also too big to fit at home. This specialized machinery can process frozen meat and fat. A bowl cutter can cleanly chop meat particles as small as 1/16" (1.5 mm). The minced meat is mixed and stuffed under a vacuum, which removes oxygen, which could interfere with color and flavor development and promote the development of fat rancidity later. Modern curing chambers can mimic any type of climate as the temperature, humidity, and airflow are computer controlled. 3. A commercial plant employs highly trained food technologists and personnel.

Advantages of a Hobbyist Working at Home

There are some good news for a hobbyist, too:

- For hundreds years we have been making wonderful salami with knife only so they can be made great again.
- He can make hundreds different sausages and modify each recipe at will. A commercial producer cannot do as his production depends on orders from supermarkets, they order products which are profitable and easy to sell.
- He is not a subject to visits by meat inspector.
- He has all time in the world for making his sausage as it is a hobby and fun.

Although it can be assumed that people intending to make salami have prior experience with making regular sausages, they could have developed a false sense of security, given that they never fell ill. However, it must be realized that there is almost no risk involved when making fully cooked sausages, given that the heat kills all bacteria, making products safe. Additionally, they are kept under refrigeration anyhow. Traditionally made salami-type products are made from raw meat; in many cases, they are not cooked at all but can be stored at room temperature. Clearly, there must be some "tricks" to make it possible. Well, what we called tricks or secrets before is today known as Good Manufacturing Practices (GMP), and this chapter is all about it.The manufacture of fermented sausages at home formidable hazards because:

- Temperatures in the kitchen will be much higher than in a commercial meat plant, even with a fully running air conditioning system.
- The temperature of the sausage mince may be higher than recommended.
- Home sausage making equipment processes meats very slowly, increasing the temperature.
- Mixing and stuffing are not performed under a vacuum which may affect color and make fats rancid later.
- Fermenting and drying chambers often lack the proper temperature, humidity and air speed controls.
- Lack of proper testing equipment (pH, Aw) and the list goes on.

The only way fermented sausages can be successfully made at home is to follow good manufacturing practices exactly. This becomes even more important if one intends to produce a traditional salami without using a starter culture. The kitchen becomes a little meat plant, and Suzie and Paul must become not only proficient sausage makers but also competent meat technologists. Once sufficient knowledge of the subject is acquired, control of microorganisms will become a part of the sausage making procedure, almost like a new tool that is needed to produce a good product. We will realize that not only is there nothing to be afraid of bacteria, but that they can be a helpful partner. The rest will fall into the proper place. And remember, we have been making those products for thousands of years, and books were not even around.

FSIS (Food Safety and Inspection Service), 9 CFR 430.1 **Ready-to-Eat Fermented, Salt-Cured, and Dried Products Guideline, May 5, 2023:**

Ready-to-eat meat and poultry is a meat or poultry product that is in a form *that is edible without additional preparation* to achieve food safety and may receive additional preparation for palatability or aesthetic, epicurean, gastronomic, or culinary purposes.

Shelf-stable for the purposes of meat and poultry products is defined as the condition achieved when meat and poultry products *can be stored under ambient temperature and humidity conditions;* if the package integrity is maintained during storage, shipping, and display at retail and in the home; and the product will not spoil or become unsafe throughout the manufacturer's specified shelf-life.

Outgrowth of the following are hazards in raw products that fermentation, salt-curing, or drying steps should be designed *to limit* in the finished RTE product:

- *Staphylococcus aureus (S. aureus)*
- *Clostridium perfringens (C. perfringens)*
- *Clostridium botulinum (C. botulinum)*

The following are hazards present in raw products that the fermentation, salt curing, or drying steps should be de (signed *to destroy* in the finished RTE product:

- *Salmonella*
- *STEC (E.coli 0157:H7*
- *Listeria monocytogenes*
- *Trichinella spiralis (T. spiralis)* and *Toxoplasma gondii (T. gondii)* (greater risk of infection for feral or non-confinement raised swine).

These hazards may be of concern at various points in the production process and multiple hurdles may be needed to address each hazard.

Lethality is the process or combination of processes that ensures that *no Salmonella organisms remain* in the finished product, *as well as reduces* other pathogens and their toxins or toxin metabolites. Examples of lethality processes include cooking, fermentation, salt-curing, and drying.

Stabilization is the process of *preventing or limiting the growth of spore-forming bacteria capable of producing toxins* either in the product before consumption or in the human intestine after consumption. Establishments may use a variety different stabilization processes such as cooling, hot-holding, or meeting and maintaining certain pH or water activity levels.

Fermentation and drying alone are not particularly effective lethality treatments. It is not enough to only meet degree-hours, follow a drying or salt-curing method for *Trichinella*, and achieve a final water activity for shelf-stability. *Degree-hours are intended to control the outgrowth of S. aureus.* To reduce levels of other pathogens such as *Salmonella,* products often need to be fermented to *a lower pH than 5.3.*

Shelf-Stability Targets

Fermented, salt-cured, and dried products typically achieve shelf-stability through a combination of hurdles such as reduced pH, reduced water activity, or a combination of both, along with other extrinsic factors, such as reduced oxygen and packaging. **S. aureus is the main pathogen of concern during storage of shelf-stable products because it can grow at a lower water activity than other pathogens. To achieve of shelf-stability, no outgrowth of S. aureus may occur in the product.** Minimizing available water (e.g., by achieving a sufficiently low water activity) is necessary to achieve shelf stability, provided measures are taken to address undesirable mold growth. Such measures to prevent undesirable mold growth may include using short inventory pull dates, low pH, antimycotics (such as potassium sorbate sprays and dips), coatings, packaging, or any combination of these measures.

Sausage Type	Aw	pH
Very perishable	> 0.95	> 5.2
Perishable	0.95 - 0.91	5.2 - 5.0
Shelf stable	< 0.90	< 5.3
	single hurdle enough →	4.6
	0.85	← single hurdle enough

Note: In Europe, fermented meat with a pH of ≤5.2 and a water activity (Aw) of 0.95 or less is considered shelf stable. A shelf-stable foods are foods that can safely sit on the pantry shelf for at least one year and be safe to consume.

Types of Safety Hurdles

A sophisticated alarm system consists of many layers: perimeter protection, motion detectors, sirens and central station connection. Hurdles are like an alarm - they need many levels of security measures to stop intruding bacteria. Generally, *one step is not sufficient* to eliminate or destroy pathogens such as *Staphylococcus auereus, Clostridium botulinum, Clostridium perfringens, E. coli O157:H7, Salmonella, Listeria monocytogenes,* or parasites like *Trichinella spiralis, Toxoplasma gondii,* instead a *combination of processing steps* known as *hurdles* is needed:

- Processing meats with a low bacteria count at low temperatures.
- Using cold equipment.
- Adding sufficient amount of salt.
- Adding nitrite/nitrate.
- Lowering pH to < 5.3 with bacterial fermentation or chemical acidulation within prescribed time.
- Lowering Aw (water activity) by drying to < 0.91.
- Using bio-protective cultures.
- Smoking.
- Cooking.
- Spices.
- Cleanliness and common sense.

How Do Bacteria Get Into Meat?

The meat of a healthy animal is clean, and any invading bacteria will be destroyed by the animal's immune system. Once the animal is slaughtered, these defense mechanisms are destroyed, and the meat enters rapid decay. Although unaware of the process, early sausage makers knew that once the animal was killed, it was a race between external preservation techniques and the decomposition of the raw meats to decide the ultimate fate of the issue. Most bacteria are present on the skin and in the intestines. The slaughtering process starts introducing them into the exposed surfaces. For example, the infamous *E. coli O157:H7* is a dangerous pathogen that was involved in recalls of fermented sausages. It is carried by cattle, and incorrect washing and removing beef hides or punctuating intestines will infect the meat. Then bacteria can cross-contaminate live pigs or pork meat when unsanitary conditions are present on the premises.

Given time bacteria will find their way inside the meat anyhow, but the trouble starts when we create a new surface cut with a knife. This creates an opening for bacteria to enter the meat from the outside and start spoiling it. We must realize that they don't appear in some magical way inside of the meat, they always start from the outside and they work their way in.

Meat Surface Area and Volume Relationship

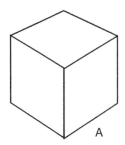 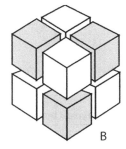

Fig. 6.1 Relationship of surface area and volume.

A. Cube A is 1 inch on each side and has a volume of 1 cubic inch and the surface area of 6 square inches.

B. Three complete cuts (two vertical and one horizontal) produce eight small cubes with a volume of 0.125 cubic inch.

Total volume remains the same - 1 cubic inch, but total *surface area has doubled* and is 12 square inches.

This is what happens when the meat is cut; the surface area increases. When the grinder cuts meat through a 1/8" (3 mm) plate, it creates an infinite number of small particles that are exposed to air. Spoilage bacteria need air to live. The more cuts, the more air and free water available to bacteria and the more spoils of meat. This is the reason why ground meat has the shortest shelf life. In a large piece of meat, the outside surface serves as a natural barrier that prevents access to bacteria. They have a long distance to travel to reach the center of the meat.

Working with Meat

Meat muscles are surrounded with a connective tissue which also *acts as a protective sheath and so does the outside skin*. Duties like cutting meat, grinding, mixing or stuffing all increase meat temperature and should be performed at the lowest attainable in the kitchen temperatures. If working at higher temperatures try to process meats as fast as possible and then place them back in a refrigerator. *Take only what you need.*

Some bacteria are present on our hands, others live in our nose and throat so personal hygiene is of utmost importance. In addition, each meat processing facility develops its own microbiological flora in which bacteria live on walls, ceilings, machinery, tools etc. All those bacteria are just waiting to jump on a piece of meat and start working in. This is the reason why meat plants have to be continuously sanitized and cleaned.

Going into detail on selecting meats according to their pH or using terms like PSE, DFD, or MDM meats is beyond the scope of these pages and will make them confusing to read. What we want to stress is that meat must be as fresh as possible with the lowest count of bacteria possible. A home-based sausage maker must make sure that:

- *Meat is very fresh and always kept cold.*
- *Facilities and tools are very clean.*
- *Working temperatures are as low as possible.*
- *Take only what you need rule always applies.*

Temperature Control

It is crucial to maintain *the lowest possible temperature* during the first processing steps, such as meat selection, cutting, grinding, mixing and stuffing. During those periods, meat is hopelessly unprotected and left at the mercy of spoilage and pathogenic bacteria. Until salt and nitrite are added, the only defense against meat spoilage is the low initial bacteria count of fresh meat and the low processing temperature.

Typical temperatures of cooling units

Home refrigerator	Butcher's cooler
36 - 40 F° (2°- 4° C)	32 F ° (0° C)
Home freezer	Butcher's freezer
0° F (-18° C)	-25° F (- 32° C)

Meat Thawing

People living in metropolitan areas generally purchase meat in large supermarkets or from local butchers, quite often being motivated by the attractive price. Such meat should be processed as soon as possible. However, it can be frozen. No meat should be thawed at room temperature, even if wrapped around with foil or paper, since it is not protected yet. The number of bacteria will reach dangerous levels, which will create detrimental conditions for the production of fermented products. The simplest thawing method is holding meat in the refrigerator until partially frozen and ready for processing.

Salt

Bacteria hate salt and different bacteria strains possess different degrees of tolerance. For example, *Lactobacillus* lactic acid bacteria as well as curing bacteria S*taphylococcus* and *Kocuria*, show more resistance to salt than spoilage or pathogenic types. By competing for nutrients with spoilage and pathogenic bacteria they prevent them from growing.

To stop bacteria from growing by salt alone, the salt levels will have to be so high that the product will not be edible. Applying salt at more than 4% will inhibit lactic bacteria from producing lactic acid, and as a result, little fermentation will take place. Since stopping them with salt entirely is not a practical solution then how about making life for them just miserable? And this is exactly what we do by adding between 2.5% – 3% salt into the minced meat.

Nitrite

Nitrite (at 100 - 156 ppm), in combination with salt (2.5%), completely inhibits the growth of *C. botulinum,* and greatly inhibits the growth of *C. perfringens*. It also slows the growth of *Salmonella* and *Listeria monocytogenes*. Although cases of food poisoning by *Cl.botulinum* are rather rare, they have one thing in common - they are fatal.

Lowering pH

Once the pH reaches 5.3 or less, *Staphylococcus aureus* and other pathogens are kept in check and further lowering pH supported by drying or precooking will create a microbiologically stable product. There are three methods of lowering pH:

- Lowering pH with bacterial fermentation.
- Lowering pH with chemical acidification.
- Combining natural fermentation with acidification together.

Lowering pH with Bacterial Fermentation

When using acidity as a main safety hurdle, most fast-fermented sausages are microbiologically stable when pH drops to 4.6 within a prescribed time. Depending on the culture and fermentation temperature, this can be easily accomplished within 12-36 hours for a fast-fermented sausage and 48-72 hours for a medium-fermented type. In traditional slow-fermented sausages, the acidity of meat increases very slowly and never reaches the point that might guarantee the safety of the sausage. Those sausages depend on drying to become microbiologically stable.

Lowering pH with Chemical Acidulation

Providing safety by increasing acidity with chemical acidulants is based on the principle that bacteria cannot grow in acidic environment. Immerse any sausage in vinegar and it can be stored at room temperature without spoiling.

There are two common acidulants that can be used for making fermented sausages:
- Gdl (Glucono-delta-lactone).
- Citric acid.

It shall be noted that pH drop can be accomplished with Gdl acting alone or the Gdl can be added to meat which is fermented with bacteria. In such a case some sugar was added already what will lower the pH of the meat. Adding Gdl will lower the pH even more.

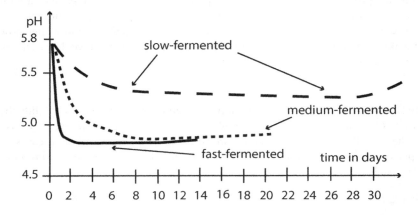

Fig. 6.2 Decrease in pH in slow, medium and fast-fermented sausages

Lowering Aw

Removing water content by drying a sausage is a slow process and may be compared to stealing water from bacteria to prevent their growth. Just adding 3% salt reduces the initial water activity in meat to 0.97. The sausage starts to lose moisture from the time it enters the fermentation room and continues to do so through the drying process. In about 3-6 days, the Aw drops to about 0.95 and the sausage is more stable as some pathogenic bacteria (*Salmonella, Bacillus*) stop multiplying. Most microorganisms do not grow below Aw 0.91, with a few exceptions, notably *Staphylococcus aureus,* which remains active until 0.86. Molds, of course, show great resistance to low moisture levels. The activity of most spoilage and pathogenic bacteria stops when Aw of 0.89 is reached. Aw drop is little affected by pH or the number of bacteria, and is more linear in nature. Stated simply, the drying process is time-dependent and factors that affect drying will also influence a decrease in water activity.

> *"The higher Aw, the lower pH is needed to protect sausages against undesirable bacteria and vice versa"*

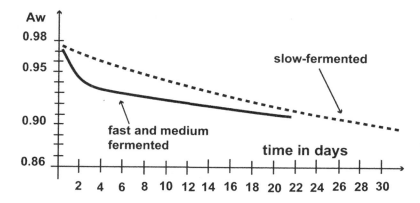

Fig. 6.3 Decrease in Aw in fast, medium and slow-fermented sausages.

Starter Cultures

The addition of any commercial culture provides introduces millions of bacteria which compete for food (moisture, oxygen, sugar, protein) with a small number of bacteria residing in meat, preventing them from growing. Keep in mind that all cultures, although in varying degree, go through a lag phase, which is generally longer for slow fermenting types and lasts 6-14 hours, the shorter time corresponding to higher temperatures.

Bio-protective Cultures

Bio-protective cultures may be added to produce fermented sausages with a short production type where a higher count of *Listeria monocytogenes* bacteria may be suspected. Chr-Hansen SafePro® cultures contain *Pediococcus acidilactici* which can control *Listeria* while performing as a classic starter culture for fermented sausages. *Pediococcus acidilactici* and *Lactobacillus curvatus* strains produce *pediocin* and *curvacin* (kind of "antibiotics") that destroy the *Listeria monocytogenes'* cell membrane and reduce their numbers. This is known as *competitive exclusion* - using desirable competitive microorganisms to inhibit undesirable organisms.

Smoking

Smoking is of lesser importance as a safety hurdle. However, it provides some protection against bacteria on the surface area and inhibits the formation of mold. Since it is a part of a drying process, it contributes to the removal of moisture.

Cooking

Cooking is a very effective way to kill bacteria, but it is hard to imagine cooking a traditional salami since this will alter its texture, taste, and flavor. In order to comply with the latest regulations, many fast-fermented semi-dry sausages are often partially cooked.

Cooking fermented sausages makes them safer, as the heat kills bacteria. On the downside, this heat also kills bacteria that are instrumental in developing meat flavor. For example, raw semi-dry products exhibit higher sensory values than cooked products. The texture of a fully cooked sausage will suffer, as the individual specs of fat so typical in these sausages will melt down and be less visible; the sausage will become creamier.

Many recipes ask for cooking sausages to 137° F (58° C) as the risk of *trichinosis* is eliminated at this temperature. In the USA, it is assumed that a pig, due to a strictly controlled diet, is trichinae-free. In Europe, every slaughtered pig is inspected for *trichinosis*. Freezing pork also prevents the possibility of contracting *trichinosis,* and such meat can be used in sausages that will not be cooked. Cooking meat fully to 160° F (72° C) takes care of *Trichinae* and all other bacteria.

Spices

Spices alone cannot be used as a hurdle against meat spoilage as the average amount added to meat is only about 0.1% (1 g/1 kg). To inhibit bacteria, the amounts of spices will have to be very large, which will alter the taste of the sausage. The latest research establishes that spices such as mustard, cinnamon, and cloves are helpful in slowing the growth of molds, yeast, and bacteria. Use of fresh spice in fermented products is generally not a good idea. Fresh spices being moist may contain bacteria, insects, and molds, which will be introduced into the sausage and may affect the process. Most cases of illness associated with *Campylobacter* are caused by handling raw poultry or eating raw or undercooked poultry meat, and only garlic offers some protection. Fresh garlic at a concentration of 5% demonstrated the most potent effect, but such a high concentration may not be acceptable to many people because of its strong flavor.

Cleanliness and Common Sense

Home made sausages are subject to the ambient temperature of the kitchen and a dose of a common sense is of invaluable help:

- Take only what you need from the cooler.
- When a part of the meat is processed put it back into the cooler.
- Keep your equipment clean and cold.
- Work as fast as possible.
- Try to keep meat always refrigerated.
- Work at the lowest possible temperature.
- Wash your hands with soap often.
- Use food grade heavier gloves for mixing. Our hands are at 98° F (37° F) and 10 minutes of mixing will raise the temperature of the ground mix.
- Clean food preparation area with diluted bleach.

The table below indicates the factors which can affect growth of pathogenic microorganisms associated with meat.

Factors Restricting Growth of Pathogenic Bacteria				
Pathogen	Salt tolerance	Needs pH at or above this value to grow	Moisture tolerance- needs Aw at or Above	Remarks
Cl. botulinum	5%	pH 4.6	Aw 0.94	nitrite effectively inhibits its growth, oxygen restricts its growth, grows best at 80-130° F (26-54° C)
Cl. perfringens	5-10%	pH 5.0	Av 0.95	grows best at 80-130° F (26-54° C), does not grow below 59° F (15° C)
St. auerus *	10%	pH 4.2-4.6. Does not produce toxin at pH ≤ 5.2	Aw 0.85	tolerates nitrite, likes oxygen, hates acidity, grows slow below 60° F (15.6° C), grows fast above this temperature and may produce toxin.
E. coli 0157:H		pH 4.4	Aw 0.95	mainly in beef and lamb, also in pork
Salmonella		pH 3.8	Aw 0.94	mainly in pork, also in beef, inhibited by nitrite
Listeria	10%	pH 4.4	Aw 0.90	good until Aw 0.93, can grow at ≥ 31° F (-1° C)
Campylobacter	1%	pH 4.9	Aw 0.98	mainly in chicken,

* Growth of St. aureus and production of toxin are greatest at approximately 68-98° F (20–37° C), but growth can occur between 45-118° F (8-48° C). This toxin is heat stable, being tolerant to boiling for 1 h. Canning under pressure at 249° F (121° C) for 30 min is sufficient to destroy the toxin.

Factors Restricting Growth of Other Microorganisms				
Spoilage bacteria	poor when salt added above 2%	poor tolerance to acidity	Aw 0.95	inhibited below Aw 0.97-0.96. Need oxygen, hence removal of air during processing is important.
Lactic acid bacteria	up to 6%	pH 3.3	Aw 0.95	performance drops when: more than 3.3% salt added or Aw drops to ≤ 0.91. Need little oxygen.
Curing and flavor forming bacteria	5%	pH 5.0	Aw 0.95	less effective below pH 5.5. Stop working at pH 5.0.
Molds	good	pH 1.2	Aw 0.80	need oxygen, sensitive to smoke
Yeasts	good	pH 2.0	Aw 0.85	need little oxygen. sensitive to smoke

The U.S. Standards And Regulations

With growing popularity of fermented meat products it was inevitable, that some sausage-related outbreaks would follow:

USA			Other Countries		
Product	Year	Pathogen	Product	Year	Pathogen
Salami sticks	2021	*Salmonella*	Dry sausage	2020 France	*Salmonella*
Italian-style meats	2021	*Salmonella*	Fuet (made in Spain)	2020 France	*Salmonella*
Lebanon Bologna	2011	*E. coli O157:H7*	Coppa (made in Italy)	2019 France	*Salmonella*
Prosciutto, capocollo, calabrese, sopressata	2010	*E. coli O157:H7*	Beef salami	2018 Denmark	*E. coli (STEC)*
Lebanon Bologna	1995	*Salmonella*	Pork sausage	2018 Denmark	*Salmonella*
Salami	1994	*E. coli O157:H7*	Duck prosciutto	2015 Australia	*Salmonella*
Basturma	1982	*Salmonella*	Biltong	2008 UK	*Salmonella*

After 1994 salami outbreak, the United States Department of Agriculture's "Food Safety and Inspection Service" panicked, and acting in good intentions, introduced new measures to protect consumers, which as a result affected organoleptic properties of some fermented and dried (jerky) products. In 1997, FSIS (Food Safety and Inspection Service) initiated intensified and expanded microbiological testing of dry and semi-dry fermented sausages for *E. coli O157:H7, Listeria sp., Salmonella sp.* and *Staphylococcus aureus.*

Stringent regulations were issued, which became a nightmare for small establishments. Some producers tried to address the *E. coli O157:H7* problem by removing beef from their recipes; others stopped production altogether, but most started cooking sausages to satisfy new standards. However, this brought changes to their texture and flavor. This led to a larger variety of fermented sausages having a greater percentage of acidity, given that acidity is a potent and easy-to-measure tool against the growth of dangerous bacteria. This increased acidity, followed by heating, made the production of the sausages safer, faster, and more profitable. On the downside, the sausages acquired a sour taste, which somehow was accepted by American consumers. As a result, we have the American style of fermented sausages, which are fast-fermented, medium-fermented, acidified (non-fermented), fermented and fully cooked, and others.

Does Pork Gets Infected with E. coli 0157:H7 ?

There are *many strains of E. coli;* most are harmless to animals including humans, howevwr, *E. coli 0157:H7* is a major dangerous strain to humans and is shed (excreted) in the manure of cattle.

Quote from Federal Register: Feb 27, 2001 (Vol 66. # 39): *"Cattle and sheep may carry E. coli O157:H7 in the intestinal tract at the time of slaughter. However, among commercially-prepared meat products, only those that contain beef have been implicated in a number of foodborne illnesses associated with this pathogen."* Healthy cattle carry *E. coli O157:H7* in their digestive tract, and it can contaminate the surface area of beef during slaughter. The bacteria will only be found on the surface, not within the muscle fibers. However, if contaminated meat is cut or ground, the bacteria can be carried down into the meat or mixed throughout ground meat. The answer to the question above is that *although pigs do not carry E. coli O157:H7, they may get bacteria through cross-contamination. E. coli O157:H7* also survives well in the environment and can be found in fruits and vegetables. Secondly, in rural areas cattle and pigs are often raised on the same farm and an employee can spread bacteria on his rubber boots. *Note:* meat purchased from reputable sources such as butcher shops or supermarkets should not contain *E. coli O157:H7*.

The Degree-Hours Concept for Establishing Safety of the Fermented Sausages

The following procedure is widely used in the USA for establishing microbiological safety of fermented sausages. However, it is the "American" way to consider safety and for the rest of the world the concept is of lesser importance. The American concept is based on acidity whereas in other countries prolonged drying establishes safety. American products are usually cooked after fermentation, while European salami are not cooked.

The US Degree-Temperature Tables For Choosing Temperature and Length of Fermentation

Adapted from Good Manufacturing Practices (The American Meat Institute, 1997).

Dry sausages are products that, as a result of bacterial action or direct acidulation should reach a pH of 5.3 or less and are then dried to remove 25-50% of the moisture, resulting in a moisture/protein ratio complying with the standards.

Semi-dry sausages are products, that as a result of bacterial action or direct acidulation should reach a pH of 5.3 or less and are then dried to remove 15% of the moisture, resulting in a moisture/protein ratio of 3.1:1 or less. Some semi-dry sausages receive a pasteurization treatment following the fermentation period and and some are shelf stable. FSIS (Food Safety and Inspection Service(requires that these shelf-stable products be nitrite cured, fermented, smoked, reach a final pH of 5.0 or less, and have a moisture/protein ratio of 1.9:1 or less.

Fermented and acidulated sausages (citric acid, lactic acid or GDL added) shall attain a pH of 5.3 or lower *within the proper time frame* (defined in temperature-degrees below) in order to control the growth of pathogenic bacteria such as *E. coli 0157:H* and *Staphylococcus aureus*. **During fermentation of sausages to a pH 5.3, it is necessary to limit the time during which the sausage is exposed to temperatures exceeding 60° F (15.6° C),** otherwise the product will spoil, even though the recommended pH was attained. This time frame is temperature dependent and these are the following criteria:

Time in F degree-hours **above** 60° F	Fermentation temperature
less than 1200	less than 90° F (32° C)
< 1000	90 - 100° F (32 - 38° C)
< 900	greater than 100° F (38 °C)

Constant Temperature Fermentation

Degree-hours **above** 60° F	Fermentation temperature		Maximum hours to pH 5.3
	° F	° C	
1200	75	24	80
1200	80	27	60
1200	85	30	48
1000	90	32	33
1000	95	35	28
1000	100	38	25
900	105	41	20
900	110	44	18

The above table provides maximum hours that a product may be fermented at given **constant** fermentation temperature (measured in ° F) to obtain pH 5.3. For example, at 80° F (27° C) constant temperature a sausage must reach pH 5.3 within 60 hours *or less*. Those hours can also be calculated for any temperature and the following examples demonstrate how.

Example A: Sausage fermented for 46 hours at 85° F to pH of 5.3.
Degrees: 85°F - 60°F = 25 degrees. Hours: 46.
Degree-hours = 25 degrees x 46 hours = 1150 degree-hours. The process passes the **limit of 1200 degree-hours** by 50 hours. *Therefore, products that reach a pH of 5.3 in 46 hours at 85°F are considered safe from enterotoxin production during fermentation.*

Example B: Constant temperature 90° F for 40 hours with a pH decline to 5.3.
Degrees: 90° F - 60°F = 30 degrees. Hours: 40.
Degree-hours: 30 degrees x 40 hours = 1200 degree-hours.
Process B **fails** the guideline limit of 1000 degree-hours.

Variable Temperature Fermentation

In many cases fermentation proceeds at different temperatures and *for each temperature setting, a separate degree-hours are calculated and then added together.* In testing each process, each step-up in the progression is analyzed for the number of degree-hours it contributes, *with the highest temperature used in the fermentation process determining the degree-hour limitation.* Degree hours is calculated *for each temperature* during fermentation.

Example C:

F Degree - hours above 60° F	Chamber ° F	Adjusted Temperature	Degrees Result	Maximum hours to pH 5.3
10 hrs	75	75 - 60 =	15	10 x 15 = 150
10 hrs	85	85 - 60 =	25	10 x 25 = 250
14 hrs	95	95 - 60 =	35	14 x 35 = 490
			Total degree-hours:	890

In the above example a product was fermented at three different temperatures (75, 85 and 95° F) for a total time of 34 hours.

The total sum of the calculated degree-hours is 890 hours which is less than the maximum of 1000 hours for 90 - 100° F temperature range. Process C **passes** the guidelines.

Example D:

F Degree hours above 60° F	Chamber ° F	Adjusted Temperature	Degrees	Maximum hours to pH 5.3
10 hrs	75	75 - 60 =	15	10 x 15 = 150
12 hrs	85	85 - 60 =	25	12 x 25 = 300
18 hrs	98	98 - 60 =	38	18 x 38 = 684
			Total degree-hours:	1134

Process D **fails** the guideline because the limit is set at 1000 degree-hours for these times and temperatures and the process has taken 1134 degree-hours to reach pH 5.3

Canadian Fermentation Standards (MH MOP, Chapter 14.10.3 (15) - **Fermented Meat Products**).

As most of the world uses the metric system we are enclosing Canadian Food Inspection Agency standards for fermentation times which are based on degrees Centigrade. Those standards are based on degree/temperatures and the same starting temperature of **15.6° C** (60° F) is used as in the US Standards. At this temperature **15.6° C** (60° F) *Staphylococcus aureus* starts to grow and produce toxins.

Degree/hours are the product of time as measured in hours at a particular fermentation temperature multiplied by the degrees over 15.6° C (60° F).

Degree/hours = *time (hours) x temperature in excess of 15.6° C (60° F).*

Note: degrees measured *as the excess over 15.6° C. Explanation:* if the sausage is fermented at the constant temperature of 26° C for 20 hours its degrees value is 26° C - 15.6° C = 10.4 degrees. Then, 10.4 degrees x 20 hrs = ***208 degree-hours.***

*Fermented sausages must reach **pH 5.3 or lower within a certain time, depending on temperature.*** The reason being that at pH < 5.3 *Staphylococcus aureus* growth is inhibited.

Time in C degree-hours **above** 15.6° C	Maximum chamber temperature
less than 665	less than 33° C, (91° F)
< 555	33-37° C (91 - 99° F)
< 500	greater than 37° C, (99° F)

Constant Temperature Fermentation

The table below provides the maximum hours that a product may be fermented at a given **constant** fermentation temperature (measured in ° C) to obtain pH 5.3. For example at 30° C (86° F) constant temperature a sausage must reach pH 5.3 within 46.2 hours or less. The following examples demonstrate how to calculate degree-hours for various fermentation temperatures.

C ° degree-hours limit for the corresponding temperature	Chamber Temperature		Maximum hours to pH 5.3
	° F	° C	
665	68	20	150.0
665	71.6	22	103.4
665	75.2	24	78.9
665	78.8	26	63.8
665	82.4	28	53.6
665	86	30	46.2
665	89.2	32	40.5
555	91.4	33	31.8
555	93.2	34	30.1
555	95	35	28.6
555	96.8	36	27.2
555	98.6	37	25.9
500	100.4	38	22.3
500	104	40	20.5
500	107.6	42	18.9
500	111.2	44	17.6
500	114.8	46	16.4
500	118.4	48	15.4
500	122	50	14.5

Example A: Fermentation room temperature is a constant 26° C. It takes 55 hours for the pH to reach 5.3.
Degrees above 15.6° C: 26 - 15.6 = 10.4. Hours to reach pH of 5.3: 55.
Degree/Hours calculation: (10.4) x (55) = 572 degree/hours
The resulting degree/hours limit (less than 33° C) is 665 degree/hours. Conclusion: Process A **passes** the test because its degree/hours is less than the limit.

Example B: Fermentation room temperature is a constant 35° C. It takes 40 hours for the pH to reach 5.3.
Degrees above 15.6° C: 35 - 15.6 = 19.4. Hours to reach pH of 5.3: 40.
Degree/Hours calculation: (19.4) x (40) = 776 degree/hours
The corresponding degree/hours limit (between 33 and 37°C) is 555 degree/hours.
Conclusion: Process B **fails** the test because its degree/hours exceeds the limit.

Example C: Fermentation room temperature is a constant 25° C. It takes 60 hours for the pH to reach 5.3.
Degrees above 15.6° C: 25 - 15.6 = 9.4. Hours to reach pH of 5.3: 60.
Degree/Hours calculation: (9.4) x (60) = 564 degree/hours
The corresponding degree/hours limit (less than 33° C) is 665 degree/hours.
Conclusion: Process C **passes** the test, its degree/hours is less than the limit.

Variable Temperature Fermentation

When fermentation proceeds at different temperatures, separate degree-hours are calculated for each temperature and then added together. In testing each process, each step-up in the progression is analyzed for the number of degree-hours it contributes, with the highest temperature used in the fermentation process determining the degree-hour limitation.

Example D: It takes 35 hours for a product to reach a pH of 5.3 or less. Fermentation room temperature is 24° C for the first 10 hours, 30° C for second 10 hours and 35° C for the final 15 hours.

Time in C degree hours **above** 15.6° C	Chamber ° C	Adjusted Temperature	Degrees Result	Maximum hours to pH 5.3
10	24	24 - 15.6 =	8.4	8.4 x 10 = 84
10	30	30 - 15.6 =	14.4	14.4 x 10 = 144
15	**35**	35 - 15.6 =	19.4	19.4 x 15 = 291
			Total C degree-hours:	519

The highest temperature reached = **35° C**
The corresponding degree/hour limit = 555 (between 33 and 37° C). Conclusion: Process D **passes** the test because its degree/hours is less than the limit.

Example E: It takes 38 hours for a product to reach a pH of 5.3 or less. Fermentation room temperature is 24° C for the first 10 hours, 30° C for second 10 hours and 37° C for the final 18 hours.

Time in C degree hours **above** 15.6° C	Chamber ° C	Adjusted Temperature	Degrees Result	Maximum hours to pH 5.3
10	24	24 - 15.6 =	8.4	8.4 x 10 = 84
10	30	30 - 15.6 =	14.4	14.4 x 10 = 144
18	**37**	37 - 15.6 =	21.4	21.4 x 18 = 385.2
			Total C degree-hours:	613.2

The highest temperature reached = **37° C**
The corresponding degree/hour limit = 555 (between 33 and 37° C)
Conclusion: Process E **fails** the test because its degree/hours exceeds the limit.

Safety Options And Examples of Validated Processes

Prior to 1994 there were no specific rules controlling the manufacture of fermented sausages in the USA. Following the 1994 US outbreak a set of new regulations was issued that required commercial producers of dry and semi-dry fermented sausages to follow 1 of 5 safety options:

1. Utilize a heat process as listed in 9 Code of Federal Regulations, 318.17 - achieve a 5-log kill using a heat process 145° F (63° C) for 4 minutes (*5-log kill is the time required to destroy 90% of the organisms present*).

2. Include a validated 5 log inactivation treatment.

3. Conduct a "hold and test" program. This option requires finished product testing and is expensive.

4. Propose other approaches to assure 5-log kill.

5. Initiate a hazard analysis critical point (HACCP) system that includes raw batter testing and a 2-log inactivation in fermentation and drying.

Note: log inactivation treatments are very technical as they require the knowledge of logarithms, so the following simplified information should clarify the subject.

Let's assume that we are dealing with a pathogenic bacteria colony unit (cpu) with the population of 1 million (1,000,000) and we want to reduce this number. A *one log reduction* (1-log kill) reduces the number of bacteria by 90% so we have 100,000 bacteria left in our colony unit. A *two log reduction* in population reduces that same population by another 90%; this would be a total *reduction of 99% from the original population count.* Thus, there are 10,000 spores in the colony still left. A 5-log kill means that there are only 10 bacteria remaining frrom the original population of 1 million. The below charts show the population at various log reductions.

Log Reduction	Number of Spores	Percent Reduction
0	1,000,000	0%
1	100,000	90%
2	10,000	99%
3	1,000	99.9%
4	100	99.99%
5	10	100%
6	1	100%

All those options must address *Salmonella, Trichinella* and *Staphylococcus.* FSIS expanded the *Staphylococcus aureus* monitoring program to include *E.coli 0157:H7*. Since some fermented products are fully cooked, it should be reiterated that thorough cooking destroys *E.coli 0157:H7*, post process contamination must be avoided. At the same time, it has been concluded that *Salmonella* may also be found in the resulting product.

These regulations created a nightmare for little producers and some stopped making fermented products altogether, others *removed **beef*** from recipes and others reluctantly started to cook the sausages. Although ground beef is usually associated with *E.coli 0157:H7* nevertheless there were many instances of pork being infected, too.

   *It is strongly advisable that the reader becomes familiar with **the first two options** as they can be easily adapted to home conditions.*

Options 3-5 require in house laboratory testing and will be utilized by commercial meat processors.

Option 1. Include as part of the manufacture of the sausage, one of the following heat processes which is recognized as controlling *E. coli 0157:H7.*

Minimum Internal Temperature		Minimum processing time in minutes after the minimum temperature has been reached
° F	° C	
130	54.4	121 min
131	55.0	97 min
132	55.6	77 min
133	56.1	62 min
134	56.7	47 min
135	57.2	37 min
136	57.8	32 min
137	58.4	24 min
138	58.9	19 min
139	59.5	15 min
140	60.0	12 min
141	60.6	10 min
142	61.1	8 min
143	61.7	6 min
144	62.2	5 min
145	**62.8**	**4 min**

It can be noted that the above heat treatment of the sausage for destruction of *E. coli 0157:H7* will take care of *trichinae* problem in pork as well.

Note: smoke may be applied during Option 1 heat process.

Option 2. Use a manufacturing process (*combination of fermentation, heating, holding and/drying*) which has already been scientifically validated to achieve a 5 log kill of E. coli *0157:H7*.

The following processes have been scientifically validated as achieving a 5-log kill or greater reduction of *E. coli 0167H:7.*

Fermentation chamber temperature		pH at the end of fermentation process	Casing diameter	Subsequent process (dry, hold or cook)	Reference
° F	° C				
70	21	> 5.0	< 55 mm	heat (1 hr @ 110° F and 6 hours @ 125 ° F)	1
90	32	< 4.6	< 55 mm	hold @ 90° F for > 6 days	1
90	32	< 4.6	< 55 mm	heat (1 hr @ 110° F then 6 hrs @ 125° F)	1
90	32	< 4.6	56 - 105 mm	heat (1hr @100° F, 1 hr @ 110° F, 1 hr @ 120° F, then 7 hrs @125° F)	1
90	32	> 5.0	56 - 105 mm	heat (1hr @100° F, 1 hr @ 110° F, 1 hr @ 120° F, then 7 hrs @125° F)	1
96	36	< 5.0	< 55 mm	heat (128° F internal product temperature x 60 minutes) and dry (at 55° F and 65% relative humidity to a moisture protein ratio of < 1.6:1)	2
110	43	< 4.6	< 55 mm	hold @ 110° F for > 4 days	1
110	43	< 4.6	56 - 105 mm	hold @ 110° F for > 4 days	1
110	43	> 5.0	56 - 105 mm	hold @ 110° F for > 4 days	1

Ref. 1: Nicholson, R., et al, *Dry fermented sausages and Escherichia coli 0157:H7*. National Cattlemen's Beef Association, Research Report Number 11-316, Chicago, Illinois, 1996.

Ref. 2: Hinkens, J.C., et al, *Validation of Pepperoni Processes for Control of Escherichia coli 0157:h7*, Journal of Food Protection, Volume 59, Number 12, 1996, pp.1260-1266.

Examples of Validated Processes

Because there are many different combinations of factors that impact the safety and stability of fermented sausages, it is hard to come up with one validation study that will apply in each case. A commonly used process that has been validated is to achieve a pH < 5.0, followed by a heat process to achieve 128° F (53.3° C) internal temperature for 1 hour.

Summer Sausage - the sausage is fermented with a starter culture at 110° F, (43.3° C) until the pH is 4.7 or lower, then cooked to 152° F (66.7° C) internal meat temperature. The final pH 4.4, Aw 0.964.

Pepperoni - the sausage is fermented with a starter culture at 102° F, (38.9° C) until the pH is 5.7 or lower, then cooked to 128° F (53.3° C) internal meat temperature. The final pH 4.7, Aw 0.896.

Lebanon Bologna. Traditionally made Lebanon Bologna was not cooked. To comply with increasingly tougher government regulations for preventing the growth of *E. coli 0157:H7*, most manufacturers subject this sausage to a heat treatment. *Instructions are listed for the purpose of stressing the importance of the control of some of the pathogenic bacteria, in this case E.coli 0157:H7 which creates a safety hazard in products made with beef. This is how the commercial producer will make the sausage in order to be on the safe side.*

Process to achieve a 7-log10 reduction of *Salmonella* and *E.coli 0157:H7.*

Ingredients:	boneless lean beef - 10% fat
	salt - 3.5%
	potassium nitrate - 12 ppm * see *Our Note* below
	sodium nitrite - 200 ppm * see *Our Note* below
Fermentation:	12 hrs at 80° F, then at 100° F until pH of 4.7 or 5.2 is reached
Heat:	110° F (44° C) for 20 hrs, OR
	115° F (47° C) for 10 hrs, OR
	120° F (49° C) for 3 hrs

Reference: Ellajosyula, K.E., S. Doores, E.W. Mills, R.A. Wilson, R.C. Anantheswaran, and S.J. Knabel. 1998. *Destruction of Escherichia coli 0157:H7 and Salmonella typhimurium in Lebanon Bologna by interaction of fermentation, pH, heating temperature, and time.* J. Food Prot. 61(2):152-7.

Our Note: * Cure #2 is a mixture of 6.25% sodium nitrite, 4% of sodium nitrate and 89.75% of salt. Cure #1 is a mixture of 6.25% sodium nitrite and 93.75% of salt and can be used instead of Cure #2.

In most cases, fermented sausages are made from a combination of pork and beef. Using safety option 1 or 2 takes care of *E. coli 0157:H7* and *Salmonella.* Cold temperature, cleanliness, and proper sanitation procedures take care of *Listeria monocytogenes.* Nevertheless, pork must be taken care of as it may be contaminated with trichinae.

Trichinea

From: Code of Federal Regulations, Title 9: Animals and Animal Products
Part 318.10 Prescribed treatment of pork and products containing pork to destroy trichinae.

Trichinae can be killed by freezing pork in home refrigerator.

(i) Group 1 comprises product in separate pieces not exceeding 6 inches in thickness, or

Required Period of Freezing at Temperature Indicated			
° F	° C	Group 1 (Days)	Group 2 (Days)
5	- 15	20	30
- 10	- 23.3	10	20
- 20	- 28.9	6	12

arranged on separate racks with the layers not exceeding 6 inches in depth, or stored in crates or boxes not exceeding 6 inches in depth, or stored as solidly frozen blocks not exceeding 6 inches in thickness.

(ii) Group 2 comprises product in pieces, layers, or within containers, the thickness of which exceeds 6 inches but not 27 inches, and product in containers including tierces, barrels, kegs, and cartons having a thickness not exceeding 27 inches.

If pork meat was not previously frozen for destruction of *trichinae* it must be heat treated:

Heat treatment to ensure destruction of Trichinella in pork		
Minimum internal temperature		Minimum time in minutes
° F	° C	
130	54	60
131	55	30
133	56	15
135	57	6
136	58	3
138	59	2
140	60	1
142	61	1
144	62	1
145	**63**	**instant**

Note that the **Option 1** for the heat treatment of the sausage for destruction of *E. coli 0157:H7* will take care of *trichinae* as well.

Pathogen Modeling Programs

From: **FSIS** (Food Safety and Inspection Service), 9 CFR 430.1 **Ready-to-Eat Fermented, Salt-Cured, and Dried Products Guideline, May 5, 2023:**

Establishments should not rely on the results of pathogen modeling programs alone unless those models have been validated. The following *are validated models FSIS recommends* for supporting decisions related to fermented, salt-cured, or dried meat and poultry products:

1. University of Wisconsin Shelf-Stability Predictor

https://meathaccp.wisc.edu/st_calc.html

This predictor is a *wonderfully designed, user-friendly* program that can be of great value to a hobbyist. Shelf Stability Predictor predicts the growth of *Listeria monocytogenes* and *Staphylococcus aureus* on fully cooked, ready-to-eat (RTE) meat products as a function of pH and water activity.

Use these tools to help you decide if your product is shelf stable.* This predictor identifies products as shelf stable if the product is fully cooked and:

- Will not support the growth of *L. monocytogenes* (*LM*) and,
- Will not support the growth of *Staphylococcus aureus* (*Staph*).

* Note, this predictor may not be used with products in the Not Heat-Treated, Shelf Stable HACCP category.

Instructions:

1. Enter the pH and water activity of your product in the spaces indicated.
2. Select Calculate.

The predictor will indicate the probability of *L. monocytogenes* and *S. aureus* growth on this product, on a scale of 0 = growth very unlikely to 1 = growth very likely. A value of 0.20 or lower is a clear indicator that *L. monocytogenes* and *S. aureus* will not grow, while a value of 0.80 or higher indicates that *L. monocytogenes* and *S. aureus* are likely to grow.

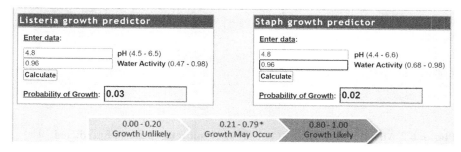

Photo. 6.1 University of Wisconsin-Madison Shelf Stability Predictor.

The Shelf Stability Predictor is only to be used with product that has received a full cook/lethality step. It is not to be used with products in the Not Heat-Treated, Shelf Stable category. The results of this predictor apply only to products that are fully cooked prior to drying to establish shelf stability. *Processors are required* to establish shelf stability of products based on pH and water activity. The pathogens most likely to grow on dried and/or acidified RTE products are toxin-producing molds, *Staphylococcus aureus,* and *Listeria monocytogenes.* A semi-dry sausage produced at home is a safe ready-to-eat product when kept in refrigerator. However, if it is submitted to additional drying at 53 - 57° F (12-14° C) the sausage will become in time a shelf-stable cooked dry salami.

A hobbyist is not going to spend thousands of dollars to buy Aw meter. However, he can estimate Aw by checking the weight loss of the sausage. The following numbers, though not scientifically reliable, can offer some guidance: Aw 0.95 - 15% weight loss, Aw 0.94 - 20% weight loss, Aw 0.90 - 30% weight loss, Aw 0.85 - 40% weight loss. Then, he can punch numbers into the predictor and verify wether the sausage is shelf-stable to be kept at room temperature. He must, of course, check also the pH of the sausage.

2. Danish Technological Institute (DMRI) ConFerm model

http://dmripredict.dk

This DMRI Predict is a *technically advanced* set of modeling programs that might be of value to commercial producers, however, it will require some time to learn. It has been validated to predict the growth of: *L. monocytogenes, C. botulinum, Yersinia enterocolitica* - reduction of *Yersinia enterocolitica* during production of salami, *Staphtox predictor - Staphylococcus* enterotoxin formation and growth of *S. aureus.*

Its modeling program, **ConFerm**, predicts the reduction of pathogens during the production of fermented and matured sausages, which can help a hobbyist decide whether the product is safe and shelf-stable.

Danish Technological Institute DMRI Predict

ConFerm

Reduction of pathogens during the production of fermented and matured sausages.

Input

Recipe variables	
NaCl (%)	3.3
KCl (%)	0
Na-nitrite (ppm)	150
Process parameters	
Fermentation temperature (°C)	26
pH Start	5.8
pH 48h	5.2
pH final	5
Total weight loss (%)	35
Total process time (days)	24
Water in final product (%)	50
Meat in the mince (only for the risk module) (%)	70

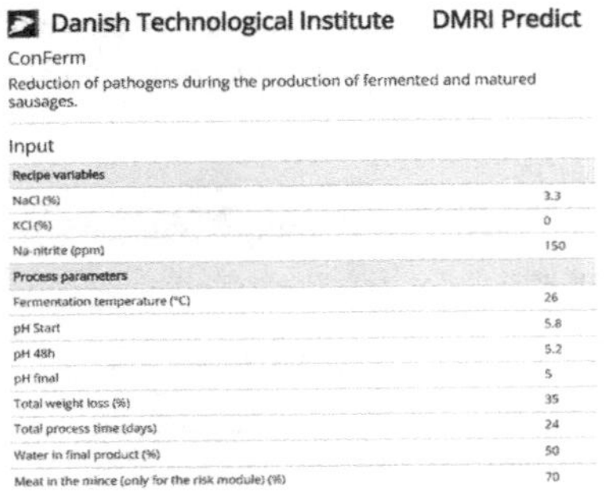

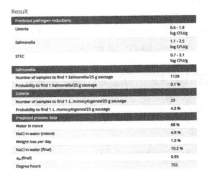

Photo. 6.2 After submitting input parameters, the predictor generates detailed data, including graphs.

Result

Predicted pathogen reductions	
Listeria	0.6 - 1.8 log CFU/g
Salmonella	1.1 - 2.5 log CFU/g
STEC	0.7 - 2.1 log CFU/g
Salmonella	
Number of samples to find 1 Salmonella/25 g sausage	1129
Probability to find 1 Salmonella/25 g sausage	0.1 %
Listeria	
Number of samples to find 1 *L. monocytogenes*/25 g sausage	23
Probability to find 1 *L. monocytogenes*/25 g sausage	4.3 %
Predicted process data	
Water in mince	68 %
NaCl in water (mince)	4.9 %
Weight loss per day	1.5 %
NaCl in water (final)	10.2 %
a_w (final)	0.93
Degree hours	752

Photo. 6.3 Result of predicted pathogen reductions.

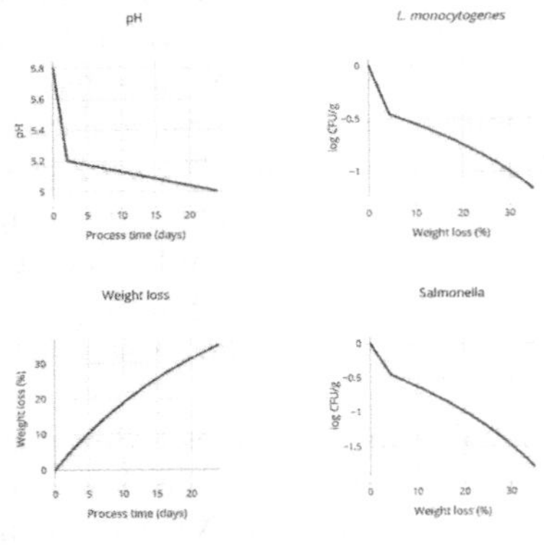

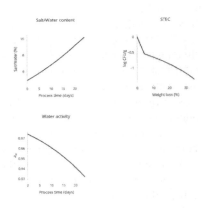

Photo. 6.4 Predicted graphs: pH, *L. monocytogenes*, weight loss, *Salmonella*.

Photo. 6.5 Predicted graphs: salt/ water content, *STEC*, water activity.

PART II

Manufacturing Process and Recipes

Chapter 7

Fermented Sausages

What is a Fermented Sausage?

Fermented sausage is a product in which natural fermentation plays a role in developing the color, texture, and flavor of the sausage. Fermentation is a food preservation process based on a simple principle that acidity preserves foods. In order for fermentation to occur, the basic material must contain some sugar, given that vegetables such as onions, garlic, and peppers. Cabbage beets contain both around 2 - 3% sugar and naturally present lactic bacteria; natural fermentation can occur, providing that salt is added to keep spoilage bacteria away. Adding additives such as Gdl or citric acid alone will also generate acidity, and this method can be used alone or in combination with natural fermentation.

The early sausages were not fermented because the sugar was not available.

Meat contains a small number of lactic acid bacteria and also around 0.2-0.3% of sugar (glycogen), but this is not sufficient for any meaningful fermentation to occur. It is possible that on some occasions, a slightly fermented sausage was produced if meat from fast-running animals was selected. The meat of fast-running animals such as a horse or deer contains more sugar, which they use as an energy source for sudden bursts of acceleration. Given that horse meat contains ~ 0.9% of glycogen, natural fermentation can occur. It is a known fact that horse meat tastes sweetish. In the past, a local butcher could create a mildly fermented dry sausage not on purpose but by chance, and most likely, his secret was guarded in his family. Nevertheless, it can be stated that: "Our original salami sausages occasionally could have been unknowingly mildly fermented, but generally, they were salt-cured and dried sausages."

Discovery of Sugar

Today, we can cause rapid meat fermentation by adding sugar; however, in early Europe, the only sweetener was honey. Sugar was first produced from sugarcane plants in India sometime after the first century AD. By the sixth century AD, sugar and processing had reached Persia, and from there, it was brought by Arabs into the Mediterranean. Sugar was still a luxury, and it was not yet generally used. After Christopher Columbus' discovery of America in 1492, the Europeans established sugar cane plantations on Caribbean islands, and although the prices fell, sugar was still a luxury. In 1747, German Andreas Sigismund Marggraf discovered sugar in sugar beets and devised a method to extract it. In time, sugar finally became available for the production of sugary foods and drinks.

Brief History of Fermented Sausages

Salt-cured dry salami were known in Rome way over a thousand years ago. Curing meats and salami allowed for long-term storage, which was crucial to feeding soldiers in the Roman army. Given that the Roman empire stretched from Asia to England, it did not take long before other countries discovered the basics of making this sausage, which became popular due to its shelf-keeping qualities. Caravan traders were moving goods, including salami, throughout Europe, so other countries would try to duplicate the technology. From Italy to Greece, Spain and France, from Spain to Portugal, salami became a ready-to-eat sausage that did not spoil.

Spanish records mention Longanissa de Vic, also known as SalchichÓn de Vic dry sausage, already in 1456. The sausage is still produced today and carries a prestigious European Certificate of Origin. Although the first starter cultures started to show up in research papers in the 1950s, the production of fermented sausages on a large scale took off only after introducing Lactobacillus plantarum bacteria culture in 1966. The culture worked well at 68-72° F (20-22° C) and is still produced today. Since 1984, various studies and technical papers have been published in many countries explaining the important role played during the production of this type of sausages. Today, government agencies and most major universities provide excellent information on food technology, including fermented sausages. Starter cultures have become available not only to meat processors but also to hobbyists who can purchase them online. Due to advances in science and technology, especially in areas like bacteriology, fermentation, and refrigeration, it became possible to produce fermented sausages with different characteristics safely at home.

Modern production is independent of outside conditions and parameters such as temperature, humidity, and air speed are computer controlled in sophisticated drying chambers. This latest technology combined with a universal use of bacterial cultures permits producing fermented sausages of constant quality at any time of the year.

Why Certain Salami Were Better Than Others?

Traditionally, the production of fermented meats relied on bacteria present at the butcher's premises. The facility developed its own microbiological flora in which microorganisms lived. Meat brought from outside had already been infected with bacteria. In some places, the slaughter of the animal was performed right on the premises, which also contributed to new bacteria infecting the meat. Summing it up, there was no shortage of microorganisms, and this combination of bacteria from the meat and from the premises often created favorable conditions for making fermented sausages.

Facilities developed different bacterial flora, and sausages of different qualities were made depending on the location. In the past, meat facilities were not sanitized as scrupulously as they are today, which helped create more favorable conditions for the bacteria to survive in the plant. These conditions were unique to each establishment, and it was impossible to duplicate them elsewhere. By the same token, sausage makers were unable to produce a fermented sausage in two different locations that would have exhibited the same quality.

Some places in Italy developed a specific flora, which was instrumental in producing a high-quality product of a particular taste and flavor. Such establishments suddenly developed fame and a brand name for making wonderful meat products. They probably were not better sausage makers than their counterparts working in different locations. They were lucky to have their shop located in an area that was blessed by Mother Nature for making fermented sausages. They did not have much clue as to what was happening, but they passed this empirical knowledge on to their sons, and it worked like magic.

Climatic differences were a significant factor in the development of different methods of smoking, drying, and preserving meat products. The South had a drier climate with steady winds, and the best-air-dried hams originated there (Spanish Serrano, Italian Parma). In the North, the weather was less predictable, with cooler temperatures and higher humidity. Those conditions were ill-suited for making air-dried products, and cold smoking became the preferred drying method. For those reasons, Mediterranean countries produced slow-fermented sausages that were only dried, and countries in Northern Europe produced fermented sausages that were smoked and dried.

Three Styles of Fermented Sausages

Given that there are so many ways to classify fermented sausages, it would be simpler to start classifying them by their organoleptic qualities, such as flavor, texture, and color. Generally, there are three styles of fermented sausages:

- South European (Mediterranean basin) - Italy, Spain, France.
- North European - Germany and neighbor countries.
- American - USA.

Style	Fermentation Temperature	Time to pH of 5.3	Aw	Time
South European	18-24° C 60-75° F	longer than 40 hours	less than 0.90	3 weeks or longer. nitrite/Nitrate added.
Milano salami, Naples salami, Spanish salchichón, Dry Chorizo, Fuet, French saucisson				
North European	22-26° C 70-80° F	less than 30 hours	more than 0.90	less than 3 weeks. nitrite added.
Danish salami, German Mettwurst				
American	above 32° C 90° F	less than 15 hours	more than 0.90	2-3 weeks or less. Nitrite added.
American pepperoni, summer sausage				

Southern European Products

The climate dictated how much drying time was available during a year for making uncooked dry or semi-dry sausages. The southern countries were blessed with the right amount of humidity due to proximity to the Mediterranean Sea, agreeable temperatures and prevailing winds. In most of the areas, save places in the mountains, there was a little need to prevent meats from freezing by starting a fire, hence people did not develop the liking for smoked meats.

Southern European countries were the last ones to accept the practice of using cultures and, in the beginning, limited their choices to flavor and color-producing *Staphylococcus xylosus, S. carnosus, and Micrococcus spp.* for making dry sausages. The sausages were fermented at <75° F (24° C) to a final < pH 5.2-5.6. This resulted in mild sausage without a sour taste. Given that lactic acid cultures produce a sour taste, which was generally disliked, it took a while before they found their way into the general market. They were fermented with 0.4-0.8% dextrose to a typical pH of 4.8 - 5.0. The end product had an acceptable quality and was microbiologically safe.

Northern European Products

In North Europe, the climate was harsh, with long periods of rain and snow and temperatures too cold for drying sausages in the air for most of the year. The pigs were slaughtered before Christmas and processed immediately into a variety of sausages. The sausages were hung in a large smokehouse that acted as a storage facility. To prevent meats from being frozen, a small fire burned inside, producing thin, cold smoke, which then dried and preserved sausages. This explains why smoked meats were and still are popular in Northern Europe, as that was the only way to preserve meat in the past. Northern European countries embraced lactic acid starter cultures as soon as they became available as they introduced a new safety feature, easily controllable acidity, which eliminated the need for prolonged drying.

Fermentation temperatures could be set up to 113° F (45° C), and pH drop was easily controlled with sugar. This has led to a greater variety of fermented products, however, due to higher acidity levels, North European sausages exhibit more sourly taste, unlike the ones from the South

History of Fermented Sausages in the USA

Native Indians knew how to dry meats and make "pemmican"- a pounded/shredded dry meat mixed with buffalo fat, herbs, and some berries, but knew nothing about sausages. European immigrants brought sausage-making technology to America. About 32 million European immigrants came to America between 1820 and 1930; Italians alone accounted for over 5 million. Between 1800 and the present, over seven million German speakers emigrated to the U.S., the majority of whom arrived between about 1840 and 1914. It is estimated that more than 2 million Poles had immigrated by the 1920s. Many newcomers brought sausage-making skills to the USA, and the ethnic butcher shops were in all large cities competing for customers and offering a variety of quality meats and sausages, salami type included.

In the 1900s, using additives, colorants, and curing accelerators was not popular, and meat science was still developing. A big step forward was the availability of lactic acid starter culture in 1966, although the Europeans showed little enthusiasm for it in the beginning. In the USA, the industry embraced the culture as it simplified production and allowed constant quality products. The acidic taste did not matter much as an average person was not familiar with European traditional salami. Given that a fast-fermented semi-dry sausage can be produced within a week, it should not be surprising that those sausages are available everywhere.

Over the years, European sausage makers trained and licensed in their countries found it hard to compete with established meat processors supplying supermarkets with products of lesser quality but at lower prices. A little butcher was being pushed out of business. What made matters worse was that the owner's sons did not want to continue the family tradition of making sausages at 4'clock in the morning. Within one hundred years, most neighborhood sausage shops were gone, and the quality of the products, too. To compound the problem, the meat processors started to add ingredients that would shorten the processing time to maximize profits. Using acidulants such as encapsulated acids, Gdl, or citric acid cut fermentation time in half, however, at the cost of the taste, which became acidic and sour.

American Products

With the growing popularity of fermented meat products, it was inevitable that some sausage-related outbreaks would follow, and there were many: 1982, 1994, 1995, 2008, 2010, 2011, 2018, 2019, and 2020 in the USA, Canada, Europe, and Australia. After the 1994 salami outbreak, the United States Department of Agriculture's "Food Safety and Inspection Service" forced manufacturers of fermented sausages to change their operating procedures, which, as a result, affected the organoleptic properties of some fermented and dried (jerky) products. A set of stringent regulations was issued in 1997, which became a nightmare for small establishments. Some producers tried to address the *E. coli O157:H7* problem by removing beef from their recipes; others stopped production altogether, but most started to cook sausages in order to satisfy new standards. However, this brought changes to their texture and flavor. As a result, we have American style of fermented sausages, and they are fast-fermented, medium-fermented, acidified (non-fermented), fermented and fully cooked, and others.

Although semi-dry sausages can be made shelf-stable by fermentation and drying, it is faster, safer, and more practical for commercial producers to finish the process by cooking sausages, as thermal treatment kills dangerous pathogens. It is all about the profits and much less about the taste and the flavor.

American-made whole-piece non-heated dry sausages are rarely available in supermarkets. However, they can be purchased online. Although they carry original Italian names such as Salami Calabrese, Salami Toscano, Salami Napoli, etc., the label clearly states the country of origin as the USA. There are some websites that offer original Italian salami. However, they are very expensive due to transportation costs.

American semi-dry sausages are fermented to pH 4.8-4.6 by rapid fermentation, either naturally with fast-fermenting cultures or through chemical acidification. Unfortunately, this is done at the expense of taste and flavor, although the finished products are very safe. New regulations, which sometimes require cooking sausages, were created to protect the customer from contracting a sickness. However, the truth is that today's semi-dry fermented sausages are becoming more and more like regular cooked products with a "tangy" or sour flavor. Southern Europeans made salami for centuries, people got used to their shape, texture, flavor and aroma and could identify them by looks alone. Given that in the USA there is no long tradition of sausage making plus the fact that Americans have less rigid rules and are more open to experimenting, the sausages with a "tangy" taste were generally accepted.

Who Makes The Best Fermented Sausages

It is not possible to choose one company or country and say they make the best sausages; however, if we narrow our criteria to salami-type products, the answer is easy: Southern European countries make the best sausages. There is a bigger sausage diversity in European stores which may be explained by a long tradition and hundreds years of sausage making. There are many European dry and semi-dry sausages which have been made in certain way for centuries and people got used to their shape, texture, flavor and aroma. It is not easy to change the history or a person's definition of quality.

Over the years, hundreds of European fermented sausages have been awarded European Certificates of Origin. Families, small local manufacturers, and even whole cities are proud of such products. It takes a lot of effort and several years to be granted such a certificate, which is not easy. The certificate specifies how a sausage must be made, in many cases from locally grown animals and herbs, and what natural casings can be selected. This is done to preserve the acclaimed products' look, texture, and flavor and prevent others from making duplicates. The selected producers receive the license and logo for each product, which must be displayed on each sausage. In addition, they are subject to supervision by meat inspectors who verify that the sausage is made the way it is specified in the license agreement. Generally, being awarded a medal or carrying a European Certificate of Origin guarantees a product a lot of attention, credibility, fame, and international recognition.

European Certificates of Origin

Throughout Europe, there is a vast assortment of great foods. When a product acquires a reputation extending beyond national borders, it can face competition from other products, which may pass themselves off as the genuine article and take the same name. In the 1930's, the French invented how to protect their regional wines. The idea gave birth to an elaborate system known today as the appellation d'origine contrôlée (AOC). Items that meet geographical origin and quality standards may be endorsed with a government-issued stamp, which acts as an official certification of the origins and standards of the product to the consumer.

In 1992, the European Union created the systems to promote and protect food products which is similar to the French Appellation d'Origine Contrôlée (AOC) system, the Denominazione di Origine Controllata (DOC) used in Italy and the Denominación de Origen system used in Spain. The law (enforced within the EU and being gradually expanded internationally via bilateral agreements of the EU with non-EU countries) ensures that only products genuinely originating in that region are allowed in commerce as such. *The purpose of the law is to protect the reputation of the regional foods and eliminate the unfair competition and misleading of consumers by non-genuine products, which may be of inferior quality or of different flavor.* These laws protect the names of wines, cheeses, hams, sausages, olives, beers, and even regional breads, fruits, and vegetables.

Photo 7.1 Protected Designation of Origin (PDO) - covers the term used to describe foodstuffs which are produced, processed and prepared in a given geographical area using recognized know-how.

Example: Italy - Prosciutto di Parma.

Photo 7.2 Protected Geographical Indication (PGI) - the geographical link must occur in at least one of the stages of production, processing or preparation.

Example: Spain - Salchichón de Vic (dry sausage).

Photo 7.3 Traditional Speciality Guaranteed (TSG) - does not refer to the origin but highlights traditional character, either in the composition or means of production.

Example: Spain - Jamon Serrano.

As such, foods such as Gorgonzola, Parmigiano Reggiano, Asiago cheese, Camembert de Normandie and Champagne can only be labelled as such if they come from the designated region. To qualify as Roquefort for example, cheese must be made from the milk of a certain breed of sheep and matured in the natural caves near the town of Roquefort in the Aveyron region of France where it is infected with the spores of a fungus (*Penicillium roqueforti*) that grows in those caves.

Italy has a long history in the production of traditional fermented sausages and almost every part of the country offers many great products, many of which have been awarded Protected Designation of Origin and Protected Geographical Indication certificates.

In order to preserve the original taste and flavor *these products are made without starter cultures* and sold in local markets. Countries which were granted most Certificates of Origin for Fermented Meat Products are: Italy, Hungary, Spain, Portugal, France, Germany. The complete list can be obtained from the European Commission/Agriculture & Rural Development.

Indication of Quality

Traditionally made sausages were made from leaner meats than commercially produced products of today. In addition, mass-produced sausages often include ingredients such as starches, antioxidants, nitrates, curing accelerators, colorants, protein concentrates, color stabilizers, sugars, hydrocolloids (gums), powdered milk, phosphates, and more. All those ingredients decrease production time, lower costs, and extend the shelf life of the products, giving supermarkets sufficient time to sell them. To buy the best quality sausage, read the label. A good indication of quality is the casing - is it natural or synthetic? All sausages carrying European Certificates of Origin are stuffed in natural casings and do not contain chemicals.

Photo 7.4 Chorizo de Cantipalos. Label attached to the twine. Each sausage has its own serial number. The list of ingredients is also included.

Almost all countries in Europe produce sausages that hold such a prestigious certificate, which makes people extremely proud. Not only fermented, but all types of sausages, including meats like hams, carry those medals. Given that travel distances among countries are very short, and no visa or travel restrictions exist in 27 countries of the European Common Market, great sausages can be found in every supermarket. They can also be ordered online and delivered within 2-3 days.

Spanish Fermented Sausages Carrying Eutopean Certificates of Origin

Photo 7.5 Sobrasada de Mallorca, PGI 1966.

Photo 7.6 Sobrasada de Mallorca de cerdo negro, PGI 1966.

Photo 7.7 Salcichón de Vic: Longanissa de Vic, PGI 2001.

Photo 7.8 Botillo del Bierzo, PGI 2001.

Photo 7.9 Chorizo Riojano, PGI 2010.

Photo 7.10 Chorizo de Cantipalos, PGI 2011.

Photo 7.11 Chosco de Tineo, PGI 2011.

Photo 7.12 Sobrasada de Mallorca, PGI 1966 can be found all over Spain.

The U.S. Official Classification of Fermented Sausages

Dry sausages are chopped or ground meat products that, as a result of bacterial action or direct addition acidulation, reach a pH of 5.3 or less and are then dried to remove 25 to 50% of the moisture. According to USDA/FSIS, dry salami must have a moisture/protein ratio (MPR) of 1.9 to 1, pepperoni - 1.6 : 1, and jerky 0.75 : 1, to be labeled as such, the smaller MPR the drier the product.

Semi-dry sausages are chopped or ground meat products that, as a result of bacterial action or direct addition of organic acids, reach a pH of 5.3 or less and are then dried to remove 15% - 20% of the moisture. Semi-dry sausages are usually smoked and often receive a heat treatment following the fermentation period to make them shelf stable. If the semi-dry sausage has a pH of 5.0 or less and a moisture protein ratio of 3.1 to 1 or less, it is considered to be shelf stable. The sausages which are not shelf stable are refrigerated.

	Dry Sausages (Slow-fermented)	Semi-dry (Fast-fermented)
Fermentation	slow, with or without cultures,	fast, with fast-fermenting cultures
Fermentation temperature	20-24° C (68-75° F)	26-45° C (78-113° F)
Processing time*	3 weeks - 6 months	2-5 days - 3 weeks
Salt	3 - 3.3%	2.2 - 2.5%
Dextrose/sugar	0 - 0.5%	up to 1%
Final pH	5.2 - 5.6 **	4.6 - 5.0
Weight loss	> 30%	5-20%
Aw	Aw ≤ 0.90	Aw > 0.90
Smoking	varies from country to country	usually yes
Texture	hard	soft - medium hard
Cooking	no	often partially cooked
Flavor	cheesy, mushroomy, aromatic	sourly, acidic
Storage	room temperature	room temperature, refrigerated
Examples	Salami, Chorizo, Pepperoni, salchichón, Saucisson	Summer Sausage, Lebanon Bologna, Sobrasada, Mettwurst

* The total time will vary on the temperature, the kind of product, and its diameter.
** Southern European dry salami do not usually drop below pH 5.3.

Spreadable sausages are classified as semi-dry sausages. They are usually smoked, non-cooked and kept under refrigeration. Processing time: 3-5 days, weight loss <5%.

Early Production Methods

There was something magical about making salami, an aura of mystery surrounding early butchers who basked in the glory claiming that they discovered the secrets. They were simply lucky to own premises which were hardly sanitized by today's standards, but were blessed by being infected with bacterial flora that meat needed to transform itself into a product that not only displayed a pleasant aroma, but could last indefinitely at ambient temperatures. This empirical experience was passed from father to son and some places became famous for their sausages. Others tried to follow the trend, however, mother nature did not reward them with the suitable strains of bacteria and their products were lower quality.

Chance Contamination

This traditional method is called chance contamination because *a chance was taken* that everything will proceed according to the plan, that much for science. The meat or a stuffed sausage was pre-cured: the meat was cut into 1-2" thickness pieces, mixed with salt, sugar, and nitrate, and left for 2 - 3 days at ~ 46° F (8° C); then, it was processed, stuffed into a casing and dried. Today, we know that the reason for this cold storage is to give time for naturally occurring lactic acid and curing bacteria to multiply. Cool temperatures offered less opportunity for bacteria to grow, but given time they would. If everything proceeded according to the plan, there would be enough lactic acid bacteria to start a healthy fermentation. Unfortunately, not only lactic bacteria but all other microorganisms would grow as well, and the end product would definitely have a shorter shelf life. However, we can still make great products this way as long as we create favorable conditions for beneficial bacteria and an unfavorable environment for spoilage and pathogenic ones.

Back Slopping

Back-slopping relies on reintroducing about 5% of the sausage mix from the previous successful production. This mix is taken after the fermentation step and before any heating or drying and is frozen for later use. This procedure inoculates a new batch of sausages with a proven quality meat paste that contains living bacteria. As those bacteria produced a high-quality sausage before, we may expect that they would introduce the same qualities into a new production. In other words, the quality of the new sausage batch should be as good as that of the previous one.

The contamination problem still remains, as it is impossible to predict what spoilage and pathogenic bacteria are present in a new batch of sausages. A new production can be contaminated with unknown bacteria and the problem will become evident only after a few back slopping cycles. By that time the whole premises might be contaminated with a new and undesired strain of bacteria.

Note: With today's rigid safety standards and scrupulous sanitizing, the amount of surrounding bacteria in a production facility is certainly lower, which is detrimental to natural bacterial fermentation.

Using Starter Cultures

Reliance on natural bacteria is like flipping a coin since the composition, number, and amount of bacteria are unknown. Some lactic bacteria strains may produce an excellent flavored product, while others will produce undesirable substances like acetic acid, alcohol, and gases.

Using a standard formula, the same culture, and maintaining the same processing parameters will certainly produce each time a product of the same quality. Naturally present in meat, bacteria have no chance to compete with 10 million laboratory-grown bacteria introduced by the culture. This, however, creates limits on the flavor development of flavor in non-heated dry sausages as the flavor of the end product becomes constant and entirely predictable.

On the other hand, using traditional methods of production without computerized chambers and cultures resulted in sausages whose quality could change from being good to excellent or even outstanding, given that it was impossible to control the type or the number of bacteria that developed the flavor of the sausage. Naturally fermented sausages without cultures carry this small amount of suspense; the sausage can be mediocre or excellent. However, a sausage made with culture and computerized equipment will always be good and safe. Today, most fermented sausages are produced in computer-controlled chambers throughout the year. Temperature, humidity, and air speed are precisely controlled, and pH and Aw can be automatically monitored. However, small processors and hobbyists cannot afford such expensive equipment. They have to restrict production to suitable seasons or use improvised solutions to adjust the climate of the production chamber.

Adding Culture

Starter cultures should not be mixed with salt, nitrite, or spices in advance as unpredictable growth of culture bacteria may occur (all they need is a bit of moisture from spices). As a result, starter cultures with different characteristics will be introduced into the sausage. Nitrite can retard culture growth if it comes in contact with it during mixing.

Since the majority of recipes in this book is calculated for 1 kg (2.2 lb) of meat the required amount of culture will be very small around 0.1 g about (1/10 of the teaspoon), hence it will be difficult to measure, unless a highly accurate digital scale is available. If you have to estimate the amount is better to add a little more culture. You will not damage the sausage with more bacteria, they will simply produce the expected results faster.

How Much Culture

Cultures for a hobbyist are of a freeze-dried type and come packed in little envelopes that specify the optimal fermentation temperature and the amount of culture to add. To weigh culture for making 1 kg (2.2 lb) sausage requires a very accurate scale; however, when in doubt, err on the plus side and add more culture as this offers some benefits:

- The rate of fermentation will increase as a larger number of lactic acid bacteria will consume more sugar. The lag phase of the culture will remain the same, however, more acid will be produced.
- More flavor in fast-fermented semi-dry sausages. Add culture containing *Staphylococcus xylosus, Staphylococcus carnosus,* or both. During the first day fermentation can run at low temperatures in order to limit production of lactic acid. This allows flavor forming bacteria to create flavors. Then, the fermentation temperature is raised to reach $\leq$ pH 5.3 within time specified in degree-temperature tables for variable temperature fermentation.
- More flavor in dry salami. An even stronger flavor can be produced when the culture contains only *Staphylococcus xylosus* and no lactic bacteria, for example Bactoferm® S-SX. There is no need to worry about acidity as long as only little sugar was added.

Molds

Natural molds will usually be present in dry, non-heated sausages, however, their color can vary from white, yellow, gray, green or even black. In addition, some may contain toxins called mycotoxins that can cause severe allergic reactions. To avoid such problems cultures that produce white noble are often added. Since molds need oxygen to survive, they are concentrated on or near the surface since there is no air below. Besides, the hard surface of the sausage does not create good conditions for the mold to move deeper.

The presence of mold creates a soft layer, contributing positively to more uniform drying with less chance for case hardening. The final pH of molded dry sausages is usually higher (pH>5.5), *even if the pH was lower after fermentation,* because molds consume lactic acid and produce ammonia, which being alkaline forces pH higher. For those who object to mold presence for visual appearance, the easiest solution is to wipe it off with cloth soaked with vinegar or oil. Molds are added prior to fermentation by dipping or spraying the sausage casings with a mold culture.

Do People Eat Mold?

When a small-diameter sausage is stuffed into a soft, delicate natural casing, it is not practical to remove the skin, and most people will consume the mold. Dry sausages are packed into larger diameter casings and are sliced thin, so it is quite easy to peel off the skin. Bear in mind that sheep casings are very tender, and most pig casings are also soft, but beef casings are tougher. Commercially produced sausages are often stuffed into strong synthetic casings and discarded with mold. If you object visually to mold on the sausage, it can be easily wiped off with a piece of cloth soaked in oil or vinegar.

Note: many mass-produced fermented sausages are dipped in talc powder or flour to create illusion of a molded sausage. Such thin fake mold which sticks to the fingers when humidity is present.

Factors Restricting Growth of Bacteria

Fresh meat is totally defenceless against bacteria and it needs our help. That is why we need to understand the strength and weakness of all bacteria types.

Factors Restricting Growth of Pathogenic Bacteria				
Pathogen	Salt tolerance	Needs pH at or above this value to grow	Moisture tolerance- needs Aw at or above	Remarks
Cl. botulinum	5%	pH 4.6	Aw 0.94	nitrite effectively inhibits its growth, oxygen restricts its growth, grows best at 80-130° F (26-54° C).
Cl. perfringens	5-10%	pH 5.0	Av 0.95	grows best at 80-130° F (26-54° C), does not grow below 59° F (15° C)
S. auerus	10%	pH 4.2-4.6. Does not produce toxin at pH ≤ 5.2	Aw 0.85	tolerates nitrite, likes oxygen, hates acidity, will not grow below 42° F/6.7° C, grows slow below 60° F/15.6° C, grows fast above this temperature and may produce toxin.
E. coli 0157:H		pH 4.4	Aw 0.95	mainly in beef and lamb, also in pork.
Salmonella		pH 3.8	Aw 0.94	mainly in pork, also in beef, inhibited by nitrite, often in chicken-destroyed by heating to 156° F/69° C.
Listeria	10%	pH 4.4	Aw 0.90	good until Aw 0.93, can grow at ≥ 31° F (-1° C)
Campylobacter	1%	pH 4.9	Aw 0.98	mainly in chicken.
Factors Restricting Growth of Other Microorganisms				
Spoilage bacteria	poor when salt added above 2%	poor tolerance to acidity	Aw 0.95	inhibited below Aw 0.97-0.96. Need oxygen, hence removal of air during processing is important.
Lactic acid bacteria	up to 6%	pH 3.3	Aw 0.95	performance drops when: more than 3.3% salt added or Aw drops to ≤ 0.91. Need little oxygen.
Curing and flavor forming bacteria	5%	pH 5.0	Aw 0.95	less effective below pH 5.5. Stop working at pH 5.0.
Molds	good	pH 1.2	Aw 0.80	need oxygen, sensitive to smoke
Yeasts	good	pH 2.0	Aw 0.85	need little oxygen. sensitive to smoke

Growth of *St. aureus* and production of toxin are greatest at approximately 68-98° F (20–37° C), but growth can occur between 45-118° F (8-48° C). This toxin is heat stable, being tolerant to boiling for 1 h. Canning under pressure at 249° F (121° C) for 30 min is sufficient to destroy the toxin.

With the advancement of meat science and technology and faster processing techniques, new variants of fermented sausages have appeared. What once was salt-cured dried sausage has evolved into a myriad of salami type products that meet the description of a fermented sausage.

Complete Classification of Fermented Sausages

The term non-heated sausage appears throughout this book. This means that the sausage was not cooked, neither partially nor fully, regardless of whether it was fermented, acidulated or dried. Traditionally made salami or spreadable fermented sausage are non-heated sausages, however, some sausages for example can be non-heated (dry) of heated (semi-dry).

1. Non-heated slow-fermented dry sausages.

2. Non-heated semi-dry sausages.

3. Heated-semi-dry sausages.

4. Spreadable-fermented sausages (refrigerated).

5. Acidified sausages

6. Cold smoked and dried sausages.

7. Fully-cooked fermented sausages.

8. Non-fermented salami type heated sausages (faked look-like salami.

9. Smoked-cooked-shelf-stable sausages

10. Non-heated or heated fermented sausages made from poultry or other meats.

11. Wild game fermented sausages.

Many of the above sausage evolved in the last 40 years from non-heated dry salami due to technological advances in meat processing equipment, better starter cultures and government regulations which were created to address food outbreaks in The US, Canada, Europe and Australia.

Manufacturing Process

Although the first steps of sausage making, such as meat selection, curing, grinding, mixing, and stuffing, initially seem to be the same, they must be tuned to new safety requirements. All tasks involved in the manufacture of fermented sausages must always be performed in such a way that meat safety is never compromised. Producing regular sausages does not present safety problems as they are usually fully cooked, which kills all bacteria. However, fermented sausages are made differently. A mistake in any processing steps can later spoil the sausage or harm the consumer. The processing steps unique to making fermented sausages are fermenting, ripening, and drying.

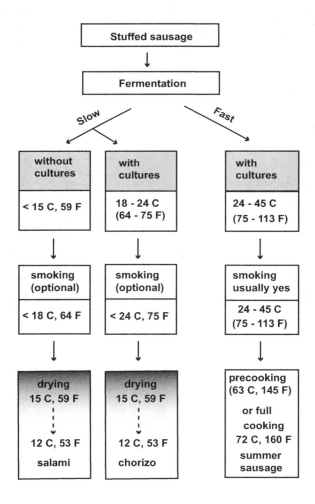

Fig. 7.1 Basic production methods.

The main difference between home production and commercial manufacturing is that commercial plants use much better equipment that allows for processing meats at lower temperatures: chilled meat pieces (usually below 24° F (-4° C) although sometimes they may be at 35° F - 33° (-2° C to 1° C) and frozen fat tissues below 17° F (-8° C) are chopped and ground in a grinder. The mincing may be performed simultaneously or by separate plates with a latter mixture. The size of lean and fat particles will depend on the plate size during grinding. However, the bowl cutter will produce the smallest particles.

General Characteristics of Dry and Semi-dry Fermented Sausages		
Sausage Type	Dry Sausages (Slow-fermented)	Semi-dry (Fast-fermented)
Salt	3% (30 g/kg)	2.5% (25 g/kg)
Dextrose/sugar	0.3 - 0.5% (3 - 5 g/kg)	0.6 - 1.2% (6 - 12 g/kg)
Nitrates	cure #2 (nitrite and nitrate)	cure #1 (nitrite)
Fermentation without culture:	59° F/15° C, 3 days	59° F/15° C, 3 days
Culture type*	T-SPX	F-LC, LHP
Fermentation with culture	64 - 72° F/18 - 22° C, 2-3 days	78-115° F/ 26-46° C 2 - 1 days
Gdl/citric acidulants	usually not	optional
Processing time **	3 weeks - 6 months	3 days - 3 weeks
pH drop	5.2-6.0 ***	4.6 - 5.3
Aw	≤ 0.90	0.93
Mold presence	optional, usually yes in Europe	no
Texture	hard	medium hard or soft
Smoking	varies from country to country	usually yes
Moisture (weight) loss	33% or more	10-20%
Cooking	no	often partially or fully cooked
Flavor	cheesy, aromatic	sourly, acidic
Storage	room temperature, <59° F/15° C	room temperature or refrigerated

* These Danish Chr-Hansen cultures are easily obtainable in the USA. With starter culture fermentation temperature should fall into culture's optimal range. Other cultures can also be selected.
* *The total time will vary on the temperature, the type of product, lean/fat ratio and the sausage diameter.
*** At the end of prolonged drying pH is known to raise due to molds consuming some of the lactic acid what creates *reversed fermentation*.
Processing conditions: meat temperature <36° F/2° C, pH of fresh meat ≤ 5.8.

Meat Selection

The suitability of meat for making fermented sausages depends mainly on its pH, water-holding capacity, and, to a lesser degree, its color. Generally, it is said that meat with pH 5.6-5.8 is an ideal meat for processing. Since fermentation and other processing steps are usually performed at elevated temperatures, the perfect meat should contain minimal bacteria. Otherwise, they will multiply to dangerous levels. Meat must be fresh and well-trimmed of glands and blood clots. Additionally, gristle, sinews and connective tissue must be removed as they will be hard and annoying to chew on, especially in a dry sausage. Such defects are less apparent in finely minced sausages but will strike out in coarsely ground sausage. Offal meat should not be used as it spoils quickly. Fat should be white and fresh to minimize the development of rancidity. If frozen for a short time, the fat can be used. However, it must be pointed out that freezing fat will not prevent rancidity.

Meat Color

The color of fresh meat is determined largely by the amount of myoglobin a particular animal carries. The more myoglobin, the darker the meat; it is that simple. Going from top to bottom, meats that contain more myoglobin are horse, beef, lamb, veal, pork, dark poultry, and light poultry. The amount of myoglobin present in meat increases with the age of the animal.

Different parts of the same animal, such as the turkey, will display a different color of meat. Muscles that are exercised frequently such as legs need more oxygen. As a result they develop a darker color unlike the breast which is white due to little exercise. This color is pretty much fixed and there is not much we can do about it unless we mix different meats together.

Meat from older animals contain more myoglobin which produce stronger cured color. In cured meat nitrite reacts with myoglobin and creates nitrosomyoglobin which is responsible for a deep red color. As the meat is heated the pink color is permanently fixed. Slow-fermented dry sausages are never cooked, however, the red color of nitrosomyoglobin becomes stabilized by drying.

Dark spices like nutmeg, caraway, cloves, and allspice can darken the color of the sausage. Paprika is a known colorant and will impart a reddish color into the sausage. Spanish pimentón paprika is added to Spanish dry Chorizo in large amount making its color orange-red.

Meat Tenderness and Flavor

Meat tenderness depends on the animal's age, chilling methods, and acidity. The way the meat is cooked is another important factor that must be considered, and the cook decides the tenderness of the final product here.

Meat flavor increases with the age of the animal. The characteristic flavors of aparticular animal are concentrated more in the fat than in the lean meat. Low-fat meats exhibit weaker flavors. Freezing and thawing have little effect on meat flavor; however, prolonged frozen storage can affect meat's flavor due to the rancidity of fat.

Importance of Meat pH

The average pH of meat in the living animal is between 6.8 - 7.2 with pork at pH 6.3 - 6.6. After slaughter, the pH in pork drops in 2 - 4 hours to 5.3 - 5.4 which is close to the isoelectric point of meat at which *removal of unbound water is the easiest which contributes positively to faster drying.* When animal dies its blood circulation and respiration stops and there is no more oxygen supply. Muscle glycogen (sugar) is depleted, lactic acid build up and the meat enters stiffening stage called "rigor mortis" (*stiffness of death*) which lasts 3 - 5 hours for pork and 24 -36 hours for beef.

During this phase, there are changes in meat pH due to metabolism (glycolysis) and the conversion of glycogen (muscle sugar) into lactic acid. Such meat is still tough and needs to rest at cool temperatures until it becomes tender again. This resting period which follows "post-mortem" phase is known as "meat aging" and is a familiar term to most people. Aged meat is distributed to the general market.

Meat Aging Time	
Poultry	24 - 48 hours
Pork	4 - 10 days
Beef	7 - 10 days
Lamb	7 - 14 days

Meat can be selected from different cuts of the animal or other animals. Remember that meat cuts originating from the same animal can have different pH values. Although the breast, due to its lower pH, would ferment faster, chicken thigh, due to its darker color, would be a better choice for a fermented sausage. Lean meat contains more moisture than fat and will ferment faster.

pH of Some Meats	
Raw meat	5.6 - 6.0
Stuffed sausage	5.6
Chicken breast/thigh	5.6 - 6.4
Turkey	5.7 - 6.1
Pork	5.6 - 5.8
Wild Boar	5.7
Deer	5.6
Beef	5.4 - 5.9
Lamb	6.0 - 6.8
Sheep	5.6 - 5.8
Goat	6.2
Horse	5.9
Fish	6.2

Normal, PSE and DFD Meat

When animal is freshly slaughtered its meat has a certain pH and its value depends on many factors: type and the age of the animal, the proportion of lean meat to fat and conditions under which was the animal slaughtered.

DFD (dark, firm, dry) meat. When an animal is stressed before slaughter or a deer is not instantly killed, it is in panic mode, and its glycogen reserves deplete rapidly, which decreases acidity, resulting in a higher pH of 6.0-6.2. Such meat holds more water, needs more time for pH drop, and is generally not suitable for making fermented sausages. Meat with high pH offers more unbound water to bacteria and slows the removal of moisture during drying.

PSE (pale, soft, and exudative) meat. PSE pork is caused by a very rapid drop in pH to 5.5-5.3 immediately after slaughter (in less than one hour) while muscle temperatures are still high. Although it may have an acceptable pH reading, PSE meat is lighter and may result in inferior texture. However, it is a better choice than using DFD meat.

Normal meat needs about 3 - 5 hours to reach pH 5.6 - 5.7 and has reddish-pink color which is associated with a good quality pork. Selecting meat with lower acidity (5.7-5.8) provides more safety, as it creates less favorable conditions for the growth of undesirable bacteria. It also shortens the fermentation time needed to drop pH to a safe level.

Given that bacteria hate acidity, initial pH of raw meat is important and a low pH (higher acidity) is desirable. Generally, meat intended for fermentation should have a pH of 5.8 and below.

What is Glycogen

Glycogen is only found in animals and can be compared to starch in plants, as both store carbohydrates. Glycogen converts easily to glucose, the simplest form of sugar, which then acts as a source of energy when needed. Animals display a different pH acidity level in meat which is related to the amount of glycogen (sugar) they carry. They use glycogen as a source of energy when stressed or facing an emergency.

Pigs and cattle are slow mowing, so they own a small amount of glycogen, but fast runners such as horses or deer contain more glycogen, which supplies more energy for sudden bursts of acceleration or facing emergency. This probably explains why horse meat taste somewhat sweetish, although most people cannot differentiate it from beef. Consumption of horse meat is legal and popular in many European countries.

In live animals glycogen is stored mainly in liver and some in muscles, but after the death of animal its glycogen converts to lactic acid what lowers slightly pH of the meat.

Meat type	Sugar (glycogen)	pH
Pork	0.2% (2 g/kg)	5.6 - 5.7
Beef	0.3 - 0.6% (3 g - 6 g/kg)	5.5 - 5.7
Horse	0.9% (9 g/kg)	5.92
The data are for meat that has completed aging process - meat which is available in supermarket.		

The glycogen level in large wild game runners like deer is hard to determine as it depends on the animal's stress level. Fast runners are seldom killed with one shot, so they may still keep on running, depleting their glycogen reserve until collapsing.

Using glycogen alone will not result in meaningful meat fermentation or protect meat from bacteria. To ensure meat safety through fermentation, we need to add sugar or use chemical acidulants to increase the acidity of the ground mixture.

Fat

Fat comprises about 85% fatty tissues, 10-15% water, and 10% connective tissue. The composition of fatty tissues varies from animal to animal, as well as their color and flavor. Generally, sausages with a higher proportion of fat taste better. This is why we often hear "that fat is a carrier of flavor." Soft-muscular fatty tissues should not be used as they cannot be cleanly chopped into clearly defined particles. The slices would have a somewhat blurred, unclear appearance. Soft fat also increases the risk of early rancidity. Soft fat smears easily and may adhere to the inner casing surface, clogging up the pores and affecting drying. It can coat meat particles with fat film, which will affect the drying of slow-fermented products. However, soft fat is used in fermented spreadable sausages as it contributes to better spreadability.

Melting temperature of some fats		
Pork	38 - 44° C	100 - 111° F
Beef	42 - 47° C	107 - 116° F
Lamb	31 - 46° C	87 - 114° F
Chicken	35 - 37° C	95 - 98° F

Beef, lamb, and pork have more saturated fat and less moisture than chicken and turkey and, therefore, are more suitable for making the sausage with a firmer texture. They are also less susceptible to rancidity and off flavors.

Choice of Fat for Fermented Sausages		
Sausage type	Fat	Remarks
Dry-sausages	pork hard fat: back and neck fat	a firm texture is needed for a thin clear-cut
Semi-dry sausages	pork hard or medium-hard fat, jowls	a firm texture is desired for a medium thickness cut, some sausages are cooked
Spreadable sausages	pork soft fat: belly, jowls, 10% vegetable oil	soft texture is needed for spreadability, use the smallest grinder plate
Fat Color and Flavor		
Pork	white, best taste and flavor	
Beef	yellowish, poor taste and flavor	
Chicken	yellowish, acceptable flavor but melts too fast	
Lamb	white, poor taste	

In large cities, it may be challenging to get back fat, and ethnic butcher stores may be the only place to find it. Many supermarkets carry heavily salted pork fat, which needs to be de-salted in cold water before use. If no back fat is available, grind whole cuts of fatty meat. Instead of struggling with fat smearing when processing it at warm temperatures, it is better to use cuts that contain a higher proportion of fat.

Fat Rancidity

Use fresh fat or fat that has not been stored for a long time because, in time, fat develops rancidity. Rancidity is the process that causes a substance to become rancid, that is, having an unpleasant smell or taste. The development of meat rancidity is a slow process, which is why we usually don't sense the problem, as meat spoils before rancidity occurs. The meat can be prevented by freezing. However, rancidity will appear in about three months. Such meat is safe to consume, but it carries off-flavor. Rancidity is the process that causes a fatty substance to develop off-flavor created by meat's reaction with oxygen, which is accelerated by exposure of meat to light. It is not reserved for meat only, but affects all fats and even oils; The best example is butter: unwrap a stick of butter, leave it on a plate for five days at room temperature, and then taste it. It will have an unpleasant taste due to rancidity, which will get stronger in time.

Given that dry sausages can be stored for a long time, the fat in them will develop some rancidity. Fat rancidity cannot be avoided, but it can be slowed down by selecting the freshest fat material and conducting drying/ripening process at <68° F (20° C) and 75-80% humidity. The following ingredients are credited with slowing fat rancidity: nitrates, ascorbic acid (vitamin C), tocopherol, spices rosemary, thyme, sage, and smoke application.

Curing

Without understanding the process, it was known for centuries that cured meats developed a nice pink color, had better flavor and lasted longer. It was also known that when meat was cured it was easier to produce consistent quality salami. Today, curing is performed when making dry or semi-dry sausages without starter cultures. Its purpose is to increase the number of lactic acid and color and flavor forming bacteria that are present in meat. The disadvantage of this process, which would often last for 10 days, was that not only beneficial bacteria but others, such as spoilage and dangerous ones, would multiply as well.

Traditional Method of Curing Meat

1. Meat is cut into 2" cubes and mixed with salt and sodium nitrite (Cure #1). Then, the meat is packed tightly (to remove air), about 6-8" high, into containers. Then, the meat is covered with a clean cloth to prevent air from discoloring it and to allow gases to escape.
2. The containers are held in a refrigerator for 3-4 days. Given that smaller particles will cure faster, the time of curing could be shortened to 24 - 48 hours by grinding the meat.

If potassium nitrate is added alone, the curing temperature should be 46° F (8° C). As mentioned earlier, the curing step is seldom practiced today given that starter cultures permit a better control of the process and help to produce a safe product of a better and constant quality. Nevertheless, curing is still a fine and recommended procedure for making top quality smoked meats and sausages.

Cutting/Grinding

As the definition implies, a grinder grinds meat using force and pushes it through the plate; it does not produce a perfectly clean cut. There is a large amount of pressure on meat in the feed chamber, which leads to tearing between the auger and the walls of the chamber. As a result, the meat is not cut as well as with a bowl cutter. This will be more pronounced when the knife is blunt.

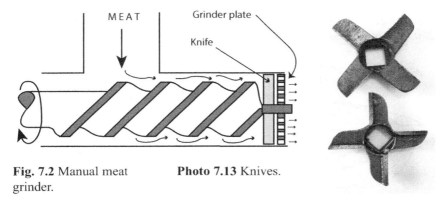

Fig. 7.2 Manual meat grinder.

Photo 7.13 Knives.

Photo 7.14 Grinder #10.

Photo 7.15 Assortment of grinder plates.

Grinders generate some heat, so to produce a clean cut, the meat must be cold or partially frozen. In commercial production, cutting/grinding temperatures are 28-30° F (-2-1° C) for meats and 27-26° F (-3-2° C) for fats. This produces easily distinguishable meat and fat particles. In-home production, we must keep the cutting knife sharp and supply meat and fat very cold. The fat contains less moisture than lean meat so it can be added partially frozen.

Bowl Cutter

To have the cleanest distribution of meat and fat particles, commercial producers process cold meat and frozen fat in bowl cutters, and these machines cut meat and fat down to very fine particles. Another benefit is that all ingredients can be introduced to the rotating bowl, and cutting and mixing can be accomplished in one step. Bowl cutters work at high speeds and generate large amounts of heat which is usually controlled by adding about 30% of ice to the bowl. The introduction of ice/water cannot be permitted when making fermented sausages, so *the low temperature is maintained by adding frozen fat and cold or partially frozen meat.*

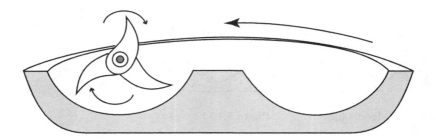

Photo 7.3 A small bowl cutter. The speed of the turning bowl and rotating knives are adjustable.

Photo 7.16 Small bowl cutter.

Meat contains 75% of water, which becomes hard ice in a frozen state. Adding frozen meat will damage the bowl cutter's knives. However, frozen fat can be cut in a bowl cutter or ground through the grinder as fat contains only 10-15% water, so there are fewer frozen water crystals to inflict damage to the knives. When a fine grind was desired, two-step grind technique was employed in the past:

- grind partially frozen meat with a larger plate, for example 3/8" (10 mm).
- place the mince for 20 minutes in a freezer.
- grind again with 1/8" (3 mm) plate.

Keep in mind that the smallest particles a grinder can produce is around 3 mm (1/8"). Obtaining 2 mm particles requires a bowl cutter.

Photo 7.17 Very small particles can be generated in a bowl cutter as seen in the upper right corner.

Note: A home food processor can be employed for making emulsified or liver sausages; however, it cannot compete with a bowl cutter. It is more difficult to monitor meat's temperature, even in pulse mode, with a home processor. Besides, the blades will not last long when frozen meat and fat are introduced.

Importance of Keeping Equipment Cold

There are two reasons why meat should always be processed cold:

1. Cold meat, especially fat can be cleanly cut, ground, mixed and stuffed. There will be a nice visible particle distribution and no fat smearing. If the fat is not cold the smearing will occur. Meat particles become surrounded with fat film and the drying will be slower. Fat smearing negatively affects removal of moisture.

2. The warmer the meat, the faster the growth of all types of bacteria. By the time minced warm meat is mixed with salt, nitrite and other ingredients, its bacterial load might be twice as high.

Keeping meat cold is extremely important when making traditional non-heated salami without a starter culture. As they are made with very small amounts of sugar and unknown type and a number of lactic acid bacteria, the fermentation will produce too little acidity to protect meat from undesirable bacteria. Keeping meat and equipment cold increases the chances of making a safe product:

- Take only as much meat from refrigerator as you can process in a short time, then put it back into refrigerator.
- Keep the head of electric grinder, knife, plates in refrigerator until ready to use.
- Use stainless steel mixing bowl and also keep it refrigerated. The bowl can be placed on ice to keep it cold. Bowl cutter's mixing bowl is often filled with crushed ice; then the ice is removed, bowl wiped off-dry, and ready for use.
- Piston stuffer's cylinder can be kept in refrigerator as well.
- Plastic gloves will prevent heat transfer from the hands into the meat.

Mixing

During the production of regular sausages, spices are often mixed with water in a blender and then added to meat. This helps to distribute all ingredients more evenly and makes mixing and stuffing sausages easier. In fermented sausages, the addition of water to the sausage mass should be avoided as this creates favorable conditions for the growth of bacteria and prolongs drying. Occasionally, wine or vinegar is added. However, both of those liquids are very acidic, and they make up for water by increasing the acidity of the sausage mix. The temperature of the sausage mix should be between 32-40° F (0-5° C). If this temperature increases, the sausage mix should be cooled down in a refrigerator before proceeding to the stuffing step. When mixing meat with ingredients, it is best to follow this sequence:

1. Minced meats, salt, nitrite/nitrate, sugar, spices, starter culture.

2. Minced fat.

Air should be removed from the mixture before it is stuffed into casings, given that oxygen promotes the growth of spoilage bacteria. When making regular sausage, forceful mixing/kneading is employed to extract proteins, so a sticky "exudate" helps to bind meat particles together. The purpose of mixing in fermented sausages is to uniformly distribute the ingredients; hence, over-mixing should be avoided as it may lead to fat smearing and excessive particle binding. This, in turn, will negatively affect the removal of moisture.

Photo 7.18 A paddle mixer, if available, is a preferred device for mixing, however, in home production manual mixing is usually performed.

Note: a sign of over mixing is the accumulation of fat on the paddles or sides of the mixer.

Stuffing

The majority of hobbyists stuff sausages using grinders and the attached stuffing tube. This arrangement has served us well for centuries, but it is a labor consuming operation normally requiring two persons.

Sausage mass can firm up very fast and should be stuffed firmly without much delay. It cannot be expected that a hydraulic vacuum stuffer will be used at home, however, it is recommended to have a vertical or horizontal piston stuffer equipped with *air valve release* which will make stuffing faster, more enjoyable and the mince will contain less air.

Always use the largest diameter tube that will fit the casing. Don't feed the cylinder with small amount of the mixture, but rather form a large balls and throw them forcefully down the cylinder. This will introduce less air.

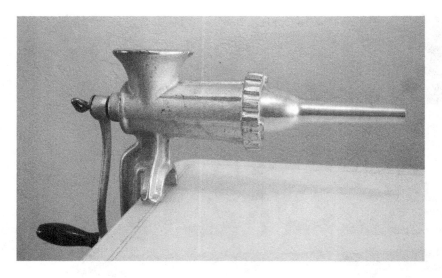

Photo 7. 19 Number 10 grinder with stuffing tube.

Photo 7. 20 DIfferent size stuffing tubes.

Fig. 7.4 Spacer.

The knife and the grinder plate are always removed for stuffing. It is recommended to use the spacer, although not absolutely necessary. The spacer supports the auger shaft and prevents the unit from wobbling.

Note: the money that is saved by not buying an electrically operated grinder can be reinvested into a purchase of a piston stuffer. If you can afford it, buy all top of the line industrial automated equipment, but keep in mind that a quality manual grinder is an incredibly efficient device that can be successfully deployed in any production that requires 20 pounds or less of meat.

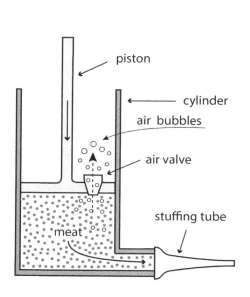

Fig. 7.5 Manual piston stuffer with air valve.

Photo 7.21 15-lb capacity manual piston stuffer..

Spoilage bacteria *(Pseudomonas spp.)* need oxygen to live, so applying vacuum during mixing and stuffing effectively inhibits their growth. To remove air, commercial producers perform mixing and stuffing under a vacuum at around 32° F (0° C). At home, a precaution must be made so that the sausage mix is stuffed firmly and any air pockets which are visible in a stuffed casing are picked with a needle. However, many sausage makers prick stuffed sausage regardless of whether air pockets are present or not, especially when making large diameter dry sausages.

Most prickers come with three or more needles; however, a long pin or a finishing nail will do the job, although it is slower. It is important not to leave any air pockets inside as they can discolor the meat, show up as little pores later, and provide oxygen to spoilage bacteria. In addition, oxygen affects the development of curing color and promotes rancidity in fats. For home production with a manual stuffer, a smart precaution is to prick stuffed sausages with a needle regardless of whether the air pockets are visible or not.

Photo 7.22 Italian round pricker.

Notes
- Sausages stuffed in natural casings should not lie on a table, but should be hung and rinsed with water or wiped off with a wet cloth. This removes any remaining water and salt that was left after soaking the casing prior to stuffing.
- The stuffed sausages should enter the fermentation stage as soon as the sausages reach the room temperature.
- Try to make sausages of the same diameter and always have a test sausage, which should be weighed before the start of fermentation. It can be shorter but must be of the same diameter as other sausages. Weighing a test sausage allows you to monitor the moisture loss. It can also be sliced to check the inside for any off-flavors.
- Dry salami should never be filled into waterproof casings as they will prevent smoke penetration and moisture removal.
- Unfilled minced meat, acidified with Gdl, should never be kept in the refrigerator overnight.

Casings

Natural and synthetic casings are used as long as they allow moisture and smoke to go through. They must be able to cling to meat and shrink with it throughout the drying process. Generally, casings for fermented sausages range from 25 mm to 110 mm (1 - 4"), given that different products use different sizes. Slow-fermented dry sausages shrink and lose more than 30% of the original weight; hence, they are packed into 60-90 mm (2.3 - 3.5") casings. The exceptions are semi-dry fermented meat sticks which may be stuffed into 10 - 13 mm (3/8 - 0.5") casings.

Casing can be classified into two groups:
- Natural casings - pig, cattle, sheep, horse.
- Synthetic - cellulose and collagen.

Natural casings are perfect for home production as they give the product a traditional appearance, which many customers find attractive. With thousands of tiny pores, they acquire smoke well and permit moisture removal. They cling to the meat and follow the shrinkage of the sausage during drying. Sheep casings are less popular with salami-type products due to their small diameter.

All types of pork and beef casings are used for making salami; however, the fact that beef casings are much thicker than pork ones should be taken into consideration when drying sausages. Given that natural casings are often stored for extended periods of time, they may be contaminated with some bacteria. Generally, they are rinsed and kept in water for 20-30 minutes; however, quite often, as an extra precaution, they are also briefly submerged in diluted vinegar. Some experts claim that natural casings are more flexible and facilitate drying if soaked in 5% solution of lactic acid. This definitely decreases the chances of growing mold or developing slime during fermentation. Natural casing must never be soaked together with other casing types.

Synthetic Casings

Synthetic casings must be permeable to permit moisture evaporation, gas removal, and smoke acquisition. They need to cling to the meat and follow the sausage's shrinkage. Because of their uniformity, synthetic casings are preferred for commercial production and are available in any diameter required. Synthetic casings are inedible. There are two types of synthetic casings: collagen and cellulose.

Collagen casings - are made from collagen extracted from pork and beef skins and other natural materials. They are preferred casings for commercial producers due to their uniform shape and diameter. They are compressed using process called "shirring" which significantly increases the length of the casing per section. They are easy to insert on a stuffing horn and their uniform diameter allows automated linking machines to produce sausages of any desired length and weight. Collagen casings used for small diameter sausages are usually edible.

Cellulose casings - are strong and uniform. There are two types of cellulose casings, and both are permeable to smoke and moisture: non-fibrous and fibrous. Cellulose casings are made from viscose, which is made up of cellulose from wood or cotton processing. These casings are inedible and must be peeled.

Fibrous casings - are popular for making fermented and cooked salami and regular large-diameter smoked and cooked sausages. They can be treated inside with a material that reduces the cling between the casing and the meat, which results in easy skin peeling. However, a protein is often applied to the inside of the casings. Protein-lined fibrous casings adhere strongly to meat and shrink together with the sausage without becoming loose, which is important when drying sausages.

Come-Up Time/Conditioning

Come-up time is a period required to bring cold sausage to a higher temperature for further processing. It is desired that starter culture bacteria start working as soon as possible; however, since the manufacturing process is undertaken at low temperatures, the sausage is often too cold to make it possible. If such a cold sausage is placed in a warmer room, the condensation will appear on the surface of the casing. To correct this, the sausage must "rest" in the fermentation chamber at around 60% humidity, which generally corresponds to humidity in a typical room. No airflow is applied until the moisture evaporates. At home, the manufacturing process will take place at higher temperatures, so condensation might not occur or be very short.

Inserting cold sausage into warm fermentation chamber is not going to trigger an immediate fermentation due to the following:

- Starter culture bacteria available online are of freeze-type variety and need to go through a "lag phase" before they "wake up" and start reacting with meat. This might take 6 - 12 hours depending on a culture.

- The sausage must reach at least 53° F (15° C) core temperature before lactic acid bacteria start producing lactic acid. Depending on a diameter of the sausage and a temperature of the chamber the "come-up" time may last a number of hours.

Reactions Taking Place Inside The Sausage After Stuffing

Once the sausage is filled, the first physical part of the production is completed. If everything was done according to good manufacturing processes, the raw minced meat inside of the stuffed sausage would become, in time, a great product. Now, the meat will go through many reactions, which will ultimately develop its texture, taste, and flavor. Regardless of what precautions are taken, some bacteria will always be present and will start multiplying rapidly in the first hours of fermentation. During this period, which may last hours or a day, the meat is only protected by salt, culture (if added), nitrite, low temperature, and good manufacturing practices, which were hopefully respected during processing.

The temperature of the sausage should increase to the recommended fermentation temperature of a prticular culture as fast as possible to create the best starting conditions for the growth of starter culture bacteria. Once when the sausage "warms up," the temperature of the fermentation chamber is set to the recommended temperature for a particular starter culture. Until this happens, the natural wild bacteria that are present in meat might have favorable conditions to grow before culture bacteria start competing with them.

Fermentation

The activity of the culture starts when it reaches the minimum growth temperature. Of course, at the minimum temperature, everything works rather slowly. At the optimum temperature, it works fast. It is essential to heat the sausages to the desired temperature as fast as possible. It means in the most cases, when the chamber is full start immediately the fermentation with the desired fermentation temperature. us.This is easier said than done due to the weak power of the fermentation/climate chambers. A chamber may be set to 75° F (24° C) for fermentation, but it sometimes takes more than 12 hours to reach this temperature in the chamber or in the core of the large-diameter sausage.

Fermentation starts at high humidity (> 90%) to slow the moisture removal from the sausage. Adding 3% salt will drop Aw water activity to 0.96-0.97. At low humidity, the drying can proceed too quickly. As a result, Aw may drop below 0.95, which will slow the growth of lactic acid bacteria, and fermentation may run slow. All bacteria types need free water to survive, and lactic acid bacteria are no exception. High humidity with restricted air speed inhibits drying, indicated by slime on the sausage. Once lactic bacteria start producing acid and moisture starts going away, the odds change in our favor.

Spoilage and pathogenic bacteria don't tolerate acidity well and will eventually stop growing. During this time moisture evaporates from the sausage, and that makes life for bacteria even more difficult as they need free water to survive. Once the fermentation has started the drying can be more aggressive.

Although the moisture evaporates from the sausage, the salt remains inside, which makes it even saltier to bacteria. The scale starts slowly tipping in our favor, and there comes a moment when the sausage is shelf-stable and safe to consume, given that bacteria either cannot grow or simply die.

Smoking Fermented Sausages

Smoking alone is not a preservation method, however, it offers some benefits:

- Provides microbiological safety against bacteria in the *surface area.*
- Prevents growth of mold. It is generally applied at the end of fermentation to not interfere with lactic acid bacteria. Applying warm smoke for a few hours will prevent mold growth, albeit for some time, as it may reappear again later, depending on humidity and temperature. Given that, the mold may be wiped off and smoke re-applied again.
- Retards development of fat rancidity.

Cold and hot smoking are two distinctive methods of smoking with warm smoking falling in between:

- Cold smoking, usually at 59-77° F (15-25° C).
- Warm smoking, 77-140° F, (25-60° C). These temperatures fall into the "danger zone" - 40-140° F (4-60° C) when all types of bacteria grow fast.
- Hot smoking, 140-160° F (60-71° C). Higher temperatures adversely affect the texture of the sausage, fat melts and texture becomes crumbly. Once the temperature exceeds 200° F (93° C) , we are entering barbecuing zone.

Sausage type	Smoking Method	Fermentation Temperature	Cooking	Remarks
Slow-fermented, or only dried	Cold (optional)	64-80° F/18-27° C	None	Can be kept at room temperature.
Fast-fermented	Hot *	> 80° F/27° C	Yes	Shelf stable when thermally treated.
Spreadable	Cold (optional)	64° F/18° C	None	In northern Europe always smoked.
The temperature of the smoke should correspond to the prevailing temperature during fermentation or drying or cooking. If a semi-dry sausage is cooked to 145-160° F/63-72° C the smoke temperature will be gradually raised as well.				

The fermentation temperature determines whether cold or hot smoke will be applied. The temperature of the smoke should correspond to the temperature of the chamber where the fermentation occurs. This temperature usually falls within the optimal range at which a particular culture ferments best.

Which Wood is Best for Smoking?

Any hardwood is fine, but soft evergreen trees like fir, spruce, pine, or others cause problems. They contain too much resin and the finished product has a turpentine flavor to it. It also develops a black color due to the extra soot from the smoke, which in turn makes the smokehouse dirtier, too. Make sure that the surface of the sausage is dry after fermentation as there are invisible to the eye particles in the smoke which will adhere to the wet surface and will discolor the sausage.

We don't use wet wood for cold smoking because we want to eliminate moisture, not bring it in; however, soaking wood chips for 30 minutes is fine. Cold smoke warms the surface of the meat up very finely, just enough to allow the moisture to evaporate. Wet chips or sawdust produce more smoke, but this is not true. The extra smoke is only water vapor (steam) mixed with smoke. There are dozens of wood chips available on the Internet: alder, beech, cherry, apple, citrus, oak, hickory, mesquite, walnut, pecan, and people argue about the best. Well, people who smoke meat a lot have an easy answer: use hardwood that grows in your area. It is a simple, convenient, inexpensive, and practical solution that always works.

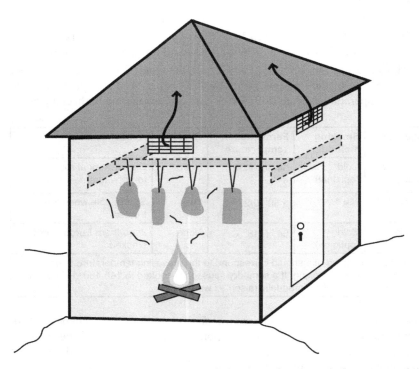

Fig. 7.6 American XVIII century smokehouse. A large smokehouse was also a storage facility where smoked meats and sausages were hung away from the source of the smoke. They continued to receive some smoke, but technically speaking, *they were dried with smoke.*

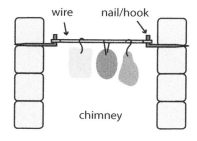

Fig. 7.7 Direct placement in chimney.

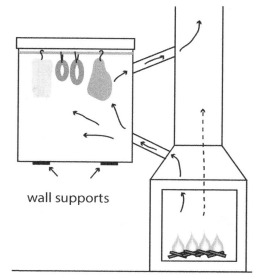

Fig. 7.8 - right. Box on the wall.

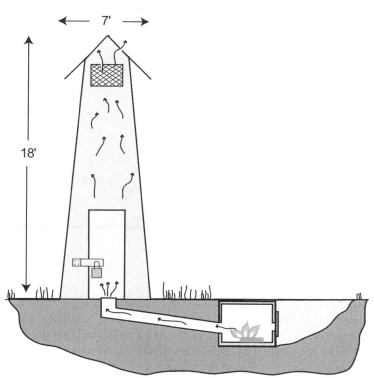

Fig. 7.9 Old Lithuanian smokehouse.

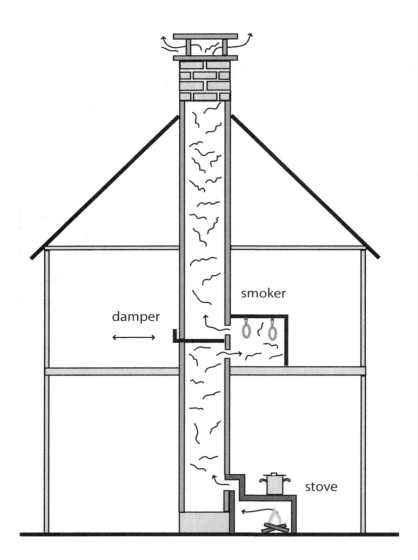

Fig. 7.10 Home chimney smoker.

Spanish traditional method of smoking meats above the kitchen stove was known as "la campana de Lareira" - old kitchen stoves used wood for fuel and had removable top plates. Removing the plates or partially covering the fire allowed control of room temperature or application of smoke. As an additional bonus, the sausages acquired different flavors from foods cooked on the stove. For example, in traditional production, Spanish marinated pork loins were stuffed in pork bungs and hung above the stove for 3-4 days. Then, the drying continued in any suitable chamber for about 3 months.

Photo 7.23 & 7.24 Using the weather to his advantage, Waldemar Kozik has no problems with cold smoking sausages in Catskill Mountains of New York.

Given that smoke contains thousands ingredients (phenols, carbonyls, acids and others), applying it early during fermentation may decrease the rate of fermentation and interfere with action of oxygen hungry flavor forming bacteria which usually reside in the surface.

Ripening - Maturing - Aging - Drying

Ripening needs time. Also termed *maturing* or *aging* the process follows fermentation and is a part of the drying process. During the ripening of dry sausages, flavor-forming bacteria naturally present in meat enzymes break proteins and fats, developing flavors and aroma, giving the sausage its individual character. Sausages are usually ripened at 53-59° F (12-15° C), below 60° F (15.6° C) when *Staphylococcus aureus* starts growing fast. Given that ripening is basically a drying process, humidity is gradually lowered to prevent mold growth on the surface. The airspeed is also lowered to avoid excessive drying; besides, due to the continuous removal of moisture, less air velocity is needed. It is impossible to say when maturing ends as there are always some reactions present in a dry sausage, even during storage.

During all processing steps, the sausage continuously loses moisture, but not the original amount of salt that remains inside. This will change the proportion of salt in the meat, so the sausage should taste saltier. However, this is hardly noticeable due to the bacterial action on proteins and fats, which somehow makes it hard to sense.

Cooking

This process is optional and depends on the type of sausage that is being made. Slow-fermented dry sausages are not cooked. Partial or full cooking is applied to the majority of fast-fermented semi-dry sausages. Regular sausages such as smoked, liver, frankfurters, and others are generally cooked in water, given that water conducts heat faster than air, so the process is shorter than baking a product in a smokehouse or in an oven. However, all fermented sausages are dried to some degree; it makes no sense to cook them in water as they will acquire moisture again, which will lower the microbiological safety of the sausage. A sausage heated in the air will lose more moisture and will become a safer product.

Storing

Sausages should be kept in a dark room to prevent color change and fat rancidity. A little airflow (0.05-0.1 m/sec) keeps the air fresh and inhibits mold formation. The temperature is set to about 50-60° F (10-15° C). The humidity should remain at around 75% as a lower humidity will increase drying, and the sausage will lose more weight. Higher humidity and temperature may create favorable conditions for the development of mold. If any mold develops, it can be easily wiped off with water and vinegar. Molds need air to live, so they are present only on the surface, and in most cases, there is nothing wrong with the meat itself. Then, the sausage can be cold smoked for a few hours, inhibiting the growth of a new mold.

Definition of Quality

This is difficult to formulate because there are many factors to consider, and not all of them are common to each sausage type. In many cases, quality is preconceived by tradition and local preference. A child growing up in one country develops a liking for products made in his area and might not like similar food originating from a different area. A good example is smoked sausages; the northern Europeans love them, and people in Mediterranean countries like Italy and Spain don't. The factors that define quality are appearance, texture, taste, flavor, and aroma.

Sausage Appearance. The type of sausage that will be produced dictates the manufacturing process, which determines attributes like color, mold, firmness, particle size, lean meat, fat, or the presence of mold. Since people buy food with their eyes, the looks are of the utmost importance. Sausage appearance depends on factors such as the choice of the casing, its color, meat color, smoking, lean-to-fat particle ratio, and particle size.

Texture. Dry sausages are hard, semi-dry sausages are softer, and semi-dry spreadable sausages are moist and soft, and as the name implies, they can be spread on a roll. When a good dry sausage is thinly sliced, the meat and fat particles should be easily distinguishable. Meat for dry sausages can be ground course, but for spreadable sausages, a fine grind is needed. Thus, the choice of meat, fat, and processing steps such as cutting, grinding, and mixing will initially decide the texture, and then fermentation and drying will add the final touch.

Taste. The taste is relatively easy to describe: salty, sweet, bitter, or sour. The taste components are mainly established during fermentation. In dry sausages, time and drying will be the major factors affecting the taste of the sausage. In semi-dry sausages, fermentation temperature and the amount of sugar will influence the acidity and taste of the sausage, and the flavorings will contribute to its flavor.

Flavor and Aroma. The flavor is harder to define as it usually consists of hundreds of components, many of which can be defined as aroma. Given that dry sausages have the longest ripening stage, they also possess the best flavor and aroma. The variety of flavors in traditionally made dry sausages was due to the fact that they were fermented with wild strains of lactic and flavor-forming bacteria. This resulted in sausages having different flavor profiles. Using starter cultures results in a less but more predictable number of flavors. The flavor of fermented sausages was often described as fruity, cheesy, mushroom, earthy, popcorn, butter, sweaty socks, leather, vomit, soap, and others. Some unpleasant flavors/odors were probably the result of undesirable effects of ripening, such as fat rancidity, formation of hydrogen peroxide (sulfur components - rotten eggs odor), and others. These could have been the results of breaking the rules of good manufacturing practices, processing warm meat, or ripening at warm temperatures.

Flavor and aroma are criteria that separate exceptional products from mass-produced products. We can replace natural fermentation with chemical acidulation, accelerate color development, or even add color additives, but it is harder to duplicate the natural meat's flavor that was developed during one or three months of drying.

In the past the sausages hanged on hooks or were kept in weaved baskets. A customer could smell aroma of smoked or dried meats the moment he opened the door. A friendly owner-butcher would offer a sample slice to try. When one tries a slice of Spanish *Longanissa de Vic/Salchichón de Vic,* he can smell its wonderful aroma before the first bite. Generally, aroma is absent in most fast produced semi-dry sausages given that develop acidity (low pH) so fast that flavor forming bacteria (*Staphylococcus spp.*) being acidity sensitive, have no chance to react with meat.

Nowadays, it is impossible to smell aroma of a sausage as most products are pre-sliced and packed under vacuum or in a modified atmosphere. This eliminates any kind of aroma that might have been present, so a customer buys the product blindly. That much for sensing aroma.

Various compounds are needed to develop the aroma and flavor of fermented sausages. Salt, spices, smoke, contribute to taste; bacteria and enzymes form flavor and aroma during ripening. Adding nitrite develops a desired "curing meat flavor" when meat is traditionally cured. About half of nitrite is depleted within hours for creating color, but the remaining part reacts with meat developing intricate flavors.

Lactic acid bacteria produce lactic acid with small amounts of acetic acid (vinegar) which give the sausages a tangy taste and some vinegar flavor. An acid flavor dominates in semi-dry products which were fermented to a low pH so they cannot compete with the flavor of dry sausages. However, a semi-dry sausage fermented to pH 5.3, then dry/ripened for 2-3 weeks will acquire a much better flavor, even if they end up partially cooked.

The noticeable difference in flavor between South European, North European, and American fermented sausages is not as much due to spice combinations as to the employment of different manufacturing methods. These methods influence the choice of starter cultures, fermentation temperatures, amounts and types of sugars, and the extent of acidity.

- South European Sausages - generally not smoked.
- North European Sausages, including Eastern Europe - smoked.
- American Sausages - either way.

The absence of smoky flavor is another factor that differentiates southern sausages from the ones from the north, which might be a positive factor in salami-type products. A pleasant meat aroma can be sensed in southern salami. Were the sausage smoked, its delicate aroma would be partially overridden by a smoky flavor. Now, let's sum up all this information with one sentence that defines a good quality sausage produced at home. For a hobbyist who makes his own products the definition of quality is very simple:

"if you like what you have made, it's a good sausage."

Chapter 8

Slow-Fermented Non-Heated Dry Sausages

Time makes the best salami. Time is the main factor that develops complex flavor in dry sausages. Time is a luxury that a commercial plant can hardly afford, but a hobbyist has plenty of it. Hence, high-quality, slow-fermented products can easily be made at home. Salami-type dry sausages are often called slow-fermented because they are fermented at low temperatures when the rate of fermentation slows down.

The US Official Classification says that "*Dry sausages are chopped or ground meat products that, as a result of bacterial action or direct addition acidulation, reach a pH of 5.3 or less and are then dried to remove 25 to 50% of the moisture.*"

We should be aware that dropping pH below 5.0 will introduce a sour taste, which may be fine for a semi-dry sausage but not for a European-style dry salami. The technology of making dry sausages relies on drying and not on generating acidity through fermentation. The water content of finished salami-type dry sausages is below 33%, which corresponds to Aw ≤ 0.89. Their texture should be firm as they are usually sliced thin. When stored at $60°$ F ($15°$ C), 70-75% humidity, such a sausage lasts at least one year. They might be called dry-cured or slow-fermented dry salami, but the definition applies to traditionally made sausages with a bit of sugar or none. Flavor-forming bacteria create their characteristic cheesy flavor during a long drying process. Traditional salami is a one-piece baton-shaped sausage that is neither pre-sliced nor packed in vacuum pouches.

They are seldom carried in American supermarkets as most manufacturers stopped making them due to a number of regulations that make production complicated. They can, however, be purchased online from a few manufacturers that still make them. Although they usually carry original Italian, Spanish, or French names, nevertheless, on the label, there is a statement: country of origin: USA. A limited number of European-made salami may also be found online, but they are expensive. Salami-type dry sausages, including the ones carrying a European Certificate of Origin, can be found in every European country, which means they are made the same way they were made in the past.All Southern European countries produce great dry sausages which can be have a distinct name, but they are all basically salami type products: salami (Italy), fuet, salchichón, longanissa (Spain), saucissón sec (France).

The production od traditional salami is challenging because:

- There is not enough acidity to inhibit *S. aureus,* hence there is no pH safety hurdle.
- Sausages are not heated; hence this safety hurdle is also eliminated.

Dry salami can be produced in two different ways:

1. Without starter cultures - not recommended as this is a complicated process which requires great operating skills.
2. With starter cultures - easy.

1. Since it is impossible to predict the type and number of different strains of bacteria residing in meat, the production without culture is a gamble, remaining a flipping the coin. We might get lucky and produce an outstanding sausage, or it might be unsafe and unedible. For example, wild lactic bacteria are of a hetero-fermentative variety, which means there might be different strains of *Lactobacillus spp.* or *Pediococcus spp.;* some may produce pure lactic acid, but others may additionally develop acetic acid (vinegar), alcohol and substances which may create unpleasant odors.

For sausages made with a little sugar, there is a weak fermentation and little acidity, and that does not offer protection against the growth of toxin producing *Staphylococcus aureus* which starts growing fast at 60° F (15.6° C) and may produce toxin. In the past we knew nothing about *S. aureus,* but it was accepted practice to introduce a stuffed sausage into the drying chamber at 42-58° F (6-15° C), where it remained for the rest of the process. For example Hungarian téliszalámi was fermented and dried at 46-53° F (8-12° C).

Adding sugar at 0.3% (3 g) does not drop pH below 5.0, so the fermentation alone does not create the safety hurdle. The sausage's microbiological safety is accomplished by drying. In slow-fermented sausages, *Staphylococcus spp.* flavor-producing bacteria (not to be confused with *pathogenic S. aureus*) are never threatened and can continue reacting with meat proteins and fat particles, developing hundreds of different aromatic flavors. The flavor of fermented sausages improves during ripening and storage, given that yeasts and molds consume some lactic acid and produce ammonia. Ammonia being alkaline (pH 11.5) forces pH higher and decreases acidity. The result is a mellower flavor and aroma. Their final pH falls between 5.3 - 5.6.

Authentic salami's flavor and aroma are developed by *Staphylococcus carnosus* and *Staphylococcus xylosus* color and flavor-forming bacteria. Since they are sensitive to acidity, they perform poorly below pH 5.5 and stop reacting with meat at pH 5.0. Hence, the quality of traditional salami is inversely proportional to the amount of sugar: less sugar equals higher quality and vice versa. Thus, the rate and extent of acid production must be limited to permit the acidity-sensitive *Staphylococcus spp.,* develop flavor and aroma.

Water Activity, Moisture and Weight Loss

Given that technology of making true dry salami depends od drying, there is always a question *how long to dry the sausage* to make it microbiologically stable. A weight loss of 30% corresponds to around Aw 0.90. It is generally accepted that dry salami should lose at least 33-40% of its original weight.

Aw 0.95 - 15% weight loss
Aw 0.94 - 20% weight loss
Aw 0.90 - 30% weight loss
Aw 0.88 - 35% weight loss
Aw 0.86 - 40% weight loss
Aw 0.85 - 45% weight loss

The above figures are not perfect, but can be at least used as a reference point. Although Aw, moisture and loss of weight curves all decrease during drying, nevertheless, there is no fixed relationship among them. There are many factors that affect the speed of drying such as: casing diameter, type of casing, temperature, humidity and air speed in a chamber, the ratio of lean meat to fat, type of meat, the particle size, the amount of salt and so on. For example, a sausage with a large proportion of fat will dry faster than a lean one, however, the latter one will loose more moisture and weight in time, given that lean meat contains more moisture than fat. Aw meter disregards all those factors and simply states how much free water remains to bacteria.

Determining pH drop is easy as the pH meters are inexpensive, easy to use, and provide instant and accurate results. On the other hand, water activities are very expensive, difficult to use, and do not provide an instant readout. They are used by labs and commercial meat plants. In-home production, we rely on the knowledge and years of experience of experts who made those sausages. For making dry sausages at home, the practical solution is to estimate moisture loss by checking the weight loss of the sausage, which is basically the amount of lost moisture.

Calculating Weight Loss

% weight loss = (a - b) / a x 100

a - the original weight of the stuffed sausage
b - the latest weight of the sausage

For example the stuffed sausage weighed 850 g and its latest weight was 550 g.
% weight loss = (a-b)/a x 100 = (850 -550) / 850 x 100 = 300/850 x 100 = 0.3529 x 100 = 35%. The sausage lost 35% of its original weight.

The weight loss can be attributed to a loss of water, however, there is no fixed relationship between the two as different meat and fats contain different percentages of water. Lean meat contains around 75% of water, but fat only ~ 15%. Given that a weight loss of 33% corresponds to around Aw 0.86 water activity it may be stated accepted that dry salami type sausages are shelf stable when they lose 33 - 50% of weight. However, the relationship between the moisture loss (weight) and the drying time is not a linear one.

In the production of traditional-style sausages, the fermentation profile must have a short lag phase to ensure the growth of the added starter culture at the expense of the unwanted bacteria. The acidification profile must be rather flat, not going below pH 4.8-5.0 at any time. This will ensure that *Staphylococci* maintain their activity over a longer period of time, foremost their nitrate reductase and flavor-forming activities.

	Slow Fermented (Dry) Sausages	
	With culture	**Without culture ***
Fermentation temp.	20°-24° C, 68°-75° F	15° C, 59° F
Ferm. humidity %	90 → 85	90 → 85
Fermentation time	2-3 days	3 days
Drying temperature	16° → 14° C, 60°-57° F	14° → 12° C, 57°- 54° F
Drying humidity %	90 → 80	90 → 80
Drying time **	6 weeks - 3 months	6 weeks - 3 months
Salt	3-3.3%	3-3.3%
Sugar 0.3-0.5%	1/3 dextrose, 2/3 sucrose ****	1/3 dextrose, 2/3 sucrose ****
Curing salt 120 - 150 ppm	Nitrite (cure #1) OR nitrite plus nitrate (cure #2)	Nitrite (cure #1) OR nitrite plus nitrate (cure #2)
Final pH ***	5.2-5.6	5.2-5.6
Expected final Aw	0.88	0.88
Weight loss	>30%	>30%

* *Prior to fermentation, meat is cured.*
** Most slow-fermented sausages are stable from 6 weeks - 3 months *depending on diameter*, however, the ripening process will continue during additional drying and storing.
*** If pH drops below 5.0 the sausage will exhibit a sourly taste. During the fermentation of Italian and Hungarian salamis which are made with Lucke: little sugar, the pH usually drops by not more than 0.5 units.
**** Sugar - use a combination od dextrose and sucrose in a 1/3 dextrose 2/3 sucrose ratio.

Drying

Sausages are dried at 54-62° F (12-16° C), 80-75% humidity. Dry sausages require 30-40% moisture loss, which should be reached in 6-8 weeks, but remember that drying times are influenced by casing type and diameter, the size of meat particles, humidity, and air speed. When sausage loses 30% of its weight, its Aw is around 0.89. The larger the diameter of the sausage, the longer the drying process. Pork blind caps, bungs, or beef casings are much tougher than natural pork casing, so the moisture escapes more slowly. Drying starts from the moment the sausage is stuffed, even at refrigerator temperature. Keep in mind that slow-fermented dry sausage stuffed into a 24 mm casing will lose at least 30% of its moisture when ready for distribution, and its diameter will become accordingly smaller. Such a fermented sausage is usually defined as a meat stick and can be dried within a week. A sausage stuffed into a 90 mm casing will be at its best after 3 months of production time.

Influence of Casing Diameter and Humidity on Drying

Casing diameter is essential in determining fermentation rate and drying time. Large-diameter sausages typically have a slower fermentation rate due to a lower temperature penetration rate, and fermentation will also be more difficult to stop with heat treatment or drying due to a slow heat transfer rate. A smaller (20-60 mm) diameter casing is used to encourage fermentation and drying. There is no need to explain that a sausage packed into a 30 mm casing will become a stable dry sausage in 3 weeks, and another one stuffed into a 90 mm casing might need 3 months to achieve the same.

There is a greater danger of a case hardening in a large-diameter sausage, given that the water has to travel a longer distance from the core to the surface. This means that less water can be removed within a certain time, and the drying must take place at a slower rate, which can be compensated by decreasing speed or increasing humidity. In small-diameter sausage, the distance from the core to the surface is shorter, so the moisture travels fast. The sausage can be dried at lower humidity. It should be noted that larger particle sizes create more space for moisture to travel.

Classical dry-fermented sausages are the hardest to manufacture. They also require the most time and care. Therefore it is advised to start with small diameter sausages first as they are faster, easier and safer to produce. Then, as more experience is gained more difficult sausages can be attempted.

Micro-Climate Around The Sausage

Freshly stuffed sausage creates its own microclimate around its surface. Sausages contain plenty of moisture, and some of it must be removed to make dry salami shelf-stable. Sausages dry from the inside out, from its core to the surface. In an ideal case, the evaporated moisture should be replaced by diffusing moisture coming from the inside. When diffusion rate = evaporation rate, there is a balanced moisture removal. This is very important in the initial stages of production when most of the moisture is being removed. Incorrect removal of moisture may lead to case hardening and discoloration in surface area or even to spoiling the meat inside. After a few weeks, less moisture is removed each day, and humidity and air speed can be lowered.

When a freshly stuffed cold sausage enters a warmer fermenting/drying chamber, its surface becomes wet. There is 100% humidity around the sausage, although there might be only 60% humidity inside the chamber. A large 90 mm diameter sausage may need to rest for 4-6 hours at 59° F (15° C), 60% humidity, without air flow until its surface becomes dry; the small diameter sausage may not have moisture at all. This resting period, known as "conditioning," is a common procedure for regular-type smoked sausages as well. Then, once the sausage enters the proper fermentation/drying stage, the humidity needs to be controlled. A large-diameter sausage, due to its large surface area, is able to evaporate so much moisture that we need to slow the drying process down.

Look at the humidity sensor when a large-diameter sausage goes inside a small fermenting chamber. The humidity reading jumps significantly higher. Since we don't want fast removal of moisture at the beginning of the process, we aim to maintain high humidity in the chamber so it will act as a buffer zone and will push back the evaporating moisture. Increasing the speed of airflow removes the moisture from the surface of the sausage faster. There should be ample free space among the sausages. Both humidity in a chamber and airflow can control moisture removal from the sausage's surface.

Commercial producers employ sophisticated computer-controlled chambers to control factors like increasing/decreasing humidity and air speed, using humidifiers and entry/exit fans. A hobbyist usually modifies a refrigerator with a line voltage controller and a small humidifier. Temperature and humidity sensors are needed, too. A small computer cooling fan is a great addition to creating airflow. Opening the door a few times a day will let the moisture out. Increasing humidity can be accomplished by inserting a pan filled with water. There are many videos on YouTube explaining how to build a small fermenting/drying chamber.

Tip: check the end of the sausage for the following symptoms:

Sausage end	Drying conditions
Soft	good
Dry	humidity too low or air speed too fast
Wet, dripping	humidity too high or air speed too slow

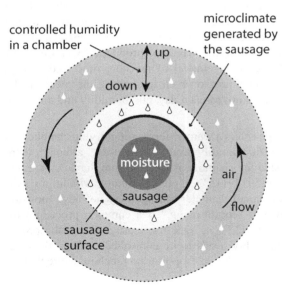

Photo Fig. 8.1 Microclimate of the sausage.

On a cloudy day, it might take most of the day to dry clothes in humid Florida (60-75% humidity), yet the same task can be accomplished in two hours in Nevada (10-15% humidity). Humidity and air speed are like brake and accelerator pedals in a car, they can slow or accelerate removal of moisture from the sausage.

Higher humidity = slower removal of moisture and vice versa.
Higher air speed = faster removal of moisture and vice versa.

Day	Process	Temp.		Humidity %	Air speed m/sec
		° C	° F		
1	fermentation *	24	75	95	0.8
2		22	72	95	0.6
3		22	72	93	0.5
4		22	72	93	0.5
5		20	68	90	0.4
6		20	68	90	0.4
7	drying	18	64	88	0.3
8		18	64	88	0.3
9		18	64	85	0.2
10		18	64	85	0.2
11		18	64	80	0.1
12		18	64	80	0.1
13........	drying continues until desired weight loss is obtained (1-2 months)	16-12	60-54	80-75	< 0.1
	storing	10-15	50-59	75-80	< 0.1
* Fermentation can last for 2 days at 24 → 22° C or 3 days at 20° C. Conditioning (if needed) may precede fermentation.					

Sugar. The amount of sugar (if used) is usually small 0.1% - 0.3% which is 1 g - 3 g/kg of meat), just enough to provide enough acidity to protect meat against spoilage bacteria in the initial stage of the process. A smart solution is to use only dextrose or the following combination:

1/3 of dextrose (glucose) at 0.1% (1 g/1 kg of meat).

2/3 of sucrose (table sugar), at 0.2% (2 g/1 kg of meat).

Dextrose will be immediately metabolized by bacteria, and a small pH drop will be obtained. This slight amount of acidity, however small, will stall the growth of bad bacteria, allowing the good bacteria to grow. This phenomenon is known as competitive exclusion and is a good example of how cultured bacteria eliminate wild strains of bacteria in meat. At the same time, bacteria are trying to break sucrose into dextrose, so even more acidity will be produced. However, there is some delay as bacteria need some time to extract dextrose from sugar. This delay will give the flavor-forming bacteria more time to do their job of reducing nitrates and breaking down proteins and fats.

Assuming that we have a ground meat of pH 5.8 and, we need to lower its pH to pH 5.3. Given that each 0.1% (1 g/kg) of dextrose lowers the pH of meat by 0.1 pH unit, we need to add 0.5% (5 g/kg of meat) of dextrose (about 1 teaspoon) to arrive at pH 5.3. Using T-SPX slow-fermenting culture, which ferments well at 68 - 75° F (20-24° C), we choose 75° F (24° C) as our fermentation temperature. It can be seen in the Constant Temperature Fermentation Table (Chapter 6) that at 75° F (24° C), we need to finish fermentation in less than 80 hours. At this temperature, T-SPX will drop pH to 5.3 within 48 hours. Generally, it can be stated that in slow-fermented sausages, adding dextrose/sugar at 0.3-0.5% (3-5 g/kg) and fermenting sausage using T-SPX culture at 68 - 75° F (20 - 24° C) delivers satisfying results.

Salami Flavor

The complex flavor of dry sausage is being developed in all process stages: fermentation, drying, ripening, and storage. The true salami flavor of a slow-fermented sausage depends mainly on the breakdown of sugars, fats and proteins during the fermentation and drying processes. These reactions are products of microbiological action of color and flavor forming bacteria end naturally occurring enzymes in meat.

Note: the traditional method of making dry salami was perfected in hundreds of years and was not chosen for its outstanding qualities, but it was the only way we knew about making sausages that could be stored at room temperature. Our ancestors would be more than happy to use starter cultures and Gdl to produce stable sausages in as little as three days, but the technology was not available then.

Making Dry Salami Without Culture

Sugar indirectly protects meat against spoilage and protects consumers from dangerous bacteria. To start fermentation, we need sugar and lactic acid bacteria (LAB), which naturally occur in meat or can be introduced in huge numbers by the culture. Depending on the number of LAB, the amount of available moisture, and the quantity of available sugar, a different amount of acidity will be generated, and how fast that happens depends on fermentation temperature and the type of culture. A trade-off is needed, as increasing acidity is inversely proportional to the quality of dry salami. Increasing acidity increases the microbiological safety of the sausage, however, at the cost of flavor and aroma. As mentioned earlier, acidity is the best way to control pathogenic *Staphylococcus aureus*. Still, the acidity present in dry sausages is not large enough to offer protection. Since we can not rely on acidity, removal of moisture becomes the main safety hurdle.

Technically speaking it is impossible to produce a sausage without any fermentation even if no sugar is added, given that meat contains a tiny amount of glycogen (sugar) and unknown number of naturally present lactic acid bacteria. Therefore, some minute fermentation will take place, however, the amount of generated acidity will be too small to prevent *S. aureus* from growing.

Given that this is a difficult sausage to make we should:

Select fresh lean meat with pH of 5.7-5.8
Select pork hard fat - back fat, neck fat or hard fat trimmings.
Use 3% salt.
Use 0.3% dextrose (3 g/kg of meat). Adding dextrose will allow LAB to produce lactic acid and drop pH to ~5.3 which will introduce a degree of safety to the process.
Use Cure #2 or just Cure #1 at 156 ppm (parts per million) - around 2.5 g per 1 kg (2.2 lb) of meat. This will add additional 2.3 g of salt, so the total salt is 3.23% (3.23 g/kg). Sodium nitrite (cure # 1 or #2) is the most effective known substance for inhibiting growth of *Clostridium botulinum*. It also restricts growth of *Salmonella*.

Curing meat. Cut meat and fat into 1-2" cubes. The fat does not contain myoglobin so it will not react with sodium nitrite and no pink color will be developed. Mix with salt and cure #2, it is fine if only cure #1 is available. Pack tightly into a 6" tall container to remove air, cover with a clean cloth to separate the surface from but air. The cloth allows gases to escape and prevents the surface of the meat to become grey. Using a plastic zip-lock bag is also fine. Hold for 2-3 days in refrigerator. The purpose of curing is to increase the number of lactic acid producing bacteria.

Lactic acid bacteria (LAB) tolerate ≤ 4% salt very well; however, spoilage bacteria do not, so they will grow slowly. The theory behind this process is simple: the salt (above 2%) and tightly packed meat inhibit spoilage bacteria, which are sensitive to salt and need air. On the other hand, lactic bacteria grow rapidly at 3% salt. All bacteria types rapidly consume air, leaving less oxygen for spoilage bacteria. All those factors favor the growth of lactic bacteria, and although they may grow slow due to low temperature, nevertheless their number will double. On the down side some pathogens will also multiply, however, not to sufficient degree to present danger. As an extra bonus, curing not only develops stronger color, but also develops "curing flavor" which positively contributes to quality of the sausage.

Processing Steps

Grinding. Grind cured meat and fat with 6-8 mm (1/4-3/8") plate.

Mixing. Add 0.3% dextrose (3 g/kg of meat) to meat and and mix with black pepper and spices of your choice. Spices as desired. The following apices are said to contribute to stronger fermentation: paprika and other powdered hot peppers, garlic, allspice, nutmeg, mace, cinnamon, ginger. Add ground fat last. Don't over mix in order to prevent fat smearing.

Stuffing. Stuff firmly into 40 mm hog casings, remember that finished sausage will have much smaller diameter.

Fermenting. Ferment for 3 days at 57-59° F (14-15° C), 90 → 85% humidity. Lactic acid bacteria start consuming dextrose and produce lactic acid. Staying below 60° F (15.6° C) prevents *S.aureus* from growing and producing toxin. Flavor forming bacteria will start producing flavor and aroma by breaking proteins and fats.

Drying. Dry sausages at 57-53° F (14-12° C), 85-75% humidity, until they lose 35% of its original weight. Once, the sausage loses about 35% of its original weigh it can be considered shelf-stable and can be kept at room temperature. Aw of traditionally dried sausages is usually ≤ 0.89.

Storing. Store at 53-50°F (12-10° C), 70-75% humidity.

Smoking. Given that a presence of mold is often desired on dry sausages, they cannot be smoked as smoking prevents mold from growing. A practical solution is to cold smoke chunks of back fat before they are minced. Adding liquid smoke to minced meat is risky as it may interfere with flavor forming bacteria.

Reversed Fermentation

In naturally fermented dry products the pH is known to slightly raise at the end of the drying process, especially when yeasts or mold are present which happens often in Southern European products. This induces a "reversed" fermentation as these microorganisms consume some of the lactic acid that was produced during fermentation and leave behind a small amount of ammonia which is alkaline (pH 11-13). Also, as the proteins and fats breakdown, one of the by-products is ammonia which is slightly basic (alkaline). This alkalinity decreases the overall acidity of the sausage and tend to raise the pH slightly as the salami dries with age. This contributes to a milder flavor in slow-fermented products.

Dry Salami Without Culture and Without Extra Sugar

Since it is impossible to predict the type and numbers of different strains of lactic acid, color nad flavor forming, spoilage and pathogenic bacteria that reside in meat, the production without culture and without added sugar is a gamble, remaining a flipping the coin. We might get lucky and produce an outstanding sausage or produce an unsafe and non-edible product.

It should be noted that sausages was made in Europe in December when pigs were slaughtered at Christmas. The evening temperatures were around 50° F (10° C) or lower, hence there was no problem with keeping meat and equipment cold.

Processing Steps

Follow the instructions for *Making Dry Salami Without Culture.*

Given that no sugar is added, lactic acid bacteria will metabolize only glycogen (meat's sugar) which will produce very little acidity. For all practical purposes the production process may be thought of as one long drying step. German books define it as "Reifung" and although exact translation means *maturing* or *ripening* in reality it covers steps such as fermentation and drying.

Within this time frame, many reactions take place. At first, the pH drops, but thanks to yeasts and mold, it can rise again. New enzymes are created that break proteins and fats, the color changes, and so on. It can be said that slowly fermented dry sausage is a living organism in which there is plenty of action that never stops.

So, the fermenting/ripening/drying process takes place at 53-57° F (12 - 14° C), 90 → 85 → 80% humidity and medium air speed, which could be supplied and controlled by a small computer cooling fan. As the sausage loses moisture, the humidity in the drying chamber will increase so some means of removing it should be provided, for example using a little exhaust fan. After a week the humidity can be lowered to 80% and air speed also decreased, however, some air movement must be present throughout entire process. Once, the sausage loses about 35% of its original weigh it can be considered shelf-stable and can be kept at room temperature. Store at 53-50°F (12-10° C), 70-75% humidity.

The chances of a successful outcome can be improved by a faster removal of moisture: *by not lowering humidity or increasing air speed* as this will produce contrary results, but by:

- Using a small diameter casing, for example 36 mm natural casings.
- Increasing the percentage of fat as the fat contains only about 15% moisture and lean meat around 75%.
- Using a larger grinder plate 6-8 mm (1/4-3/8") as coarse grind creates more space among particles for the moisture to escape from the inside to the surface.

Trace amounts of sulfur, manganese, magnesium, and cobalt act as catalysts for fermentation. This is why you will see trace amounts of both wine and garlic in traditional style Italian salami that are made without culture.

Making Dry Salami with Gdl

An important function of fermenting sausages is to lower the pH. A little pH, let's say to pH 5.3, creates a degree of safety in the initial phase of making sausages. Going lower will inhibit action of *Staphylococcus spp.* flavor forming bacteria and it will introduce tangy taste, which is not desired in traditional dry sausages.

Adding starter culture with 0.3% dextrose will result in a higher quality, but culture must go through a *lag phase* first before lactic bacteria start producing acid, so there is a *delay*.

Gdl being a chemical reaction does not need sugar and *reacts with moisture in meat immediately*, even at refrigerator temperatures, hence it offers a degree of extra safety which is important in home production. The main benefit of using Gdl instead of natural fermentation is that we don't have to worry about the number of wild lactic acid bacteria that the meat contains given that a curing step is not needed as the natural fermentation does not take place.

Given that adding 0.1% of Gdl (1 g of Gdl added to 1 kg of meat) lowers pH by about 0.1 point, adding 0.3-0.4% (3 - 4 g/kg) of Gdl will create a safety hurdle. For example adding 0.3% Gdl to meat having pH 5.8, will drop it to pH 5.5.

Making Dry Salami with Gdl Without Culture and Without Sugar

Increasing acidity is the primary safety hurdle against undesirable bacteria; however, without sugar, any meaningful fermentation will not occur, negatively affecting the meat's safety. The processing steps will have to be performed at low temperatures, and drying becomes the main safety hurdle. We can, however, increase the margin of safety by generating acidity not through fermentation with sugar but by acidifying the process with Gdl.

Select fresh lean meat with pH of 5.7-5.8
Select pork hard fat - back fat, neck fat or hard fat trimmings.
Use 3% salt. Use 0.4% of powdered Gdl (4 g/kg of meat). Adding Gdl generates gluconic acid which will drop pH to ~5.3 which *will introduce a degree of safety* to the process. Use Cure #2 or just Cure #1 at 156 ppm (parts per million) - around 2.5 g per 1 kg (2.2 lb) of meat. This will add additional 2.3 g of salt, so the total salt is 3.23% (3.23 g/kg). Adding 3-3.3% salt will drop original Aw 0.95 to 0.96-0.97, so less moisture will affect all bacteria, except *Staphylococcus aureus* which can grow well at low moisture levels. It also tolerates salt well, however, it grows slow at cold temperatures.

Processing Steps

Stuff without delay mixture into 40 mm hog casings, beef middles or 3" protein lined fibrous casings, otherwise the sausage batter will firm up and becomes harder to stuff. Leave the sausages in the refrigerator for two days to acidify, then move them to the drying room. Dry at 59-54° F (15 → 12° C), 85 → 80% humidity for 2-3 months until sausages lose 35% of their original weight. Store sausages at 50-54° F (10-12° C), 75% humidity. If desired, you can apply cold smoke at 64° F (18° C) at any time after acidification. Smoking need not to be continuous.

Acidic Liquids. Couldn't you just use vinegar or lemon juice to lower the pH? Yes, you can. Many professional sausage makers do it this way, but it is difficult to estimate the dosage. Using Glucono-delta-lactone offers better control of pH and does not require sugar, hence the process is called acidification and not fermentation. Gdl is guaranteed to work, 100% safe and works while the sausage is in the fridge.

Note: encapsulated Gdl cannot be used for non-heated sausages as the temperatures will never reach 135 - 150° F (57 - 66° C) to melt down the encapsulating protective cover.

A Simple to Make Dry Salami Stick

Select fresh lean meat with pH of 5.7-5.8
Select pork hard fat - back fat, neck fat or hard fat trimmings.
Use 3% salt.
Use 0.3% Gdl (3 g/kg of meat). Adding Gdl generates gluconic acid which will drop pH to ~5.3 which will introduce a degree of safety to the process. Use Cure #2 or just Cure #1 at 156 ppm (parts per million) - around 2.5 g per 1 kg (2.2 lb) of meat. This will add additional 2.3 g of salt, so the total salt is 3.23% (3.23 g/kg).

Production

Grind partially frozen meat and frozen fat with 6 mm (1/4") plate. Mix with salt Cure #2, black pepper and spices of your choice.

Add 0.4% (4 g/kg) Gdl to meat and mix again, but don't over mix in order to prevent fat smearing. Stuff into 32 mm hog casings. Acidify sausages at 58° F (14° C), 90 → 85% humidity for two days.

Dry at 58° F (12° C), 85-80% humidity for ~30 days until sausages lose 35% of their original weight. The drying time will depend on the diameter of the sausage.

Store sausages at 50-54° F (10-12° C), 75% humidity.

Making Dry Salami with Culture

2. This version of salami is much easier and safer to produce given that we have friendly bacteria willing to work with us together. There is no need to cure meat to increase the number of lactic acid bacteria which might be about 1000 per gram of meat as the culture introduces from 1 to 10 millions of them. Basically, we have to make sure that they work slow and do not generate too much acidity as this will inhibit bacteria which develop flavor and aroma by breaking proteins and fats. As long as we do not add too much sugar and keep fermentation temperature at 64-71° F (18-22° C) a quality product will be produced.

Starter cultures make the entire process easier, safer and well controlled. Starter cultures are homo-fermentative, that means that they contain bacteria which perform a well design purpose, unwanted products of fermentation like alcohol, acetic acid or unpleasant odors are eliminated. On top of that they allow fermentation to run at temperatures from 64 - 113° F (18 - 45° C), depending whether dry or semi-dry sausage is desired. Since we can precisely select fermentation temperature we can inhibit growth of *Staphylococcus aureus* by staying within limits of temperature-degree tables.

For dry sausages the optimum fermentation temperature is around 68° F (20° C) as it stimulates the growth of lactic acid while suppressing the growth of spoilage ones which don't tolerate acidity well. Nevertheless the culture will ferment at 64° F (18° C) or 75° F (24° C) as well, however, the rate of fermentation is faster at higher temperature. Be aware that the action of color and flavor forming bacteria is adversely affected by acidity so the fermentation should not proceed too fast. The higher the temperature the faster fermentation and the faster pH drop. Lactic acid bacteria start metabolizing sugar slowly and the acidity in the meat starts to build up. This gives curing and flavor forming bacteria time to develop flavor so typical of traditionally fermented dry sausages. Adding 3-3.3% salt will drop original Aw 0.95 to 0.96-0.97, so less moisture will affect all types of bacteria, except *Staphylococcus aureus* which can grow well at low moisture levels. It also tolerates salt well, however, it grows slow at cold temperatures.

A variety of cultures can be selected, however, there are cultures which were specifically designed for Mediterranean type of salami type products. They usually include combination of bacteria strains that produce lactic acid and others that contribute to a stronger color, flavor an aroma.

A typical traditionally produced salami process with culture

Pork pH 5.9 Beef pH 5.8	Temp.	Humidity %	Air Speed m/sec	Time	pH	Aw
Conditioning	20-25° C 68-77° F	60-70	none	~ 6 hrs	5.7-5.9	
Fermenting	18-25° C 66-77° F	95-92	0.8-0.5	2-3 days	5.3-5.2	0.96-0.94
Drying	22-18° C 72-66° F	90-85	0.5-0.2	5-10 days	5.2-5.0	0.95-0.90
Drying	< 15° C < 60° F	80-75	0.2-0.1	4-8 weeks	5.2-5.0	0.92-0.85
When the sausage achieves acidity pH of 5.2 or lower and water activity Aw 0.89, it is considered microbiologically stable.						
Storing	15-10° C 60-50° F	80-75	0.1-0.05	--	pH increase up to 5.4	0.84-0.89
During the storage period the pH will increase, the sausage will be less acidic and its flavor will be more mellow and more cheesy.						

When starter cultures are used, fermentation temperatures should correspond to those recommended by by the manufacturer. For European style dry sausages, temperatures of 18 to 24° C (64 to 75° F) are generally used. Lactic bacteria might start fermenting at 59° F (15° C), but the fermentation rate will be very slow. Any significant fermentation requires temperatures higher than 64° F (18° C).

Adding glucono-delta-lactone alone at 0.5% can provide immediate chemical acidulation dropping pH by ~0.6 pH unit), but this usually introduces some tangy sand flavor.

Glucona delta lactone (0.25%) can be combined with starter cultures for lowering the pH in tandem.

Meats and Ingredients

Select fresh lean meat with pH of 5.7-5.8
Select pork hard fat - back fat, neck fat or hard fat trimmings.
Use 0.3% dextrose (3 g/kg of meat). Adding dextrose will allow lactic bacteria to produce lactic acid and drop pH to ~5.3 which will introduce a degree of safety to the process.
Use Cure #2 or just Cure #1 at 156 ppm (parts per million) - around 2.5 g per 1 kg (2.2 lb) of meat. This will add additional 2.3 g of salt, so the total salt is 3.23% (3.23 g/kg).
Black pepper and spices.

Processing Steps

Grind cured meat and fat with 6 mm (1/4") plate.

Add 0.3% dextrose (3 g/kg of meat) to meat and and mix with black pepper and spices of your choice. Add ground fat and starter culture last. Don't over mix in order to prevent fat smearing. The culture should not come in direct contact with salt and sodium nitrite, hence add it to meat either first or the last. Stuff firmly into 40 mm hog casings, beef middles or 3" protein lined fibrous casings.

Ferment at 69° F (20° C) for 2-3 days, 90 → 85% humidity.

Ripening/drying. The drying takes place at 59-54° F (15 →12° C), 85-80% humidity for 2-3 months until sausage lost 35% of its original weight. The must be some ventilation and air speed which could be supplied by a small computer cooling fan. As the sausage loses moisture, the humidity in the drying chamber will increase so some means of removing it should be provided, for example using a little exhaust fan. After a week the humidity can be lowered to 80% and air speed also decreased, however, some air movement must be present throughout entire process. Once, the sausage loses about 33% of its original weight it can be considered shelf-stable and can be kept at room temperature.

Store sausages at 50-54° F (10-12° C), 75% humidity.

Notes: if desired, you can apply cold smoke at 64° F (18° C) at any time after fermentation. Smoking need not to be continuous.

In the past most regular sausages were made with nitrate alone and it was well known though not understood, that sausages that were cured at higher temperatures 46° F (8° C) exhibited stronger color and better quality. Years later we discovered, that at higher temperatures curing bacteria grew and reacted with meat and nitrate faster which led to stronger color and better flavor. The serious drawback to this method was that other bacteria also grew faster at higher temperatures. Although the end product will be safe, nevertheless, its shelf life will be severely shortened.

Smoking

If a smoky flavor is desired, you may apply a thin cold smoke at 64° F (18° C) or lower after fermentation has ended or during drying. The length of smoking time depends on the diameter of the casing and the color desired.

In order to produce quality dry sausages follow these three basic rules:

1. Keep fermenting and the first stage of drying around 64-68° F (18-20° C).
2. Control humidity in such a way that the casing of the sausage is not overly wet or dry.
3. Apply cold smoke at 59-68° F (15-20° C). (Optional step).

Storing Sausages

Store sausages in a dark room at 50-60° F (10-15° C), 75-80% humidity where the process of color and flavor development will continue. Sausage will keep on drying what will additionally contribute to its stability. A weak draft should be present (0.05-1.0 m/sec), which is found in a typical ventilated room.

Heating and Drying. Slow-fermented sausages are usually dried only, but they can be submitted for heat treatment as well. The product can be partially cooked to 120-145° F (49-63° C) or fully cooked to 155-160° F (68-71° C), both methods provide a means of destroying pathogens potentially present in meat. Applying heat too early is not recommended as heat will kill the color and flavor-forming bacteria, and no more flavor development will take place.

When subjected to heating, the sausage initially dries fast, but then the drying slows down due to surface drying and skin formation. Sausages not submitted to high temperatures exhibit more of a "raw" taste and firm bite with a definite fat and lean meat differentiation. Fully cooked sausages exhibit a hard bite and little fat and lean definition due to fat melting.

Molds

Mold is desired on many traditionally made dry sausages. The distinction must be made between the wild mold, which is produced by unknown strains of mold present in the air, and the cultured mold grown in a laboratory and packed as a starter culture. The wild mold can be grey, green, or black, while the cultured mold will be white or creamy. The sausage covered with questionable color of mold should be discarded. The fault lies partly with the operator needing to pay attention to the process, as mold needs time and plenty of moisture to grow. That, of course, is due to high humidity and insufficient air speed. More moisture is produced than being removed, the equilibrium is shaken and the mold appears. In these conditions, the sausage becomes slimy to the touch, and mold appears. This can easily be corrected by wiping the mold off with a cloth soaked in salt solution or vinegar.

Mold needs oxygen to survive, so it is present only on the surface. The inside of the sausage should be fine. Smoking is an effective temporary method of mold control, but it only prevents mold for a specific time. If mold reappears, it should be wiped off again and cold smoke should be applied for 3-4 hours.

Using cultured mold offers two benefits:

1. It creates a secondary skin which slows down drying. Slower drying provides more time for curing and flavor producing bacteria to develop more intense color and flavor.

2. At the end of the drying process molds start to consume lactic acid which lowers acidity and develops a milder flavor. It may be considered a *reversed pH drop*.

Mold covered sausages exhibit more complex and aromatic flavor.

The smoke should not be applied to molded sausages as soot and unburned smoke particles will adhere to white mold and the result will be a black unsightly surface. If both the smoky flavor and white mold are desired, the acceptable method is to cold smoke back fat before grinding.

There are mold starter cultures made by Chr-Hansen, for example Mold-600 which promote the desirable mold growth. A solution of culture mold and water is applied onto the surface of the casing where it will grow in the form of a white mold through the drying/ripening process.

Molds can be applied to sausages by dipping them into a mold-solution straight after filling, or the solution can be sprayed later on again if mold growth is unsatisfactory. It is a good idea to spray solution on smokesticks and carts as well, however, be advised that it might be difficult to get rid of mold from the drying chamber later on. It is recommended to have *a separate chamber* for sausages that will be covered with mold. Home improvised drying chambers such as refrigerators are easy to sanitize with a bleach solution so recurring mold should not be the problem. Molds need at least 75% humidity to grow. Higher temperatures also favor their growth.

Photo 8.1 Molded and unmolded salami.

When *Penicillium* mold cultures are used, they are applied to sausages just before the sausages enter the fermentation room. If mold develops and it is not desired, it can be easily wiped off with a cloth saturated with a salt solution or vinegar. Commercial producers dip sausages into 10-20% solution of potassium sorbate which effectively prevents mold growth, but the fact must be mentioned on the label. Wild growing mold on the sausage surface is of dubious nature and poses the risk to the sausage. Its color can be white, grey, yellow, brown, or black and the length and density may vary. Generally white or white-grey molds are fine but it is still a naturally developed wild mold, and it would be much wiser to use mold growing starter cultures.

Mold - To Eat or Not to Eat

The question of what to do with mold, for example, fuet sausage. In home production it is stuffed into a soft delicate natural casing. It is not practical to fight removing it and most people will consume the mold. The same reasoning applies to small diameter dry sausages like secallona or somalla. As dry sausages are sliced thinly it is quite easy to peel off the skin. When sausages are stuffed into tough synthetic casings it is best to discard the casing with mold. If you object visually to having mold it can be easily wiped off with a cloth soaked in oil or vinegar. According to a poll conducted in 2012 by the Spanish magazine La Vanguardia on preferred ways of consuming fuet: 38.5% consumers eat the sausage with mold, 55.82% consumers eat the sausage without mold, 5.68% do not care.

Talc and Rice Flour

Mold is often developed to improve drying, but then is removed and the sausages are sprinkled with talc powder or rice flour. As molds often don't grow uniformly an uneven surface coverage may be expected. Applying flour is the common fix.

Dips

Dips are decorative edible solutions, based on gelatin that are applied to the surface of the sausages. They must adhere to the surface fast and well and they should be elastic enough to shrink with the sausage. The sausages must be mature and dry in order not to shrink too much in time.

Preparation

- If the sausage was kept in a refrigerator it should be brought to room temperature.
- The casing is fully removed to expose the meat. If it is oily it should be wiped off with a paper towel. The casing is discarded.
- A mixture of desired spices, crushed peppers, herbs, dried fruits, nuts or shredded cheese is prepared. The mixture is spread on the table.
- Gelatin is mixed with water at around 122-140° F (50-60° C). The gelatin solution is poured into a narrow and long pan.
- The sausage is immersed into gelatin solution.
- The sausage is rolled all around over the decorative mixture.
- The sausage is hung for 30 minutes to allow gelatinized mixture to adhere.
- The procedure is repeated (immersion, rolling, hanging).
- The sausage is placed in a storage room.

Chapter 9

Semi-Dry Fermented Sausages

Semi-dry fermented sausages are very popular, given that they are faster, easier and safer to produce. Their safety depends mainly on acidity, however, additional safety hurdle such as drying or partial/full cooking are usually employed.

The U.S. Official Standards state that: semi-dry sausages are chopped or ground meat products that, as a result of bacterial action or *direct addition of organic acids,* reach a pH of 5.3 or less and are then dried to remove 15%-20% of the moisture. The European standards are similar for example German semi-dry sausages have pH values of 4.8-5.0, Aw around 0.93, and a weight loss of about 18%.

The standards are created to protect customer from getting sick, they do not dictate how a product must look or taste. Using starter cultures and organic acids allows producing a microbiologically safe *semi-dry sausage* within days, instead of weeks. With starter cultures they can be fermented at a wide range of temperatures from 78 - 113° F (26-45° C) and can reach pH 5.3 in 12 hours. Semi-dry sausages are usually smoked and often receive a heat treatment following the fermentation period to make them shelf stable. During smoking the sausage loses more moisture becoming more microbiologically stable. *Spreadable* fermented sausages are softer and moister. Given their limited shelf life they are refrigerated and should be consumed within 3-5 days.

The semi-dry fermented sausages are medium-coarse ground products that can be fermented with native bacteria or with starter cultures. In all cases acidification (bacterial fermentation, acidulation or both) is the main method of production. The sooner the acidity is achieved, the faster the sausage becomes microbiologically stable and can be distributed to stores.

Given that a pH drop to 4.6 makes sausage microbiologically safe, a large percentage of sugar, usually dextrose, is added, and the fermentation runs at high temperatures using fast-fermenting cultures. The fast conversion of sugar into lactic acid by lactic bacteria is directly responsible for the tangy or sour taste in fast fermented sausages. Fast-fermented sausages need about 1-2 days to drop pH to 4.8, and medium-fermented sausages need about 2-3 days. If used, the fermentation rate depends on the starter culture, fermentation temperature, the amount and type of sugar, and extra additives such as Gdl or citric acid.

Although not recommended, semi-dry sausages can be made without starter cultures. In such a case, it is recommended that meat is first cured. If the sausage is fermented to pH 4.6, the production can end with smoking/drying. Additional drying will create a dry sausage, however, it will not have the flavor of traditional salami.

When the sausages are heat treated, the loss of moisture and application of smoke are less critical. Smoking becomes a flavoring stop that can end when the desired color is obtained. Be aware that a small-diameter sausage might taste bitter if smoked for many hours.

Semi-dry sausages are shelf-stable when:

- pH ≤ 5.3 is reached within prescribed times and the Aw reaches ≤ 0.90 *OR*
- pH ≤ 5.3 is reached within prescribed time and the sausage is heated to 145° F (63° C) for 4 minutes (or other values) as specified in Option 1 - controlling *E. coli 0157:H7* (see Chapter 6).

Time needed to decrease pH value of the sausage to 5.0		
Fast-fermented	**Medium fast-fermented**	**Slow-fermented**
0.5-2 days	2-4 days	usually does not drop below 5.2

If the cooking option is chosen, the temperature in the smokehouse is gradually raised, which heats the core of the sausage and makes the cooking process shorter. The time of cooking depends on the diameter of the casing and the temperature of the chamber. Keep in mind that the texture of a partially cooked semi-dry sausage is softer than that of a non-heated dry sausage.

Improving the Taste

Adding sugar to meat develops acidity, which contributes to taste but not much to flavor. The taste is relatively easy to describe: salty, sweet, bitter, or sour. The taste components are mainly established during fermentation.

Given that the acidity is the primary factor that establishes the safety of fast-fermented sausage, a rapid fermentation to pH 4.6-5.0 is required. This calls for fast-fermented cultures and around 1% of dextrose or using acidulants. The final product will exhibit a sourly taste, unless we introduce some changes to the formula. The point to remember is that cooking the sausage will stop the fermentation by inactivating or killing lactic bacteria - therefore, no more acidity will be generated. Any sugar that remains unfermented will "sweeten" the sausage and off-set some of the tangy taste. The taste of fermented sausage is adversely affected by the processing temperatures, more so during fermentation. The higher the fermentation temperature, the faster the rate of pH and the more acidic taste of the sausage. When making fast-fermented sausages, the pH drop below 5.0 can be obtained within 12-24 hours, but that inhibits color and flavor-forming bacteria, which are acid sensitive, from reacting with meat. As a result, no proteolysis (protein breakdown) or lipolysis (fat breakdown) will take place, so the sausage will not develop a traditional salami flavor.

The simplest solution is to lower the temperature to give flavor-forming bacteria more time to perform. However, the length of fermentation can also be extended by introducing complex sugars.

Sucrose, maltose, and lactose are only partially fermented by lactic bacteria; thus, using them in tandem with dextrose will result in a lower pH and lower rate of fermentation. Increasing the amount of dextrose is less effective than using common sugar as dextrose is approximately 70% as sweet as sucrose (common table sugar). Fructose is 1.7 times sweeter than common sugar so it will bring a lot of sweetness (*see* Table of Sweetness in Chapter 5).

Improving the Flavor

The flavor is harder to define as it usually consists of hundreds of components, many of them can be defined as aroma. The flavor and aroma would be established during the *ripening* stage. Given that dry sausages have the longest ripening stage, they also possess the best flavor and aroma. The flavor and aroma are created in meat by natural enzymes that break down proteins and fats and by *Staphylococcus spp.* flavor forming bacteria which occur in meat in small numbers, but are included in all starter cultures that are designed for making Southern European style sausages. Most of those cultures *include* lactic bacteria such as *Lactobacillus spp.* or *Pediococcus spp., and color and flavor forming bacteria* such as *Staphylococcus xylosus, Staphylococcus carnosus* or both.

Starter cultures designed for *ultra-fast fermentation* do not even include *Staphylococcus spp.* color and flavor forming bacteria as the rapid onset of acidity would give them no chance to develop complex flavors associated with dry sausages. In order to produce a semi-dry sausage with a natural "meaty" flavor the starter culture must include flavor forming bacteria such as *Staphylococcus xylosus* and fermentation rate must be slow in the first 24 hours giving *S. xylosus* a chance to react with meat.

Other than using different combinations of sugars to influence sausage flavor, many alcoholic beverages, such as rum, red wine, sherry, brandy, Cointreau, or even beer, are used. Of special interest are homemade herbal infusions/flavorings, which are made by mixing about 20% fruit or whole spices with 80% spirit (vodka, rum, red wine) and leaving it in a closed container for about 3 days (*see* Flavorings and Herbal Infusions in Chapter 5).

Given that the majority of semi-dry sausages are heated to 145° F (65° C) for at least 4 minutes or fully cooked to 160° F (72° C), the fermentation will definitely end as the lactic bacteria stop working or, in the latter case, die. Any remaining unfermented sugars or flavorings will contribute to a better taste and flavor.

Note: cooking will not prevent acidulants (Gdl, citric acid) from generating acidity as acidification will continue until all acidulant is exhausted.

Improving Flavor by Slowing Fermentation

In order to make a sausage fast we need to conduct fermentation at high temperature, however, this prevents *Staphylococcus spp.* flavor forming bacteria, which are acid sensitive, from developing flavor and aroma. Their growth slows down around pH 5.5 and at pH 5.0 they are ineffective or dead. The conclusion is simple, let's slow down the generation of acid for as long as possible, being at the same time in compliance with the degree-hours tables *(covered in detail in Chapter 6)* which specify within how many hours at given temperature pH of the sausage must drop to 5.3 or lower. Thus, instead of fermenting sausage at 100° F (38° C) constant temperature for 25 hours, let's use variable temperature criteria and *break fermentation into two stages.*

The example that follows demonstrates how a particular culture can influence the length of fermentation by running fermentation at different temperatures. For demonstration purpose we use T-SPX culture consisting of *Pediococcus pentosaceus* and *Staphylococcus xylosus*. The culture is listed at 78-100° F (26-38° C), optimum being 90° F (32° C). The culture will ferment as well at 68-75° F (20-24° C), but slower. Dextrose is added at 0.5%.

Example 1

Constant Temperature Fermentation		Variable Temperature Fermentation	
Temperature	Time, no longer than	Temperature	Time in hours
68° F/20° C	150 hours	1st stage: 68° F/20° C	48 hours
--	--	2nd stage: 100° F/38° C	no longer than 3 hours
100° F/38° C	25 hours	Total fermentation time:	< 51 hours

Example 2

Constant Temperature Fermentation		Variable Temperature Fermentation	
Temperature	Time, no longer than	Temperature	Time in hours
75° F/24° C	80 hours	1st stage: 75° F/24° C	24 hours
--	--	2nd stage:100° F/38° C	no longer than 16 hours
100° F/38° C	25 hours	Total fermentation time:	< 40 hours

Example 3

Constant Temperature Fermentation		Variable Temperature Fermentation	
Temperature	Time, no longer than	Temperature	Time in hours
78° F/26° C	66 hours	1st stage:78° F/26° C	24 hours
--	--	2nd stage:100° F/38° C	no longer than 14 hours
100° F/38° C	25 hours	Total fermentation time:	< 38 hours

The above examples deal with two-stage fermentation, however, more stages can be added. It shows how the length and the rate of fermentation is influenced by changing temperature. The simplest approach is to take the lower end of a recommended fermentation temperature for particular culture and apply it for the first 24 hours (stage 1). Then, use the higher end of culture temperature and determine from temperature-degrees table for *variable* fermentation the number of fermentation hours for stage 2, *(see Chapter 6 for detailed calculations).*

Discussion: the best quality sausage will be produced at 68° F/20° C (Example 1) *with constant or variable* temperature fermentation as it provides more time for *Staphylococcus xylosus* flavor forming bacteria to react with meat. Example 2 and 3 also provide 24 hours for *S. xylosus* to develop meat flavor, which is sufficient.

The poorest quality will be obtained at 100° F/38° C with *constant* temperature fermentation as *S. xylosus will have no time to develop flavors* due to the rapid generation of acidity, hence T-SPX *should not be even selected* for fermenting at such a high temperature.

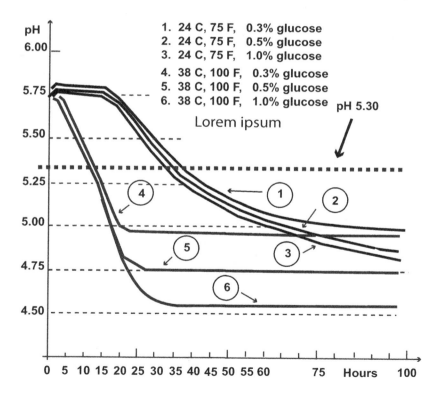

Fig. 9.1 Influence of amount of glucose on the pH-decrease induced by the traditional fermenting culture T-SPX, containing a *P. pentosaceus* bacteria strain, at two temperatures: 24° C (75° F), 38° C (100° F).

Data of Chr. Hansen

Fast-Fermented Sausages

The strategy behind making fast-fermented sausages relies on a *rapid increase in acidity* which can be accomplished in two ways:

- Addition of a fast-fermenting *starter culture* plus a sufficient amount of sugar.
- Addition of Gdl alone, slow fermenting sugars, spices and flavorings.

Adding Gdl must be carefully monitored as too much may be added. This will increase the acidity so rapidly that the growth of all bacteria will be adversely affected. The sausage will be safe to consume but its flavor will suffer.

Characteristics	Fast-fermented
Fermentation temperature	24°- 40° C (76°-104° F)
Ferm. humidity	92-90%
Fermentation time	1-2 days (depending on ferm. temperature)
Smoking	optional
Cooking	Yes
Salt	2.5%
Curing agent	nitrite (Cure # 1)
Sugar	dextrose, 0.75-1%
Flavor	tangy, sourly
Final pH	4.6 - 5.0
Weight loss %	< 15
Starter cultures/Gdl	yes
Production time	3-4 days

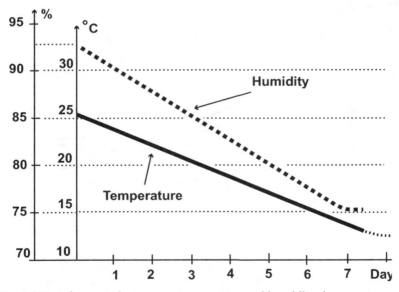

Fig. 9.2 Fast-fermented sausages, temperature and humidity decrease.

In industrial drying chambers temperature and humidity levels are lowered on a daily basis. The above graph is a good approximation of those conditions, there is about a 2 degrees drop in temperature every day.

Fermentation process is fast and pH drop is large, the latter contributing to a firmer texture. As the pH drops below pH 5.3 the forces binding water become weaker, releasing water become easier and the sausage becomes firmer. This is known as "iso-electric point" and happens around pH 4.8. More water will be removed during the following smoking step. The firmer texture greatly improves sliceability which is a desired feature in all but spreadable fermented sausages. Given that fast-fermented sausages usually lose only 10-15% of their original weight, the drying step may not be needed at all as the sausages are usually partially cooked what can take place during smoking.

Medium Fast-Fermented Sausages

Medium-fast fermented sausages fall between fast-fermented and slow fermented sausages. Sausages become stable due to the combined effect of pH drop and drying even without subsequent heat treatment. The flavor of the sausage is tangy and is influenced by spices, sugars and to some degree by *Staphylococcus spp.* flavor producing bacteria. Most semi-dry sausages (fast and medium-fast fermented) are smoked during the fermentation stage which elevates the temperature in the fermentation chamber to about 90-110° F (32-43° C).

Characteristics	Medium-fast fermented
Fermentation temperature	24°- 38° C (76°-100° F)
Ferm. humidity	92-90%
Ferm. time	2-3 days
Smoking	optional
Drying temp.	22°-16° C
Drying humidity	85-75%
Salt	2.5%
Curing agent	nitrite (Cure # 1)
Sugar	dextrose, 0.5-0.8%
Flavor	tangy, sourly
Final pH	4.8 - 5.0
Weight loss %	<30
Starter cultures	yes
Production time	21-28 days

In fast fermented and medium-fast fermented sausages pH reduction is the main hurdle against bacteria which is accomplished by using cultures, adding sugar, and acidulants. With Gdl or citric acid a low level of pH can be rapidly attained resulting in a product with a noticeable tangy flavor. This, however, can be compensated for by using a combination of different sugars. flavorings and spices.

Dextrose (glucose) is added at 0.75 - 1.0%, and is readily metabolized by lactic bacteria, after fermentation ends, whatever remains flavors the sausage. Adding more than 1% may not decrease pH much lower as lactic bacteria stop growing in excess acid. Other, more complex sugars such as sucrose, maltose or lactose may be fermented to a lesser extent and will ferment slower. Adding additional *slow fermenting sugars* such as corn syrup, maltose or lactose will impart some sweetness as they may remain unfermented. Sugar like salt is able to bind free water, however, adding excessive amount of sugars can retard fermentation, given that lactic bacteria need moisture.

Stopping Fermentation

When the desired pH has been reached, but there is a suspicion that it may still drop lower, there are two ways of stopping fermentation:

- Lower the temperature to 53° F (12° C). The remaining unfermented sugar will offset the acidic taste of the fast-fermented sausage and will contribute to stronger color and flavor in slow-fermented types. Lowering temperature when Gdl was added will only slow down fermentation, which will continue until all Gdl is converted into gluconic acid.

- It is relatively easy to stop fermentation at any pH level (if no chemical acidulants were added) by heating sausages to 145° F (63° C) for 4 minutes what will kill the lactic bacteria and make sausages biologically safe. Cooking fully the sausage to 160° F (72° C) will definitely stop the fermentation by killing not only lactic, but all other bacteria, pathogenic ones a as well.

Summary of Important Issues

- Mold is not an issue in fast-fermented sausages as it does not have enough time to grow, however, it may appear when storing sausages in humid conditions.

- Once Gdl is added, the meat has a tendency to solidify so the mass should be stuffed without delay.

- Be aware that the sausages start to taste sourly when pH 5.0 is reached. Going still lower makes sausages extremely sour and somewhat bitter.

- After smoking and drying the sausages are kept in a storage room at 50-60° F (10-15° C), 75-80% humidity. Sausage will also keep on drying what will additionally contribute to its stability.

- Semi-dry sausages are usually smoked at 72-90° F (22-32° C) with a medium heavy smoke.

- Without starter cultures a large and fast pH drop may be hard to achieve within the prescribed times, thus adding chemical acidulants such as Gdl or citric acid will augment fermentation.

- Fermentation or chemical acidulation takes care of *Staphylococcus auereus,* but full cooking inhibits growth of *E. coli O157:H7, Salmonella, Listeria* and kills *Trichinosis* (if present).

- A cooked semi-dry sausage stored at 50-54° F (10-12° C) will lose in time more moisture and will become the dry sausage, however, its sourly flavor will remain and the only result will be a loss of weight.

- if a sausage was fermented to pH 5.0 the cooking step can be skipped, however, the sausage must be further dried to Aw ≤ 0.90, until it loses 33% of its original weight.

- The quantity and type of sugar influences the rate and extent of acidulation, and also contributes to flavor, texture, and yield properties.

- pH meter will indicate when the pH 5.3 has been attained.

American Style Semi-Dry Sausages

Generally, American semi-dry sausages are fermented, smoked and cooked, but usually not dried. The target pH after fermentation is pH 4.8-4.6 and this is achieved with 0.8-1% dextrose. Fermentation is usually followed by heating what shortens production time and makes it safer. Unfortunately, this is done at the expense of taste and flavor, although the finished products are very safe. The only weight loss is due to the moisture loss during fermentation and cooking. A common procedure consists of heating sausages in a smokehouse (no smoke applied) for 8-16 hours followed by a variable period of heating and smoking. Because of ever tightening safety concerns most commercially produced semi-dry products such as summer sausage are partially or fully *cooked*.

U.S. Popular Semi-Dry Sausages

Summer Sausage (similar to some of the European cervelats) - beef and pork, or beef alone. pH 4.6 - 4.8, 3-5 mm (1/8 - 3/16") grind, black pepper, coriander, mustard, occasionally whole peppers and mustard seeds, garlic. Naturally smoked or liquid smoke, 10% of cheese (optional). Casings from 40-120 mm, fibrous, collagen, or laminated natural casings (?), fabric-reinforced collagen casings. Good shelf life, up to one year.

Lebanon Bologna - from Lebanon, Pennsylvania. *All beef*, 2-5 mm (3/32-3/16") plate, long smoking, liquid smoke, pH 4.2-4.4. Typically, it is not heated to a temperature higher than 135° F (57° C). Black pepper, cinnamon, cloves, allspice, and ginger. It is heavily smoked and has a distinctly "tangy" and smoky flavor. In the traditional process, the coarse ground meat is cured and held under refrigeration for a period of up to 1 week. *Note:* Lebanon Bologna is usually fermented to a very low pH with 1.25% dextrose. The sausage is not fully cooked.

Sweet Bologna - sweet bologna is a variation of Lebanon Bologna that is made with 10-12% sugar as opposed to 2-4% in the Lebanon Bologna.

Snack Sticks - shelf-stable semi-dry sausage with a finished diameter of approximately 19-15 mm. The formulation is similar to summer sausage. Jalapeno, chili, or other spicy peppers are often added to produce a "hot" finished product. These are normally stuffed in an edible collagen casing that is designed specifically for this type of product.

Sausage for Pizza - this is a derivative of summer sausage having a spice formula similar to pepperoni. It can be used as a substitute for true pepperoni on price competitive pizzas if appropriate labeling restrictions are observed. For fast fermented sausages like pepperoni, major pepperoni manufacturers overkill at adding 1.5%-2% sugar but most of Italian processors settle out between 0.4-0.8%.

European Style Semi-Dry Fermented Sausages

Most European-style semi-dry sausages are made with 0.5-0.8% of dextrose so the final pH after fermentation is 4.8-5.0. Formulations often contain a combination of fast (dextrose) and slowly fermenting sugars (sucrose, maltose, lactose) which develops more complex flavors.

Lucke: Undried and semi-dry sausages are usually fermented at 71-78° F (22-26° C) and for American style semi-dry sausages, even higher fermentation temperatures along with shorter fermentation times are applied. Up to 2% fermentable sugar are sometimes used, especially in the production of US-style semi-dry fermented sausages. The pH may then drop to 4.5, and many consumers - particularly in Europe - will not readily accept such a "sour" sausage. The formulation of European- style sausage commonly contains a combination of "rapidly" and "slowly" fermentable sugars. In countries where regulations permit such additives, quite large amounts of lactose (milk powder) or starch (e. g., potato flour) are sometimes added to raw sausage mixtures.

Most sliceable semi-dry fermented sausages (on the German market: about 80% of the products) have aw values around 0.93. Assuming an initial fat content of 34 % and an initial aw of 0.96, this means a weight loss of about 18% and a moisture content of about 40%. To obtain dry sausages, they are dried further to aw values of 0.90 or below, bacterial growth is inhibited, and, if surface condensation of water and mould growth is avoided, they maybe stored at ambient temperature. Their water content is 35 % or less which corresponds to a weight loss of at least 25%.

Most semi-dry sausages in Belgium and Germany have pH values of 4.8 - 5.0 after fermentation which corresponds to a concentration of approximately 25 g lactic acid per kg dry weight (Deketelaere et al., 1974; List and Klettner, 1978).

Chapter 10

Acidified Sausages

The Food Safety and Inspection Service (FSIS) issues rules and the guidelines for making fermented sausages. The guidelines do not deal with topics like the taste and flavor of the sausages, they have been designed to protect consumer from getting ill. FSIS accepts both, the natural fermentation and/or chemical acidification as proper methods for generating acidity.

Acidification and Acidulants

Fermentation, a form of *naturally occurring acidification*, has long been used for food preservation. However, there is another method called acidification or acidulation, which employs natural substances known as acidulants and can be applied to control the growth of undesirable microorganisms, including pathogens. Acidulants in*crease* acidity of meat through chemical reaction *which do not involve lactic acid bacteria. Hence, there is no bacterial fermentation and no need for sugar.* Acidulation is usually performed alone, but it can be combined with starter culture, too. Acidulants *immediately* react when exposed to moisture in meat and work faster at higher temperatures. This greatly shortens the process of lowering pH; however, a high dosage of acidulant results in a harder texture and imparts a *tangy* taste to the sausage. Hence, acidification is generally used in the production of less expensive semi-dry products.

Acidulants do not cure meat directly; however, by lowering pH, they contribute to developing a red color. The acidity they develop speeds up the chemical conversion of *sodium nitrite to nitric oxide,* which in turn reacts with meat myoglobin and creates a pink color, so they act as an accelerator. Still, they do it *by reacting with sodium nitrite,* which must be present to begin with. The typical curing accelerators used in the meat industry are *sodium erythorbate and ascorbic acid.*

The benefit of acidification is that pH is easier to control, and *the sausage can be produced in a chamber that lacks temperature and humidity control.* It must be, however, realized that *acidification creates products of much lesser quality than bacterial fermentation.*

The most popular acidulants are:

- Gdl (glucono-delta-lactone - used to make cottage cheese, tofu, bakery products and fermented sausages.
- Citric acid - used to add an acidic taste to foods, soft drinks and wine.

Glucono-delta-lactone (Gdl) is manufactured by microbial fermentation of pure glucose to gluconic acid but is also produced by the fermentation of glucose derived from corn or rice. Gdl can be found in honey, fruit juices, wine and many fermented products. Since Gdl lowers the pH, it also helps preserve food from deterioration by enzymes and microorganisms. Glucono-delta-lactone is often used to make cottage cheese, tofu, bakery products and fermented sausages.

In natural bacterial fermentation, acidity is generated by lactic acid bacteria, but in chemical acidulation, Gdl, under the influence of meat's own water, breaks down to gluconic acid, decreasing the pH in a controlled manner. Gluconic acid is non-toxic and completely metabolized in our bodies. Compared to other food acids, glucono-delta-lactone can be considered to be a slow-release acidulant. After dissolving in water, gluconic acid is produced in about 60 minutes. It can reach the lowest pH within a few hours, depending on the meat's initial pH, its moisture content, the amount of Gdl, and the temperature. Gdl works well at 71-75° F (22-24° C), but like any chemical reaction, it will work faster at higher temperatures. Decreasing the temperature may only slow it down; to stop the reaction, we have to freeze the meat.

   Gdl is usually added at 0.2-0.8% (2-8 g/kg). As it is a natural acid, adding more than 1% (10 g/kg of meat) may cause more pronounced sourly flavor. Once Gdl is added to the sausage mass, the meat's pH starts dropping down and the reaction will continue for as long as there is remaining Gdl and free water inside of the sausage.

Adding 0.1% (1 g/kg of meat) Gdl lowers pH by 0.1 pH.

- initial meat pH = 5.8, adding 0.4% Gdl lowers pH to 5.4
- initial meat pH = 5.8, adding 1.0% Gdl lowers pH to 4.8

The addition of sugar lowers the meat's pH during fermentation, but adding Gdl will speed up the process. Gdl is a pH-neutral, whitish powdered natural food acid (roughly a third of the sourness of citric acid) that contributes to the tangy flavor of various foods.

In the USA, Gdl is classified as GRAS, Generally Recognized As Safe, as per 21 CFR 184.1318 for use in food with no limitation other than current good manufacturing practice as a curing and pickling agent, leavening agent; as *pH control agent* and as sequestrant (a food additive which improves the quality and stability of foods). Gdl is cleared by the Meat and Poultry Inspection Division as an acidifier in meat and poultry products at the following amount:

0.5% - 8 oz of Gdl (0.5%) to 100 lb meat or meat by products.
1.0% - 16 oz (1 lb) of Gdl to 100 lb meat (Genoa salami only).

In Europe, glucono delta-lactone, is approved *quantum satis* (as needed) unless otherwise restricted for use as an acidity regulator and a sequestrant. Gdl was a great acidulant in the past; however, with the recent entry of easy-to-administer cultures, its popularity is fading away. By introducing fast-fermenting culture with the right amount of sugar we can achieve the same results yet produce products with a better flavor.

Gdl is a slow-release acidulant which provides a slow, but continuous hydrolysis to gluconic acid, which takes place gradually in about 40-60 minutes after dissolution in moisture in meat. In water, it hydrolyzes to gluconic acid very quickly. During its hydrolysis, the initial sweet taste of Gdl becomes only slightly acidic, resulting in the final flavor much less tart than that of other acidulants.

Citric acid is a weak organic acid found in citrus fruits. It is a natural preservative that adds an acidic taste to foods, soft drinks, and wine. It is safe for human consumption. Citric acid is a white crystal material with a strong acid taste that is fully soluble in water. *It acts faster than Gdl; adding 1 g of citric acid to 1 kg of meat lowers the pH of meat by about 0.3 - 0.4 pH units.*

To lower the pH of meat from pH 5.8 to pH 4.8 (one pH 1.0 unit), around 3-4 grams of citric acid/1 kg of meat is needed. The easiest way to mix such a small amount uniformly with ground meat is to dissolve 4 g of citric acid in 60 ml (2 oz fl) of water. Add citric acid last while mixing ingredients, then stuff the mixture into the casing without delay. Although both Gdl and citric acid introduce a sour taste, it is accepted that *Gdl is slightly milder.* To protect meat from flies and spoiling bacteria, hunters mix citric acid with water and spray the meat with a spray bottle. Note that citric acid tends to lump together if stored above 75% humidity.

Acidulants are available in two forms:

- Powdered - little crystals which react immediately when exposed to moisture.
- Encapsulated - little crystals which are coated with vegetable oil that melts down at varying temperatures, from 122-150° F/50-66° C.

Adding 1% (10 g/kg) powdered Gdl or 0.3% (3 g/kg) of citric acid to meat will:

- Rapidly increase acidity and will prevent flavor forming bacteria from reacting with meat.
- Contribute negatively to binding properties of minced meat as the acid will start cooking proteins. That is why the sausage mixture should be stuffed into the casing without much delay.

Using a Fine Spray Bottle

Introducing 0.1% -0.3% (1-3 g/1000 g of meat) of powdered citric acid presents a formidable challenge as a uniform distribution of acidulant is important for proper acidification. Water removal is not a crucial factor in *heated* acidified products as it will evaporate during cooking, thus a practical approach is to dilute 1-3 g of citric acid in 30 ml (1 oz fl) of water and mix it with meat. The solution can also be dispersed as a fine mist from a fine spray bottle.

Encapsulated Acids

Applying strong substances such as citric acid, lactic acid, or Gdl (glucono-delta-lactone) will also cook (denature) proteins in meat. Thus, adding Gdl or citric acid in powdered form to minced meat will start cooking the meat to a small degree, affecting the binding between meat particles and negatively affecting the texture.

Encapsulated acids such as Gdl/gluconic, citric, lactic, and fumaric are coated with a hydrogenated cotton seed oil coating, which prevents them from reacting with meat during mixing and stuffing as these stages of processing are performed below the melting point of encapsulated acid. Then, as the meat is heated to 122-150° F (50-66° C), the coating melts down, exposing the acidulant, which starts reacting with moisture and generates acidity. Thus, *the temperature triggers the start of acidification.* The rate of acid release is basically dependent upon the temperature and the available moisture.

Why and When Use Encapsulated Acidulants?

Using powdered acidulants for making semi-dry sausages is easy to justify as they drastically shorten the processing time by eliminating natural fermentation. The benefit of using *encapsulated acidulant is that it provides more time* for *Staphylococcus spp.* flavor producing bacteria (naturally present in meat) to develop flavors. However, this requires that any heat treatment cannot be performed during the first 24 hours. The temperature must be maintained below 60° F (16° C) otherwise pathogenic *S. Staphylococcu*s will start growing. Adding 0.1% (1 g/kg) of dextrose would allow lactic bacteria to generate a slight acidity, providing some safety, yet will not prevent flavor-forming bacteria from working.

The heating requirement limits the use of encapsulated citric acid to fast-acidified semi-dry sausages such as partially cooked *pepperoni pizza toppings* or sausage. Given that summer sausage or other semi-dry sausages are cooked later in the process, adding encapsulated acidulants (citric acid, Gdl, lactic acid) is fine as encapsulated acidulants will start melting after the internal meat temperature reaches 122-150° F (50-66° C). This means the flavor-forming bacteria can receive sufficient time to develop flavor before the heat is applied and the encapsulated acidulant melts down and lowers pH. Encapsulated acid must be the very last ingredient that we add during mixing. *Heavy mixing/kneading might break the encapsulation,* releasing the acid prematurely into the meat negatively affecting the bind and texture.

Starter cultures create a better quality product, but cost money and are not available in many parts of the world. To compound the problem, in many areas, the climate is hot, refrigeration scarce, and equipment very basic. Under those conditions using Gdl or citric acid is quite practical as it allows for safe manufacture and storage of meat products.

Sausage Type	Powdered Gdl/ ascorbic acid	Encapsulated Gdl/ascorbic acid	Remarks
Fermented non-heated dry salami	no	no	Traditional dry sausages are not cooked. Their flavor and aroma are the result of bacterial reaction with meat.
Fermented non-heated semi-dry sausages	yes *	no	These are semi-dry sausages made without cultures.
Fermented heated sausages	yes	yes **	Provides time delay before acidity will inhibit action of flavor forming bacteria
Acidified cooked sausages	yes ***	yes	The purpose of acidulant is to apply "tangy" taste which is associated with naturally fermented sausages.
Fresh grill type sausages	yes	no	The purpose of acidulant is to apply "tangy" taste
Smoked/cooked sausages	yes	yes	The purpose of acidulant is to apply "tangy" taste. Acidulant can be added to any sausage that will be cooked. This also implies to acidic liquids as vinegar or lemon juice.

Note: general consensus is that sausages made with Gdl exhibit a smoother, more mellow taste, as opposed to citric acid whose taste is more "metalic."

* acidulants are added in very small amount (0.5% Gdl *OR* 0.2% citric acid) to increase safety in initial stage of processing when no culture is available. The pH should drop to <pH 5.3 within time as prescribed in temperature tables (see Chapter 6). Then, the sausage must be dried to lose at least 20% of its original weight or cooked.

** the processing steps should be performed below 59° F (15° C).

*** with powdered acidulant the process is technically more difficult: the mixture must be immediately stuffed, dispersing citric acid is difficult.

Acidic Liquids

Cooking meat is usually associated with heat treatment. Heating changes the structure of meat proteins during a process known as denaturation. Acids can change the structure of the meat in the same way as heat. The best example is the Spanish Ceviche technique, originally from Peru, for cooking fish by soaking it in lemon juice. Mild acids such as lemon juice (pH 2.5) cook fish relatively easily because its flesh has a weak collagen structure. However, intermuscular collagen links in red meat are numerous and stronger. Vinegar is another acidic liquid.

Lemon juice is an excellent substitute for citric acid. One teaspoon of powdered citric acid weighs 3.8 g, equivalent to 60 ml (1/4 cup or 2 oz fl) of lemon juice (4 Tablespoons). It should drop pH by one full unit. 1 gram of powdered citric acid equals to ~ 15 ml (1 Tablespoon or 3 tsp) of lemon juice. *Vinegar* is twice as strong as lemon juice.

pH of Acidic Liquids	
Soy sauce	4.6
Red wine	3.3
Rice wine	3.4 - 4.5
Lemon juice	2.0 - 3.0
White vinegar	2.4

Using Gdl for Making Semi-Dry Sausages

Gdl can be used not only for making super-fast semi-dry type sausages but also to increase the safety of dry sausages in the initial stage of processing. It can also be used with starter cultures to get a better flavor and aroma. If added at a low amount, the low flavor profile of Gdl itself makes it possible to acidify sausages without interrupting the work of color and flavor-forming bacteria. Minced meat, all ingredients, and Gdl are mixed together, filled into casings, and then dried at 59° F (15° C) for a day or two. After that, the sausages are cooked to be shelf-stable.

Although it is possible to use chemical acidulants to produce a fast-fermented sausage in one day, the sausage will have only a sour taste and no flavor of its own, as no bacterial reactions will take place with the meat. The pH drop will be so rapid that flavor-forming bacteria will become inactive. However, adding sugar, spices, and herbal extracts will give it its own unique flavor.

Semi-dry sausages - adding 1.0% (10 g/kg) of powdered Gdl will drop pH below 5.0 quickly. Then, the sausages can be smoked (optional) and cooked at 145° F (63° C) for at least 4 minutes. By eliminating natural fermentation time, which can last 12-18 hours, an acidified summer sausage could be made by following the recipe, including powdered or encapsulated Gdl, stuffed into casings, smoked, and cooked to 161°F (72°C) at internal temperature, all can be accomplished within one day.

Using Gdl for Making Dry Sausages

Dry sausages - if not using cultures or relying on natural fermentation, adding 0.5% (5 g/kg) of Gdl will drop the initial pH of fresh pork from 5.8 to about 5.3. It will become a safety hurdle in initial stage of the production, yet still allowing naturally occurring in meat flavor forming bacteria to react. Add 3% salt, 2.5 g sodium nitrite (Cure #1)/kg, and flavorings, then mix with minced meat and stuff into casings. Leave the sausages in the refrigerator for two days to acidify and move them to the smoking/drying chamber. Apply cold smoke < 64° F (18° C) if desired. Dry the sausages at 53-57° F (12-14° C), 75% humidity until they lose 33% of the original weight.

Dry sausage with Gdl and culture - combining 0.4% GdL with T-SPX will produce a satisfying product. Maintain humidity high during the first two days of production, as Gdl works better at high moisture levels. Then continue drying. The texture of the sausage may become a bit harder than with starter culture alone.

Stopping Acidification

Acidification is a chemical reaction, so heating will not prevent acidulants from lowering pH. The acidification rate will be even faster at higher temperatures and continue until no more acidulants remain. A very good acidification rate with Gdl (release of gluconic acid) occurs at 70-74° F (21-23° C).

Summary on Acidified Sausages

Recently, citric acid has become popular with hobbyists, but there needs to be some clarification about its applications. Many believe they create a fermented sausage because it exhibits an acidic taste or that adding encapsulated citric acid cures the meat. Relying on acidulants alone produces lower-quality sausage, as *acidulants introduce only an acidic taste and no flavor or aroma.*

On the other hand, bacterial fermentation, whether natural or with cultures, directs bacteria to react with proteins and fats, which develop complex flavors. Additionally, enzymes naturally occurring in meat react with proteins and fat. When lactic acid bacteria consume sugar, they create through fermentation not only lactic acid but many other components that enhance the flavor of the sausage. On the other hand, acidulants, by lowering pH, accelerate the development of color but do not contribute to flavor; they only supply acidity.

By using encapsulated acids, we can run bacterial fermentation in the first stage of production and then cook the sausage so that the capsules melt, freeing the acidulant. This, however, eliminates the production of traditional salami, given that they are not supposed to be heated. Adding a large amount of powdered acidulant into the mix will introduce a degree of safety. However, it will prevent lactic, curing, and flavor-forming bacteria from reacting with meat.

Acidification is a method of choice for people who need more time or are not willing to learn more about fermentation. However, it is widely employed in mass production operations, where saved production time increases profits.

The benefits of using acidulants:

- Shorten the production process by eliminating fermentation stage.
- with Gdl the pH can be lowered directly in the sausage mass and so the development of pathogen and spoilage causing microorganisms can be reduced.
- Simplify production as there is a lesser need for microprocessor controlled temperature, humidity and air speed controls.
- There is no need to worry about drying, worrying about Aw or checking moisture loss by weighing the test sausage.
- Given that natural fermentation is usually absent, control of humidity is less important. A liquid smoke flavored sausage can be acidified and then cooked.
- Faster and improved color stability allows for applying less nitrite. the color is more intense, the sausage is firmer and the cut-resistance is improved.
- Acidulants are inexpensive, available online and in stores, need no refrigeration and have almost unlimited shelf life. They can be used at the moment's notice.

Bockwurst Style Sausage Acidified with Lemon Juice

No Gdl or citric acid, just lemon juice.

Squeeze lemons to produce 60 ml (4 Tbsp) of lemon juice. Filter the juice through a paper towel or coffee filter.
Optional: for lemon aroma grate lemon skin discarding white inside pith.*

Semi-fat pork	1000 g	(2.2 lb)

Ingredients per 1 kg (2.2 lb) of meat

Salt	18 g	3 tsp
White pepper	2.0 g	1 tsp
Ginger, ground	0.5 g	1/4 tsp
Lemon peel, grated	2.0 g	1 tsp
Chives, chopped	3.0 g	1 Tbsp
Parsley, chopped	4.0 g	1 Tbsp
Nutmeg	0.5 g	1/4 tsp
Lemon juice	60 ml	4 Tbsp
Water	30 ml	2 Tbsp

Cut back fat into 1/4" (6 mm) cubes.
Grind pork, beef and veal with 1/8" (3 mm) plate slowly adding water.
Mix ground meat with all ingredients.
Add fat cubes and mix again.
Stuff into 28 - 32 mm natural casings forming 2.5" (8 cm) long links.
Cook in water at 176° F (80° C) for 30 minutes. Refrigerate.
Re-heat in hot water before serving.

* the skin of the lemon consists of both the pith and the zest. The pith is the white inside part that is closer to the pulpy interior. The pith can be bitter and can add an unpleasant note to the flavor. On the other hand, zest adds a purer more intense flavor without the bitterness.

Note: adding lemon juice to minced meat immediately starts reacting with meat proteins and may create a woody, breadcrumbs-like texture. It is recommended to use at least 30% fat, and some emulsified connective tissue will also contribute to a better binding and texture.

Chapter 11

Spreadable Fermented Sausages

Eating fresh ground beef was an accepted custom in Europe, and "steak tartare" can still be found on the menu in every European country. In the late 19th century, the Hamburg steak became popular on the menus of many restaurants in the port of New York. This kind of fillet was beef minced by hand, lightly salted, and often smoked, and it was usually served raw in a dish along with onions and bread crumbs. Cannibal sandwiches (fresh ground beef) are a longtime Milwaukee tradition in Wisconsin.

Health concerns have reduced the popularity of this meat dish in some parts of the world because of the danger of contamination by bacteria and parasites. In the United States, ground beef is not typically sold with the expectation that it will be eaten uncooked. According to the World Health Organization, when basic hygienic rules are followed, and fresh meat is used, the risk of bacterial infection is low. The best quality salami were never cooked, fermented, or acidified; hence technically speaking, they were raw meat. However, the meat was made safe for consumption by treating it with salt and nitrite and prolonged drying.

Spreadable sausages are finely ground, incorporate soft fat, and have a moderate pH drop. Since spreadable sausages are neither cooked nor strongly fermented/acidified or dried, they need to be refrigerated as their shelf life is short, as opposed to salami, which can last a year at room temperature. Thus, unlike raw ground beef steaks or sandwiches, which need to be immediately consumed, spreadable sausages can last one week in the refrigerator, although they are not cooked. They can be classified as non-heated semi-dry sausages; what separates them from other fermented products is their spreadability, soft texture, and original "meaty" taste.

Spreadable fermented sausages are popular in Germany (Mettwurst, Teewurst), Poland (Metka); and in the areas of the USA where immigrants from those countries have settled in the past. These sausages are spreadable like liverwurst, however, they are made from fermented meat that is often smoked, but not submitted to cooking. German and Polish spreadable sausages are usually smoked. In Southern Europe there is a well known Italian spreadable *Nduja* and very popular Spanish *sobrasada* sausages, the best known, of course, *the Sobrassada di Mallorca* which holds a prestigious European Certificate of Origin.

Photo 11.1 -top. Polish Metka.
Photo 11.2 Spanish Sobrasada de Mallorca, PGI.

General Guidelines

To retain their soft texture and meaty taste, spreadable sausages must:

- Be slightly fermented so there is a small pH drop, resulting in slight acidity and almost no *tangy* taste. As pH lowers, the sausage texture becomes firmer, decreasing its spreadability. *The less acidity sausage has, the easier it is to spread.*
- Have a unique, *slightly* sour taste and flavor which people like. Rapid fermentation to low pH must not be allowed as it promotes drying, hardens the texture and creates sour taste.
- Should not have low Aw as drying/removal of moisture will harden their texture, and the moisture is needed to make the sausage soft and spreadable.

The pH drop should fit into 5.1-5.4 range. Lower pH will harden the texture and make the sausage less spreadable. Acidity is obtained by adding dextrose, sucrose or lactose, starter cultures and a proper choice of fermenting temperature. The sausages are generally subjected only to one or two day's fermentation at 68-77° F (20-25° C) which is sufficient for curing color formation, but does not guarantee microbiological safety. Neither acidity, nor the amount of moisture is sufficient to make them shelf-stable, and since they are not heated, they must be kept in a refrigerator.

The best quality spreadable sausages are naturally fermented, usually with starter cultures. Acidulants such as Gdl or citric acid should be avoided, as they increase the firmness of the texture, which will negatively affect the spreadability. In addition, they develop a sour taste, which might not be accepted by a customer.

All steps prior to meat stuffing are extremely important, given that they affect the microbiological safety of the meat. The meat must be fresh or properly de-thawed, equipment and work tables should be sanitized, and the manufacturing must be performed at the lowest possible temperature. Complying with those rules will slow down the growth of spoilage bacteria and protect the meat from being infected with bacteria residing on the premises.

Adding salt and sugar will lower Aw by about 0.2 units, nitrite will inhibit the growth of pathogenic bacteria, and 10 million starter culture bacteria will compete with spoilage bacteria for oxygen and nutrients. The sausages can be stuffed into permeable synthetic casings such as collagen or cellulose to allow smoke penetration and some removal of moisture. Both processes are relatively short, so weight loss is almost negligible.

Manufacturing Process

Selection of Materials. Most spreadable fermented sausages are made of pork, but other fatty meats like beef or lamb may be used. A combination of beef and pork fat is also popular. Pork must be trichinae-free. If in doubt, freeze pork before processing as the official regulations prescribe (see Chapter 6). The texture of spreadable sausages must be soft and moist to be spreadable over a slice of bread. This requires a relatively large amount of soft fat (40-50%), such as belly fat, dewlap, and jowls; however, finely minced back fat is often used. Both fat and meat are finely minced, which adds not only to a better spreadability but also covers lean meat particles with a thin oil film that retards the removal of moisture, preserving the softness of the sausage. When not enough soft fat is available, about 1-2% of vegetable oil may be added; however, take into account the amount of intramuscular fat the meat contains. Vegetable oil offers two benefits:

- Oil is transparent so the sausage seems to be leaner.
- Oil is less prone to rancidity.

Grinding

Spreadable sausages can also be grouped by the size of minced particles:

- Fine (Teewurst) - cuts of cold meat and fat are mixed with all ingredients and then ground through 2-3 mm (1/16 - 1/8") plate and fermented at 95% humidity
- Medium coarse (Mettwurst) - cuts of meat and fat are partially frozen, mixed with all ingredients and ground through 3 - 8 mm (1/8 - 5/16") plate and fermented at 95% humidity

Commercially produced spreadable sausages like Teewurst can be chopped in a bowl cutter to 1/16" (1.5 - 2 mm) size, but at home, using a 1/8" (3 mm) grinder plate is fine, providing that partially frozen meat and frozen fat are processed.

Mixing

Mix meat, fat and all the ingredients together. If acidulant is added, proceed to stuffing without a delay.

Stuffing

Eliminate introduction of air during stuffing as much as possible. Use permeable casings as most sausages are smoked and occasionally briefly dried.

To shorten the process using Gdl at 2% (2 g/1 kg of meat), sugar (3 g/kg), and fast fermented culture brings also a satisfying result. If no culture is added use Gdl at <0.5% (5 g/kg), no sugar is necessary. However, adding slow fermenting carbohydrates such as maltose, lactose, honey or flavorings will offset some of the tangy taste.

Gdl (if used) drops pH fast; however, *it contributes to a harder texture, a feature which is not desired in spreadable sausages.* Gdl should be applied below 5 g/ kg, otherwise the taste will be too sourly and metallic, especially when sugar was also added. Potassium nitrate alone or in Cure #2 should not be used as the production cycle is short and curing bacteria will not have time to force nitrate into creating nitrite. Given that adding Gdl to minced meat immediately hardens its texture, the mixture should be stuffed without a delay.

Fermentation

Time	Temperature	Humidity	Process
1 day	64° F/18° C	80	Resting/fermenting, little air flow
1 day	72° F/22° C	90	Fermentation
1 day	72° F/22° C	85	Fermentation
12 hours	71° F/22° C	80	Smoking/Drying
Salt 2.5%, Cure #1: 2.5 g - Take into the account that Cure #1 contains 93.75% salt. Dextrose 0.3%. T-SPX culture. A weak air-speed is introduced, and a thin cold smoke applied. For large diameter casings add another day of smoking/drying.			

Smoking

After fermentation the sausages are smoked with a thin cold smoke at 64-72° F (18-22° C), 80% humidity. The surface of sausages must be dry before smoke is applied.

- Mettwurst and Teewurst - smoked for about 12 hours and refrigerated.
- Italian Nduja - smoked and dried.

Spanish Sobrassada is not smoked after fermentation, but only dried for about 34-45 days.

The process of making spreadable sausages ends with the cold-smoking stage. Since they are neither sufficiently fried nor cooked, they last for 3-5 days and must be stored in refrigerator or kept at cool temperature.

Note: when Gdl has been added, the sausage can be dried at 68° F (20° C), 90% humidity, and moderate airflow for one day. Then, it can be cold smoked. For large-diameter casings, add another day of smoking/drying,

Drying

Spreadable sausages are often shortly dried during fermentation/smoking steps. An overly dried sausage will be too hard to spread. Spreadable sausages only need a liitle drying as they are not expected to have a very long shelf life. A very weak air-speed is introduced, about 0.1 m/sec.

Note: if spreadable sausage is allowed to dry at 53-57° F (12-14° C) it will become in time a semi-dry sausage.

Emulsifiers

These two ingredients are often added as they contribute positively to better spreadability:

Guar gum has almost eight times the water-thickening potency of cornstarch and only a very small quantity is needed for producing sufficient viscosity. Guar gum will bind and prevent removal of some water, what will greatly extend the spreadability of the sausage.

Mustard flour is produced by grinding the seed of the white mustard plant to a fine powder. It is used in many foods including meat, chicken, fish, vegetables and Asian cooking. Adding mustard flour does not change the flavor of the sausage, however, it slows down the action of lactic acid bacteria what leads to a softer texture. In addition mustard flour retards fat rancidity. It binds water well and is often added to spreadable sausages at 1-1.5 ratio to extend spreadability.

Photo 11.3 Spanish Sobrasada.

The shelf life of spreadable sausages is much shorter than that of dry or semi-dry fermented sausages, which is why American supermarkets do not stock them. Secondly, they are not cooked, so it will be hard for commercial producers to satisfy the requirements of the official standards. However, their unique texture and flavor are popular in Germany and Poland. These sausages are produced by neighborhood butchers who cater to the local clientele.

Guidelines for making German and Polish spreadable sausages		
Meat	pork, beef (20-30%)	pork pH 5.6-6.0, beef pH ~5.8,
Soft fat, dewlap, belly	30-50%	belly, dewlap, jowls, occasionally vegetable oil at 1-2%
Grind	fine, 1/16-1/8" (2-3 mm)	smaller particles size improve spreadability
Salt	salt 2.2 - 2.5%,	applying more than 2.5% salt will negatively affect spreadability
Nitrite (Cure #1)	130-156 ppm,	cure #1 (nitrite) at 2.0-2.5 g/kg introduces additional 0.2% salt
Sugar	0.3%	dextrose 0.2% plus sugar 0.1%
Gdl (optional)	0.2-0.3%	more Gdl will create harder texture preventing spreadability, don't add dextrose/sugar
pH	pH ~ 5.3	the extent of pH drop must be limited in order to keep sausages spreadable
Aw	Aw ≥ 0.95	water activity should be relatively high given that more moisture contributes to better spreadability
Fermenting/drying	without culture: 24 hours at ≤ 59° F (≤ 15° C)	with culture *: 24 hours at 75° F (24° C)
Smoking is optional, but generally applied **	without culture: smoke at ≤ 64° F (≤ 18° C) for 12 hours	with culture: smoke at ≤ 64-75° F (≤ 18-24° C) for 12 hours
Storing	in refrigerator	may be stored for a day or two at ≤ 50° F (10° C), 75% humidity, a little air speed
Equipment should be cold, all processing steps at 50-53° F (10-12° C).		
* for additional safety use one of the cultures that produce pediocin which is a bacterocin with strong antagonistic properties against *Listeria*, such as: SafePro® B-LC-007, SafePro® Flora Italia LC		
** smoking can be considered to be a part of drying process. Prolonged smoking/drying will remove more moisture and will harden the texture of the sausage.		

Photo 11.4 Italian Nduja.

Chapter 12

Cold Smoked, Cooked Fermented and Cooked Non-Fermented Sausages

Cold-Smoked Dry Sausages

The technology of making North European cold-smoked sausages closely resembles the manufacturing process of making Italian salami or Spanish dry sausages. The main difference is that a small fire was warming the sausage chamber in a cold climate, just enough to prevent the sausages from freezing. In the first stages of combustion, burning wood after evaporating moisture produces smoke, so a thin, cold smoke is always present. After a while, no more smoke is produced. However, the wood continues to burn. To sum it up, the purpose of burning wood was to keep the facilities warm, and the smoke just happened to be there. The meats were simply dried with cold smoke. Italians did not need to warm up the premises as the climate was just suitable for drying sausages with air. Hence, the smoking was seldom performed.

A very interesting group of sausages were cold-smoked products made in the past in Poland and Russia before the advent of refrigeration. They were not thought of as salami, and people simply called them dry sausages. Many of these sausages were naturally fermented cold smoked products, which would fully qualify to be called salami. Starter cultures were not around yet, so the products were naturally dried. Those sausages were cured with potassium nitrate because sodium nitrite was not known yet. Fermentation was not even mentioned, but what was significant is that a small amount of sugar was added because people knew that potassium nitrate worked better with sugar; the color was more intense, and the flavor was better, too. A few decades later, it was discovered that sugar was an essential nutrient for curing and lactic acid bacteria, both naturally occurring in meat. As the amount of sugar was very minute, the final product exhibited none of the sour taste that is common in fast-fermented products today.

The procedure was as follows:

- Top quality meats were selected and cured for 3-4 days with salt, sugar, and potassium nitrate at around 42-46° F (6-8° C). Curing bacteria forced potassium nitrate to release sodium nitrite which reacted with meat's myoglobin creating a pink color.

- Sausages were cold smoked for weeks at the time. However, smoking was not continuous, as the fire was often not burning at night. This allowed natural fermentation and drying to take place inside the smokehouse. There was a steady removal of moisture, but no mold was present due to smoke. The product would become a dry sausage.
- Sausages were left hanging in a smokehouse or in the kitchen and were consumed on a need basic. The sausages kept on drying out and during this "ripening" process were developing salami like flavor.

The processing times and temperatures correspond precisely to the principles of making traditional products as practiced in Southern Europe. The only difference was that Mediterranean products were dried without smoke in the open air due to a favorable climate, while North European sausages were smoked/dried inside a smokehouse.

We could classify these sausages as:

- Cold smoked sausages - they can be considered smoked salami.
- Spreadable fermented sausages - called "Metka" sausages. Metka sausages were usually cold smoked and no further processing was performed. They had to be kept al low temperature.

What follows is the manufacturing process for making Polish cold-smoked sausages. At first glance, it looks like the process can be applied to any smoked sausages; however, when you look at the temperatures, you will see that they are much lower. Secondly, the salt was added at about 3.3% what prevented spoilage and pathogenic bacteria from growing. Although it was called cold smoked sausage, however, if the recipe is studied in detail, it could be renamed traditionally made salami.

Cold-Smoked Polish Sausages

1. Curing meat. Cut pork into 25-50 mm (1-2 inch) pieces and mix with 3% salt, 0.2% (2 g/kg) sugar and (2.5 g/kg meat) of Cure #2. Leave for 2-3 days in refrigerator.
2. Grind meat.
3. Add black pepper, marjoram and garlic and mix all together. Stuff into casings.
4. Condition for 2 days at 35-42° F (2-6° C) and 85-90% humidity.
5. Smoke with a thin cold smoke at 64° F (18° C) for 1-2 days. This could be called fermentation/drying stage.
6. Dry at 50-53° F (10-12° C) and 75-80% humidity until sausages lose 15% of the original weight. Additional drying will create a dry sausage.
7. Store at 53° F (12° C) or lower, 75% humidity.

Cold-Smoked Russian Sausages

During the era of Communism, Russia had a diverse assortment of meat products, comprising more than 200 types, varieties, and classes of sausages. Due to the lack of refrigeration, most of those sausages were either dry or semi-dry to be stable at room temperatures. Depending on the quality of the raw material (meat and fat), they were subdivided into higher class, class 1, and class 2.

Dry sausages		Semi dry sausages	
higher class	class 1	higher class	class 1
Pork, Metropolitan, Kazakh, Delicatessen, Russian, Special, Jewish, Cervelat, Tambov, Maikop, Tourist, Neva, Uglich, and Braunschweig varieties	Moscow, Fancy, Ukrainian, Orsk, Mutton sausages	Cervelat, Rostov, Summer delicatessen	Moscow, Fancy, Ukrainian, Mutton, Minsk

The smoked sausages were subdivided into raw or hard-smoked (dry sausages) and smoked and cooked (semi-dry, summer-type sausages). The meat was cured with salt and nitrate for 5-7 days at 40° F (4° C), then cold smoked for 3-5 days (below 71° F (22° C) and then dried for 25-30 days at 54-56° F (12-14° C). Of course, no starter cultures were used. In addition, they were dry sausages (higher class only-Kazakh dry sausage) made from 35% horse meat, pork, pork fat, and semi-dry sausages made in high class (35% horse meat, pork, pork fat) and class 1 (70% horse meat, pork, pork fat).

Cooked Fermented Sausages

There are two types of cooked fermented sausages:

• Fermented, dried and partially cooked sausages.

• Fermented, non-dried, fully cooked sausages.

Natural fermentation can be supported with acidulant. However, if acidulany is used alone, the sausage does not qualify to be called a fermented product.

Fast-fermented sausages must exhibit a characteristic tangy flavor. This can be produced by:

• 2 days *natural* fermentation.

• 1-2 days fermentation with starter culture and dextrose/sugar. The rate of fermentation will depend on a type of culture and fermentation temperature. The extent of fermentation (pH drop) depends on the type and the amount of sugar added.

• Using acidulants such as Gdl or citric acid which can acidify meat within one day, the acidification rate increases with temperature.

In all above cases the product will be cooked resulting in a short production time.

What differentiates it from a regular smoked and cooked sausage is the tangy flavor it has developed during the fermentation stage. All that is needed is a fast-fermenting culture like LHP or F-1, 0.5% dextrose, and 100° F (38° C) fermenting temperature. Instead of a starter culture, Gdl can be added to develop acidity. Such a fermentation process can be accomplished in 12 hours; the sausage can be smoked/cooked and be finished in one day. If such a sausage is fully cooked, the manufacturing process becomes easy as there is little to worry about pH drop or Aw water activity. What we get is a safe to consume sausage with a tangy taste. Why to cook a sausage that has always been made without cooking?

It is all about money. It is faster, safer, easier, and cheaper to create sour salami without drying the sausage. Drying a sausage is a slow and expensive process that, depending on its diameter it may take weeks or more to accomplish, but the same sausage can be fully cooked in 30 minutes. Well, it may have a different texture and flavor, but for many people, if it is hard and sour, it must be salami. And it matters little whether the slices of pepperoni on top of pizza were traditionally fermented and dried for a month or acidified and cooked in just one day.

Applying a fast-fermented culture at 104° F (40° C) and 0.5-1.0% dextrose will ferment a sausage in 12 hours, then it can be smoked if desired. Gradually increasing the temperature to 176° F (80° C) will smoke, bake, and finish the sausage within a day. The pH drop in a fully cooked sausage does not need to be very low, as the cooking step makes the sausage safe. Acidity loses its importance as a safety hurdle and becomes a flavoring step. Due to the high cooking temperature, the sausage's texture and presentation will suffer as the little specks of fat meltdown and will no longer be as distinctive. Some purists may frown upon such a technique, but making some fast snack food such as small summer sausage or meat sticks will work just fine.

Partially-Cooked Fermented Sausages

Ingredients for 1 kg of meat:

Salt 25 g, Cure #1 2.5 g, Gdl 2 g, fast-fermenting culture L-HP, dextrose 3 g, spices.

Mix ground meats with all ingredients and stuff into 60 mm casings without delay. Ferment at 72-76° F (22-24° C), 90% humidity for 48 hours. Cold smoke at 73° F (22° C) for 24 hours. Bake in smokehouse at 167° F (75° C) until meat reaches 140° F (60° C) internal temperature. Dry at 53-59° F (12-15° C), 75% humidity for 2 days. Store in refrigerator. You can store it at 53-57° F (12-14° C), 75% humidity which will count as additional drying. Two more days of drying will make sausage safe to be kept at room temperature. In order to obtain real salami texture the meat and fat must be very cold, grinder knife must be sharp and mixing performed at low temperature. It will help to mix ingredients in a very cold stainless steel bowl. Production time about 5 days.

Fully-Cooked Fermented Sausages

Natural fermentation

Ingredients for 1 kg of meat

Salt 25 g, Cure #1-2.5 g, dextrose 5 g, spices.

Cut meat into 25-50 mm (1-2 inch) pieces and mix with salt and cure #1. Leave for 3 days in refrigerator. To avoid smearing use partially frozen meat and fat. Mix ground meats with all ingredients and stuff into 60 mm casings. Hold at 59° F (15° C), 90-85% humidity for 12 hours, then ferment at 64° F (18° C) for additional 18 hours. Apply cold smoke at 64° F (18° C) for 6 hours. Bake in smokehouse at 176° F (80° C) until meat reaches 158° F (70° C) internal temperature. Processing time 40 hours.

With Starter Culture

Salt 25 g, Cure #1 2.5 g, fast fermenting culture L-HP, dextrose 5 g, spices.

Mix ground meats with all ingredients and stuff into 60 mm casings. Ferment at 72-76° F (22-24° C), 90-85% humidity for 24 hours. Smoke at 72° F (22° C) for 6 hours. Bake in smokehouse at 176° F (80° C) until meat reaches 158° F (70° C) internal temperature. Processing time 36 hours. No curing necessary.

With Gdl

Ingredients for 1 kg of meat

Salt 25 g, Cure #1-2.5 g, Gdl 1% (10 g/1 kg), spices.

Mix ground meat with all ingredients and stuff without delay. Hold at 75° F (24° C), 90% humidity for 48 hours. Apply smoke at 140° F (60° C) for 2-4 hours. Bake in smokehouse at 176° F (80° C) until meat reaches 158° F (70° C) internal temperature.

The sausage will have a tangy taste, and the meat and fat particles will be somewhat less defined than in uncooked sausages because of the higher processing temperatures, which should not exceed 176° F (80° C). Otherwise, the fat will start melting inside, and the texture will suffer.

Non-Fermented Partially Cooked Dry Sausages

Some sausages are not fermented or acidified, yet shelf stable. They are made without cultures or acidulants (Gdl, citric acid), and no fermentation takes place. Generally, after stuffing, these sausages are partially cooked to 146° F (63° C) and then dried to a water activity of < 0.86 (Aw growth limit for S. aureus). Due to the higher pH, these products must be dried to a lower water activity than fermented products to achieve shelf stability. Non-fermented dried sausages are also known as non-fermented salamis.

Non-Fermented Fully-Cooked Dry Sausages

When the Second World War ended in 1945, most people did not own refrigerators, so food preservation was necessary. Most sausages were smoked, cooked, and then air-dried at 50-59° F (10-15° C). This reduced Aw (water activity) to about 0.92, which made the product shelf stable if it was kept at 50-57° F (10-14° C). They were kept in kitchen pantries and would keep losing moisture, eventually becoming dry sausages. The majority of sausages that were made after the war in Poland, Germany, or Russia would fit into this category. They were not called salamis but had their own names: Kabanosy, Mysliwska, Krakowska and many more.

The salt was added at around 2.2% (2.2 g/kg), and potassium nitrate was the curing agent. Those sausages were always cured (salt, nitrate, a little sugar) for 3-4 days at cool temperatures, around 46° F (8° C), then cold smoked with a thin smoke for 12 hours. Then they were air dried without smoke for a few hours (sometimes just left overnight) and smoked with a thin cold smoke again. Cooking was accomplished in smokehouse by baking them w/wo smoke to 154° F (68° C) internal temperature.

Kochsalami

Kochsalami is a smoked cooked-in-water sausage that is stuffed into a large diameter casing. The meat and fat are finely ground, the color is red, and there are easily distinguishable particles of lean and fat. Without a bowl cutter, it would be impossible to achieve such a fine particle distribution. By description, a "traditional salami" is a lightly fermented and dried sausage. However, Kochsalami does not meet these criteria yet they are classified as such.

These sausages may look like salami, but they exhibit none of the traditional salami or any fermented sausage flavor, so they can be called fake salami. They can be smoked or not. Different proportions of pork and beef and different selections of spices are to be expected as they are produced in many regions of Germany. This also results in different names: Pariser Kochsalami, Hildesheimer Kochsalami, Bayerische Kochsalami, Tiroler Kochsalami, Göttinger Kochsalami. Countries such as Poland, Hungary, Czech Republic, and the USA produce their own versions of Kochsalami as well.

Fermented Chicken Sausages

Chicken is the most popular meat consumed worldwide as it is easy to raise and can be eaten by the average family in one sitting. Chicken thigh meat creates a better color than the breast as it contains more myoglobin. However, it is characterized by a high pH (6.1-6.4), which means a good water-holding capacity. Breast pH (5.6-6.8) falls into the pork pH range. Higher levels of dextrose should be used in sausages that initially have a higher pH, such as poultry.

Chicken fat contains more water and less collagen structure than other fats, which makes it soft and semi-liquid at room temperature. During heat treatment, chicken fat often melts inside the sausage creating oily pockets. To improve the texture of the sausage, some pork fat should be added.

pH of pork fat is also high (6.2-7.0) and the sausage batter consisting of chicken meat and pork fat may have an initial value well over 6.0.

The high initial pH of the sausage batter will require a longer fermentation time to drop pH below 5.3 within the prescribed time. Due to the sausage batter's high initial pH, it is essential to limit the time the sausage is left at temperatures over 15.6° C (60° F), which favors the growth of *Staphylococcus aureus*. Raw chicken meat is often contaminated with *Salmonella* which can be destroyed by heating to 156° F (69° C).

Due to chicken meat's high moisture level, its initial Aw will be around 0.98 even after salt introduction. This moisture, supported by high temperatures, creates favorable conditions for the growth of *Listeria* and *Campylobacter jejuni,* a pathogen found in poultry meat.

Starter cultures that are available online are of freeze-dry type, and they exhibit a rather long lag phase (wake-up time) before bacteria start to produce a significant amount of lactic acid. Adding a larger amount of starter bacteria will compensate for lag time and low temperatures during fermentation. Bactoferm™ F-LC bio-protective culture might be a good choice as it inhibits *Listeria monocytogenes* and can be used at a wide range of temperatures.

Fermented Wild Game Sausages

Game meat is suitable, but it is at risk of being infected with trichinosis and should treated before use as recommended by authorities. *Trichinae* is caused by consuming raw or undercooked pork or wild game meat infected with *"trichinella spiralis."* It should be assumed that wild boar, bear, raccoon, and possum may be infected with a parasitic worm. Deer is an herbivore; it eats leaves from trees, bushes, and shrubs and generally doesn't contract the disease.

The U.S. Code of Federal Regulations requires pork to be cooked for 1 minute at 140° F (60° C) to treat *trichinella*. Traditionally made dry salami is generally never cooked, so it may be risky if made from game meat. However, they are cured with a higher percentage of salt, which should kill *trichinae,* too.

Fortunately, storing pork for a prescribed time at low temperatures also kills trichinae. For a home sausage maker, there is an easy-to-apply procedure: Table 1- Required Period of Freezing at Temperature Indicated, which comes from the Code of Federal Regulations, Title 9: Animals and Animal Products, § 318.10 - Prescribed treatment of pork and products containing pork to destroy *trichinae* (See Chapter 6).

It should be noted that wild game, notably bears, that live in Northwestern U.S. and Alaska are known to develop immunity to *Trichinella* parasites, and freezing might not kill larval cysts residing in meat. Such meat must be cooked to 165° F (74 C) internal temperature. Microwraving, curing, drying or smoking is not effectiv°e in preventing *Trichinae*.

General Considerations

- Game meat is lean so it needs extra fat, however, the flavor of wild animal fat is unpredictable so replace it with pork fat. If using pork is objectionable for religious reasons add 5-10% vegetable oil.
- Using strong aromatic spices like rosemary and juniper helps to mask wild game's off flavors.
- Freezing the carcass too soon after death, for example transporting freshly killed deer in freezing temperatures, prevents aging by keeping the proteins (actin and myosin) locked together, resulting in a very tough meat.

To protect meat from flies and spoiling bacteria hunters mix citric acid with water and spray the meat using a spray bottle.

Venison. Deer meat sausages are commercially made in Canada and Alaska. Venison is lean meat so it should be mixed with pork back fat, hard fat trimmings or have some fatty pork or beef added. A proportion of 60% venison to 40% other meats is a good choice.

Factors That Influence the Selection of the Meat

Local customs - people in Alaska might use caribou, moose, reindeer or bear meat. Norwegian fermented sausages such as *Faremorr, Sognemorr gilde, Stabbur* and *Tiriltunga* contain beef, lamb and horse meat and are heavily smoked.

Religious beliefs - consuming pork is not allowed in Jewish and Islamic faith.

Economics - the consumption of higher-value meats is reserved for the upper class, and those less fortunate have to look at other combinations of meats. Sausages are made from sheep, goats, camels, horses, and other meat, but those materials will hardly appeal to the majority of Western consumers, at least not in the USA. Europeans are more tolerant; for example, Polish Kabanosy meat sticks were always made from pork but were also imported from Belgium, although those were made from horse meat. Horse meat has a slightly sweet taste reminiscent of beef. Many consumers cannot tell the difference between beef and horse meat.

Kosher Fermented Sausages

The selection of meat, casings and choice of ingredients must conform to the requirements of Kashrut - a set of dietary laws dealing with the foods that Jews are permitted to eat and how those foods must be prepared according to Jewish law. Pork is not permitted, and that includes pork fat. This forces you to choose:

- Beef, mutton or chicken.
- Edible oils as replacement for animal fat.

Fat. Chicken fat tastes good, however, it melts at room temperature so you may end up with pockets of melted fat inside your sausage.
Beef and sheep fat have a poor taste, so they should be avoided.
Adding a vegetable or olive oil is a good choice and as long you don't add more than 10% the sausage will be of acceptable quality.

Casings. Pig casings are not allowed, but there is no shortage of beef, sheep or synthetic casings which can be used.

Dry Sausages Made with Filler Material

Dry sausages that contain filler material rich in carbohydrates include Alheira de Vinhais (wheat bread), Farinheira de Portalegre (60% wheat flour), Farinato (bread, flour, oil), Chorizo de Calabaza (pumpkin), Chorizo Patatero (potatoes), Nham (rice), and others. Lactic acid bacteria can't directly ferment the carbohydrates mentioned above, but during fermentation and ripening, *enzymes from the meat can break down part of the carbohydrates, and then those sugars can be fermented partly.* This is the reason that products containing starch, potatoes, rice, etc., become quite low in pH sooner or later. Those sausages also include a large percentage of garlic, chili peppers, or paprika, which are rich in carbohydrates and sugar.

Dry and Semi-Dry Sausages Made with Nuts and Cheese

Many dry and semi-dry fermented sausages include nuts or chunks of hard cheese as those ingredients contain not enough moisture to spoil meat during production.

Nuts

Since nuts have water activities generally less than Aw 0.70, they are shelf-stable and may be added to different types of sausages. Adding walnuts or hazelnuts creates dry sausage with a new flavor profile. Additionally, the product looks visually pleasing when sliced. Add about 10-15% of nuts.

Photo 12.1 Dry salami with walnuts.

Cheese

All cured meats and salami taste great when paired with cheese, so it comes as no surprise that combining cheese with meat will make a great salami. A yellow hard cheese cut into 3/8" (1 cm) cubes will work great. A cheese with a high melting point should be selected as most semi-dry fermented sausages are heat treated to around 145° F (63° C). There is a wider range of cheeses to choose from when making a non-heated dry salami, given that there is no danger of melting the cheese, which will dry out along with the meat.

Recommended salami-cheese pairings:

Salami Calabrese - Pecorino (hard sheep's milk cheese)
Salami Milano - Asiago cheese
Salami Genoa - Provolone
Cheeses with a high melting point: Swiss Emmental, American Cheddar, Cabot,

Westphalia, a northwestern region in Germany, is famous for its smoked salami, made with Camembert cheese culture. American Summer Sausage is often made with diced Cheddar cheese.

If you find that your chosen cheese is on the softer side, don't worry. Simply open the wrapping and let it sit in the refrigerator for a few days. This will allow the cheese to lose some moisture, making it firmer and easier to handle in your recipes. Add about 10% of cheese to the meat mixture.

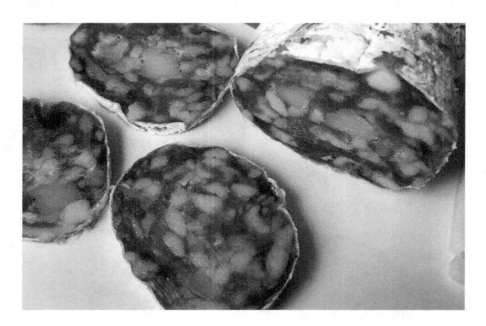

Photo 12.2 Dry salami with cheese.

Chapter 13

Troubleshooting Problems

Acidification - Final pH too low

- Too much sugar has been added.
- Fermentation has continued for too long. If thermal process did not take place or was applied late, lactic acid bacteria converted all sugar into acid.

Acidification too slow

- Temperature during fermentation has been inconsistent with recommended culture optimum - it has been too low or two high.
- Frozen culture has been allowed to thaw and subsequently held too long before dispensing into meat. I.e. the culture has exhausted nutrients in the can, reduced pH and partly inactivated itself.
- Secondary growth of contaminating microorganisms has outgrown the culture or produced components that buffered the pH-drop. Wild bacteria have outgrown culture and has taken over the process.
- Culture was introduced to the mince, however, the mince was kept too long in a cooler before stuffing. This has largely extended culture's lag phase.
- Stuffed sausages have been kept in a cooler too long becoming colder than normal, resulting in prolonged lag phase.
- Excessive salt or cure addition has inhibited the culture.
- Direct contact of culture with salt or curing components has inactivated the culture.
- Too rapid moisture loss has left insufficient water for bacteria to conduct fermentation. This will be even more pronounced in sausages with a higher fat content as the fat contains less water than a lean meat.
- Larger diameter product has given slower heat transfer.
- Insufficient carbohydrate source or not enough glucose has been added to the sausage mixture.

Acidification too fast

- Too high temperature.
- Too much water was added during processing.
- Higher proportion of lean meat introduced more moisture (higher Aw).
- The sausages were too warm when placed in fermentation chamber.
- Incorrect combination of sugars.
- Small diameter sausage was processed at higher humidity than normally.
- Leaner product has introduced more moisture (higher water activity).
- Initial meat pH was very low.

No acidification

- No culture was added.
- Culture has been inactivated by direct contact with salt, cure components, or heavily chlorinated water.
- Insufficient amount of sugar was added to sausage mince or the fat
- Too much salt has been added to the mince or the fat content is unusual high.
- Culture was stored at too high temperature.

Inconsistent acidification from batch to batch

- Inadequate distribution of culture has resulted in "hot" and "cold" spots in the meat mixture.
- Distribution of the culture, salt, cure, spices, dextrose has been inconsistent.
- Stored (laid down) mince has caused some of the mince to dry out.
- Temperatures within the sausages have been diverse.
- Batches have been made with different spice formulations, meat components, casing diameters, pH or water/fat content.
- Temperature/humidity in the fermentation and/or drying room has been uneven from batch to batch.

Moisture - Insufficient moisture loss

- Too high humidity during drying.
- Excessive air speed and/or too low humidity in the beginning of the proces has created a dry rim so that moisture cannot escape from the inside to the surface.
- Excessive smoke too early in the process has cooked surface proteins thereby retarding moisture removal.
- Fat smearing prevented moisture loss.
- Fermentation temperature was too high causing fat melting inside of the casing and preventing moisture escaping to the surface.

Too much moisture loss (drying too fast)

- Humidity too low.
- Air speed too high.
- Acidification has been too fast.
- The applied starter culture has been too fast and thereby the pH too low.

Flavor - Souring of product, post processing

- The heat treatment to destroy the microorganisms (US cooking process) has been insufficient.
- Too much sugar added, some lactic acid bacteria survived process and triggered secondary fermentation.
- Insufficient drying.
- Too high storing temperature.

Off-odor

- Poor quality raw materials were used. Some spoilage bacteria survived fermentation or were reintroduced during post-packing.
- PoorO sanitation practices introduced undesirable bacteria during processing,
- Poor sanitation practices introduced undesirable bacteria during packing or storage.
- Too fast drying created hard surface which prevented moisture removal. Inside of the sausage remained moist and became breeding ground for bacteria.
- Old, stale natural casings were used.

Color - Discoloration - green or grey coloration

- Fat smearing or hard surface ring prevented moisture removal making inside of the sausage grey.
- Insufficient amount of sodium nitrite/nitrate.
- Insufficient amount of curing and color forming bacteria (*Staphylococci* and *Micrococcaceaae*) naturally present in meat if starter culture was not added. Problem is even worse if only potassium nitrate was used.
- Chemical acidulant was used.
- Casing treated with too much potassium sorbate.
- An excessive growth of yeast on the surface.
- Smearing or dry rim have prevented water loss giving spoiled (gray) center.
- Greening can be caused by wild lactic bacteria or the excess of ascorbic acid. Wild lactic bacteria produce hydrogen peroxide (H_2O_2), which can cause an undesirable green and yellow color, which often appears as grey spots.

Texture - Mushy product

- Meat not perfectly fresh.
- Using meat with too much connective tissue.
- Over-mixing ground meat with materials.
- Grinding and mixing meat at too high temperature. This usually holds true for home production, especially when a large proportion of fat is present.
- Insufficient amount of salt.

Slimy, gassy product

- Yeast or heterofermentative (wild) lactic acid bacteria contamination in package post-processing.
- Excessive moisture content.
- Inadequate smoke concentration on the surface of the product.
- Adding a large amount of sugar may produce an excess of carbon dioxide during fermentation and the texture of the sausage may display little pinholes.

Greasing (fat melting)

- Too high heating rate (US cooking process).
- Too high fermentation temperature.
- Unstable mince, low-binding meats.
- Overworking raw mince.
- Too high smoking temperature.

Soft sausage

- Not enough salt.
- Too much soft fat.
- Too high pH.
- Too little sugar.
- Lack of culture.
- Too high processing temperature.
- Incomplete drying.

Hard surface ring

- To low humidity.
- Too fast air speed.
- Too warm smoke.

Grey surface ring

- Too high humidity during ripening or storage.
- Wet smoke.
- Too low storage temperature.

Poor meat and fat particle definition

- Too much soft fat.
- Too high processing temperature.
- Cutting/grinding knife not sharp.
- Mixing too long.

Mold

- Unwanted - too much humidity and/or not enough air speed during fermentation, drying or storage.
- Cultured - uneven distribution, starter culture old, culture applied too late, sausage was smoked.

Problems Related to Spreadable Sausages

Poor spreadability

Too much lean meat	add more fat or vegetable oil
Too many large hard fat particles	use softer fat
Fat particles too large	use smaller grinder plate
Too rapid pH drop - too much sugar or Gdl	decrease the amount

Visible grey areas inside

Too much light meat added	use meat from older animals
Too little or too much nitrite	change dosage
Bacteria count too high	use fresher meat and/or improve manufacturing conditions

Greasy sausage, dripping fat, premature rancidity

Too much soft fat	replace some soft with hard fat
Sausage mass too warm	keep below 59° F (20° C), mix materials at lower temperature
Meat and fat too warm	keep in cooler
Dull grinder knife	use sharp knife
Too warm smoke	apply cold smoke below 64° F (18° C)
High storage temperature	store at 50 - 53° F (10-12° C), 75% humidity

Loose or wrinkled casings

Fat was not distributed properly and did not envelop lean meat particles what resulted in too fast drying	increase the amount of fat, add more soft fat or some vegetable oil. Soak natural casings longer in water
Too much sugar promoted growth of undesirable bacteria	add less sugar
Too high temperature	keep temperature below 24° C

Grey rim

Too long ripening or storing at high humidity	adjust humidity
Too cold storage	store above 41° F (5° C)
Too early application of smoke	apply smoke when the texture is red
Smoke too wet	keep smoke humidity <75%

Sourly and vinegar like taste

Fermentation temperature too high	process at <75° F (<24° C)
Different strains of wild bacteria fermenting	use recommended starter culture

Black and brown spots

Salt not properly dissolved	mix properly

Chapter 14

Creating and Modifying Recipes

A recipe is what the word says: "the recipe." It does not imply that one will produce an outstanding sausage. Making quality sausages has nothing to do with recipes; it is all about meat science and the rules that govern it. Each step in sausage making influences the step that follows, and all those steps, when performed correctly, will create a quality product.

There isn't one standardized recipe for any of the sausages. The best meat science books, written by the foremost experts, list different ingredients for the same sausage. Replacing mace with nutmeg, using white or black pepper, and adding/ removing a particular spice will have little final effect on a sausage. Grinding cold meat or frozen fat is more important for making a quality sausage than a pretty arrangement of expensive spices.

By all means, look at different recipes, but be flexible and not afraid to experiment. Use ingredients that you like, as in most cases, you will make a sausage for yourself, so why not like it? When making a large amount of the product, a wise precaution is to taste the mix before stuffing, as there is still time for last-minute changes. A recipe is just a recipe; let your palate be the final judge. As mentioned earlier, if you like what you have made it is a good sausage.

Dry sausages made with *pepper only* will have the wonderful mellow cheesy flavor *created in time by the reaction of bacteria with meat.* Take Spanish *Salchichón de Vic* as an example; it is a wonderful salami that contains only one spice: black pepper. Fast-fermented sausages will always exhibit this tangy and sour flavor as flavor-forming bacteria don't get sufficient time to work with meat. In this case, various spices, sugars and syrups can somewhat offset the acidic taste.

Salt, Sodium Nitrite, Starter Cultures, Fermentation and Drying

Adding salt and nitrite (Cure #1) offers protection against undesirable bacteria; however, nitrite, if given sufficient time (during the traditional curing process), develops a desired "curing meat flavor." It can be applied at the maximum allowable limit (156 parts per million) as about half of the nitrite is depleted within hours for developing color, and the remaining part dissipates in time by reacting with meat and developing intricate flavors, and during smoking, drying, or cooking. Finished products contain about 10 ppm of nitrite. Replacing nitrite with celery powder is not recommended as it also contains sodium nitrite, and it is hard to estimate the needed amount *(see Chapter 5 - Additives).*

There are many excellent old recipes for making salami that do not mention cultures because starter cultures were not invented then. It is, however, highly recommended that those recipes be upgraded with cultures and sodium nitrite/nitrate as this increases the chances of making consistent quality and microbiologically safe products. There is no universal temperature for fermenting, drying, or storing. There is an acceptable range of temperatures that correspond to each particular process. When a starter culture is used, the manufacturer lists the optimal fermentation. It is not possible to predict the exact time needed to produce a fermented sausage as there are many factors to consider: temperature, humidity, casing diameter, particle size, ratio of lean meat to fat, the amount and type of sugar, type of a sausage desired. The book offers theory, guidelines, practical advice, and tips, including the government standards for making safe products. All this, combined with a pH meter and a weighing scale, should produce a great salami at home.

Using Acidulants

Gdl has often been added to meat whenever a fast increase in acidity is required. Nowadays, there are widely available fast-fermenting cultures that can do the same job yet create a higher-quality product. Moreover, they can work at various temperatures, which is essential in home production. A sausage of a better quality will be produced with a starter culture, as even fast-fermenting cultures contain lactic acid, color, and flavor-forming bacteria. Getting low and rapid pH using acidulants alone eliminates flavor-developing bacteria, so the sausage quality suffers, and slow-fermented carbohydrates and spices must make up flavors.

Why Dextrose is Preferred Carbohydrate

People often ask why both dextrose and sugar are added to meat. The answer is that at the beginning of the process, we need to generate acidity as fast as possible to protect the meat in the initial production stage. The meat is protected only with salt and sodium nitrite at that point, but *its safety increases when acidity arrives.* The speed at which lactic bacteria can generate acidity differs for each carbohydrate (sugar); however, the acid production rate is fastest with dextrose (see Chapter 5 Additives/dextrose).

The easiest way to explain is by following the graph that follows. A starter culture containing 0.1% dextrose and 0.3% sugar is introduced to a sausage mince. It is depicted by point A on the graph. Bacteria are waking up from the freeze (lag phase) and not much happens between A and B. Depending on the temperature this can last from a few to 14 hours. In point B lactic acid bacteria become fully active and immediately start converting *dextrose* into lactic acid. As the acid is produced the spoilage bacteria find the environment increasingly hostile. There is a fast pH drop which ends in point C (at the intersection of pH2 and T1) as there is no more dextrose left for lactic bacteria. The amount of developed acidity is too small to inhibit color and flavor forming bacteria *(Staphylococci)* which are growing and reacting with meat.

At the same time lactic acid bacteria want to consume sugar, however, there is a problem; unlike dextrose which is a simple sugar, common sugar (sucrose) is a complex carbohydrate and must be first converted into dextrose (glucose) before bacteria can consume it. *This conversion takes time so there is a delay.* As a result lactic acid bacteria processes sugar slowly, see the rather flat sugar curve from B to E. *Dextrose processing* bacteria reached pH2 (point C) in just T1 hours, however, sugar processing bacteria need T2 hours to reach the same pH drop (D). Much more time was needed to reach pH2 so more time was given to spoilage bacteria to grow and spoil the meat. Bacteria will produce lactic acid until all sugar will be exhausted in point E (pH1 and T3). Of course the total acidity will be the sum of dextrose and sugar fermentation.

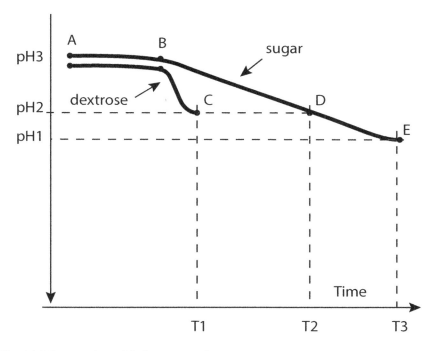

Fig. 14.1 Fermenting with dextrose and sugar.

Note: using dextrose *alone* wouldl create the fastest pH drop which might inhibit acidity sensitive *Staphylococcus xylosus* bacteria from developing flavors. Thus, adding a little dextrose jumps up the fermentation by allowing lactic bacteria to produce acidity faster. After a slight delay they start produce acidity from sugar, but at lower rate. Hence, adding a little dextrose jumps up the fermentation process by allowing lactic bacteria to produce acidity faster what creates a safety hurdle sooner.

Choosing Sausage Type

Choosing the sausage type determines fermentation and drying temperatures, total production time, amount and type of sugar used, type of starter cultures and other parameters. By now you should realize that *with one recipe you can make different types of fermented sausages* and it is entirely up to you which way you want to go. Forty years ago a hobbyist had only one choice and that was a slow-fermented sausage. Let's say you have a recipe for a fresh Italian sausage and you want to make a fermented sausage out of it. All you need is to increase the percentage of salt, add sodium nitrite, starter culture and decide whether you want to wait 3 months before it becomes a dry salami or whether you want to make a semi-dry meat stick that you you can take on a hunting trip next week.

Being familiar with different types of fermented sausages and understanding theory behind manufacturing them, can often save a product that failed to reach a planned value, by introducing a new processing step and creating a different type of the sausage. For example a semi-dry sausage that failed to reach the intended low pH for can be saved by additional drying or cooking. All ingredients remain the same, the flavor will not change either, only the texture will be different. The sausage type will change from non-heated semi-dry sausage to non-heated dry sausage or fully cooked fermented sausage. What started as a fermented spreadable sausage can easily be converted into a semi-dry sausage as long as the sausage is still in a processing stage.

Modifying Existing Sausage Recipes

The same sausage recipe can be used to produce a fresh, smoked or fermented sausage by changing parameters of manufacturing process. For example, the pepperoni recipe is presented in two forms: dry pepperoni and semi-dry pepperoni. The semi-dry pepperoni can be fermented and dried, fermented and cooked or acidified and cooked. There are hundreds of sausage recipes that can be turned into fermented sausages.

When the war ended and there was no refrigeration, all smoked sausages were hanging in Polish kitchens or pantries for weeks and months at the time and they only got drier and better. Given time they would have become shelf-stable dry sausages. Almost any sausage recipe can be converted to the fermented-cooked type by applying salt at $\geq 2.5\%$, adding sodium (Cure # 1), fermenting meat (with or without starter cultures) or acidifying with Gdl, and then cooking to a safe internal temperature of 160° F (72° C). Had the meat reached pH 4.8 or lower, the sausages would be stable at room temperature, otherwise they should be stored in a refrigerator. However, any smoked sausage that was made with 2.2% salt and 2.5 g/kg of Cure #1, which was smoked and cooked to 154° F (68° C) would become stable if stored at 50-53° F (10-12° C), 75% humidity. The sausage will keep on drying out becoming first a semi-dry and later dry sausage.

Guidelines for Creating Your Own Recipes

And why to create your own recipes? Because it will give you the great feeling knowing that you can:

- Design any type of the sausage recipe in spare of the moment *OR*
- Modifying any well known recipe the way you like.

Rule 1. Your recipes must always produce a safe to consume sausage.

Rule 2. Read Chapter 6 - Safety Hurdles. After that you can start designing recipes. If there are any questions or terms you have forgotten, look up the table of contents or the index and read the relevant material again.

Before we can do anything we need to know:

- The type of a sausage we want to produce.
- pH of the sausage mince.

Hold off sugar calculations until the initial pH of the meat is determined. Pork, beef, fat, skins, they all have a different pH and it is impossible to estimate pH of the sausage mass beforehand. Pork butts coming from different animals will have a different value. In some recipes such as Salami Milano wine is added which will increase acidity. Your pH can lie anywhere between 5.7 and 6.2 and adding 1% dextrose or 1% Gdl will drop it one full point to 4.7 and 5.2 respectively. If initial pH is 6.0 or higher, increase dosage of sugar or acidulant accordingly.

Once you know the pH of the mixed sausage mass, you can estimate the amount of dextrose that is needed. This decision will also depend on your starter culture and fermentation temperature. Decide how much acidity you are comfortable with. The taste of the sausage will be tangy if pH drops below 5.0. Check degree-hours tables (Chapter 6) to see whether the temperature and the duration of fermentation pass the requirements.

1. If acidulation alone is selected as the processing method, add powdered acidulant (Gdl) last and stuff the mixture into a casing without a delay. If using encapsulated acidulant such as Gdl or citric acid add it last be gentle when mixing.

2. Make a test sausage of the same diameter, the length can be shorter. You can check pH at the half point and at the end of fermentation. If you think pH is dropping too slow, raise the fermentation temperature by 5 degrees. Re-calculate tour degree-hours as now you are dealing with variable temperature fermentation.

3. Smoking (optional). Apply smoke after fermentation. It can count as the beginning of the cooking time. Avoid using liquid smoke with starter cultures.

4. Dry non-heated products *OR* use Option 1 (Chapter 6) to determine the temperature and the length of cooking for semi-dry products.

5. If you did not reach pH drop within desired time or have other issues save the sausage by cooking it fully to 160° F (72° C).

Grind Size

The size of the meat particles is determined by the grinder plate or the knife speed, bowl turns and duration of the process in a bowl cutter. The best answer is that is up to you, but keep in mind that larger meat particles facilitate faster removal of moisture which may be important when making dry salami. On the other hand a small meat particles will contribute to easier spreading of the sausage paste in spreadable sausages. Salami Milano and Salami Genoa are almost identical, the main difference is the particle size. The size of the particles in the sausage often determines the product type, in Germany, for instance, fermented dry sausages with large particles were named "Plockwurst", and those with small particles "Cervelatwurst"

Sugar

Although most reliable sources are in agreement that adding 0.1% (1 g/kg) of *dextrose* will result in 0.1 pH drop, thus adding 1% (10 g/kg) results in *approximate* decline of 1 pH unit, nevertheless, many sausage makers claim that less sugar is needed for dropping pH from its initial 5.7-5.8 value to pH 5.2-5.3. They claim that 0.3-0.4% (3-4 g) is all that is needed. This amount will be used for making traditional dry sausages. However, in semi-dry sausages, when the intent is to drop pH by the full point from 5.7-5.8 to 4.6-4.8, adding 1-1.2% (10-12 g) od dextrose works fine. The quantity of sugar added should be based on initial mix pH. At pH values above 6.0, a minimum of 1% would be suggested; at pH values of 5.8 or below, 0.75% would be sufficient.

Summary of Important Issues

- During all processing steps the sausage looses moisture, however, the salt remains inside. This proportionally increases the salt content and inhibits growth of bacteria.
- Both cures (#1 and #2) contain salt and this amount should be accounted for when calculating the total amount of salt in all recipes.
- Most recipes call for grinding pork with a 3/16" (3 mm) plate. If you own only 3/8" (10 mm) use this one instead, nothing will happen to the sausage.
- Minced particle size: dry sausages - coarse grind, semi-dry - medium coarse, spreadable - fine. Beef is usually ground with 1/8" (3 mm) plate.
- Dextrose (glucose) is used in semi-dry sausage recipes as fermentation times are very short and a fast pH drop is required.
- For non-heated dry sausages it is a good idea to use a combination of 1/3 dextrose and 2/3 common sugar. The reason is that dextrose being the simplest of sugars is easily metabolized by lactic acid bacteria and a small but moderately fast pH will be immediately obtained. This will provide an extra margin of safety which is very important during the first hours of the process.
- *It is easier and safer* to make fermented sausages when using small diameter casings as drying times will be much shorter.

- Cold smoking is drying with smoke and does not need to be continuous. Smoke can be applied for about one hour then the sausage "rests" for one hour. The cycle is repeated again and again.
- Spices like powdered paprika (pimentón) or garlic are rich in sugar and will contribute to stronger fermentation.
- As pH drops the texture of the sausage hardens and the removal of moisture is easier. This continues until the *isoelectric* point is reached at about pH 4.8 - 5.2. Below that point the moisture removal becomes harder again.

Recommended Equipment

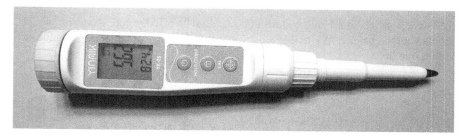

Photo 14.1 Yinmik YK 25 pH meter. pH meter is your eyes, it let you see what happens inside of the sausage. They are very inexpensive and quite reliable.

Photo 14.2 AWS Blade - 100 scale. Capacity 100 g, accuracy 0.01 g. A must scale for weighing cultures or small amount of spices. A quarter coin in lower right corner.

Photo 14.3 Humidity and temperature meter. Sensor probe goes inside of the chamber while display unit remains outside.

Many recipes are designed for 1 kg (2.2 lb) of meat. A new recipe can be tested with 1/2 lb of meat only. It is overkill to use a piston stuffer for such a small amount. Sometimes, it is easier to purchase packed ground meat in a store, then mix it with ingredients and fill into casing with a jerky gun. Remove air bubbles with a pricker. A small semi-dry sausage can enter fermenting chamber within one hour.

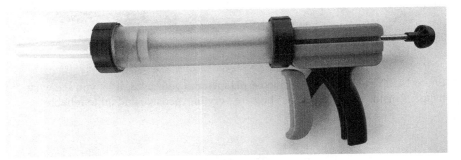

Photo 14.4 - 14.5 Weston brand jerky gun, capacity 2 pounds. The unit is easy to use, disassemble, clean and can be stored in a drawer.

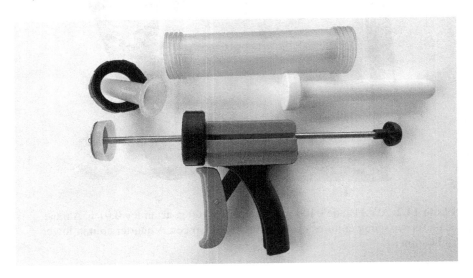

Fermented Sausages
Recipe Index
(264 Recipes)

Sausages awarded *European Certificate of Origin* are marked with *PGI* or *PDO* symbol. Those recipes often include meats and ingredients which are hard to find as they are grown locally, thus substitute them using your own judgement.

Name	Type	Country	Page
Aalrauchmettwurst	dry, smoked	Germany	216
Alheira de Barroso-Montalegre, PGI	dry, smoked	Portugal	216
Alheira de Vinhais, PGI	dry, smoked	Portugal	217
Androlla Gallega	dry, smoked	Spain	217
Androlla Maragata	dry, smoked	Spain	218
Baiona Curada	dry	Spain	218
Banski Staretz	dry	Bulgaria	219
Baranjski Kulen, PGI	dry, smoked	Croatia	219
Bauernbratwurst	dry, smoked	Germany	220
Belutak	dry	Brunei	220
Berliner Knacker	dry, smoked	Germany	221
Bispo	semi-dry	Spain	222
Boerenmetworst	dry, smoked	Holland	222
Botagueña	dry, smoked	Spain	223
Botelo or Butelo Gallego	dry, smoked	Spain	223
Botillo del Bierzo, PGI	semi-dry, smoked	Spain	224
Botillo de León	semi-dry, smoked	Spain	224
Braunschweiger	dry, smoked	Russia	225
Braunschweiger Mettwurst	spreadable, smoked	Germany	225
Buche de Costillas (Badajoz)	dry	Spain	226
Budapesti Téliszálami, PGI	dry, smoked	Hungary	226
Butelo de Vinhais, PGI	dry, smoked	Portugal	227
Butifarra Dulce Curada	semi-dry	Spain	227
Bydgoska	semi-dry, smoked	Poland	228
Cacciatore	dry	Italy	228
Calabresa	semi-dry, smoked	Brazil	229
Cervelat	semi-dry, smoked	European	229
Cervelat - Traditional	dry, smoked	USA	230
Cervelatwurst	dry, smoked	German	230
Chanfaino	dry, smoked	Spain	231
Chicken Fermented Sausage	dry, smoked	General	231

Chistorra or Txistorra - Traditional	dry	Spain	232
Chistorra with Culture	dry	Spain	232
Chorizo Andaluz	dry	Spain	233
Chorizo Asturiano	dry, smoked	Spain	233
Chorizo Candelario	dry	Spain	234
Chorizo Cantabro (Guriezo)	dry, smoked	Spain	234
Chorizo Cular (Salamanca)	dry	Spain	235
Chorizo de Aragón	semi-dry	Spain	235
Chorizo de Bilbao	semi-dry	Philippines	236
Chorizo de Bofe (Lungs Sausage)	dry	Spain	236
Chorizo de Calabaza (Pumpkin Sausage)	dry	Spain	237
Chorizo de Cantimpalo, PGI	dry	Spain	237
Chorizo de Cebolla (Onions Sausage)	dry, smoked	Spain	238
Chorizo de Cerdo	dry	Spain	239
Chorizo de la Sierra de Aracena	dry, smoked	Spain	239
Chorizo de León	dry, smoked	Spain	240
Chorizo de Mezcla	dry, smoked	Spain	240
Chorizo de Pamplona	dry, smoked	Spain	241
Chorizo de Potes	dry, smoked	Spain	241
Chorizo de Soria	dry	Spain	242
Chorizo de Villarcayo	dry	Spain	242
Chorizo Extremeño	dry	Spain	243
Chorizo Gallego	dry, smoked	Spain	243
Chorizo Ibérico de Huelva	dry	Spain	244
Chorizo Patatero de Monroy (with potatoes)	dry	Spain	244
Chorizo Patatero Rojo (with potatoes & blood)	dry	Spain	245
Chorizo Quzande de Bandeira	dry, smoked	Spain	245
Chorizo Riojano	dry	Spain	246
Chorizo-Spanish	dry	Spain	246
Chorizo Traditional	dry	Spain	247
Chorizo Zamorano	dry	Spain	247
Chosco de Tineo	dry	Spain	248
Chosco or Choscu	dry	Spain	248
Chouriça de Carne de Barroso-Montalegre, PGI	semi-dry, smoked	Portugal	249
Chouriça de Carne de Melgaço, PGI	dry, smoked	Portugal	249
Chouriça de Carne de Vinhais, PGI	dry, smoked	Portugal	250
Chouriça Doce de Vinhais	dry, smoked	Portugal	250
Chouriço	dry, smoked	Portugal	251
Chouriço Azedo de Vinhais	dry, smoked	Portugal	251
Chouriço de Abóbora de Barroso-Montalegre, PGI	dry, smoked	Portugal	252
Chouriço de Carne de Estremoz e Borba, PGI	dry, smoked	Portugal	252

Chouriço de Portalegre, PGI	dry, smoked	Portugal	253
Chouriço Mouro de Portalegre, PGI	dry, smoked	Portugal	253
Ciauscolo, PGI	spreadable, smoked	Italy	254
Csabai Kolbasz, PGI	dry, smoked	Hungary	254
Delicatessen Sausage	semi-dry, smoked	Poland	255
Deutsche Salami	dry, smoked	Germany	255
Dongguan	semi-dry	China	256
Droë Wors	dry	South Africa	256
Dürre Runde	dry, smoked	Germany	257
Eichsfelder Feldgieker, PGI	dry	Germany	257
El Xolis	dry	Spain	258
Farinato (no meat)	dry, smoked	Spain	259
Farinheira de Estremoz e Borba, PGI	semi-dry	Portugal	259
Farinheira de Portalegre, PG	semi-dry, smoked	Portugal	260
Farmer Sausage (Wiejska)	dry, smoked	Poland	261
Feldkieker (Feldgicker), PGI	semi-dry, smoked	Germany	262
Figatelli	dry, smoked	France	262
Frankfurter	semi-dry, smoked	Poland	263
Fuet	dry	Spain	263
Fuet de Barcelona	dry	Spain	264
Geräucherte Bratwurst	spreadable, smoked	Germany	264
Goan Sausage	dry	India-Goa	265
Goin Chong	semi-dry	China	265
Gornooryahovski Sudzhuk, PGI	dry	Bulgaria	266
Goteborg	dry, smoked	Sweden	266
Gothaer	semi-dry, smoked	Germany	267
Göttinger Feldkieker, PGI	dry	Germany	267
Göttinger Stracke, PGI	dry	Germany	268
Grassland (Kresowa)	dry, smoked	Poland	268
Greußener Salami, PGI	dry, smoked	Germany	269
Güeña	semi-dry	Spain	269
Gyulai Kolbász, PGI	dry, smoked	Hungary	270
Haussalami	dry	Germany	270
Hofer Rindfleischwurst	spreadable, smoked	Germany	271
Holsteiner	dry, smoked	Germany	272
Holsteiner-American	semi-dry, smoked	USA	272
Hungarian Dry Sausage	dry, smoked	Poland	273
Hungarian Smoked Sausage	dry, smoked	Poland	273
Imperial de Bolaños	dry	Spain	274
Imperial de Lorca	dry	Spain	274
Isterband	semi-dry, smoked	Sweden	275

Jauntauler Salami	dry, smoked	Germany	275
Jesus	dry	France	276
Kaminwurz	dry, smoked	Austria	276
Kantwurst	dry, smoked	Austria	277
Katenrauchwurst	dry, smoked	Germany	277
Kindziuk	dry, smoked	Poland	278
Kohlwurst	dry, smoked	Germany	278
Kohlwurst - Lippsche	dry, smoked	Germany	279
Kümmelwurst-Roh	dry, smoked	Germany	279
Lamb Sausage	dry, smoked	Russia	280
Landjager	dry, smoked	Germany	280
Lap Cheong	dry, smoked	China	281
Lebanon Bologna	semi-dry, smoked	USA	281
Lebanon Bologna-Traditional	semi-dry, smoked	USA	282
Linguíça do Baixo Alentejo, PGI	semi-dry, smoked	Portugal	282
Linguiça de Portalegre, PGI	semi-dry, smoked	Portugal	283
Lithuanian Dry Sausage	dry, smoked	Lithuania	284
Llangonisa Rotja - Alicantina	dry	Spain	285
Lomo Embuchado (Dry Whole Loin)	dry	Spain	285
Lomo Embuchado de Segovia	dry	Spain	286
Lomo Picado (Dry Formed Loin)	dry	Spain	286
Longaniza	dry	Spain	287
Longaniza Andaluza	dry	Spain	287
Longaniza de Aragón	semi-dry	Spain	288
Longaniza de Mezcla	semi-dry	Spain	288
Longaniza de Pascua	dry	Spain	289
Longaniza de Payés	dry	Spain	289
Longaniza Dominicana	semi-dry	Dominican Republic	290
Longaniza Navarra	semi-dry	Spain	290
Longaniza Traditional	dry	Spain	291
Loukaniko Pitsilias, PGI	semi-dry	Cyprus	291
Lucanica di Picerno, PGI	dry	Italy	292
Luftgetrocknete Mettwurst	dry	Germany	292
Lukanka	dry	Bulgaria	293
Medwurst	semi-dry, smoked	Sweden	293
Merguez	semi-dry	North Africa	294
Metka	spreadable, smoked	Poland	295
Metka Brunszwicka	spreadable, smoked	Poland	295
Metka Pomorska	spreadable, smoked	Poland	296
Metka Salmon Style	spreadable, smoked	Poland	296

Meetvursti	dry	Finland	297
Metworst	dry	Netherlands	297
Mettwurst - Braunschweiger-Schnittfeste	dry, smoked	Germany	298
Mettwurst - Streichfähige	spreadable, smoked	Germany	298
Morcón Andaluz	dry	Spain	299
Morcón Gaditano	dry	Spain	299
Morrpølse	dry, smoked	Norway	300
Mortadella-Dry	dry	Italy	300
Moscow Dry-Sausage	dry, smoked	Russia	301
Moscow Semi-Dry Sausage	semi-dry, smoked	Russia	301
Nduja	spreadable, smoked	Italy	302
Neva Sausage	dry, smoked	Russia	303
Nham	semi-dry	Thailand	303
Ossenworst	spreadable, smoked	Holland	304
Paio de Beja, PGI	semi-dry, smoked	Portugal	305
Painho de Portalegre, PGI	semi-dry, smoked	Portugal	306
Pafitiko Loukaniko, PGI	dry	Cyprus	307
Patatera Extremeña	dry	Spain	307
Pepperoni-Dry	dry. smoked	Italy	308
Pepperoni-Semi-Dry	semi-dry, smoked	Italy	308
Petrohan	dry, smoked	Bulgaria	309
Plockwurst	dry, smoked	Germany	309
Polish Dry Sausage-Russian Style	dry, smoked	Poland	310
Polish Sausage-Cold Smoked	semi-dry, smoked	Poland	310
Rheinische Mettwurst	spreadable, smoked	Germany	311
Rosette de Lyon	dry	France	311
Russian Sausage	dry, smoked	Russia	312
Sabadiego or Sabadeña	dry	Spain	312
Sächsische Mettwurst	spreadable, smoked	Germany	313
Sai Krok Isan	dry	Thailand	314
Salama da Sugo	dry	Italy	314
Salam de Sibiu, PGI	dry, smoked	Romania	315
Salame Brianza, PDO	dry	Italy	316
Salame Cremona, PGI	dry	Italy	316
Salame di Fabriano	dry	Italy	317
Salame di Varzi, PDO	dry	Italy	317
Salame Piacentino, PDO	dry	Italy	318
Salame S. Angelo, PGI	dry	Italy	318
Salametti	dry	Germany	319
Salami-All Beef	dry	USA	319
Salami Calabrese	dry	Italy	320

Salami de Arles	dry	France	320
Salami de Verona	dry	Italy	321
Salami Felino, PGI	dry	Italy	321
Salami Finocchiona, PGI	dry	Italy	322
Salami Genoa	dry	Italy	322
Salami - German	dry, smoked	Germany	323
Salami-Hungarian	dry	Hungary	323
Salami-Hungarian-Traditional	dry	Hungary	324
Salami-Kosher	dry, smoked	USA	324
Salami Lombardia	dry	Italy	325
Salami - Mailänder	dry, smoked	Germany	325
Salami Milano	dry	Italy	326
Salamini italiani alla cacciatora, PDO	dry	Italy	326
Salami Nola	dry, smoked	Italy	327
Salami Piemonte, PGI	dry	Italy	327
Salami-Polish	dry, smoked	Poland	328
Salami-Polish-Traditional	dry, smoked	Poland	328
Salami-Russian	dry, smoked	Russia	329
Salami Sorrento	dry	Italy	329
Salami - Spanish	dry	Spain	330
Salchicha de Zaratan	semi-dry	Spain	330
Salchichón	dry	Spain	331
Salchichón de Vic-Llonganissa de Vic, PGI	dry	Spain	331
Salchichón Gallego	dry	Spain	332
Salmon Sausage	semi-dry, smoked	Poland	332
Salpicão de Vinhais, PGI	dry	Portugal	333
Salsiccia di Calabria, PDO	dry	Italy	333
Salsiccia Sarda	dry, smoked	Italy	334
Saucisson au Camembert	dry	France	334
Saucisson aux Noisettes	dry	France	335
Saucisson aux Noix	dry	France	335
Saucisson d'Alsace	dry	France	336
Saucisson d'Ardenne, PGI	dry	France	336
Saucisson de Lacaune	dry	France	337
Saucisson de L'Ardéche, PGI	dry	France	337
Saucisson sec au Beaufort	dry	France	338
Saucisson sec d'Auvergne, PGI	dry	France	338
Schlackwurst	dry, smoked	Germany	339
Schmierwurst	spreadable, smoked	Germany	340
Sebreljski Želodec, PGI	dry	Slovenia	340
Secallona-Somalla-Petador-Espetec	semi-dry	Spain	341

Servolatka	spreadable, smoked	Poland	341
Skilandis	dry, smoked	Lithuania	342
Slavonski Kulen, PGI	dry, smoked	Croatia	342
Snijworst	dry	Holland	343
Sobrasada	dry	Spain	343
Sobrasada de Mallorca, PGI	spreadable	Spain	344
Sobrasada de Mallorca de Cerdo Negro, PGI	spreadable	Spain	344
Sobrasada Picante Casera	dry	Spain	345
Sobrasada Valenciana	dry	Spain	345
Soppressata	dry	Italy	346
Sopressata di Calabria, PDO	dry	Italy	346
Soprèssa Vicentina, PDO	dry	Italy	347
Soviet	dry	Russia	347
Stolichnaya	dry, smoked	Russia	348
Sucuk	semi-dry	Turkey	348
Sucuk-Traditional	dry	Turkey	349
Summer Sausage	semi-dry	USA	349
Szegedi Szalámi, PDO	dry, smoked	Hungary	350
Tambov	dry, smoked	Russia	350
Teewurst	spreadable, smoked	Germany	351
Teewurst Rugenwalder Art	spreadable, smoked	Germany	351
Thuringer	semi-dry, smoked	Germany	352
Touristenwurst	dry, smoked	Germany	352
Tourist Sausage-Russian-Dry	dry, smoked	Russia	353
Urutan	dry	Indonesia	353
Venison Salami	dry, smoked	USA	354
Westfälische Mettwurst	spreadable, smoked	Germany	354
Zervelatwurst	dry, smoked	Germany	355
Zgornjesavinjski Želodec, PGI	dry	Slovenia	355

Note: to simplify sausage recipes, they are standardized on Charles-Hansen starter cultures, first introduced to American hobbyists almost 20 years ago. Since then, Chr-Hansen created more cultures bearing new names; however, they still include the same strains of bacteria. Chapter 4 lists all the latest cultures. For example, F-LC culture for acidification, color and flavor formation, and prevention of *Listeria* included three bacteria strains: *Lactobacillus curvatus, Pediococcus acililactici,* and *Staphylococcus xylosus.*

The latest cultures for *Listeria* control, such as SafePro® B-LC-007 and SafePro® Flora Italia LC, contain different bacteria strains, even yeasts, but the former and the latest cultures will perform equally well. It may be harder to obtain the latest types as online distributors have grown accustomed to storing the previous cultures.

Aalrauchmettwurst
(Eel Smoked Mettwurst Sausage)

Aalrauchmettwurst is a fermented sliceable sausage that is listed (2.211.12) in the German government publication Guide to Meats and Meat Products - Leitsätze für Fleisch und Fleischerzeugnisse. This medium-grind, heavily smoked mettwurst sausage is made of fatty pork or pork with some beef. The word "aal" signifies "eel" in German. However, no eel (fish) is added. The sausage derives its name from the fact that it was smoked with eels together over beech wood. The sausage usually has a slender, elongated shape of an eel. Manufacturers often paint the facial features of an eel in white, which is printed on the black sausage casing.

Lean pork	600 g	1.32 lb
Back fat or		
hard fat trimmings	250 g	0.55 lb
Beef	150 g	0.33 lb

Ingredients per 1 kg (2.2 lb) of meat

Salt	28 g	4.5 tsp
Cure #2	2.5 g	1/2 tsp
Dextrose	2.0 g	1/2 tsp
Sugar	2.0 g	1/2 tsp
Pepper, ground	2.0 g	1 tsp
Paprika	0.5 g	1/4 tsp
Cumin	0.5 g	1/4 tsp
Mustard seeds, ground	0.5 g	1/4 tsp
T-SPX culture	0.12 g	use
scale		

Grind pork through 6 mm (1/4") plate.
Dice partially frozen fat into 6 mm (1/4") cubes.
Grind beef through 3 mm (1/8") plate.
Mix pork, beef, salt, cure #1 and starter culture together. Add remaining ingredients, diced fat and mix again.
Stuff into 36 mm pork casings forming 40 cm (16") links.
Ferment at 20° C (68° F), 90 → 80% humidity for 72 hours.
Cold smoke at 18° C (64° F) for 24 hours.
Dry at 15→12° C (58 →53° F), 80-75% humidity for 3 weeks - until the sausage looses 33% of its original weight.
Store at 10-12° C (50-53° F), <75% humidity.

Notes
Eat cold as a snack or with bread. Mustard, horseradish or cucumber pickle go well with it.
Beef is added at 15-20%.

Alheira de Barroso-Montalegre

A Portuguese smoked sausage made in the municipality of Montalegre, in the Vila Real district.

Pork	500 g	1.10 lb
Pork fat	200 g	0.44 lb
Poultry meat (chicken, turkey, duck) or rabbit	200 g	0.44 lb
Wheat bread	100 g	0.22 lb

Ingredients per 1 kg (2.2 lb) of material

Salt	28 g	5 tsp
Cure #1	2.5 g	1/2 tsp
Pepper	2.0 g	1 tsp
Sweet paprika	4.0 g	2 tsp
Freash parsley, chopped	4.0 g	1 Tbsp
Onion	50 g	1/2
Olive oil	30 ml	1 oz fl

Chop meat and fat into pieces suitable for cooking. Place meat and fat in a pot, add some salt and cover with water. Occasionally soup greens are added for better flavor. Simmer the meat until soft; fat needs less cooking time. Drain meats but save the meat stock.
Spread the meat on the table and separate meat from bones when the meat is still warm.
Break up or cut up white bread (the crust can be left on) and soak in the hot meat stock for 60 minutes. Drain and squeeze the excess stock out.
Chop the onion and fry in a little fat until glassy.
Mix shredded (chopped) meat and fat with bread, onions, chopped parsley, salt and spices. Stuff into 32 mm hog casings.
Using oak wood apply a thin smoke at 18° C (64° F) for 3-4 days.
Dry at 12-15° C (54-59° F), 75% humidity for 4 days.
Store at 12° C (54° F), 70% humidity or refrigerate.

Note: Alheira de Barroso-Montalegre carries PGI 2007 classification.

Alheira de Vinhais

Portuguese smoked sausage, made from the meat of pigs of the Bisaro breed or of cross-breeds that must be 50 % Bisaro.

Pork meat: head, belly, shoulder, meat trimmings	800 g	1.76 lb
Wheat bread	200 g	0.44 lb
Poultry meat - for making stock only.		

Ingredients per 1 kg (2.2 lb) of material

Salt	28 g	5 tsp
Cure #1	2.5 g	1/2 tsp
Pepper	2.0 g	1 tsp
Sweet paprika	4.0 g	2 tsp
Garlic, minced	4.0 g	1 clove
Olive oil	30 ml	2 Tbsp

Chop meat into sizes suitable for cooking. Place all meats in a pot, add some salt and cover with water. Occasionally soup greens are added for better flavor. Simmer the meat until soft. Drain meats but save the meat stock. Spread the meat on the table and separate meat from bones when the meat is still warm. Poultry meat is not used for making the sausage.

Break up or cut up white bread (the crust can be left on) and soak in the hot meat stock for 60 minutes. Drain and squeeze the excess stock out.

Mix shredded (chopped) meat with bread, salt, oil and spices.

Stuff into 28 mm hog casings forming rings about 12" (30 cm) long.

Using oak wood apply a thin smoke at 18° C (64° F) for 3-4 days.

Hold at 12-15° C (54-59° F), 75% humidity for 4 days.

Store at 12° C (54° F), 70% humidity or refrigerate.

Note: Alheira de Vinhais carries PGI 2008 classification.

Androlla Gallega

Androlla Gallega is a popular semi-dry sausage in Lugo and Qurense (Viana do Bolo) province situated in the Galicia region of Spain. Galician Androlla includes rib bones; however, in Androlla Maragata, the bones are removed. Maragatería is a historic region in León, Spain.

Pork spare ribs with attached meat	900 g	1.98 lb
Pork skins	100 g	0.22 lb

Ingredients per 1 kg (2.2 lb) of meat

Salt	24 g	4 tsp
Cure #2	2.5 g	1/2 tsp
Pimentón, sweet	25 g	4 Tbsp
Pimentón, hot	3.0 g	1 tsp
Garlic	7.0 g	2 cloves
Oregano, ground	2.0	1 tsp
White dry wine	60 ml	2 oz fl

Chop ribs into 2 cm (3/4") long pieces. The bones are not removed. Cut skins into smaller strips. Mix wine, salt, cure #2 and spices together. Add ribs and skins and mix all together. Place in refrigerator for 48 hours. Stuff firmly into 50 mm natural casing. Make links 20 cm (8") long. Smoke/dry for 8-10 days by hanging sausages above the kitchen stove. Move the sausages to a different area of the kitchen and dry them for 1-2 months.*

Notes: Androlla is always cooked in water before consumption. It is usually served with boiled potatoes and turnip greens, known in the UK as *rapini* and in the US as *broccoli raab or broccoli rabe.* Pieces of rib bones are easy to spot and separate from meat easily. The sausage exhibits an intense red color. The texture is rather loose and varied, unlike the one in dry, smoked or emulsified sausages. The average weight of the sausage is about 1/2 kg (1 lb). The flavor of the sausage is strongly influenced by the quality of the meat that comes from locally grown and free-roaming "celta" pigs.

* traditional method of smoking known as "la campana de Lareira." Today, the process will be shorter: apply a thin smoke at 18° C (64° F) for 10 hours. Dry at 12-15° C (53-59° F) for 30-40 days. Store at 10-12° C (50-53° F), <70% humidity or refrigerate.

Androlla Maragata

Androlla Maragata is a popular sausage in the communities of el Bierzo and la Maragatería in Castilla y León region of Spain. The sausage is similar to Galician Androlla as both sausages are made with pork ribs, however, in Androlla Maragata *the bones are removed and only the meat is processed.* Due to the high content of connective tissue (ribs, skins and jowls) the sausage contains a lot of collagen which gels upon heating and provides the pleasant experience upon eating.

Jowls	500 g	1.10 lb
Spare rib meat (no bones)	400 g	0.88 lb
Back fat, skins	100 g	0.22 lb

Ingredients per 1 kg (2.2 lb) of meat

Salt	24 g	4 tsp
Cure #2	2.5 g	1/2 tsp
Pimentón, sweet	25 g	4 Tbsp
Pimentón, hot	3.0 g	1 tsp
Oregano, rubbed	2.0 g	3 tsp
White dry wine	60 ml	2 oz fl

Cut rib meat and jowls into 20 mm (3/4") pieces. Cut skins into smaller strips.
Mix salt, cure #2, spices, meat and skins together. Place in refrigerator for 48 hours.
Stuff firmly into a 50 mm casing. Make links 20 cm (8") long. Smoke/dry for 8-10 days by hanging sausages above the kitchen stove.
Move the sausages to a different area of the kitchen and dry them for 1-2 months.*

Notes
Androlla is always slow cooked in water before consumption. Add soup greens to water for best results. It is usually served with boiled potatoes and turnip greens, known in UK as *rapini* and in US as *broccoli raab or broccoli rabe.*
The sausage exhibits an intense red color.
The average weight of the sausage is about ½ kg (1 pound).

* traditional method of smoking known as "la campana de Lareira."

Today, the process will be shorter: apply a thin smoke at 18° C (64° F) for 24 hrs.
Dry at 12-15° C (53-59° F) for 30-40 days.
Store at 10-12° C (50-53° F), <70% humidity or refrigerate.

Baiona Curada

Baiona curada, also known as little ham (*jamoncito*) is made with boneless pork butt (*paletilla*) which is the upper part of a shoulder. It is somewhat similar to lomo embuchado in that both products are made from whole cut of meat, stuffed in casings and dried. Baiona is most popular in the Spanish Basque country.

Pork butt, boneless 2-3 kg   4.4-6.6 lb

Ingredients per 1 kg (2.2 lb) of meat

Coarse salt for salting loin, *as needed.*

Cure #2	5.0 g	1 tsp
Pepper	2.0 g	1 tsp
Sugar	3.0 g	1/2 tsp
Oregano, ground	2.0 g	1 tsp
Cumin, ground	1.0 g	1/2 tsp
White wine or vinegar	30 ml	2 Tbsp

Trim off the skin from the butt. Using force rub in a generous amount of coarse salt (as needed) all over butt. The butt should rest in a suitable container on a layer of salt and be well covered with salt all around leaving no exposed areas.
Hold in refrigerator for 24 hours.
Brush off the salt, wash briefly in running water and pat dry with paper towels.
Mix all ingredients with wine to form the marinade paste. Remainder: *multiply the above ingredients per weight of butt.* No more salt is needed.
Apply the paste all around the butt. Hold in refrigerator for 48 hours.
Stuff the butt into pork bungs that will tightly accommodate the piece.
Ferment/dry at 22-24° C (72-75° F), 85-90% humidity, for 2 days.
Dry at 15 → 12° C (59 → 53° F), 85 → 75% humidity for 2 months. The butt should lose about 35% of its original weight.
Store at 10-12° C (°F), <75% humidity.

Banski Staretz

Banski Starets is a Bulgarian slow-fermented dry sausage having origin in the town of Bansko, Bulgaria's largest and number-one ski resort.

Pork, lean	800 g	1.76 lb
Back fat	200 g	0.44 lb

Ingredients per 1 kg (2.2 lb) of meat

Salt	28 g	4.5 tsp
Cure #2	2.5 g	1/2 tsp
Dextrose	2.0 g	1/2 tsp
Sugar	3.0 g	1/2 tsp
Black pepper	2.0 g	1 tsp
Paprika, sweet	2.0 g	1 tsp
Cumin	2.0 g	1 tsp
Garlic	3.0 g	1 clove
T-SPX culture	0.12 g	use scale

Grind lean pork through 8 mm (5/16") plate. Grind partially frozen fat through 8 mm (5/16") plate.
30 minutes before mixing dissolve starter culture in 15 ml (1 tablespoon) de-chlorinated water.
Mix lean pork with salt and Cure #2. Add spices and wine. Lastly, add culture, ground fat and mix all together.
Stuff tightly into 60 mm pork or beef casings.
Ferment at 20° C (68° F) for 72 hours, 90 → 85% humidity. Flatten with weight and wooden planks to develop a characteristic for this sausage shape.
Dry at 15→12° C (59→53° F), 80-75% humidity for 6 weeks.
Dry at 10-12° C (50°-55 F), 75% humidity for 10 weeks.
Store at 10-12° C (50°-55 F), 75% humidity.

Baranjski Kulen

The "Baranja kulen" is a large fermented dry sausage produced in the Baranja in the northeastern part of Croatia.

Lean pork (legs, loin)	800 g	1.76 lb
Semi-fat pork (shoulder)	200 g	0.44 lb

Ingredients per 1 kg (2.2 lb) of meat

Salt	28 g	5 tsp
Cure #2	5.0 g	1 tsp
Dextrose	2.0 g	1/2 tsp
Sugar	2.0 g	1/2 tsp
Paprika, sweet	5.0 g	2 tsp
Paprika, hot	5.0 g	2 tsp
Garlic	7.0 g	2 cloves
Red wine	15 ml	1 oz fl
T-SPX culture	0.12 g	use scale

Grind meat through 8 mm (5/16") plate.
30 minutes before mixing dissolve starter culture in 1 tablespoon de-chlorinated water.
Mix lean pork with salt and Cure #2. Add spices and wine. Lastly, add culture and mix all together.
Stuff tightly into pork caecum (blind cap), bung or bladder.
Ferment at 20° C (68° F) for 72 hours, 90-85% humidity.
Apply a thin cold smoke at 18° C (64° F) for 2-3 weeks using oak, beech or a mixture of both. Maintain high humidity. Smoking does not have to be continuous as long as a low temperature is maintained. Cold smoking is drying with smoke.
Dry at 15 →12° C (59 → 53° F), 80-75% humidity for 6 weeks.
Dry at 10-12° C (50°-55 F), 75% humidity for 10 weeks.
Store at 10-12° C (50°-55 F), 75% humidity.

Notes
Baranjski Kulen carries PGI 2015 classification.

Bauernbratwurst
(Farmers Dry Bratwurst)

Bauernbratwurst is listed (2.211.17) in the German government publication Guide to Meats and Meat Products - *Leitsätze für Fleisch und Fleischerzeugnisse.* Bauer means "farmer" and there are a number of sausages that carry this prefix: *Bauernbratwurst, Bauerleberwurst, Bauerwurst.*

Lean pork without sinews and connective tissue	200 g	0.44 lb
Pork belly (about 30% visible fat), no skin	650 g	1.43 lb
Semi-fat beef, connective tissue allowed	150 g	0.33 lb

Ingredients per 1 kg (2.2 lb) of material

Salt	24 g	4 tsp
Cure #1	2.5 g	1/2 tsp
Dextrose	2.0 g	1/2 tsp
Sugar	2.0 g	1/2 tsp
Pepper	3.0 g	1.5 tsp
Paprika	1.0 g	1/2 tsp
Caraway , ground	0.5 g	1/2 tsp
Cumin, ground	0.5 g	1/2 tsp
Garlic, diced	3.0 g	1 clove
T-SPX culture	0.12 g	use
scale		

Grind beef through 3 mm (1/8") plate and mix with starter culture.
Grind pork through 6 mm (1/4") plate. Mix with all ingredients.
Grind partially frozen pork belly through 6 mm (1/4") plate.
Mix all meats and ingredients together.
Stuff into 28-32 mm pork casings, forming 15 cm (6") links.
Ferment at 20° C (68° F) for 3 days, 95 → 85% humidity.
Cold smoke at 18° C (64° F) for 12 hours.
Dry at 15 → 12° C (58 → 53° F), 80-75% humidity for 3 weeks - until sausage looses 33% of its original weight.
Store at 10-12° C (50-53° F), <75% humidity.

Belutak

Belutak is a fermented meat product made in a tiny nation on the island of Borneo, surrounded by Malaysia, Vietnam, and the Philippines. The sausage was originally produced by the water village people of Kampung Ayer, who lived on stilt houses on the Brunei River, which flows to Brunei Bay and the South China Sea. The original inhabitants were fishermen whose diet consisted mainly of seafood and rice, and the popular animal was a large water buffalo, which spent most of their time in water grazing on aquatic plants. Every part of buffalo was eaten or made into other products.

Belutak is a salty, slightly acidic, and chewy sausage that is made of meat trimmings with a mixture of salt, sugar, chilies, garlic, and spices. The salt is applied in a large amount as it must inhibit the growth of spoilage and pathogenic bacteria in the first stage of production. Naturally present in meat, lactic acid-producing bacteria start breaking sugar-producing lactic acid that immediately creates acidity, which further inhibits the growth of undesirable bacteria types. Chillies and garlic also contain sugar and contribute to a better fermentation.

After fermenting for 24 hours at a high ambient temperature of 28-30° C (82-86° F) and humidity, the sausage was submitted to at least 5 days of sun drying. The sun-dried product had a shelf life of about 3 months at 30° C (86° F). (Abu Bakar 2000), so it is no surprise that it was a popular product among locals who did not have access to refrigeration. Due to its high salty taste, Belutak is usually eaten with rice and vegetables. The sausage is thickly sliced, fried with chilies and onions, and served with rice.

Belutak - **Traditional** recipe:

Buffalo meat trimmings: lean and fat	1000 g	2.2 lb

Ingredients per 1 kg (2.2 lb) of meat

Salt	33 g	5.5 tsp
Sugar	24 g	6 tsp
Garlic	15 g	5 cloves
Chopped chillies	15 g	0.5 oz

Chop or grind meat and fat into 10 mm (3/8")
pieces. Chop very fine or grind through 3 mm
(1/8") any connective tissue.
Finely chop garlic and chillies.
Mix chopped meat and fat with salt, garlic,
chilliest and sugar. Stuff into small intestines of
buffalo or cow.
Ferment for 24 hours at 28-30° C (82-86° F),
high humidity.
Sun-dry for at least 5 days.

Belutak - Modern recipe

Beef, lean	700 g	1.54 lb
Beef brisket	300 g	0.66 lb

Ingredients per 1 kg (2.2 lb) of meat

Salt	28 g	4.5 tsp
Cure #2*	2.5 g	1/2 tsp
Dextrose	2.0 g	1/2 tsp
Sugar	3.0 g	1.2 tsp
Garlic	12 g	3 cloves
Chopped chillies	10 g	0.3 oz
F-LC culture**	0.25 g	use
scale		

Grind all beef through 6 mm (1/4").
Chop finely chillies and garlic. Dilute culture in
30 ml (2 tsp) of distilled water.
Mix ground beef with salt, Cure #1, all
ingredients and starter culture.
Stuff into 40 mm beef rounds.
Ferment at 28° C (82° F) for 48 hours, 90-85%
humidity.
Dry for 1 day at 18° C (63° F), 85% humidity
Dry for 1 month at 16→12° C (60→54° F), 85-
75% humidity.
Store sausages at 10-15° C (50-59° F), 75%
humidity.

Notes:
Belutak is a common side dish alongside
ambuyat, the national dish of Brunei. Ambuyat
is a dish made from the solids of interior trunk
of the sago palm.
* Cure #2 is recommended for safety.
** Culture is recommended for reliable and
stronger fermentation.

Berliner Knacker
(Berlin Knacker)

Berliner Knacker,   also known as Berliner
Knackwurst is listed (2.211.17) in the German
government publication Guide to Meats and
Meat Products-*Leitsätze für Fleisch und
Fleischerzeugnisse.* The name supposedly was
invented in the 16th century after the crackling
noise when chewing the sausage. This recipe
is for fermented sliceable knacker, however,
they are many knackers that belong to boiled
sausages (*Brühwurst*) group.

Lean pork, no connective tissue	300 g	0.66 lb
Pork belly (max 50% visible fat)	500 g	1.10 lb
Beef, little fat, some connective tissue ...	200 g	0.44 lb

Ingredients per 1 kg (2.2 lb) of material

Salt	22 g	3.5 tsp
Cure #2	2.5 g	1/2 tsp
Dextrose	2.0 g	1/2 tsp
White pepper	2.0 g	1 tsp
Mustard seed, ground	1.0 g	1/2 tsp
T-SPX culture	0.12 g	use
scale		

Grind beef through 3 mm (1/8") plate.
Grind pork through 6 mm (1/4") plate.
Grind pork belly through 6 mm (1/4") plate.
Mix all meats with ingredients together.
Stuff into 32 mm pork casings.
Hold at 18-20° C (64-68° F), 90-85% humidity
for 96 hours.
Smoke at 18° C (64° F) for 24 hours.
Dry at 15 → 12° C (58 → 53° F), 80-75%
humidity for 3 weeks - until the sausage looses
33% of its original weight.
Store at 10-12° C (50-53° F), <75% humidity.

Bispo

Bisbo is a large cooked sausage popular in Pyrenees valleys of Aragón in northeastern Spain. It is made from pork head meat, pork mask (face), including the tongue and cuts of lean pork. Meats are ground, mixed with spices, stuffed in pork blind cap (caecum) and dried.

Pork head meat, tails, tongue, ribs with attached meat	1000 g	2.2 lb

Ingredients per 1 kg (2.2 lb) of meat

Salt	30 g	5 tsp
Cure #1	2.5 g	1/2 tsp
Pimentón, sweet	25 g	4 Tbsp
Pimentón, hot	2.0 g	1 tsp
Oregano, ground	1.0 g	1/2 tsp
Garlic, smashed	7.0 g	2 cloves

Chop ribs and tails into smaller pieces. Do not remove bones.
Chop other meats.
Mix salt with all spices adding a little water to create a paste.
Mix meats with the paste and hold for 24 hours in refrigerator.
Stuff firmly into pork blind cap (caecum) or large diameter casing.
Using oak wood apply cold smoke at 18° C (64° F) 3-4 days. Try to deliver smoke at least 8 hours each day.
Dry at 12-15° C (53-59° F), 65-75% humidity, for at least 3-4 days.
Refrigerate.

Notes
Cook in water (below the boiling point) for about 2 hours before serving, it is usually served with potatoes and vegetables.

Boerenmetworst

Boerenmetworst is a Dutch specialty dry sausage.

Pork	500 g	1.10 lb
Lean beef	200 g	0.44 lb
Back fat or hard fat trimmings	300 g	0.66 lb

Ingredients per 1 kg (2.2 lb) of meat

Salt	28 g	5 tsp
Cure #2	2.5 g	1/2 tsp
Dextrose (glucose)	3.0 g	1/2 tsp
Pepper	3.0 g	1.5 tsp
Coriander	2.0 g	1 tsp
Mustard powder	2.0 g	1 tsp
T-SPX culture	0.12 g	use scale

Grind pork and back fat through 5 mm (3/16") plate. Grind beef with 3 mm (1/8") plate.
Mix all ingredients with meat.
Stuff firmly into 36-40 mm hog casings. Form 24-30" long links, tie ends together to make a ring.
Ferment at 20° C (68° F) for 72 hours, 90-85% humidity.
Apply cold smoke at 18-22° C (64-72° F) for 12 hours. Dry at 16-12° C (60-54° F), 85-80% humidity. In about 6-8 weeks a shrink of 30% should be achieved.
Store sausages at 10-15° C (50-59° F), < 75% humidity.

Spices such as ginger and cloves are sometimes added.

Botagueña

Botagueña, also known as *tarángana* in Castilla la Vieja, *güeña* in La Nueva, *virica* in Navarra, is a blood sausage made with *encallado* (pieces of lungs, heart or stomach) which is also called offal meat. Botagueña, unlike typical blood sausages, *is not cooked* after stuffing. The sausage is smoked, dried and stored in a cool well ventilated room and is characterized by its long shelf life.

Pork fat, fat trimmings	300 g	0.66 lb
Pork lungs, heart, stomach	550 g	1.21 lb
Pork blood	150 ml	5 oz fl

Ingredients per 1 kg (2.2 lb) of meat

Salt	28 g	4.5 tsp
Cure #1	2.5 g	1/2 tsp
Pimentón, sweet	25 g	4 Tbsp
Pimentón, hot	2.0 g	1 tsp
Red pepper or cayenne	1.0 g	1/2 tsp
Cinnamon	0.5 g	1/4 tsp
Anise	0.3 g	1/8 tsp
Cilantro, ground	0.5 g	1/4 tsp
Oregano, ground	1.0 g	1/2 tsp

Cook lungs, heart and stomach until soft. Cool and grind through 6 mm (1/4") plate.
Grind fat through 6 mm (1/4") plate.
Mix meat, fat and all ingredients together. Hold for 24 hours in refrigerator.
Stuff into 32 mm pork casings.
Apply a thin cold smoke 18° C (64° F) for 10 days. Traditionally, the sausage was hung above the wood fired kitchen stove where it acquired different flavors and smoke from everyday cooking.
Dry at 12-15° C (53-59° F), 75-85% humidity for 2 weeks.
Store in cool, not humid and well ventilated place. The sausages keep well for up to 6 months.

Botelo or Butelo Gallego

Butelo also known as butelo or botillo, is a popular sausage in Lugo province, situated in the Galicia region of Spain. Botelo is especially popular in el Barco de Valdeorras; a municipality in Ourense. The sausage is similar to Androlla, however, it is stuffed into a larger casing.

Pork spare ribs	700 g	1.54 lb
Pork skin	100 g	0.22 lb
Meat trimmings*	150 g	0.33 lb
Back fat, belly, fat trimmings	50 g	0.11 lb

Ingredients per 1 kg (2.2 lb) of meat

Salt	25 g	4 tsp
Cure #2	2.5 g	1/2 tsp
Sugar	5.0 g	1 tsp
Pimentón, sweet	20 g	3.5 Tbsp
Pimentón, hot	2.0 g	1 tsp
Garlic, diced	10 g	3 cloves
Oregano, ground	2.0 g	1 tsp
White dry wine	60 ml	2 oz fl

Chop ribs into 20 mm (3/4") long pieces. The rib bones are not removed. Chop other bones with attached meat. Cut skins into smaller strips. Mix wine, salt and spices together. Add ribs, meat and skins and mix all together. Place in refrigerator for 48 hours.
Stuff firmly into a large diameter casing like pork caecum, stomachs or bladders. The casings are not uniform so the shape of the sausage will vary – caecum being long and oval, round and bag-shaped for bladders and stomachs.
Apply a thin cold smoke 18° C (64° F) for 8-10 days. Traditionally, the sausage was hung above the wood fired kitchen stove or in chimneys for where it acquired different flavors and smoke from everyday cooking.
Dry at 12-15° C (53-59° F) for 2-3 months.
Store in a cool, well ventilated and dark room or refrigerate.

Notes: Botelo is always cooked before serving. The sausage exhibits an intense red color. The texture is rather loose and different meat cuts are easy to distinguish.
* Meat trimmings attached to skeleton and bones, shoulder, head meat. Bones may be included. It is usually served with boiled potatoes and turnip greens, known in UK as *rapini* and in US as *broccoli raab or broccoli rabe.*

Botillo del Bierzo

Botillo del Bierzo is a type of semi-dry smoked sausage which is stuffed into pig's cap (caecup), a large diameter pouch that is the beginning of a large intestine. The weight of Botillo del Bierzo averages 1is kg (2.2 lb).The El Bierzo region made up of 38 municipalities located to the west of the province of Leon (Castile-Leon), Spain.

Pork rib meat	700 g	1.54 lb
Bone-in tails	100 g	0.22 lb
Meat trimmings: tongue, jowls, spine meat, shoulder	200 g	0.44 lb

Ingredients per 1 kg (2.2 lb) of meat

Salt	25 g	4 tsp
Cure # 1	2.5 g	1/2 tsp
Pimentón, sweet	15 g	3.5 Tbsp
Pimentón, hot	10 g	2.5 Tbsp
Oregano, rubbed	2.0 g	2 tsp
Garlic, minced	10 g	3 cloves

Chop ribs and tails into smaller pieces about 20 mm (3/4"). Do not remove bones.
Chop other meats.
Mix meats with salt, cure and all ingredients.
Place in refrigerator for 24 hours.
Stuff firmly into a large diameter casing like pork cap or bung.
Using oak wood apply cold smoke at 18° C (64° F) for 4 days (one day being the minimum).
Dry at 16-12° C (60-54° F) for 9 days.
Store at 12° C (60° F), <65% humidity or refrigerate.

Notes: the required amount of ribs 65-90%
The required amount of tail meat 10-20%
Trimmings from the following parts may be also incorporated: tongue, jowls, shoulder, backbone meat, no more than 20% total and none of the trimmings should account for more than half of this 20%.
Weight - 500-1600 g
Botillo del Bierzo is usually served in a form of a stew which is made by boiling botillo with cabbage, potatoes and a few fresh chorizos, a task that requires from 2 -2.5 hours.
Botillo del Bierzo carries PGI 2001 certification.

Botillo de León

This is a large sausage from Castlla-León region of Spain, weighing 1-1.5 kg and stuffed into pork blind cap (caecum) or stomach. It is called botelo or butelo in Galicia, but in Castilla-León its name is "botillo."

Pork tails, ribs and jaws with attached meat	1000 g	2.2 lb

Ingredients per 1 kg (2.2 lb) of meat

Salt	30 g	5 tsp
Cure #1	2.5 g	1/2 tsp
Pimentón, sweet	15 g	7 tsp
Pimentón, hot	10 g	5 tsp
Oregano, dry, rubbed	1.0 g	1 tsp
Garlic, smashed	7.0 g	2 cloves

Cut meats into 50-60 mm (2 ") long pieces.
Mix salt with all spices adding a little water to create a paste.
Mix meats with the paste and hold for 24 hours in refrigerator.
Stuff firmly into pork blind cap (caecum).
Using oak wood apply cold smoke at 18° C (64° F) 3-4 days. Try to deliver smoke at least for 8 hours each day.
Dry at 12-15° C (53-59° F), 65-75% humidity, from 3-4 days to 15-20 days for a drier sausage.

Notes
Serve by cooking in water (below the boiling point) for about 2 hours. Botillo de León is usually served with potatoes and vegetables.

Braunschweiger
(Браунивейгская колбаса)

Russian style of dry Braunschweiger.

Lean beef	450 g	0.99 lb
Lean pork	250 g	0.55 lb
Pork back fat	300 g	0.66 lb

Ingredients per 1 kg (2.2 lb) of meat

Salt	30 g	5 tsp
Cure #1	5.0 g	1 tsp
Sugar	2.0 g	1/2 tsp
Black pepper	1.0 g	1/2 tsp
Cardamom	0.3 g	1/4 tsp

Curing: cut meat into 25 mm (1") pieces. Place beef, pork and back fat in separate food grade containers. Mix pork and beef with salt, Cure #1 and sugar according to the recipe (estimate amounts). Back fat needs salt only. Pack tightly to eliminate air and cover with clean cloth. Place for 72 hours in refrigerator. Discard any liquid brine (if present) and submit meat to grinding.

Grind beef through 3 mm (1/8") plate. Grind pork through 3 mm (1/8")) plate. Dice back fat into 5 mm (3/16") cubes.

Mix ground meat with spices. Add fat cubes and remix everything together. Don't add any water.

Stuff sausages firmly into 45-50 mm beef middles or fibrous casings about 50 cm (20") long.

Hang sausages for 5-7 days at 2-4° C (34-38° F), 85-90% humidity.

Apply cold smoke at 18-22° C (64-72° F) for 2-3 days.

Dry sausages for 5-7 days (depending on sausage diameter) at 11-15° C (52-59° F), 80-84 humidity. Dry additional 20-23 days at 10-12° C (50-54° F), 74-78% humidity.

The finished sausage should retain about 60% of its original weight.

Braunschweiger Mettwurst

German spreadable sausage. Braunschweiger Mettwurst is listed (2.212.2) in the German government publication Guide to Meats and Meat Products - *Leitsätze für Fleisch und Fleischerzeugnisse.* The sausage gets its name from a town in Germany called Braunschweig.

Beef	300 g	0.66 lb
Pork butt	300 g	0.66 lb
Pork belly, jowls	400 g	0.88 lb

Ingredients per 1 kg (2.2 lb) of material

Salt	23 g	4 tsp
Cure #1	2.5 g	1/2 tsp
Dextrose	1.0 g	1/4 tsp
Sugar	1.0 g	1/4 tsp
Pepper	2.0 g	1 tsp
Paprika	2.0 g	1 tsp
Mace	0.5 g	1/4 tsp
Juniper extract*	2.0 g	1/2 tsp

Grind all meats through 3 mm (1/8") plate. Re-freeze meats and grind again. You may grind once and then emulsify in the food processor without adding water.

Add all ingredients during this step.

Stuff firmly into 40-60 mm beef middles or fibrous casings. Form 20-25 cm (8-10") links. Ferment for 24 hours at 18° C (64° F), 75-80% humidity.

Cold smoke at 18° C (64° F) for 12 hours. Refrigerate.

Notes

* insert 20 g of crushed juniper berries into 120 ml (½ cup) vodka or cognac and leave in a closed jar for 2-3 days. Filter the liquid from berries.

Buche de Costillas *(Badajoz)*

Buche de Costillas originates in Badajoz, the capital of the province of Badajoz in the region of Extremadura, Spain. The sausage is made from pieces of spare ribs, tails, snouts, and tongues, plus lean pork and fat. The mix is spiced, stuffed into pork stomachs, and dried and aged. The buche sausage was produced and consumed in winter. The sausage was stored in stone jars filled with lard. The buche sausage was served by cooking it in large Dutch ovens over an open fire. About 2 hours were needed to cook buche weighing 1 kg (2.2 lb). Chorizo sausage, pork shoulder, whole garlic cloves, and red peppers were usually added and cooked in the same pot. Cabbage was always added to the pot during the last 30 minutes of cooking. Next, the meats and vegetables were removed, and rice was cooked in the remaining meat stock. Then, all were presented on a plate and served with red wine. Eating Buche in Extremadura was a social gathering, a party.

Lean pork	500 g	1.10 lb
Back fat	250 g	0.55 lb
Tails	50 g	0.11 lb
Tongues	50 g	0.11 lb
Spare ribs	50 g	0.11 lb
Pig mask*	100 g	0.22 lb

Ingredients per 1 kg (2.2 lb) of meat

Salt	30 g	5 tsp
Cure #2	2.5 g	1/2 tsp
Dextrose	5.0 g	1 tsp
Pimentón	25 g	4 Tbsp
Garlic, smashed	15 g	4 cloves

Cut all lean pork, fat, tails, tongues, spare ribs and face meats into smaller (finger length) pieces.
Mix meats with salt and spices. Hold for 24 hours in refrigerator.
Stuff into pork stomachs.
Dry at 20° C (68° F) for 20 days.
Dry at 15-10° C (59-50° F) for 1-2 months depending on the size of a stomach.

Notes
* pig mask is the face of the pig (cheeks, snout, ear) - skin with attached meat and small bones. It will not be easy to obtain in metropolitan areas so use dewlap (chin) or jowls (cheeks). Consume sausage raw or cooked.

Budapesti Téliszálami

Hungarian salami from the capital, Budapest.

Lean pork: leg, shoulder, loin	700 g	1.54 lb
Back fat or hard fat trimmings	300 g	0.66 lb

Ingredients per 1 kg (2.2 lb) of meat

Salt	30 g	5 tsp
Cure #2	5.0 g	1 tsp
White pepper	2.0 g	1 tsp
Sweet paprika	10 g	3 tsp
Allspice, ground	2.0 g	1 tsp

Meat is manually boned, which enables the thorough removal of sinews, gristle and connective tissue.
Cut the meat into 6 mm (1/4") pieces.
Cut fat into 3 mm (1/8") pieces.
Mix lean meat with all ingredients. Add fat and remix.
Stuff into horse or 40-85 mm fibrous casings forming (33-50 cm (13-20") long links.
Apply a thin cold smoke at 16° C (60° F) for 12-20 days using beech wood. Cold smoking is not a continuous process, it can be interrupted often, however, the temperature of 16° C should be maintained. You are *drying* the meat with smoke.
Place sausages in a fermenting/drying room at 10-14° C (50-56° F), 86-90% humidity to permit the growth of mold.
The fermentation/drying process continues for 2-3 months depending on the diameter (not the length) of the sausage. Once the mold appears the relative humidity can be lowered, however, it should not drop below 45% as the drying will be too fast.
The total production time from filling the sausages is at least 90 days.

Note: Budapesti Téliszálami carries PGI, 2009 classification. No starter cultures are allowed.

Butelo de Vinhais

Butelo de Vinhais originates in the Vinhais area in the Bragança district of Portugal.

Pork meat - cuts of meat, fat and trimmings obtained from the ribs and spine of the pig	1000 g	2.2 lb

Ingredients for making marinade per 1 kg (2.2 lb) of meat

Salt	18 g	3 tsp
Cure #1	2.5 g	1/2 tsp
Sugar	3.0 g	1/2 tsp
Paprika, sweet	4.0 g	2 tsp
Bay leaf	1 leaf	1 leaf
Garlic	7.0 g	2 cloves
Dry wine	120 ml	1/2 cup
Water	120 ml	1/2 cup

Mix all ingredients together to create a marinade. Cut meat into small pieces. Immerse meat in the marinade and hold for 3 days in refrigerator. Drain.

Stuff into pig's stomach, bladder or a large diameter casing.

Apply a thin cold smoke at 18° C (64° F) for 15 days. Smoking need not be continuous, for example the fire can be put out at night and restarted in the morning as long as the temperature inside of the smokehouse stays below 18° C. The sausage is smoked with oak, chestnut or a mixture of both.

Dry at 12-15° C (54-59° F), 75% humidity for 14 days.

Store at 12° C (54° F), 70% humidity.

Note: Butelo de Vinhais, also registered as Bucho de Vinhais or Choriço de Ossos de Vinhais carries PGI 2015 classification.

Butifarra Dulce Curada

Sweet Butifarra is a traditional Spanish sausage that is presented fresh or dried, like a salami. The sausage is popular in the Catalonia region of Spain, especially in Gorona which is North of Barcelona. It is said that this sausage was one of the favorite dishes of the painter Salvador Dali. This is a dry version of Sweet Butifarra.

Pork, lean	700 g	1.54 lb
Pork back fat or hard fat trimmings	300 g	0.66 lb

Ingredients per 1 kg (2.2 lb) of meat

Salt	28 g	5 tsp
Cure #1	2.5 g	1/2 tsp
Dextrose	3.0 g	1/2 tsp
Honey	20 g	1 Tbsp
Pimentón, sweet	4.0 g	2 tsp
Lemon zest, grated	1/2 lemon	1/2
Cinnamon	2.0 g	1 tsp

Grind meat and fat through 6 mm (1/4") plate. Mix all ingredients with ground meat and fat. Hold for 24 hours in refrigerator.

Stuff firmly into 32 mm hog casings. Make 60 cm (24") long links.

Ferment/dry at 25° C (77° F) for 24 hours, 90-85% humidity.

Dry at 16-12° C (60-54° F), 85-80% humidity for 14 days. Store sausages at 10-12° C (50-54° F), <75% humidity or refrigerate.

Notes

Starter culture such as F-LC or L-HP, 0.25 g/kg of meat can be used.

Dry sweet butifarra can be served like fresh sweet butifarra (with apples):

Butiffara sausage, 2
Sugar, 2 Tbsp
Lemon peel, 1 lemon
Golden apples, 4
Cinnamon stick, 1
Water, 120 ml (1/2 cup)
Sweet wine or grape juice, 60 ml (1/4 cup)
Sweet butter, 20 g (1 oz)

Peel the apples, remove the core and cut into wedges. Put everything in a skillet, less apples, and cook uncovered for 10 minutes. Prick the sausages with a fork and add with apples to the skillet. Cook for additional 10 minutes.

Bydgoska - Dry
(Kiełbasa bydgoska surowa)

Polish semi-dry sausage.

Pork butt	1000 g	2.2 lb

Ingredients per 1 kg (2.2 lb) of meat

Salt	21 g	3.5 tsp
Cure #1	2.5 g	1/2 tsp
Pepper	1.5 g	1 tsp
Marjoram	1.0 g	1/2 tsp
Sugar	2.0 g	1/2 tsp

Curing: cut meat into 2.5-5 cm (1-2") pieces and mix with salt and Cure #1. Pack tightly in container, cover with cloth and keep in refrigerator for 72 hours.
Grind meat through 10 mm (3/8") plate.
Mix ground meat with spices until sticky.
Stuff into 32-36 mm hog casings forming 15 cm (6") long links. Leave links in long coils.
Apply cold smoke at 18-22° C (64-72° F) for 1-1.5 days until the casings develop yellow-light brown color.
Dry at 10-12° C (50-53° F) and 75-80% humidity until the 87% yield is obtained. This should take about 2 weeks. Divide sausage coils into pairs.
Store at 12° C (53° F) or lower.

Note: 87% yield means that the finished sausage has retained 87% of its original unprocessed weight. In other words it has lost 13% of the moisture.

Cacciatore

Italian small dry sausage. Cacciatore means "hunter" in Italian as the hunters carried this sausage as a snack on long hunting trips.

Lean pork	600 g	1.32 lb
Lean beef	100 g	0.22 lb
Back fat	300 g	0.66 lb

Ingredients per 1 kg (2.2 lb) of meat

Salt	28 g	5 tsp
Cure #2	2.5 g	1/2 tsp
Dextrose (glucose)	3.0 g	1/2 tsp
Pepper	3.0 g	1.5 tsp
Coriander	2.0 g	1 tsp
Caraway	2.0 g	1 tsp
Red pepper	1.0 g	1.5 tsp
Garlic powder	1.5 g	1.5 tsp
T-SPX culture	0.12 g	use
scale		

Grind pork and back fat through 5 mm (3/16").
Grind beef with 3 mm (1/8") plate.
Mix all ingredients with meat.
Stuff firmly into 36-40 mm hog casings or beef rounds. Make 6" long links.
Dip into surface mold growing solution - Bactoferm Mold 600.
Ferment at 20° C (68° F) for 72 hours, 95-90% humidity.
Dry for 2 days at 18-16° C (64-60° F), 90-85% humidity.
Dry at 16-12° C (60-54° F), 85 -80% humidity.
In about 6-8 weeks a shrink of 30% should be achieved.
Store sausages at 10-15° C (50-59° F), <75% humidity.

Calabresa

Calabresa is a common sausage in Brazil. The name Calabresa comes from the Calabria region in southeastern Italy, which is the origin of this sausage. The main difference between the two is that the Brazilian Calabresa is smoked. Calabresa, like many other Portuguese and Brazilian sausages, is often served as part of a heavy meal, typically accompanied by rice, beans, and other pork products.

Lean pork (butt, ham)	800 g	1.76 lb
Back fat or hard fat trimmings	200 g	0.44 lb

Ingredients per 1 kg (2.2 lb) of meat

Salt	28 g	5 tsp
Cure #2	2.5 g	1/2 tsp
Pepper	2.0 g	1 tsp
Dextrose (glucose)	2.0 g	1/2 tsp
Sugar	2.0 g,	1/2 tsp
Fennel, ground	2.0 g	1 tsp
Paprika, sweet	6.0 g	2 tsp
Cayenne	2.0 g	1 tsp
Garlic, granulated	3.0 g	1 tsp
T-SPX culture	0.12 g	use scale

Grind pork through 10 mm (3/8").
Grind fat through 10 mm (3/8") plate.
Dilute starter culture in 1 tablespoon of de-chlorinated water.
Mix lean meat with salt and Cure #2 until sticky. Add spices, culture and fat and mix again.
Stuff firmly into 38 mm hog casings forming 6" (15 cm) links.
Ferment at 20° C (68° F) for 72 hours, 90-85% humidity.
Apply thin cold smoke (< 20° C, 68° F) for 4 days.
Dry at 16-12° C (60-54° F), 85-80% humidity for 1 month. The sausage is dried until around 30-35% in weight is lost.
Store sausages at 10-15° C (50-59° F), 75% humidity.

Cervelat

European semi-dry sausage, very popular in Switzerland, is an equivalent of American summer sausage. The definition covers countless recipes and sausages with the name Cervelat, made in many countries. You can call a sausage Thuringer, the Thuringer Cervelat, Summer Sausage, or the Cervelat Summer Sausage, and all names are correct and describe the same type of sausage.

Beef	700 g	1.54 lb
Pork	300 g	0.66 lb

Ingredients per 1 kg (2.2 lb) of meat

Salt	25 g	4 tsp
Cure #1	2.5 g	1/2 tsp
Dextrose	10 g	2 tsp
Sugar	10 g	2.5 tsp
Black pepper, gnd	3.5 g	1.5 tsp
Black pepper, whole	2.0 g	1 tsp
Coriander, ground	2.0 g	1 tsp
Paprika	2.0 g	1 tsp
Mustard seeds, whole	4.0 g	2 tsp
Ginger	1.0 g	1/2 tsp
F-LC culture	0.25 g	use scale

Grind pork and beef through 5 mm (3/16").
30 min before use mix culture with 15 ml (1 Tbsp) de-chlorinated water.
Mix all ingredients with meat.
Stuff into 60 mm beef middles or fibrous casings forming 30" links.
Ferment at 38° C (100° F) for 24 hours, 90-85% humidity.
Introduce warm smoke at 43° C (110° F), 70% humidity for 12 hours. Gradually increase smoke temperature until meat reaches 60° C (140° F) internal temperature.
For a drier sausage dry 2 days more at 22-16° C (70-60° F), 65-75% humidity or until desired weight loss has occurred.
Store sausages at 10-15° C (50-59° F), 75% humidity or refrigerate.

Cervelat-Traditional

Pork trimmings	700 g	1.54 lb
Lean beef	200 g	0.44 lb
Pork back fat	100 g	0.22 lb

Ingredients per 1 kg (2.2 lb) of meat

Salt	28 g	4.5 tsp
Cure #2	5.0 g	1 tsp
Sugar	5.0 g	1 tsp
Black pepper	2.0 g	1 tsp
Paprika, sweet	2.0 g	1 tsp
Coriander, ground	1.0 g	1 tsp

Take a slab of skinless back fat and rub in 5% salt (50 g salt per 1 kg of back fat) on all sides. Place in refrigerator at 4° C (40° F) for 2 weeks. Rinse with cold water to remove any crystallized salt. Cut into 12 mm (1/2") cubes.
Grind pork with 10 mm (3/8") plate.
Grind beef with 3 mm (1/8") plate.
Mix all meats and back fat with salt, Cure #2 and spices. Pack tightly in a container about 6" (15 cm) deep and hold for 4 days in refrigerator. Stuff firmly into hog bungs, beef middles or large diameter synthetic protein lined fibrous casings.
Dry for 3 weeks at 10° C (50° F).
Apply cold smoke at 18° C (68° F) for 2 days.
Store at 10-12° C (50-53° F).

Cervelatwurst

Cervelatwurst is listed (2.211.08) in the German government publication Guide to Meats and Meat Products - *Leitsätze für Fleisch und Fleischerzeugnisse.* Cervelatwurst or Zervelatwurst is a fine-grind-salami type smoked sausage made from pork and beef.

Lean pork	400 g	0.88 lb
Beef, little fat and		
some connective tissue	300 g	0.66 lb
Back fat/neck fat	300 g	0.66 lb

Ingredients per 1 kg (2.2 lb) of material

Salt	28 g	4.5 tsp
Cure #2	2.5 g	1/2 tsp
Dextrose	2.0 g	1/2 tsp
Sugar	2.0 g	1/2 tsp
Pepper, ground	2.0 g	1 tsp
Pepper, whole	2.0 g	1 tsp
Nutmeg	0.5 g	1/2 tsp
Ginger	0.3 g	1/8 tsp
T-SPX culture	0.12 g	use
scale		

Grind all meats through 3 mm (1/8") plate.
Cool and grind again.
Grind partially frozen back fat through 3 mm (1/8") plate.
Mix meats, and all ingredients together. Add fat and mix again.
Stuff into 60 mm beef middles or synthetic protein lined fibrous casings.
Ferment at 3 days at 20° C (68° F), 95 → 90% humidity.
Smoke at 18° C (64° F) for 24 hours.
Dry at 15→12° C (58 →53° F), 80-75% humidity for 6 weeks until sausage looses 33% of its original weight.
Store at 10-12° C (50-53° F), <75% humidity.

Chanfaino

Chanfaino or *chanfaina*, also known as *Longaniza Gallega* originates in the Lugo province of Galicia region. The sausage is made with pork heart, lungs, fat and typical galician spices such as Pennington, garlic, oregano and onions. It might be as well called *sabadeña* or *sabadiego* which are made in Galicia and in other parts of the country. The sausage is smoked and dried and served hot with boiled potatoes, turnips and other vegetables.

Pork, semi-fat, shoulder ...	200 g	0.44 lb
Pork offal meat (heart, lungs, spleen, stomach diaphragm)	800 g	1.76 lb

Ingredients per 1 kg (2.2 lb) of meat

Salt	24 g	4 tsp
Cure #1	2.5 g	1/2 tsp
Pimentón, sweet	25.0 g	4 Tbsp
Pimentón, hot	5.0 g	1 Tbsp
Garlic	10 g	3 cloves
Oregano, rubbed	2.0 g	2 tsp

Grind pork meat with 10 mm (3/8") plate.
Chop offal meat into smaller pieces.
Mix meats with all other ingredients and hold in refrigerator for 24 hours.
Stuff firmly into 32 mm hog casing forming links or rings.
Smoke at 18° C (64° F) with oak wood for 2-3 days. The smoking process may be interrupted as long as the temperature stays below 18° C (64° F).
Dry at 12-15° C (53-59° F) for 21 days.
Store at 12° C (53° F), <75% humidity.

Chicken Fermented Sausage

American sausage. Chicken thigh meat will create a better color than the breast. Chicken fat becomes semi-liquid already at room temperature and should be replaced with pork hard fat (back fat or hard fat trimmings). The moisture level of chicken meat is high and its skin is often microbiologically dirty (contains undesirable bacteria). In addition to common pathogens that may be present in chicken meat, *Campylobacter jejuni* is typically associated with poultry meat.

Bactoferm™ F-LC bio-protective starter culture is a good choice as it inhibits *Listeria monocytogenes* and can be used at a wide range of temperatures.

Chicken meat	800 g	1.76 lb
Back fat or pork hard fat trimmings	200 g	0.44 lb

Ingredients per 1 kg (2.2 lb) of meat

Salt	28 g	5 tsp
Cure #2	2.5 g	1/2 tsp
Dextrose (glucose)	10 g	2.5 tsp
Sugar	3.0 g	1.2 tsp
Pepper	3.0 g	1.5 tsp
Coriander	2.0 g	1 tsp
Ground mustard	2.0 g	1 tsp
Allspice	2.0 g	1 tsp
Garlic	5.0 g	2 cloves
F-LC culture	0.5 g	use scale

Grind chicken and back fat through 5 mm (3/16") plate. Mix all ingredients with meat. Stuff firmly into 36-40 mm hog casings.
Ferment for 24 hours at 22° C (72° F), 85% humidity.
Optional: during fermentation cold smoke from time to time at 22° C (72° F) or lower.
Dry for 21 days at 14-12° C (58-54° F), 75% humidity.
Store at 10-12° C (50-53° F), <75% humidity.

Chistorra or Txistorra

Chistorra also known as Txistorra is a popular sausage in Navarra region of Spain. Similar to chorizo, but shorter and stuffed into narrower casings, Chistorra has high fat content, usually around 50%, sometimes even more. The sausage is shortly dried and looks like a meat stick.

Pork, lean	250 g	0.55 lb
Beef	250 g	0.55 lb
Back fat	250 g	0.55 lb
Pork belly	250 g	0.55 lb

Ingredients per 1 kg (2.2 lb) of meat

Salt	28 g	5 tsp
Cure #1	2.5 g	1/2 tsp
Dextrose	2.0 g	1/2 tsp
Sugar	3.0 g	1/2 tsp
Pimentón, sweet	25 g	4 Tbsp
Pimentón, hot	2.0 g	1 tsp
Garlic	3.5 g	1 clove

Cut meats into 25 mm (1") pieces. Mix with all ingredients.
Hold in refrigerator for 24 hours.
Grind meats through 10 mm (3/8") plate.
Stuff into 20-24 mm sheep casings, forming 15 cm (6") straight links.
Ferment/dry at 15° C (59° F), 85-90% humidly for 48 hours.
Dry at 15-12° C (59-53° F), 80-85% humidity for 16-25 days (depending on a size). Hold semi-dry sausage in refrigerator. Drying sausage for 25 days or more will produce ready to eat dry sausage.

Notes
Chistorra can be made from all pork (replace beef with pork shoulder).
The sausage is usually fried or added to stews. If this is the case the sausage can be removed from the drying chamber at any time.

Chistorra with Culture

Chistorra is a type of dry sausage from Aragon, the Basque Country, and Navarre, Spain.

Lean pork	700 g	1.54 lb
Back fat, jowls, hard fat trimmings	300 g	0.66 lb

Ingredients per 1 kg (2.2 lb) of meat

Salt	28 g	5 tsp
Cure #2	2.5 g	1/2 tsp
Dextrose (glucose)	3.0 g	1/2 tsp
Sugar	3.0 g	1/2 tsp
Sweet Pimentón (smoked paprika)	10 g	3 tsp
Hot Pimentón	4.0 g	1.5 tsp
Garlic powder	4.0 g	1.5 tsp
F-LC or L-HP culture	0.25 g	use scale

Grind pork through 8 mm (5/16") plate.
30 min before use, mix culture with 15 ml (1 Tbsp) de-chlorinated water.
Mix all ingredients with ground pork.
Stuff firmly into 24 mm sheep casings. Make 24" (60 cm) long links.
Ferment at 24° C (75° F) for 48 hours, 90-85% humidity.
Dry at 16-12° C (60-54° F), 85-80% humidity for 3 weeks. (Larger diameter casing will require longer drying time). The sausage is dried until around 30-35% weight is lost. Store sausages at 10-15° C (50-59° F), 75% humidity.

Note: The sausage is usually fried or added to stews. If this is the case the sausage can be removed from the drying chamber at any time.

Chorizo Andaluz

Chorizo Andaluz originates in the southern region of Spain, which is known as Andalusia.

Pork, semi-fat	1000 g	2.2 lb

Ingredients per 1 kg (2.2 lb) of meat

Salt	25 g	4 tsp
Cure #2	2.5 g	1/2 tsp
Pimentón, sweet	25 g	4 Tbsp
Pimentón, hot	2.0 g	1 tsp
Pepper, black	1.0 g	1/2 tsp
Garlic, smashed	3.5 g	1 clove
Water	30 ml	1 oz fl

Grind meat through 6 mm (1/4") plate.
Mix meat with all ingredients. Hold for 24 hours in refrigerator.
Stuff into 36 mm pork or beef casings.
Apply a thin smoke at 20-24° C (68-75° F) (smoking step is optional) or ferment/dry sausages at 20-24° C (68-75° F) for 24-48 hours.
Dry at 15-12° C (59-54° F), 75-80% humidity for 15 days.
Store sausages at 10-12° C (50-53° F), 65-70% humidity or refrigerate.

Chorizo Asturiano

Chorizo Asturiano is produced in Asturias province in north-west Spain, where a large number of sausage types are produced. Asturian sausages are often smoked.

Lean pork	600 g	1.32 lb
Back fat and meat trimmings with attached fat	400 g	0.88 lb

Ingredients per 1 kg (2.2 lb) of meat

Salt	22 g	3.5 tsp
Cure #2	2.5 g	1/2 tsp
Sugar	3.0 g	1/2 tsp
Pimentón, sweet	20 g	5 tsp
Pimentón, hot	5.0 g	5 tsp
Oregano, rubbed	2.0 g	2 tsp
Garlic, minced	7.0 g	2 cloves

Grind pork and fat through 8 mm (5/16") plate.
Mix all ingredients with ground meat. Hold for 24 hours in refrigerator.
Stuff into 32-34 mm pork casings forming 30 cm (12") loops OR into 50-60 mm pork bungs making straight sections.
Ferment/dry at 25-30° C (77-86° F) 2-3 days, 80-85% humidity. Apply a thin cold smoke at <25° C (77° F) during this step.
Dry 32-34 mm sausages at 12-15° C (53-59° F), 70-75% humidity for 14 days OR pork bungs for 2 months.
Store sausages at 10-12° C (50-53° F), 65-70% humidity.

Notes
Consume cold or cooked.

Chorizo Candelario

Chorizo Candelario originates in the municipality of Candelaria in the Salamanca province of Castilla y León region of Spain. It is made from lean pork and pork fat and is always seasoned with pimentón, oregano and garlic. The sausage is stuffed into straight or U-shaped casing. The same area produces another well-known chorizo called "White Chorizo Candelario" (*Chorizo Blanco Candelario*) which is made without pimentón. All other ingredients and processing steps remain the same as in Chorizo Candelario.

Lean pork: head, loin, shoulder, legs	1000 g	2.2 lb

Ingredients per 1 kg (2.2 lb) of meat

Salt	28 g	4.5 tsp
Cure #2	2.5 g	1/2 tsp
Dextrose	2.0 g	1/2 tsp
Sugar	2.0 g	1/2 tsp
Black pepper	1.0 g	1/2 tsp
Pimentón, sweet	20 g	10 tsp
Pimentón, hot	2.0 g	1 tsp
Oregano, ground	2.0 g	1 tsp
Garlic	3.5 g	1 clove
Wine	15 ml	1 Tbsp
Water, as needed	30 ml	1 oz fl

Smash garlic and using mortar and pestle grind it with wine into the paste.
Lean cuts from pork head, loin, shoulder, legs. Remove all membranes, sinews, gristles etc.
Grind meat through 8 mm (5/16") plate.
Mix ground meat with all ingredients adding as little water as needed for proper texture of the meat mass. Hold in refrigerator for 48 hours.
Stuff into 40-55 mm pork middles, tying off 8-10 cm (4") links or into 50-90 mm pork bung.
Prick each sausage with a needle, especially in visible air pockets. Ferment/dry at 22-24° C (72-75° F) for 48 hours, 90-85% humidity.
Dry sausages for 30 days at 12-15° C (53-59° F), 75-80% humidity. Dry pork bungs longer, depending on diameter, until the sausage looses 33% of its original weight.
Store at 10° C (53° F) in a cool and ventilated area or refrigerate.

Chorizo Cántabro *(Guriezo)*

Chorizo Cántabro is a Basque chorizo popular in Cantabria, an autonomous region on Spain's north coast. The sausage is made with the "choricero pepper" (pimiento choricero), a variety of sweet red pepper (a variant of the species *Capsicum annuum*) that is usually dried in the air in strings to preserve it better. Chorizo Cántabro is also known as Chorizo de Guriezo. Guriezo is a municipality located in the autonomous community of Cantabria, Spain.

Pork, lean	600 g	1.32 lb
Pork belly	400 g	0.88 lb

Ingredients per 1 kg (2.2 lb) of meat

Salt	21 g	3.5 tsp
Cure #1	2.5 g	1/2 tsp
Dextrose	2.0 g	1/2 tsp
Sugar	2.0 g	1/2 tsp
Chorizo pepper (choricero)*	15 g	7 tsp
Pimentón, hot	2.0 g	1 tsp
Garlic	7.0 g	2 cloves

Grind meat and belly through 10 mm (3/8") plate.
Mix with all spices. Hold the mixture for 12 hours in refrigerator.
Stuff into 32-36 mm hog casings forming links, Tie the ends together.
Apply a thin cold smoke and dry at 18° C (64° F) for 2 days. Cold smoking does not have to be a continuous process.
Dry sausages for 14 days at 12-15° C (53-59° F), 75-80% humidity.
Store at 10-12° C (50-53° F), <75% humidity or refrigerate.

Notes
Sausage can be consumed raw, fried or cooked in white wine or cider.
* In US the chorizo pepper (*Choricero*) can be ordered from Edwards Greenhouse, Boise, ID
https://www.edwardsgreenhouse.com
It is a common practice in northern Spain to cook (simmer) chorizos in white wine. Cook them whole or cut into 7-10 cm (3-4") pieces and heat in wine for 30 minutes. Fat will leak into the wine, pimentón will color the liquid red and the sausage is enjoyed with soaked in wine bread.

Chorizo Cular *(Salamanca)*

Chorizo cular is a very popular sausage in Salamanca and de la de Ávila provinces of the Castilla and León region of Spain. This is a large chorizo sausage, 45-70 mm in diameter, 50-60 cm (20-24") in length, weighing about 850 grams (1.87 lb). In the traditional home production method, sausages are suspended below the kitchen range hood for 2-3 days. Old kitchen stoves were wood fired and had removable top plates. Removing plate allowed to smoke/dry products hanging above. The sausages acquired different flavors from foods which were being cooked on the stove. This chorizo derives its name from the pork casing it is stuffed in - tripa "cular" which is a pork bung (the last section of casing).

Lean pork*	800 g	1.76 lb
Back fat	200 g	0.44 lb

Ingredients per 1 kg (2.2 lb) of meat

Salt	30 g	5 tsp
Cure #2	2.5 g	1/2 tsp
Sugar	2.5 g	1/2 tsp
Pimentón, sweet	20 g	3.5 Tbsp
Pimentón, hot	4.0 g	2 tsp
Oregano, dry	3.0 g	3 tsp
Garlic	10 g	3 cloves
Cinnamon	1.0 g	1/2 tsp
Nutmeg	0.5 g	1/4 tsp
Cloves	0.3 g	1/8 tsp
Ginger	0.3 g	1/8 tsp
White wine	30 ml	2 Tbsp
Olive oil	30 ml	2 Tbsp

Grind meat through 8 mm (5/16") plate. For better particle definition manually cut partially frozen fat into 6-10 mm cubes. Mix meat, fat and all other ingredients and hold in refrigerator for 48 hours. Stuff into 40-60 mm pork bungs (*"tripa cular"*) forming 50-60 cm (20-24") straight sections.
Dry/ferment for 24 hours at 24° C (75° F), 85-90% humidity.
Dry at 12-14° C (53-57° F), 70-80% humidity for 2 months. Store at 10-12° C (50-53° F), <75% humidity or refrigerate.

Notes
* preferably from Iberian pig. In traditional home production the stuffed sausages were hung for 2-3 days below kitchen range hood ("campana de cocina") and then dried in natural homemade drying chambers for 3-4 months.

Chorizo de Aragón

Chorizo de Aragón is a Spanish semi-dry sausage popular in the region of Aragón, especially around its capital Zaragoza. The sausage is made with lean pork, fatty pork cuts like pork belly, dewlap and classical Spanish chorizo spice combination: pimentón paprika, oregano and garlic.

Pork, lean	700 g	1.54 lb
Pork belly, dewlap or back fat	300 g	0.66 lb

Ingredients per 1 kg (2.2 lb) of meat

Salt	30 g	5 tsp
Cure #1	2.5 g	1/2 tsp
Pepper	2.0 g	1 tsp
Pimentón, sweet	24 g	4 Tbsp
Pimentón, hot	2.0 g	1 tsp
Oregano, ground	2.0 g	1 tsp
Nutmeg	0.5 g	1/4 tsp
Garlic, smashed	7.0 g	2 cloves

Grind lean meat through 8 mm (5/16") plate. Grind fat cuts through 8 mm (5/16") plate. You can manually cut partially frozen fat into 8 mm pieces for better particle definition.
Mix ground meat with all ingredients, then add ground fat and mix again. Pack the mixture in container and place for 24-36 hours in refrigerator.
Stuff into 28-32 mm pork or sheep casings forming 10 cm (4") long links.
Dry/ferment at 22-24° C (72-75° F), 85-90% humidity for 24 hours.
Dry for 48 hours at 15-18° C (59-64° F), 70-80% humidity.
Dry at 12-15° C (53-59° F) for 48 hours. At this point Chorizo de Aragón can be classified a semi-dry sausage which is served fried or cooked.

Notes
To make a dry sausage continue drying at 12-14° C (53-57° F), 75-80% humidity until the sausage looses 33% of its original weight. The dry sausage can be consumed raw.
Nowadays, commercial producers stuff sausage into horseshoe loops about 40 cm (16") long.

Chorizo de Bilbao

Chorizo de Bilbao is a spicy semi-dry sausage popular in the Philippines.

Beef, lean	500 g	1.10 lb
Pork, lean	300 g	0.66 lb
Pork back fat	200 g	0.44 lb

Ingredients per 1 kg (2.2 lb) of meat

Salt	28 g	5 tsp
Cure #1	2.5 g	1/2 tsp
Dextrose	2.0 g	1/2 tsp
Sugar	3.0 g	1/2 tsp
Pimentón, sweet	20 g	3.5 Tbsp
Pimentón, hot	3.0 g	1.5 tsp
Cumin	2.0 g	1 tsp
Oregano, ground	2.0 g	1 tsp
Garlic	7.0 g	2 cloves

Grind beef through 6 mm (1/4") plate. Grind pork through 8 mm (5/16") plate.
Dice partially frozen fat into 6 mm (1/4") cubes. Mix ground meats, fat and all ingredients together. Hold in refrigerator for 24 hours.
Stuff firmly into 36 mm casings forming 15 cm (6") long links.
Ferment for 24 hours at room temperature, 90-85% humidity.
Refrigerate.
Cook before serving.

Notes
After fermenting instead of refrigerating, the sausages may be submitted to the drying process:
Dry at 15-12° C (59-54° F), 75-80% humidity for 3 weeks. (Larger diameter casing will require longer drying time). The sausage is dried until around 30-35% in weight is lost. Store dried sausages at 10-12° C (50-53° F), 70% humidity or in refrigerator.
If making dry sausage TSPX starter culture (0.12 g per 1 kg meat) can be added just before stuffing for better control of the process.

Chorizo de Bofe

Chorizo de bofe (*bofe* means lungs) is made with offal meat (lungs, spleen, stomach), skins and other meat by-products which are hard to obtain in metropolitan areas; however, in rural areas, such meats and blood are usually processed first for sausages. The sausage is also known as *sabadeño* in Castilla, *sabadiego* in León and *bofeños* in Extremadura.

Lean pork	300 g	0.66 lb
Beef, semi-fat	200 g	0.44 lb
Lungs, spleen, stomach, skins	400 g	0.88 lb
Trimmings rich in connective tissue, skins .. 100 g		0.22 lb

Ingredients per 1 kg (2.2 lb) of meat

Salt	24 g	4 tsp
Cure #1	2.5 g	1/2 tsp
Pimentón, sweet	30 g	5 Tbsp
Pimentón, hot	5.0 g	1 tsp
Oregano, ground	1.0 g	1/2 tsp
Nutmeg	1.0 g	1/2 tsp
Garlic, smashed	7.0 g	2 cloves
Wine	60 ml	2 oz fl

Take heart, lungs, stomach, skins and trimmings and cook in water (below boiling point) until soft. Drain and cool.
Grind beef and pork through 8 mm (5/16") plate. Grind cooked meats through 3 mm (1/8") plate.
Mix meats and all ingredients together. Hold for 12 hours in refrigerator.
Stuff into 40-50 mm pork or beef middles.
Ferment/dry at 22-24° C (72-75° F), 90% humidity for 48 hours.
Dry at 14-15° C (57-59° F), 70% humidity for 30 days.
Store at 10-12° C (50-52 F), 60-65% humidity or refrigerate.

Chorizo de Calabaza

Pumpkin is used in Spanish sausage known as Chorizo de Calabaza or in Portuguese Chouriço de Abóbora de Barroso-Montalegre which carries the prestigious PGI award.

Pork butt	500 g	1.10 lb
Pumpkin	500 g	1.10 lb

Ingredients per 1 kg (2.2 lb) of material

Salt	25 g	4 tsp
Cure #1	2.5 g	1/2 tsp
Dextrose	1.0 g	1/4 tsp
Sugar	2.0 g	1/2 tsp
Allspice	0.5 g	1/2 tsp
Pimentón, sweet	10.0 g	5 tsp
Bay leaf	1 leaf	1 leaf
Nutmeg	1.0 g	1/2 tsp
Cinnamon	2.0 g	1 tsp
Cloves, ground	0.3 g	1/8 tsp
Ginger, ground	0.5 g	1/4 tsp
Sherry wine	30 ml	1 oz fl

Cut meat into small pieces and marinate with salt, Cure #1, bay leaf, all spices and wine. Scrape the flesh of the pumpkin, discard the seeds. Mash the flesh with potato masher. Wrap around with a cheese cloth, place in a colander, add some weight on top and let it drain overnight. Mix meat, pumpkin and all ingredients together. Hold for 24 hours in refrigerator. Stuff into 36 mm hog casings. Ferment at 20° C (68° F) for 72 hours, 90-85% humidity. Dry at 16-12° C (60-54° F), 85-80% humidity for 30 days. The sausage is dried until around 30% in weight is lost.
Store sausages at 10-12° C (50-53° F), <75% humidity or refrigerate.

Notes
To make 1 kg of cooked pumpkin you need about 4 kg of raw pumpkin. *Pumpkin puree:* cut pumpkin into smaller sections, remove seeds and fiber. Cook pumpkin for 25 minutes in water, 15 minutes in steam or bake for 30 minutes at 176° C (350° F). Remove the skin (it peels off easily) and cut the pieces into smaller parts. Place the pumpkin flesh in food processor and emulsify it into the puree. Don't add any water as pumpkin has plenty of it. Place pumpkin puree in a draining bag, place some weight on top and let it drain overnight. TSPX starter culture (0.12 g per 1 kg meat) can be added just before stuffing for better control of the process.

Chorizo de Cantimpalos

This classic, dry chorizo originates in the municipality of Cantipalos in the province of Segovia of the autonomous region de Castilla y León in the middle of Spain. For hundreds of years, the area of Cantipalos was highly regarded for making sausages, but 1900 is the date that is credited as the official beginning of the sausage-making industry in Cantipalos. By 1928, the sausages from Cantipalos were regularly shipped (packed in cans) to Mexico and other countries. Chorizo de Cantimpalos is a cured sausage product made from fresh fatty pork, with salt and pimentón as basic ingredients, to which garlic and oregano may also be added and subjected to a drying and maturing process.

Since 2008, all matters related to Chorizo de Cantimpalos have been handled by the Regulatory Council of Cantimpalos (Consejo Regulador) in the province of Segovia in the Castilla y León region of Spain. For example, it is required that all pigs chosen for Chorizos de Cantimpalos be marked since birth with the CS symbol; only white pigs are used; in their last 3 months of life, their diet must consist of at least 75% wheat and barley, they must be 7-10 months old and weigh 115-160 kg when slaughtered, each chorizo must have its own etiquette and serial number, the ends of the sausage must be connected with wine having 3-color threads (white, red and black).

Meat composition: lean pork 70-80%, fat 20-30%. No previously frozen meat is permitted.
Pimentón - applied at 15-25 g per 1 kg of meat and at least 50% of Pimentón de La Vera must be used.
Sea salt is added at 15-22 g per 1 kg of meat.
Garlic - no more than 4 g per 1 kg of meat.
Oregano - dry oregano at no more than 0.2 g per 1 kg of meat.
Sugar - permitted only for chorizo stuffed into pork bungs.
Phosphates - are allowed.
Anti-oxidants - ascorbic acid or citric acid are allowed.
Proteins - only non-fat dry milk is allowed.
Nitrite/nitrate - not allowed.

Lean pork	700 g	1.54 lb
Back fat or hard fat trimmings	300 g	0.66 lb

Ingredients per 1 kg (2.2 lb) of meat

Sea salt, finely ground	22 g	4 tsp
Pimentón de la Vera, sweet	20 g	3.5 Tbsp
Pimentón de la Vera, hot	2.0 g	1 tsp
Oregano, rubbed	0.2 g	1/4 tsp
Garlic, diced cloves	4.0 g	1.5

For chorizos *sarta* and *achorizado* style grind meat through 10-16 mm (3/8-1/2") plate.
For chorizos *cular* style grind meat through 18-26 mm (3/4-1") plate.
Mix salt, spices and meats together. Hold for 12-36 hours in refrigerator.
Stuff into natural casings:

- 34-40 mm pork ring shaped casings (***sarta*** style), the ends tied together.
- a string of several chorizo sausages (***achorizado*** ristra style) about 12 cm (5") long, 36-50 mm in diameter, tied or wired together with ends connected together with twine forming a long U-shaped loop.
- pork bungs (***cular*** style) of more than 38 mm in diameter, an irregular cylindrical shape straight sections.

Dry at 6-16° C (43-60° F), 60-85% humidity for 1/2 of the total drying time.
Dry at 12-15° C (57-59° F), 60-80% humidity for the remaining drying time.

- *sarta* style - total drying time 21 days.
- *achorizado* ristra style - total drying time 24 days.
- *cular* - total drying time up to 40 days.

Store at 10-12° C (50-52° F), 60-70% humidity.

Notes
The sausage develops a thin white mold.
The sausage is finished when it loses about 30% of its original weight.

Chorizo de Cantipalos carries protective geographical indication certificate PGI 2011

Chorizo de Cebolla

Chorizo de cebolla (*cebolla* means onion) is a popular dry sausage from the Galicia region of Spain.

Pork belly, jowls	400 g	0.88 lb
Offal meat: diaphragm muscle, lungs, heart, skins	300 g	0.66 lb
Diced onions, cooked	300 g	0.66 lb

Ingredients per 1 kg (2.2 lb) of material

Salt	25 g	4 tsp
Cure # 1 *	2.5 g	1/2 tsp
Sweet pimentón	20 g	3.5 Tbsp
Hot pimentón	2.0 g	1 tsp
Garlic, diced	3.5 g	1 clove
Oregano, ground	2.0 g	2 tsp
Parsley, dry	1.0 g	1 tsp
Bay leaf, crushed	1 leaf	1 leaf

Remove tendons, sinews, hard connective tissue from offal meats, then cook the meats in water (below boiling point) until soft. Drain and cool. Chop the onions and cook in water for 45 minutes. Drain and let the moisture evaporate. Grind meats through 6 mm (1/4") plate and mix with salt and spices. Hold for 24 hours in refrigerator.
Mix the sausage mix with cooked onions and stuff without delay into 40 mm pig casings forming links ~ 15 cm (6") long.
Apply cold smoke at 15-18° C (53-64° F) for 7-10 days. Smoking need not to be continuous.
Dry at 15-12° C (59-53° F), 75-80% humidity for 45 days.
Store sausages at 10-12° C (50-53° F), 65-70% humidity or refrigerate.

Notes
For home production it is recommended to cook the onions as that will eliminate a lot of moisture, otherwise drying will be prolonged and unsafe.
* Sodium nitrite/nitrate and sugars are not added in the traditional manufacturing process.

TSPX starter culture (0.12 g per 1 kg meat) can be added just before stuffing for better control of the process.

Chorizo de Cerdo

This is a typical example of chorizo-making technology, which can be applied to most chorizo sausages. The quality chorizo is made from well-trimmed lean cuts of pork and hard fat, the preferred cut being the back fat. Salt, pimentón, and garlic are the main ingredients; the rest follow proper processing.

Lean pork	750 g	1.65 lb
Hard fat (back fat) or		
hard fat trimmings	250 g	0.55 lb

Ingredients per 1 kg (2.2 lb) of meat

Salt	25 g	4 tsp
Cure #2	2.5 g	1/2 tsp
Pimentón, sweet	25 g	4 Tbsp
Pimentón, hot	5.0 g	1 tsp
Oregano, ground	1.0 g	1/2 tsp
Garlic, smashed	3.0 g	1 clove

Grind meat through 8 mm (5/16") plate.
Grind fat through 8 mm (5/16") plate.
Mix meat with all ingredients. Hold for 24 hours in refrigerator.
Stuff into 36 mm pork or beef casings.
Apply a thin smoke at 22-24° C (72-75° F) (smoking step optional) or dry/ferment sausages at 22-24° C (72-75° F) for 24-48 hours.
Dry at 15-12° C (59-53° F), 75-80% humidity for 15 days.
Store sausages at 10-12° C (50-53° F), 65-70% humidity or refrigerate.

Notes
TSPX starter culture (0.12 g per 1 kg meat) can be added just before stuffing for better control of the process.

Chorizo de la Sierra de Aracena

Chorizo de la Sierra de Aracena owes its name to Sierra de Aracena and Picos de Aroche Natural Park, a protected area in the Sierra de Aracena range, part of the Sierra Morena mountain system which lies in Huelva province in Andalusia region of southwestern Spain. This mountain range and national park abound with many oak forests ("dehesas") where Iberian pigs roam free and feed between December and April on oak acorns ("bellota").

Lean Iberian pork	600 g	1.32 lb
Pork belly and		
dewlap (chin)	400 g	0.88 lb

Ingredients per 1 kg (2.2 lb) of meat

Salt	28 g	4.5 tsp
Cure #1	2.5 g	1/2 tsp
Pimentón, sweet	25 g	4 Tbsp
Pimentón, hot	2.0 g	1 tsp
Garlic, diced	3.5 g	1 clove

Grind meats into 8 mm (5/16") pieces.
Mix meats with salt and spices. Marinate for 24 hours in refrigerator.
Stuff into 40-45 mm beef middles forming small 15 cm (6") rings. Tie the ends together.
Apply a thin smoke at 22-24° C (72-75° F) and dry/ferment sausages at 22-24° C (72-75° F) for 24-48 hours.
Dry at 15-12° C (59-53° F), 75-80% humidity for 30 days.
Store sausages at 10-12° C (50-53° F), 65-70% humidity or refrigerate.

Notes
Consume raw, cooked, fried or grilled.
TSPX starter culture (0.12 g per 1 kg meat) can be added just before stuffing for better control of the process.

Chorizo de León

Chorizo de León is a dry sausage from León region of Spain. This is rather a fat sausage that is heavily smoked during fermentation. The sausage is made from white pig quality meats such as pork shoulder, rear leg (ham) trimmings, pork belly, dewlap, and back fat.

Pork, lean	750 g	1.54 lb
Pork back fat, belly	250 g	0.55 lb

Ingredients per 1 kg (2.2 lb) of meat

Salt	25 g	4 tsp
Cure #2	2.5 g	1/2 tsp
Dextrose	3.0 g	1/2 tsp
Pimentón, sweet	20 g	3.5 Tbsp
Pimentón, hot	2.0 g	1 tsp
Oregano, ground	2.0 g	1 tsp
Garlic, diced	3.5 g	1 clove

Grind meat and pork fat through 10 mm (3/8") plate.
Mix meats with all ingredients and hold for 24 hours in refrigerator.
Stuff into 36 mm pork casings forming U-shaped loops with ends tied together.
Apply cold smoke at <18° C (64° F) and dry sausages at 12-15° C (53-59° F), 85-75% humidity.
Apply a thin cold smoke at 22-24° C (72-75° F) and dry/ferment sausages at 22-24° C (72-75° F) for 24-48 hours.
Dry at 15-12° C (59-53° F), 75-80% humidity for 30 days. The temperature in León can reach low levels so a slow burning fire is started to warm up the drying chamber. This means that the sausages are additionally cold smoked during the drying stage .
Store sausages at 10-12° C (50-53° F), 65-70% humidity or refrigerate.

Notes
Sodium nitrite/nitrate and sugars are not added in the traditional manufacturing process.
TSPX starter culture (0.12 g per 1 kg meat) can be added just before stuffing for better control of the process.

Chorizo de Mezcla

Most chorizos are made with pork, but occasionally other meat is combined with pork, usually beef.

Pork meat	300 g	0.44 lb
Pork fat	300 g	0.66 lb
Beef	400 g	0.88 lb

Ingredients per 1 kg (2.2 lb) of meat

Salt	25 g	4 tsp
Cure #2	2.5 g	1/2 tsp
Pimentón, sweet	25 g	4 Tbsp
Pimentón, hot	5.0 g	2 tsp
Oregano, ground	1.0 g	1/2 tsp
Garlic, smashed	7.0 g	2 cloves
Red wine	60 ml	2 oz fl

Grind pork through 6 mm (1/4") plate.
Dice fat into 6 mm (1/4") cubes.
Grind beef through 3 mm (1/8") plate.
Mix ground meats, fat and all ingredients together. Hold for 24 hours in refrigerator.
Stuff into 36 mm pork or beef casings.
Apply a thin smoke at 22-24° C (72-75° F) (smoking step optional) or dry/ferment sausages at 22-24° C (72-75° F) for 24-48 hours.
Dry at 15-12° C (59-54° F), 75-80% humidity for 15 days.
Store sausages at 10-12° C (50-53° F), 65-70% humidity or refrigerate.

Notes
TSPX starter culture (0.12 g per 1 kg meat) can be added just before stuffing for better control of the process.

Chorizo de Pamplona

Chorizo de Pamplona is a large dry sausage
that is very popular not only in the Navarra
region of Spain, where it originates from but
everywhere else in Europe as well as in the
USA. It is a large diameter (min 40 mm), one-
piece sausage, about 30-40 cm (12-15") long,
weighing around 1.5 kg (3.3 lbs). The sausage
is made with pork and beef or pork only (80/20
lean/fat). Unlike other chorizos, the meats in
Chorizo de Pamplona are finely ground.

Pork	450 g	0.99 lb
Beef	200 g	0.44 lb
Back fat	350 g	0.77 lb

Ingredients per 1 kg (2.2 lb) of meat

Salt	28 g	4.5 tsp
Cure #1	2.5 g	1/2 tsp
Dextrose	3.0 g	1/2 tsp
Pimentón, sweet	25 g	4 Tbsp
Pimentón, hot	5.0 g	2 tsp
Garlic	3.5 g	1 clove

Grind pork and beef through 3 mm (1/8") plate.
Dice partially frozen back fat 3-5 mm (1/8-
1/4") cubes.
Mix ground meats with all ingredients. Add
ground fat and mix all together. Hold for 24
hours in refrigerator.
Stuff into 55-80 mm natural or artificial
permeable (allowing liquids or gases to pass
through) casings. Make straight links ~20 cm
(8") long. Prick with needle to remove air.
Dry/ferment sausages at 22-24° C (72-75° F) for
48 hours.
Dry for 45-60 days at 15→12° C (59→53° F),
65-85% humidity. You can apply cold smoke
(<18° C/64° F) during this step. Cold smoking
is performed with a thin smoke and the process
is usually interrupted at night time and resumed
in the morning, however cold smoking can be
interrupted at any time.
Store sausages at 10-12° C (50-53° F), 65-70%
humidity or refrigerate.

Notes
Cold smoking is not required, it is usually
introduced when the temperatures are dropping
below 12° C (53° F).
TSPX starter culture (0.12 g per 1 kg meat) can
be added just before stuffing for better control
of the process.

Chorizo de Potes

Chorizo de Potes is a well-known smoked
and dried sausage from Cantabria region of
Spain. What differs Chorizo de Potes from the
majority of Spanish chorizos is that in addition
to pimentón it also contains regular pepper.
Using thyme is another characteristic of the
sausages.

Pork, lean	500 g	1.10 lb
Pork belly	500 g	1.10 lb

Ingredients per 1 kg (2.2 lb) of meat

Salt	25 g	4 tsp
Cure #1	2.5 g	1/2 tsp
Pepper	2.0 g	1 tsp
Pimentón, sweet	24 g	4 Tbsp
Pimentón, hot	2.0 g	1 tsp
Garlic	3.5 g	1 clove
Oregano, dry	2.0 g	3 tsp
Thyme, dry	2.0 g	3 tsp

Grind meat and belly through 10 mm (3/8")
plate.
Mix with all ingredients and hold in refrigerator
for 12 hours.
Stuff into 36 mm hog casings and form links
using one continuous string of butcher twine.
Smoke and dry with oak wood at 15-18° C
(59-64° F), 70-80% humidity for 25 days.
The smoking process can be interrupted, so
it is smoking-drying-smoking-drying etc.
Usually drying at night and smoking by day.
As the process continues start lowering slowly
temperature.

Notes
The sausage is served in many forms; sliced
and consumed raw, in sandwiches, or in bean
stews.

Chorizo de Soria

Soria is a city in north-central Spain, the capital of the province of Soria in the region of Castile and León. The sausage is made of lean pork and fat, although adding some beef is permitted. Just a few spices - salt, pimentón and garlic are added and the sausage is stuffed into large diameter pork or beef casings and dried.

Lean pork	700 g	1.43 lb
Back fat, pork belly	300 g	0.55 lb

Ingredients per 1 kg (2.2 lb) of meat

Salt	28 g	4.5 tsp
Cure #2	2.5 g	1/2 tsp
Dextrose	2.0 g	1/2 tsp
Sugar	3.0 g	1/2 tsp
Pimentón	25 g	4 Tbsp
Garlic, smashed	3.5 g	1 clove

Dice a half of the partially frozen fat (150 g) into 6-8 mm (1/4-3/8") cubes.
Grind pork meat and remaining fat (150 g) through 10 mm (3/8") plate. Mix meat, fat with all ingredients. Hold in refrigerator for 24 hours. Stuff into 26-80 mm pork or beef casings. Thin sausages were linked with butcher twine (*rastra* style) or formed into rings with ends tied together (*herradura* style), and the thick ones left in straight sections (*vela* style). Dry/ferment sausages at 22-24° C (72-75° F) for 48 hours. Dry at 15-12° C (59-53° F), 70-80% humidity, for 30-50 days depending on diameter. The sausages are considered dry when they lose about 33% of their original weight.

Notes: originally, the sausages were dried at 10-28° C (50-82° F), 40-90% humidity, for 16-50 days, depending on time of the year and the diameter of the sausage. When the temperature dropped low a small wood burning fire was started to warm up the drying facility. The sausage was stuffed into pork or beef casings of different diameters - 26-80 mm. Nowadays, large diameter synthetic protein-lined fibrous casings can be used.
Chorizo de Soria can be made with the following combination of meats: lean pork-60-70%, beef-0-15%, back fat, pork belly or both – 25-28%. TSPX starter culture (0.12 g per 1 kg meat) can be added just before stuffing for better control of the process.

Chorizo de Villarcayo

As the name implies Chorizo de Villarcayo originates in Villarcayo, a municipality in Burgos province of Castilla y León region of Spain. It is situated about 75 km from Burgos, the capital of the province and 79 km from Bilbao, the port in Bay of Biscay in Atlantic. The sausage is made from pork and the principal spices are pimentón and garlic.

Lean pork	800 g	1.96 lb
Pork belly or lean meat trimmings with attached fat	200 g	0.44 lb

Ingredients per 1 kg (2.2 lb) of meat

Salt	28 g	4.5 tsp
Cure #2	2.5 g	1/2 tsp
Pimentón	20 g	10 tsp
Oregano	1.0 g	1 tsp
Cinnamon	0.5 g	1/4 tsp
Cloves	0.3 g	1/8 tsp
Garlic	3.5 g	1 clove

Cut meat and fat into 30 mm (1.3") pieces. Mix meat and fat with salt and spices. Hold for 24 hours in refrigerator.
Stuff into 40-60 mm pork bungs (tripa *cular*) or beef bungs (tripa *roscal*) forming 50-60 cm (20-24") straight sections (*vela*) or make loops with ends tied together (*herradura*).
Dry/ferment with a thin oak smoke at 22-24° C (72-77° F) for 48 hours.
Dry at 15-12° C (59-53° F), 60-80% humidity, for 40-60 days, depending on the diameter of the sausage until it loses about 33% of its original weight.
Store sausages at 10-12° C (50-53° F), 65-70% humidity or refrigerate.

Notes
Consume raw or cooked.
TSPX starter culture (0.12 g per 1 kg meat) can be added just before stuffing for better control o the process.

Chorizo Extremeño

Chorizo Extremeño is a dry sausage made from Iberian meat, oregano, garlic, white wine and pimentón. Extremadura, an autonomous region of western Iberian Peninsula is an important area for wildlife, particularly with the major reserve at Monfragüe, which was designated a National Park in 2007, and the International Tagus River Natural Park (Parque Natural Tajo Internacional). Wild black Iberian pigs roam in the area and feed on acorns in oak forests known as *dehesas*.

Lean Iberian pork	800 g	1.76 lb
Back fat, belly	200 g	0.44 lb

Ingredients per 1 kg (2.2 lb) of meat

Salt	22 g	3.5 tsp
Cure #2	2.5 g	1 tsp
Pimentón, sweet	25 g	4 Tbsp
Pimentón, hot	5.0 g	1 Tbsp
Oregano, dry	2.0 g	2 tsp
Garlic, diced	7.0 g	2 cloves
Dry sherry	30 ml	2 Tbsp
Water	60 ml	2 oz fl

Grind lean pork and fat through 6 mm (1/4") plate.

Mix meats with all ingredients. Hold in refrigerator for 48 hours.

Stuff into 40-50 mm hog casings. Form 5-10 cm (3-4") links or 45 cm (18") straight sections or 45 cm (18") rings.

Dry/ferment at 12-15° C (53-59° F), 80-85% humidity, for 2-3 days.

Dry at 12-15° C (53-59° F), 80% humidity for 1-2 months depending on the diameter of the sausage.

Store sausages at 10-12° C (50-53° F), 65-70% humidity or refrigerate.

Notes

Pimentón brand "de la Vera" recommended.

Consume raw, cooked, fried or grilled.

Chorizo Gallego

Chorizo Gallego is the most popular sausage in Galicia. The sausage is produced by commercial meat plants and hobbyists at home from quality meats: lean pork (70-80%) and back fat (20-30%). It is characterized by a dark red color and visible and generous distribution of fat pieces. Sausage is safe to eat after losing 30% of its original weight. Chorizo Gallego is consumed raw, fried, grilled or becomes an ingredient in many dishes.

Pork, lean (shoulder, ham) 700 g		1.54 lb
Pork back fat, belly or fat trimmings	300 g	0.66 lb

Ingredients per 1 kg (2.2 lb) of meat

Salt	22 g	3.5 tsp
Cure #2	2.5 g	1 tsp
Pimentón, sweet	20 g	3 Tbsp
Pimentón, hot	5.0 g	1 Tbsp
Garlic	7.0 g	2 cloves

Cut or grind meat and fat into 8 mm (5/16") pieces.

Mix salt, Cure #2 and spices together. Mix with meats.

Hold for 24 hours in refrigerator.

Stuff firmly into 36 mm pork casing forming 15 cm (6") links.

Smoke at 18° C (64° F) with oak wood for 12-48 hours.

Dry at 12-15° C (53-5°9 F) for 30-45 days.

Store in a dark place at 12° C or less, <65% humidity.

Notes

Chorizo Gallego was traditionally smoked in home chimneys.

The sausage was traditionally preserved by keeping it in oil or in lard.

The sausage can be consumed raw, cooked, fried or grilled, but is usually served with boiled potatoes and turnip greens, known in UK as *rapini* and in US as *broccoli raab or broccoli rabe*.

It is also added to bean stew. There are local variants of the sausage, often onion is added (chorizo de cebolla or "ceboleira"), sometimes pumpkin (chorizo de calabaza).

TSPX starter culture (0.12 g per 1 kg meat) can be added just before stuffing for better control of the process.

Chorizo Ibérico de Huelva

Chorizo Ibérico de Huelva originates in Huelva, an old port city in southwestern Spain, the capital of the province of Huelva in the autonomous region of Andalusia. To the north of the city, there is a number of mountain ranges and national parks with oak forests ("dehesas") where Iberian pigs roam free and feed between December and April on oak acorns. During that time an average Iberian pig (Pata Negra) consumes 10 kg (22 lbs) of acorns each day. This diet influences the flavor and the texture of its meat and fat.

Lean Iberian pork	800 g	1.76 lb
Back fat	200 g	0.44 lb

Ingredients per 1 kg (2.2 lb) of meat

Salt	28 g	4.5 tsp
Cure #1	2.5 g	1/2 tsp
Pimentón, sweet	25 g	4 Tbsp
Pimentón, hot	2.0 g	1 tsp
Garlic, diced	3.5 g	1 clove

Cut chilled lean pork into 35 mm (1.5") pieces.
Dice partially frozen fat into 12 mm (1/2") cubes.
Mix meats with salt and spices. Marinate for 24 hours in refrigerator.
Stuff into 50-55 mm pork bungs or beef middles, about 40-50 cm (16-20") long.
Dry/ferment at 22-24° C (72-77° F), 80-85% humidity, for 48 hours.
Dry at 12-15° C (53-59° F), 80% humidity, for about 45 days. When temperatures were dropping low a slow burning fire provided heat in a chamber.
Store sausages at 10-12° C (50-53° F), 65-70% humidity or refrigerate.

Notes
Consume raw.
TSPX starter culture (0.12 g per 1 kg meat) can be added just before stuffing for better control o the process.

Chorizo Patatero de Monroy

Chorizo Patatero ("patata" means potato in English) originates in Monroy, a municipality in Cáceres province, in the autonomous community of Extremadura, Spain. The meat and fat come from the Iberian pig; the main ingredient is boiled potatoes. The typical spices are salt, pimentón, and garlic. However, chopped parsley and a little wine are occasionally included, too.

Lean pork and pork belly....................	100 g	0.22 lb
Hard fat trimmings	400 g	0.88 lb
Boiled potatoes	500 g	1.10 lb

Ingredients per 1 kg (2.2 lb) of material

Salt	25 g	4 tsp
Pimentón, sweet	25 g	4 Tbsp
Pimentón, hot	2.0 g	1 tsp
Garlic, diced	7.0 g	2 cloves

Grind meat and pork belly through 8 mm (5/16") plate.
Dice partially frozen hard fat into 6-8 mm (1/4-5/16") cubes.
Mix meats, fat, potatoes, salt and spices together. Hold for 6 hours in refrigerator.
Stuff into 45-50 mm beef middles forming 20 cm (8") links.
Dry at 10-12° C (50-53° F), 80% humidity, for 35 days.
Dry at room temperature (below 15° C/59° F) until fully cured what will take about 60 days total, depending on the diameter of the sausage and drying conditions.

Notes
Meat and fat should come from Iberian pig.
Pimentón de la Vera is recommended.

Chorizo Patatero Rojo

Chorizo Patatero Rojo is a well-known sausage in the Ciudad Real province of Castilla-La Mancha region in Spain. Its composition differs from others mainly in that it is made with a touch of blood and potatoes.

Lean pork	250 g	0.55 lb
Back fat	490 g	1.08 lb
Potatoes, cooked	250 g	0.55 lb
Blood	10 ml	2 tsp

Ingredients per 1 kg (2.2 lb) of material

Salt	21 g	3.5 tsp
Pimentón, sweet	25 g	4 Tbsp
Pimentón, hot	2.0 g	1 tsp
Garlic, smashed	7.0 g	2 cloves

Boil potatoes until cooked, but do not overcook. Drain and cool.

Cut potatoes, lean pork and fat into 6-8 mm (1/4-5/16") cubes.

Mix the mixture with salt, blood and spices.

Hold for 24 hours in refrigerator.

Stuff into 28-40 mm natural casings forming links or loops 15-20 cm (6-5") long.

Dry at 14-16° C (57-60° F), 75% humidity, for 10-21 days, depending on the diameter of the sausage.

Store at 10-12° C (50-53° F), <65% humidity or in refrigerator.

Notes

Adjust the hotness of the sausage by changing the proportion of sweet and hot pimentón.

Consume raw or grilled.

Chorizo Quzande de Bandeira

Chorizo Quzande de Bandeira Chorizo Quzande de Bandeira is a short pork sausage popular in La Estrada, Pontevedra province, Galicia. It is made with lean pork, back fat and a classical Galician spice combination: pimentón and garlic.

Pork, lean	700 g	1.54 lb
Back fat	300 g	0.66 lb

Ingredients per 1 kg (2.2 lb) of meat

Salt	24 g	4.5 tsp
Cure #1	2.5 g	1/2 tsp
Pimentón, sweet	25.0 g	4 Tbsp
Pimentón, hot	4.0 g	2 tsp
Garlic, smashed	7.0 g	2 cloves
Oregano, ground	2.0 g	1 tsp
Red dry wine	60 ml	2 oz fl

Grind meat with 10 mm (3/8") plate.

Mix with all ingredients and place in refrigerator for 24 hours.

Stuff into 32-34 mm hog casings linking sausages every 10 cm (4").

Apply a thin smoke at 22-24° C (72-75° F) and dry/ferment sausages at 22-24° C (72-75° F), 80-85% humidity for 48 hours.

Dry at 15-12° C (59-54° F), 75-80% humidity for 21 days.

Store sausages at 10-12° C (50-53° F), 65-70% humidity or refrigerate.

Notes

Consume raw, cooked or fried.

Quzande de Bandeira was stored in the past in lard in clay jars.

Chorizo Riojano

Chorizo Riojano (*Chorizo de la Rioja*) is made in the autonomous community of La Rioja in Spain. The sausage carries the Protective Geographical Indication (PGI 2010) award. This recipe is for PGI-certified products, which are made by six licensed manufacturers, all located in La Rioja. There are other versions of Chorizo Riojano, some stuffed into 26-28 mm loops, others into 40-50 mm pork or beef middles straight sections. The proportion of meat/fat can vary from 20-40% fat and 60-80% lean, but the spices remain the same: salt, pimentón and garlic.

Lean pork	700 g	1.54 lb
Pork belly or meat trimmings		
with attached fat	300 g	0.66 lb

Ingredients per 1 kg (2.2 lb) of meat

Salt	28 g	5 tsp
Pimentón, sweet	25 g	4 Tbsp
Pimentón, hot	2.0 g	1 tsp
Garlic, minced	7.0 g	2 cloves

Grind all meat through 3/8" plate (10 mm).
Mix meat with all ingredients.
Hold the sausage mass for 24 hours in refrigerator.
Stuff into 30-40 mm pork casings making 30 cm (12") rings (*sarta*) or U-shaped loops (*herradura)* style, about 300 g in weight.
Dry/ferment at 22-24° C (72-75° F), 80-85% for 2-4 days. In home production the temperature of the chamber was controlled by burning oak wood.
Dry at 14-16° C (57-60° F), 75-80% humidity for 15-20 days.
Store sausages at 10-12° C (50-53° F), 65-70% humidity or refrigerate.

Notes
Consume raw or on sandwiches.
For your own version of the sausage you can add Cure #1 (2.5 g, 1 tsp) and sugar (5.0 g, 1 tsp).

Chorizo-Spanish

In Spain and South American countries, the chorizo sausage is made from coarsely chopped pork and seasoned with pepper, paprika and garlic. Spanish smoked paprika (sweet, bittersweet or hot) known as pimentón gives Spanish chorizo its deep red color. Mexican Chorizo is made from pork that is ground and seasoned with chile peppers, garlic and vinegar. It is moister and much hotter than the Spanish chorizo.

Pork butt	1000 g	2.2 lb

Ingredients per 1 kg (2.2 lb) of meat

Salt	28 g	5 tsp
Cure #2	2.5 g	1/2 tsp
Dextrose	2.0 g	1/2 tsp
Sugar	2.0 g	1.2 tsp
Pepper	6.0 g	3 tsp
Pimentón, sweet	10 g	5 tsp
Oregano	2.0 g	1 tsp
Garlic	9.0 g	3 cloves
T-SPX culture	0.12 g	use
scale		

Grind pork through 8 mm (5/16").
Mix all ingredients with meat.
Stuff firmly into 32-36 mm hog casings, form 6" links.
Ferment at 20° C (68° F) for 72 hours, 90-85% humidity.
Dry at 16-12° C (60-54° F), 85-80% humidity, for 1-2 months.
Store sausages at 10-15° C (50-59° F), 75% humidity.

Chorizo Traditional

This is a traditional recipe for pure Spanish chorizo. Spanish chorizo is a dry sausage made from pork, pimentón, oregano and garlic. Pork is coarsely chopped and seasoned with oregano, garlic and pimentón which gives the sausage its deep red color.

Lean pork, ham or butt	750 g	1.65 lb
Back fat or		
hard fat trimmings	250 g	0.55 lb

Ingredients per 1 kg (2.2 lb) of meat

Salt	25 g	4 tsp
Cure #2	2.5 g	1/2 tsp
Pimentón, sweet	28 g	4.5Tbsp
Pimentón, hot	5.0 g	1 Tbsp
Oregano, ground	2.0 g	1 tsp.
Garlic, diced	3.5 g	1 clove

Grind meat and fat through 8 mm (5/16") plate. Mix all ingredients with meat. Hold in refrigerator for 24 hours.
Stuff firmly into 32-36 mm hog casings, form 15 cm (6") long links.
Ferment/dry at 22-24° C (72-75° F) for 48 hours, 90-85% humidity. A thin smoke at 22-24° C (72-75° F) can be applied during this step.
Dry for 6-8 weeks at 16-12° C (60-54° F), gradually decreasing humidity from 85 to 75%.
Store sausages at 10-12° C (50-53° F), <75% humidity or refrigerate.

Notes
In the past chorizo was made without cure (#2 or #1) as most people were not aware of them.

Chorizo Zamorano

Chorizo Zamorano is a dry pork sausage popular in Zamora province of the Castilla-León region of Spain. The sausage is usually covered with a light white mold. The color is intense red with visible particles of fat. The sausage is stuffed in different casings, so it acquires different shapes: straight links, continuous links, horseshoe loops or cylindrical straight sections when pork bungs are used (tripa *cular*).

Lean pork	800 g	1.76 lb
Back fat	200 g	0.44 lb

Ingredients per 1 kg (2.2 lb) of meat

Salt	28 g	4.5 tsp
Cure #1	2.5 g	1/2 tsp
Pimentón, sweet	25 g	4 Tbsp
Pimentón, hot	2.0 g	1 tsp
Oregano, ground	3.0 g	1.5 tsp
Garlic	7.0 g	2 cloves

Grind meat through 8 mm (5/16") plate.
Dice fat into 8 mm (5/16") cubes.
Mix meat and fat with salt and spices. Hold in refrigerator for 12 hours.
Stuff into 20-25 mm sheep casings forming rings about 30 cm (1 foot) long OR into 50-60 mm pork bungs or beef casings forming straight sections.
Dry/ferment at 18-20° C (64-67° F), 85-90% humidity for 3 days.
Dry for 4-8 weeks, depending on diameter, at 15-12° C (59-53° F), gradually decreasing humidity from 85 to 75%.
Store sausages at 10-12° C (50-53° F), <75% humidity or refrigerate.

Notes
The sausage is ready to eat raw or cooked.
Pimentón de la Vera is required.
The development of a thin white mold is natural and accepted.
TSPX starter culture (0.12 g per 1 kg meat) can be added just before stuffing for better control of the process.

Chosco de Tineo

Chosco de Tineo is produced in Tineo municipality in the Asturías region in Spain. Chosco de Tineo is made exclusively from cuts of pork shoulder/neck area known in Spanish as "cabecera de lomo" and tongue. The meats are seasoned, packed by hand into pork blind cap (*caecum*), smoked, and dried, giving it characteristics that differ from those of other types of sausage. When cut, the different pieces of meat used are clearly visible. *The meat must not be minced.* It is a large (weighing 500 g - 2 kg) special sausage made with high quality cuts, which is reserved to a great extent for special occasions.

Pork butt (boneless), at least 80%, ...	800 g (1.76 lb)
Pork tongue, at least 15%, ...	200 g (0.44 lb)

Ingredients per 1 kg (2.2 lb) of meat

Salt	28 g	4.5 tsp
Pimentón, sweet	25 g	4 Tbsp
Pimentón, hot	2.0 g	1 tsp
Garlic	3.5 g	1 clove

Cut butt (*cabecera*) into 2-3 pieces. Trim off tendons, skin, membrane. Cut tongue into 25 mm (1") pieces. Mix meats with all ingredients and hold in refrigerator for 48 hours.
Stuff firmly into pork blind cap (caecum).
Apply a thin cold smoke at 18° C (64° F) for at least 8 days. Use oak, beech or chestnut wood.
Dry at 15-12° C (59-53° F), 75-80% humidity for minimum of 30 days.
Store at 10-12° C (50-53° F), <75% humidity.

Notes

In 2011 Chosco de Tineo was granted PGI certificate (Protected Geographical Indication), which brought it the fame and recognition.

Instead of drying there is an option of cooking smoked Chosco in water at 80-100° C (176-212° F). To eliminate possibility of rupturing the sausage it is recommended to cook at 80° C. This will take at least 2 hours, until the sausage reaches 72° C (160° F) internal temperature. Cooked Chosco de Tineo must be kept in refrigerator.
In home production it is recommended to add 2.5 g of cure #1. TSPX starter culture (0.12 g per 1 kg meat) can be added just before stuffing for better control of the process.

Chosco or Choscu

Chosco is a large-diameter sausage that is very popular in Asturías. This recipe is for a fully cured version of chocolate. The sausage is made from chunks of pork tongue, lean pork or pork loin, and dewlap (double chin). Pimentón delivers a characteristic red color. *Chosco is a fully cured sausage that is ready to eat at any time; however, if the same Chosco sausage is only lightly cured, it becomes Choscu and must be refrigerated and, of course, cooked before serving.* In other words, both sausages include the same ingredients, but due to different drying times, they carry different names. Fully cured (dried) chosco can be consumed raw or added to other dishes, but partially dried chosco must be cooked, usually in water, before serving. The sausage is usually served with cut-boiled potatoes (*cachelos*) or added to the famed Spanish bean stew (*fabada asturiana*).

Pork tongue	500 g	1.10 lb
Lean pork or loin	350 g	0.77 lb
Dewlap or jowls	150 g	0.33 lb

Ingredients per 1 kg (2.2 lb) of meat

Salt	28 g	4.5 tsp
Cure #2	2.5 g	1/2 tsp
Pimentón	25 g	4 Tbsp
Garlic	7.0 g	2 cloves

Cut all meats into smaller chunks.
Mix meats with all ingredients and hold in refrigerator for 2 days.
Stuff firmly into pork blind cap (caecum), 60-70 mm pork middles, or 70-90 mm pork bungs.
Dry at 15-12° C (59-53° F), 75-80% humidity in a dark, well ventilated rom for 2-3 months.
Sausage is done when it loses 30% of its original weight.
Store sausages at 10-12° C (50-53° F), <75% humidity or refrigerate.

Chouriça de Carne de Barroso - Montalegre

This Portuguese sausage is produced in the municipality of Montalegre, in the Vila Real district.

Lean pork: shoulder, leg, loin, trimmings	1000 g	2.2 lb

Ingredients per 1 kg (2.2 lb) of meat

Salt	18 g	3 tsp
Cure #1	2.5 g	1/2 tsp
Sugar	3.0 g	1/2 tsp
Pepper	2.0 g	1 tsp
Paprika, sweet	4.0 g	2 tsp
Garlic	4.0 g	1 clove
Red or white dry wine	120 ml	1/2 cup

The meat is cut into small pieces, seasoned with salt, Cure #1, garlic and wine for 5 days in refrigerator. Then it is drained and paprika is added.

Stuff the mixture into 36 mm hog casing and tie the ends together forming a ring.

Apply a thin cold smoke at ≤18° C (64° F) for 10-15 days. Smoking need not be continuous, for example the fire can be put out at night and restarted in the morning as long as the temperature inside of the smokehouse stays below 18° C. The sausage is smoked with oak wood.

Refrigerate.

Note: Chouriça de Carne de Barroso -Montalegre carries PGI 2007 classification.

Chouriça de Carne de Melgaço

Chouriço is probably Portugal's most popular sausage. A dry sausage similar to the more popular Spanish chorizo, chouriço is very garlicky, red-brown with paprika, and sold in links about 10 inches long and 1 1/2 inches in diameter.

Pork shoulder		700 g	1.54 lb
Pork back fat, hard trimmings or belly		300 g	0.66 lb

Ingredients per 1 kg (2.2 lb) of meat

Salt	30 g	5 tsp
Cure #2	5.0 g	1 tsp
Pimentón (smoked Spanish paprika), sweet	10 g	3 tsp
Onion powder	3.0 g	1/2 tsp
Garlic powder	5.0	1 tsp
Bay leaf, crushed	1	1
White wine	30 ml	1 fl oz

Grind meat through 8 mm (5/16") plate. Grind fat through 8 mm (5/16") plate. Mix meat, fat and all ingredients together. Place the mixture for 1 week in a refrigerator or a cool place where temperature will not exceed 11° C (52° F). Cover the container and stir the mixture twice a day.

Stuff firmly into small diameter (< 30 mm) hog casings forming horse-shoe shaped loops about 30 cm (1 foot) long.

Apply a thin cold smoke at 18° C (64° F) for 15 days using hard wood chips.

Dry at 16 → 12° C (60-54° F), 85 → 80% humidity for 21 days. The sausage is dried until around 30% in weight is lost.

Store sausages at 10-15° C (50-59° F), < 75% humidity.

Note: Chouriça de Carne de Melgaço carries PGI, 2015 classification.

Chouriça de Carne de Vinhais

Chouriça de Carne de Vinhais, also known as Linguiça de Vinhais, is produced in the area of Vinhais in Portugal.

Pork - loin, neck, butt, belly	1000 g	2.2 lb

Ingredients per 1 kg (2.2 lb) of meat

Salt	28 g	5 tsp
Cure #2	2.5 g	1/2 tsp
Sugar	3.0 g	1/2 tsp
Paprika	4.0 g	2 tsp
Bay leaf, crushed	1 leaf	1 leaf
Garlic	7.0 g	2 cloves
Red or white dry wine	60 ml	2 oz fl
Water	60 ml	2 oz fl

Cut meat into 25 mm (1") cubes.
Make a marinade by mixing all ingredients with wine and water.
Mix meat with marinade and place for 12 hours in refrigerator. Drain.
Stuff firmly into 32 mm hog casings. Make a ring by tying both ends together.
Hold for 1-2 hours at room temperature.
Apply a thin cold smoke at 18° C (64° F) for 14 days. Smoking need not be continuous, for example the fire can be put out at night and restarted in the morning as long as the temperature inside of the smokehouse stays below 18° C. The sausage is smoked with oak, chestnut or a mixture of both.
Dry at 12-15° C (54-59° F), 75% humidity for 21 days.
Store at 12° C (54° F), 70% humidity.

Note: Chouriça de Carne de Vinhais carries PGI 1998 certification.

Chouriça Doce de Vinhais

Chouriça Doce de Vinhais is a smoked Portuguese sausage from Vinhais. It is made from the meat of pigs of the Bisaro breed, regional bread, olive oil pig's blood, honey, walnuts, or almonds, and stuffed into a diameter pig or cow casing. It is horseshoe-shaped, approximately 20 to 25 cm long, and approximately 2 to 3 cm in diameter. The finished product is black due to blood and long smoking.

Lean pork from shoulder or head	350 g	0.77 lb
Pork belly	200 g	0.44 lb
Pork blood	150 ml	5 oz fl
Wheat bread	170 g	4 slices
Honey	40 g	2 Tbsp
Walnuts	60 g	2 oz
Olive oil	30 g	2 Tbsp

Ingredients per 1 kg (2.2 lb) of material

Salt	15 g	2.5 tsp
Pepper	2.0 g	1 tsp
Garlic powder	1.0 g	1/2 tsp
Cinnamon	0.5 g	1/4 tsp
Mace	0.5 g	1/4 tsp
Cloves, ground	0.25 g	1/8 tsp

Cut lean pork and belly into smaller pieces. Add into a pot with water and some salt and simmer below boiling point until meat is cooked. Remove the meat, save the meat stock. Cut bread into thin slices (leave the crust on) and soak in the meat stock. Remove, strain and squeeze the bread to remove excess of stock. Mix all meats (cut into smaller pieces if needed), bread, blood, nuts, honey, oil and spices together.
Stuff into 30 mm hog casings forming rings 25 cm (10") long.
Apply cold smoke at 18° C (64° F) for 8 days. Smoking does not need to be continued as long as the sausages are kept at low temperature. Then continue drying sausages at 15 → 12° C (59 → 53° F), 70-75% humidity for 15 days or more without smoke. Use oak or chestnut wood for smoking.

Notes
Chouriça doce de Vinhais carries PGI 2008 certificate.

Chouriço

Chouriço is Portugal's most popular sausage. A dry sausage similar to the more popular Spanish chorizo (which may be substituted for it in recipes), chouriço is very garlicky, red-brown with paprika, and smoked.

Pork shoulder	1000 g	2.2 lb

Ingredients per 1 kg (2.2 lb) of meat

Salt	28 g	3 tsp
Cure #2	2.5 g	1/2 tsp
Dextrose	5.0 g	2 tsp
Pepper	4.0 g	2 tsp
Sweet paprika	2.0 g	1 tsp
Smoked paprika (pimentón)	4.0 g	2 tsp
Cayenne pepper	0.5 g	1/2 tsp
Minced garlic	10 g	1 Tbsp
Red wine	15 ml	1 Tbsp

Cut meat into 10 mm (3/8") pieces.
Mix with all ingredients.
Stuff firmly into 36 mm hog casings and tie off into (25 cm (10")) rings.
Apply a thin cold smoke at 18° C (64° F) for 2 days.
Dry for 30 days at 12-15° C (54-59° F), 70-75% humidity.
Store at 12° C (54° F), 70% humidity.

Chouriço Azedo de Vinhais

Chouriço Azedo de Vinhais, also known as Azedo de Vinhais and Chouriço de Pão de Vinhais is produced in the Vinhais province in the Bragança district of Portugal.

Lean pork (head, shoulder)	700 g	1.54 lb
Fat, pork belly, back fat, fat trimmings)	300 g	0.66 lb

Ingredients per 1 kg (2.2 lb) of material

Salt	28 g	5 tsp
Cure #1	2.5 g	1/2 tsp
Pepper	2.0 g	1 tsp
Sweet paprika	4.0 g	2 tsp
Garlic, minced	4.0 g	1 clove
Olive oil	30 ml	2 Tbsp

Chop meat into sizes suitable for cooking. Place all meats in a pot, add some salt and cover with water. Occasionally soup greens are added for better flavor. Simmer the meat until soft. Drain meats but save the meat stock.
Spread the meat on the table and separate meat from bones when the meat is still warm.
Break up or cut up white bread (the crust is left on) and soak it in the hot meat stock adding strips of meat, all spices and all ingredients. Drain and squeeze the excess stock out.
Stuff into 70-100 mm hog casings (pork middles, fat ends or bungs) about 25 cm (10") long.
Apply a thin cold smoke ≤ 18° C (64° F) for 4 weeks using local wood (oak, chestnut). Smoking need not be continuous, for example the fire can be put out at night and restarted in the morning as long as the temperature inside of the smokehouse stays below 18° C.
Hold at 12-15° C (54-59° F), 75% humidity for 7 days.
Store at 12° C (54° F), 70% humidity or refrigerate.

Note: Chouriço Azedo de Vinhais carries PGI 2008 classification.

Chouriço de Abóbora de Barroso - Montalegre

Chouriço de Abóbora de Barroso-Montalegre is a very original Portuguese pork-pumpkin sausage from Barroso-Montalegre, a small area on the northern border with Spain, west of Bragança and northwest of Braga.

Pork, semi-fat	700 g	1.54 lb
Pumpkin (or squash)*	200 g	0.44 lb
Wine, red or white	100 ml	3.33 oz fl

Ingredients per 1 kg (2.2 lb) of material

Salt	18 g	3 tsp
Cure #2	2.5 g	1/2 tsp
Sugar	3.0 g	1/2 tsp
Paprika, sweet	2.0 g	1 tsp
Chili powder	2.0 g	1 tsp
Garlic, minced	7.0 g	2 cloves
Bay leaf, crushed	1 leaf	1 leaf
Cinnamon	1.0 g	1/2 tsp
Ginger	1.0 g	1/2 tsp

Cut the meat and fat into small pieces and marinate with salt, Cure #1, bay leaf, garlic and wine for up to 5 days. Stir daily.
Scrape the flesh of the squash (or pumpkin), discard the seeds. Wrap around with a cloth (or cheese cloth), place in a colander, add some weight on top and let it drain for 2 days.
Mix meat, squash, paprika, chili, cinnamon and ginger together.
Stuff into 60 mm hog casing. The casing is tied shut with two simple knots at each end, using a single piece of cotton twine, giving the sausage a horseshoe shape.
Apply a thin cold smoke at 18° C (64° F) for 30 days. Smoking need not to be continuous, for example the fire can be put out at night and restarted in the morning as long as the temperature inside of the smokehouse stays below 18° C. Think of the process as drying with smoke. The sausage is smoked with oak.
Dry at 12-15° C (54-59° F), 75% humidity for 7 days.
Store at 12° C (54° F), 70% humidity.

Note: * Both squash and pumpkin belong to the same family (*the cucurbitaceae*). A pumpkin is a type of squash.

Chouriço de Abóbora de Barroso-Montalegre carries PGI, 2007 classification.

Chouriço de Carne de Estremoz e Borba

Chouriço de Carne de Estremoz e Borba is a Portuguese sausage that originated in the municipalities of Alandroal, Borba, Estremoz, and Vila Viçosa.

Lean pork	700 g	1.54 lb
Fat pork	300 g	0.66 lb

Ingredients per 1 kg (2.2 lb) of material

Salt	28 g	5 tsp
Cure #1	2.5 g	1/2 tsp
Pepper	2.0 g	1 tsp
Sugar	3.0 g	1/2 tsp
Sweet paprika	4.0 g	2 tsp
Garlic, minced	8.0 g	2 cloves

Cut meat into (12 mm (1/2")) pieces.
Mix with all ingredients.
Stuff firmly into 30 mm hog casings. Tie the ends together making a 8-12" (20-30 cm) long loop.
Smoke with oak wood at 30° C (86° F) for at least 3 days.
Store at 5-8° C (41-46° F), 75% humidity until the sausage loses about 30% of its original weight.

Notes
The meat must come from the Alentejano pig. Chouriço de Carne de Estremoz e Borba carries PGI 2004 classification.

Chouriço de Portalegre

Chouriço de Portalegre is produced in
Portalegre's district in Portugal.

Lean pork	700 g	1.54 lb
Back fat, belly,		
fat trimmings	300 g	0.66 lb

Ingredients per 1 kg (2.2 lb) of meat

Salt	18 g	3 tsp
Cure #1	2.5 g	1/2 tsp
Sugar	3.0 g	1/2 tsp
Paprika, sweet	4.0 g	2 tsp
Chili powder	1.0 g	1/2 tsp
Garlic, minced	7.0 g	2 cloves
White wine	60 ml	2 oz fl
Water	60 ml	2 oz fl

Make a marinade by mixing all ingredients with
wine and water.
Separately cut meat and fat into 20 mm (3/4")
pieces.
Mix meat and fat with marinade. Hold for 2
days at 10° C (50° F), 80-90% humidity or keep
in refrigerator. Stir daily.
Stuff into 36-45 mm hog or beef casings. Tie
the ends together to make a loop about 40 cm
(16") long.
Apply a thin cold smoke at 18° C (64° F) for
3-10 days (depending on diameter). Smoking
need not to be continuous, as long as the
temperature inside of the smokehouse stays
below 18° C. Think of the process as drying
with smoke. The sausage is smoked with oak.
Store at 12° C (54° F), 70% humidity until the
sausage loses about 30% of its original weight.

Note: The meat must come from the Alentejano
pig.
Chouriço de Portalegre carries PGI 1997
classification.

Chouriço Mouro de Portalegre

A dark, smoked sausage form Portalegre
region. A dark, smoked sausage from the
Portalegre region. In 711, the Moors (Mouro in
Portuguese) invaded the Iberian Peninsula from
North Africa and ruled the entire region until
their expulsion in 1609. They left their mark
on Spanish flamenco music and local cuisine,
including this sausage.

Pork meat-head meat,		
hearts, kidneys,		
meat trimmings	500 g	1.10 lb
Pork belly, fat trimmings	300 g	0.66 lb
Bell peppers, fresh	80 g	3.0 oz
White wine	60 ml	2 oz fl
Water	60 ml	2 oz fl

Ingredients per 1 kg (2.2 lb) of material

Salt	12 g	2 tsp
Cure #1	2.5 g	1/2 tsp
Paprika, sweet	4.0 g	2 tsp
Pepper paste	50 g	2 oz
Garlic, minced	7.0 g	2 cloves
Cumin or caraway seeds	2.0 g	1 tsp

Pepper paste. Cut bell peppers lengthwise into
halves. Discard stems and seeds. Get a suitable
pan and sprinkle salt on the bottom. Place
peppers on salt, then cover them with more
salt. Repeat the procedure creating a multilayer
combination with salt being the top layer. Hold
for 8 days. Rinse with water, pat dry with paper
towel and grind through 3 mm (1/8") plate or
emulsify in food processor.
Make marinade by mixing salt, Cure #1, spices,
water and wine.
Chop the meat and fat into 10 mm (3/8") cubes.
Marinate the meat and fat in marinade for 3
days in refrigerator or at <10° C (50° F).
Mix pepper paste with marinated meat.
Stuff firmly into 36 mm hog casings. Tie the
ends together to form a loop.
Apply a thin cold smoke at 18° C (64° F) for
7 days. Smoking need not to be continuous,
as long as the temperature inside of the
smokehouse stays below 18° C. Think of the
process as drying with smoke. The sausage is
smoked with oak.
Store at 12° C (54° F), 70% humidity until the
sausage loses about 30% of its original weight.

Notes
Chouriço Mouro de Portalegre carries PGI 1997
certification.

Ciauscolo

Ciauscolo, sometimes also spelled *ciavuscolo* or *ciabuscolo is* a variety of Italian salame typical of the Marche region. It is made from the common meat cuts: belly, shoulder, ham and loin trimmings. A high percentage of soft fat contributes to give it its typically creamy consistency.

Pork belly	600	1.32 lb
Pork shoulder	200	0.44 lb
Ham and loin trimmings	200	0.44 lb

Ingredients per 1 kg (2.2 lb) of meat

Salt	30 g	5 tsp
Cure #2	2.5 g	1/2 tsp
Pepper	2.0 g	1 tsp
Dextrose (glucose)	2.0 g	1/2 tsp
Garlic, finely diced	3.0 g	1 tsp
Juniper berries	2	2
Vino cotto or red wine	20 ml	4 tsp

Grind lean meat through 6 mm (1/4") plate, then grind it twice through 3 mm (1/8") plate.
Cut pork belly into 25 mm (1") cubes and partially freeze.
Grind pork belly with 3 mm (1/8") plate, partially refreeze and grind again. Hold in refrigerator until needed.
Crush juniper berries and grind them in a spice mill.
Mix lean meat with all ingredients until sticky. Add ground belly and mix all again.
Stuff into beef middles or large diameter hog casings (45 - 100 mm), 6 - 18" (15 - 45 cm) long.
Apply a thin cold smoke at 15-18° C (59-64° F) for 2-3 days.
Dry sausages for 30 - 45 days (depending on diameter) at 12-15° C (53 - 59° F), 65-80% humidity.
Store at 10-12° C (50-53° F), 65-70% humidity.

Note: if available, add juniper branches to fire on the second day to impart a characteristic for this sausage flavor. This is a common practice when smoking hunter's type sausages, regardless of the country.
Ciauscolo is not sliced but is 'spread' on bread.
Ciauscolo carries PGI 2009 certification.

Csabai Kolbasz

Hungarian 'Csabai kolbász' or 'Csabai vastagkolbász' is produced within the administrative boundaries of the towns of Békéscsaba and Gyula.

Pork (shoulder, leg, loin belly)	700 g	1.54 lb
Back fat	300 g	0.66 lb

Ingredients per 1 kg (2.2 lb) of meat

Salt	28 g	3 tsp
Cure #2	2.5 g	1/2 tsp
Pepper	2.0 g	1 tsp
Paprika, sweet	9.0 g	3 tsp
Paprika, hot	9.0 g	3 tsp
Caraway, crushed	3.0 g	1.5 tsp
Garlic, smashed	7.0 g	2 cloves

Meat is manually boned, which enables the thorough removal of sinews, gristle and connective tissue.
Grind meat through 6 mm (1/4") plate.
Grind fat through 6 mm (1/4") plate.
Mix with salt, Cure #2 and spices.
Stuff into 40-60 mm hog or synthetic fibrous casings forming 20-55 cm (8-22") links.
Apply a thin cold smoke for 3-5 days at 20° C (66° F), 70-90% humidity. Original Gyulai kolbasz was smoked with beech wood.
Dry for 4 -6 weeks at 18° → 16° C (64-60° F), 90-92% humidity, then gradually reduce humidity to 70 → 65%.
Store at 12° C (54° F), 65% humidity.

Notes
Csabai Kolbász carries PGI 2010 certification.

Delicatessen Sausage
(Kiełbasa delikatesowa)

The Delicatessen sausage recipe comes from the government archives of Polish sausages.

Lean pork	400 g	0.88 lb
Beef	400 g	0.88 lb
Pork back fat or hard fat trimmings	200 g	0.44 lb

Ingredients per 1 kg (2.2 lb) of meat

Salt	30 g	5 tsp
Cure #2	5.0 g	1 tsp
Sugar	4.0 g	3/4 tsp
Pepper	2.0 g	1 tsp
Sweet paprika	1.0 g	1/2 tsp
Ginger	1.0 g	1/2 tsp
Nutmeg	1.5 g	3/4 tsp
Garlic	1.5 g	1/2 clove

Curing: cut meat into 5-6 cm (2") cubes, mix with salt, sugar and Cure #2. Keep pork, beef and fat separately. Allocate salt, sugar and cure #2 proportionally. The fat needs salt only. Pack tightly in a container and cover with a clean cloth. Place in refrigerator for 72-96 hours.
Grind all meats and fat through 6 mm (1/4") plate.
Mix ground meats with all ingredients until sticky.
Place the mixture in a container for 24 hours at 2-4° C (35-40° F).
Stuff into 60 mm synthetic fibrous casings.
Place sausages in a container one on top of another and hold for 4-5 days at 2-4° C (35-40° F), 85-90% humidity.
Hang for 2-3 days at 8-10° C (46-50° F), 80-85% humidity.
Apply cold smoke at 22° C (72° F) for 2-3 days until brown in color.
Cool in air to 10-12° C (50-53° F) or lower. Dry at this temperature and 75-85% humidity for 10 days. Continue drying for 10 days more at 75% humidity.
Store at 12° C (53° F), 65-75% humidity or refrigerate,

Deutsche Salami
(German Salami)

German salami made from beef and pork, or from pork only.

Lean beef	400 g	0.88 lb
Lean pork	300 g	0.66 lb
Back fat	300 g	0.66 lb

Ingredients per 1 kg (2.2 lb) of material

Salt	28 g	4.5 tsp
Cure #2	2.5 g	1/2 tsp
Dextrose	2.0 g	1/2 tsp
Sugar	2.0 g	1/2 tsp
Pepper	2.0 g	1 tsp
Garlic	3.5 g	1 clove
Rum or red wine	5 ml	1 tsp
T-SPX culture scale	0.12 g	use

Grind beef through 3 mm (1/8") plate.
Grind pork through 6 mm (1/4") plate.
Grind partially frozen fat through 6 mm (1/4") plate.
Mix ground meat with all ingredients.
Stuff into 55 mm beef or pork middles or synthetic protein lined casings. Form 50 cm (20") straight links.
Ferment at 20° C (68° F), 95 → 85% humidity for 3 days.
Cold smoke at 18° C (64° F) for 1 day.
Dry at 15 → 12° C (58 → 53° F), 80-75% humidity for 5 weeks until sausage looses 33% of its original weight.
Store at 10-12° C (50-53° F), <75% humidity.

Dongguan

Dongguan sausage, also called Guandong sausage, is a very popular Cantonese sausage in the Guangdong province of China and in neighboring countries. Guangdong province is located in the southernmost part of the Chinese mainland. Quoted from China Daily: Legend tells of a very short man who sold sausages for a living. As he shouldered the sausages down the street, some of the longer sausages reached the ground and were dragged through the mud. People laughed at him, saying he was too short to carry the sausages. He found ways to make the sausages shorter and taste differently from others. The aroma of his short, fat sausages could be smelled from afar, attracting many customers. Today, people still call a short, clever person a "Dongguan Sausage." It is thought that the Dongguan sausage was introduced to Guangdong by Arab merchants in the 7th century, during the rule of the Tang Dynasty.

Pork, lean	700 g	1.54 lb
Back fat or hard fat trimmings	300 g	0.66 lb

Ingredients per 1 kg (2.2 lb) of meat

Salt	25 g	4 tsp
Cure #1	3.0 g	3/4 tsp
Sugar	60 g	4 Tbsp
Soy sauce	40 ml	1.3 oz fl
Rice wine	15 ml	1 Tbsp
Star anise, powdered	0.3 g	1/5 tsp
Fennel seeds	0.5 g	1/4 tsp
Cinnamon	1.0 g	1/2 tsp
Ginger, powdered	0.5 g	1/4 tsp
Cardamom	0.3 g	1/5 tsp

Cut meat into 25 mm (1") pieces. Mix with all ingredients and marinate overnight.
Grind marinated meat with 6 mm (1/4") plate.
Grind fat with 6 mm (1/4") plate.
Mix meat and fat together. Stuff into 24-24 mm sheep casings, link every 10 cm (4").
Dry at 45-48° C (113-120° F) for 48 hours without smoke. This is a semi-dry sausage that must be refrigerated and cooked before serving. To make a dry sausage keep on drying/storing at 12° C (53° F) until the sausage loses 35% of its original weight.

Droë Wors

Droë wors in Afrikaans, literally "dry sausage," is a Southern African snack food. It is a thinner sausage, so it can dry faster and does not need to be refrigerated.

Lean beef or venison	1000 g	2.2 lb

Ingredients per 1 kg (2.2 lb) of meat

Salt	18 g	3 tsp
Cure #2	2.5 g	1/2 tsp
Dextrose	2.0 g	1/2 tsp
Sugar	2.0 g	1/2 tsp
Pepper	2.0 g	1 tsp
Coriander, ground	4.0 g	2 tsp
Nutmeg	0.5 g	1/4 tsp
Cloves, ground	0.3 g	1/8 tsp
Cider vinegar	45 ml	3 Tbsp

Cut the meat into 25 mm (1") cubes.
Mix with salt and Cure #1, pack tightly, cover with clean cloth and place for 2 days in refrigerator.
Grind through 6 mm (1/4") plate.
Mix with all remaining ingredients.
Stuff in to 24 mm sheep casings.
Dry for 2 weeks at 12-15° C (54-59° F), 75-80% humidity.
Store at 12° C (54° F), 60-70% humidity.

Note: this is a small diameter sausage so it will dry rapidly. Sausages of larger diameter are usually flattened to provide a larger surface area for drying.

Dürre Runde

Dürre Runde is listed (2.211.17) in the German government publication Guide to Meats and Meat Products - *Leitsätze für Fleisch und Fleischerzeugnisse.* This is a fermented sliceable sausage.

Lean beef with connective tissue	250 g	0.55 lb
Lean pork without connective tissue	500 g	1.1 lb
Back fat	250 g	0.55 lb

Ingredients per 1 kg (2.2 lb) of material

Salt	27 g	4.5 tsp
Cure #2	2.5 g	1/2 tsp
Dextrose	1.0 g	1/4 tsp
Sugar	2.0 g	1/2 tsp
Pepper	3.0 g	1.5 tsp
Garlic, smashed	3.5 g	1 clove
T-SPX starter culture scale	0.12 g	use

Grind beef through 3 mm (1/8") plate. Add culture and mix together.
Grind pork through 6 mm (1/4") plate. Mix with beef adding spices.
Grind back fat through 6 mm (1/4") plate. Mix everything together.
Stuff into 46 mm pork or beef casings forming loops.
Ferment at 20° C (68° F), 95 → 75% humidity for 3 days.
Cold smoke at 18° C (64° F) for 24 hours.
Dry at 15→12° C (58 →53° F), 80-75% humidity for 4 weeks until sausage looses 33% of its original weight.
Store at 10-12° C (50-53° F), <75% humidity.

Eichsfelder Feldgieker

Eichsfelder Feldgieker is a firm, fermented sausage with a typical, slightly acidic taste. The Eichsfeld is a historical region in southeastern Lower Saxony and north-western Thuringia. The region has a long tradition of sausage-making, especially the manufacture of 'Eichsfelder Feldgieker,' which is documented in many published literature sources, the earliest dated in 1718. The sausage is made from pork with the typical seasonings (pepper, black or white, coriander) stuffed into sausage casings, which are bladder-shaped (calf's bladder, linen bag, protein casing). High-quality meat from pigs with an extended fattening period and a slaughter weight of at least 130 kg is used. Deutsches Landschwein or Deutsches Edelschwein pig breeds are usually selected. The meat is from selected meat parts (muscle, thighs, back; as fat, only firm belly and back fat).

After slaughtering, the pork must still be warm when production begins. Warm meat has the best water-holding capacity, is more tender, and is better for processing. However, the time when meat must be processed is very short. The non-refrigerated meat must be transported no more than two hours and processed no more than four hours after slaughter; otherwise, the meat will enter the "post mortem" phase, and the meat will stiffen. Needless to say, the entire process, from the slaughter to the finished product, can be accomplished only when the operation takes place in one locality. The meat used to produce 'Eichsfelder Feldgieker' comes exclusively from slaughterhouses, which are licensed to deliver warm meat. "Eichsfelder Feldgieker" is the only Feldgieker sausage for which the meat is processed warm (it is not used for Göttinger Feldgieker). It is only in the Eichsfeld that Feldgieker is made from warm meat. This processing of the meat, when it is still warm, contributes to the special quality of the Feldgieker.

Traditionally the production took place in fermenting/drying chambers which had been in operation for a number of decades so they developed natural flora that would react with meat and produce a constant quality product. Nowadays, any climate controlled chamber will do as the laboratory-made bacteria flora in the form of starter cultures is introduced into the meat.

Lean pork (shoulder)	700 g	1.54 lb
Pork back fat	300 g	0.66 lb

Ingredients per 1 kg (2.2 lb) of material

Salt	28 g	5 tsp
Cure #2	2.5 g	1/2 tsp
Pepper	2.0 g	1 tsp
Dextrose	3.0 g	1/2 tsp
Sugar	3.0 g	1/2 tsp
Coriander	0.5 g	1/4 tsp
Caraway, ground	0.3 g	1/8 tsp
T-SPX culture	0.12 g	use scale

Grind meat and fat through 3-6 mm (1/8-1/4") plate.
Dissolve culture in 1 tablespoon of de-chlorinated water 30 minutes before use.
Mix ground meat with salt and cure #2. Add ground fat, spices and the culture and mix all together.
Stuff into pork or calf's bladder, blind cap (caecum) or 65 mm beef middles. Make 6-12" (15-30 cm) links.
Ferment at 20° C (68° F) for 72 hours, 90-85% humidity.
Dry at 18° C (64° F), 85-80% humidity for 24 hours.
Dry for 5-6 weeks at 15 → 12° C (59 → 54° F), 80 → 75% humidity until the sausage looses 33% of its original weight. The diameter of the sausage influences the drying time.

Notes
Eichsfelder Feldgieker sausage is often stuffed into a linen bag or bladder or pear-shaped casings.
In 1844, a full description of the "Feldkyker" *(field watcher)* was given: "Feldkyker " is a long Schlackwurst (sausage) in a thick natural casing which may have derived its name from the fact that when it – the long variety – is placed in a trouser pocket or hunting bag it sticks out of the pocket or bag and *looks* into the field. The base end is called the *Feldkyke* which at the thickest end is made of intestine *(Die goldene Mark Duderstadt, Carl Hellrung, 1844)*.
The Feldgieker, also known Feldkieker, a type of German salami was already known in 1488 in the Hessian Büraberg near Fritzlar.
Eichsfelder Feldgieker carries PGI 2013 certification.

El Xolis

El Xolis is a quality dry sausage made from lean pork, fat, and spices that is related to salchichón and fuet. The sausage has been produced for many years in the Pallars area, in the Pyrenees, in northwestern Catalonia. The sausage is made in December-January and cured in natural chambers. The area sits at around 1300 meters high, so the winter temperatures are cold, and the air is pure.

Lean pork from rear leg (ham), loin or butt (shoulder)	750 g	1.55 lb
Pork back fat or dewlap...	250 g	0.55 lb

Ingredients per 1 kg (2.2 lb) of meat

Salt	25 g	4 tsp
Cure #2	2.5 g	1/2 tsp
Dextrose	2.0 g	1/2 tsp
Sugar	3.0 g	1/2 tsp
Black pepper	3.0 g	1.5 tsp
Black pepper, whole	1.0 g	1 tsp

Grind meat and fat through 6-8 mm (1/4-5/16") plate.
Mix meat with all ingredients and stuff into pork bungs or large diameter casings. Leave both ends open for now.
Hold for 24 hours in refrigerator. Tie off the ends with twine.
Hang for 4 days at 8-10° C (48-50° F).
Place on a flat surface, place a suitable board with a weight on it (wooden planks were normally used) and flatten for 24 hours, of course, at low temperature. El Xolis is a flattened sausage, often figure "8" shaped. When the sausage lies flat it has manually created grove which runs lengthwise.
Hang at 12-15° C (53-59° F), 80-85% humidity, for 2-3 months.
Store at 10-12° C, <75% humidity.

Notes
Traditional El Xolis was made without cure #2 and sugar.

Farinato

Farinato is a sausage that contains no meat, just lard, flour and pimentón. The sausage is popular in provinces of Salamanca, Zamora and León in the Castlla-León region of Spain. There is a similar Portuguese sausage called Farinheira ("farinha" denotes flour in Portuguese). Originally thought to be the food of poor people, Farinato has gained widespread acceptance to such a degree that a native of Ciudad Rodrigo (*Rodrigo City*) is nicknamed "farinato."

White wheat bread, without crust	450 g	0.99 lb
Vegetable oil	230 ml	7.6 oz fl
Lard	230 g	0.50 lb
Flour	90 g	0.20 lb

Ingredients per 1 kg (2.2 lb) of material

Salt	12 g	2 tsp
Pimentón, sweet	16 g	8 tsp
Onion medium	90 g	1

Cook onion in water for 45 minutes. Drain. Grind onion, bread and lard together.
Mix the ground mixture with all other ingredients.
Stuff into 34-36 mm pork casings. Form 40 cm (16") loops with ends tied together.
Dry sausages at 18° C (64° F) for three days. In traditional production the sausages were hung in the kitchen above the wood fired stove for 3 days.
Move sausage to a drying chamber and dry them at 12-14° C (53 -57° F), 75% humidity, for 15 days.

Notes
The sausage is ready to eat – serve raw or fried. Often used: pumpkin, aniseed and aguardiente (aniseed flavored liqueur).

Farinheira de Estremoz e Borba

Farinheira de Estremoz e Borba is produced in the municipalities of Borba, Estremoz, Vila Viçosa, and Alandroal.

Pork soft fat: pork belly, jowls, fat trimmings	400 g	0.88 lb
Wheat flour	600 g	1.32 lb

Ingredients per 1 kg (2.2 lb) of meat

Salt	18 g	3 tsp
Cure #1	2.0 g	1/3 tsp
Pepper	2.0 g	1 tsp
Red pepper paste*	30 g	2 Tbsp
Paprika	2.0 g	1 tsp
Nutmeg	1.0 g	1/2 tsp
Ginger	0.5 g	1/4 tsp
Garlic, minced	8.0 g	2 cloves
White wine	30 ml	2 Tbsp
Water	240 ml	1 cup

* Red pepper paste. Cut bell peppers lengthwise into halves. Discard stems and seeds. Get a suitable pan and sprinkle salt on the bottom. Place peppers on salt, then cover them with more salt. Repeat the procedure creating a multilayer combination with salt being the top layer. Hold for 8 days. Rinse with water, pat dry with paper towel and grind through 3 mm (1/8") plate or emulsify in a food processor. Make marinade by mixing salt, Cure #1 and spices with wine.
Chop fat into 6 mm (1/4") or smaller pieces. Mix fat with marinade and hold for 3 days at 10° C (50° F) or lower or in refrigerator. Mix marinated fat, red pepper paste flour and water. Add more water if needed.
Mix all together adding flour and water. Add more water if needed.
Stuff into beef casings, tie the ends together making 15 cm (6") long loops.
Smoke for 10 days at 30-40° C (86-104° F) with oak wood.
Store at 12° C (54° F), 70% humidity or in refrigerator.

Home method for making red pepper paste (about 1 cup):

3 red bell peppers
24 g (4 tsp) salt
2 cloves of garlic
1 fl oz (30 ml=2 Tbsp) olive oil

Cut peppers into quarters. Remove the stems and seeds. Remove the white pulp from the inside of the peppers.

Place peppers in a jar and sprinkle them with salt. Shake the jar. Leave uncovered for 24 hours at room temperature. Rinse the peppers and pat them dry with paper towel.

Spread peppers on a pan and bake them for 20 minutes until the skins are charred and dark. Remove the tray and let the peppers cool. Remove the skins from the peppers, they come off easily.

Using a mixer blend the peppers with 2 garlic cloves gradually adding olive oil. The mixture should reach the consistency of a fine creamy paste.

The sausage is made from Alentejano pigs and only beef casings are allowed.

Athough Farinheira de Estremoz e Borba resembles any meat sausage, its taste is not meaty; it's tangy and somewhat sweet. The texture is somewhat doughy due to the large amount of flour the sausage contains.

The sausage is usually roasted, grilled or used in general cooking.

Note: * red pepper paste (in Portuguese "massa de pimentão") is an essential condiment in Portuguese cooking.

Farinheira de Estremoz e Borba carries PGI 2004 certification.

Farinheira de Portalegre

Farinheira de Portalegre is produced in the district of Portalegre.

Pork soft fat: pork belly, jowls,		
fat trimmings	400 g	0.88 lb
Wheat flour	600 g	1.32 lb

Ingredients per 1 kg (2.2 lb) of meat

Salt	18 g	3 tsp
Cure #1	2.5 g	1/2 tsp
Pepper	2.0 g	1 tsp
Red pepper paste*	30 g	2 Tbsp
Paprika	2.0 g	1 tsp
Garlic, minced	8.0 g	2 cloves
White wine	30 ml	2 Tbsp
Water	240 ml	1 cup

* Pepper paste. Cut bell peppers lengthwise into halves. Discard stems and seeds. Get a suitable pan and sprinkle salt on the bottom. Place peppers on salt, then cover them with more salt. Repeat the procedure creating a multilayer combination with salt being the top layer. Hold for 8 days. Rinse with water, pat dry with paper towel and grind through 3 mm (1/8") plate or emulsify in a food processor.

Make marinade by mixing salt and spices with wine.

Chop fat into 6 mm (1/4") or smaller pieces. Mix fat with marinade and hold for 3 days at 10° C (50° F) or lower or in refrigerator.

Mix marinated fat and red pepper paste with flour and *hot* water. Mix all well together.

Stuff into beef casings, tie the ends together making 15 cm (6") long loops.

Smoke for 7 days at 30-40° C (86-104° F) with oak wood.

Store at 12° C (54° F), 70% humidity or in refrigerator.

Note: * red pepper paste (in Portuguese "massa de pimentão") is an essential condiment in Portuguese cooking.

Home method for making red pepper paste (about 1 cup):

3 red bell peppers
24 g (4 tsp) salt
2 cloves of garlic
1 fl oz (30 ml=2 Tbsp) olive oil

Cut peppers into quarters. Remove the stems and seeds. Remove the white pulp from the inside of the peppers.

Place peppers in a jar and sprinkle them with salt. Shake the jar. Leave uncovered for 24 hours at room temperature. Rinse the peppers and pat them dry with paper towel.

Spread peppers on a pan and bake them for 20 minutes until the skins are charred and dark. Remove the tray and let the peppers cool. Remove the skins from the peppers, they come off easily.

Using a mixer blend the peppers with 2 garlic cloves gradually adding olive oil. The mixture should reach the consistency of a fine creamy paste.

Although Farinheira de Portalegre resembles any meat sausage, its taste is not meaty; it's tangy and somewhat sweet. The texture is somewhat doughy due to the large amount of flour the sausage contains.

The sausage is usually roasted, grilled or used in general cooking.

The sausage is made from Alentejano pigs and only beef casings are allowed.

Farinheira de Portalegre carries PGI 2004 certification.

Farmer Sausage
(Wiejska)

Polish sausage is coarsely ground sausage with manually cut fat pieces. Besides its rustic look and different-sized grind, the recipe differs very little from that of classic Italian salamis.

Pork (butt),	300 g	0.66 lb
beef (chuck),	500 g	1.10 lb
back fat or		
hard fat pork trimmings	200 g	0.44 lb

Ingredients per 1 kg (2.2 lb) of meat

Salt	28 g	5 tsp
Cure #2	2.5 g	1/2 tsp
Dextrose	3 g	1 tsp
Ground white pepper	3 g	1.5 tsp
T-SPX culture	0.12 g	use
scale		

Grind pork through 10 mm (3/8"). Dice back fat or pork fat trimmings into 6 mm (1/4") pieces. Grind beef with 6 mm (1/4"), partially freeze and regrind again through 3 mm (1/8") plate.
Mix all ingredients with meat.
Stuff firmly into 60 mm beef middles or protein lined fibrous casings. Make 40 cm (16") long links.
Ferment at 20° C (68° F) for 72 hours, 90-85% humidity.
Cold smoke at 20° C (68° C) or lower for 24 hours.
Dry at 16-12° C (60-54° F), 85-80% humidity, for 2-3 months. The sausage is dried until around 30-35% in weight is lost.
Store sausages at 10-15° C (50-59° F), 75% humidity.

Feldkieker (Feldgicker)

The Feldgieker, also known Feldkieker, a type of German salami was already known in 1488 in the Hessian Büraberg near Fritzlar. Friedcakes is listed (2.211.09) in the German government publication Guide to Meats and Meat Products - *Leitsätze für Fleisch und Fleischerzeugnisse.*

In 1844, a full description of the "Feldkyker" *(field watcher)* was given: "Feldkyker " is a long Schlackwurst (sausage) in a thick natural casing which may have derived its name from the fact that when it – the long variety – is placed in a trouser pocket or hunting bag it sticks out of the pocket or bag and *looks* into the field. The base end is called the *Feldkyke* which at the thickest end is made of intestine *(Die goldene Mark Duderstadt, Carl Hellrung, 1844).*

| Lean pork | 700 g | 1.54 lb |
| Back fat | 300 g | 0.66 lb |

Ingredients per 1 kg (2.2 lb) of material

Salt	28 g	5 tsp
Cure #2	2.5 g	1/2 tsp
Pepper	2.0 g	1 tsp
Dextrose	2.0 g	1/2 tsp
Sugar	2.0 g	1/2 tsp
Coriander	0.5 g	1/4 tsp
Caraway, ground	0.3 g	1/8 tsp
T-SPX culture	0.12 g	use
scale		

Grind pork through 6 mm (1/4") plate.
Grind back fat through 6 mm (1/4") plate.
Mix meat, fat and all ingredients together.
Stuff into 55 mm pork or beef middles forming loops.
Ferment at 20° C (68° F), 95 → 85% humidity for 3 days.
Cold smoke at 18° C (64° F) for 24 hours.
Dry at 14 → 12° C (58 → 53° F), 85 → 75% humidity for 5 weeks.
Store at 10-12° C (50-53° F), <75% humidity.

Figatelli - Dry

The Fratelli is a dry Corsican sausage made of liver and pork and scented with garlic and spices. The proportion of the liver varies significantly depending on whether it is located in Southern or Upper Corsica. There are many variations, and the sausage can be made as a fresh type that must be fully cooked before serving or a dry type that is ready to eat at any time, though not cooked.

Pork liver	350 g	0.77 lb
Pork shoulder, lean	300 g	0.66 lb
Pork back fat, hard fat trimmings or pork belly	300 g	0.66 lb
Pork blood	50 ml	1.4 oz fl

Ingredients per 1 kg (2.2 lb) of meat

Salt	24 g	4 tsp
Cure #1	2.5 g	1/2 tsp
Pepper	6.0 g	3 tsp
Garlic	10 g	3 cloves
Cloves, ground	0.3 g	1/4 tsp
Bay leaf, crushed	1	1

Discard all sinews, gristle and connective tissue.
Dice lean pork into small pieces and mix with blood. Dice liver into 12 mm (1/2") cubes. Dice partially frozen fat into 6 mm (1/4") cubes. Mix lean pork with liver and all spices. Add fat and mix again.
Stuff firmly into 36 mm hog casings forming 2 feet long u-shaped loops.
Cold smoke at 18° C (64° F) for 2 days.
Dry in air at 12-15° C (53-59° F) for 3 weeks.
Store at 12° C (53° F) 65% humidity. Drying and storing is often accomplished in a cellar.

Notes
Figatelli was originally smoked with beech wood.
Dry Figatelli can be enjoyed on its own or served with lentils and a sauce. It is traditionally accompanied by pulenda (Corsican bread made from chestnut flour) and brocciu (cheese) in some areas. And of course a bottle of Patrimonio, the famous Corsican wine.

Frankfurters-Smoked
(Frankfurterki wędzone)

This cold smoked sausage recipe comes from the official Polish Government archives.

Lean pork	500 g	1.1 lb
Regular pork	500 g	1.1 lb

Ingredients per 1 kg (2.2 lb) of meat

Salt	25 g	4 tsp
Cure #1	2.5 g	1/2 tsp
Sugar	2.0 g	1/3 tsp
Pepper	1.5 g	3/4 tsp
Nutmeg	0.5 g	1/4 tsp

Curing: cut meat into 2.5-5 cm (1-2") pieces and mix with salt and Cure #1. Pack tightly in a container, cover with cloth and keep in refrigerator for 3 days.

Grind pork through 8 mm (5/16") plate.

Mix pork with all ingredients until sticky.

Stuff into 22 mm or larger sheep casings.

Form 15-18 cm (6-7") links leaving them in a continuous coil.

Hang for 8 hours at 2-4° C (35-40° F), 85-90-% humidity or for 1 hour at room temperature.

Cold smoke at 18-22° C (64-72° F) for 6-8 hours until light brown.

Dry at 10-12° C (50-53° F) until 84% yield is obtained.

Store sausages at 10-15° C (50-59° F), 75% humidity.

Fuet

Fuet is a Spanish pork sausage, dry cured, like salami. The sausage is frequently found in Cataluña, Spain. Unlike the Butifarra, another in the family of Catalan sausages, fuet is dry cured. The name fuet means "whip" in the Catalan language.

Lean pork	700 g	1.54 lb
Back fat or		
hard fat trimmings	300 g	0.66 lb

Ingredients per 1000 g (2.2 lb) of meat

Salt	28 g	5 tsp
Cure #2	2.5 g	1/2 tsp
Dextrose (glucose)	3.0 g	1/2 tsp
Pepper	3.0 g	1.5 tsp
Paprika	4.0 g	2 tsp
Garlic powder	3.0 g	1 tsp
T-SPX culture	0.12 g	use
scale		

Grind pork and back fat through 5 mm (3/16")

Mix all ingredients with meat.

Stuff firmly into 38 mm hog, beef middles or protein lined fibrous casings.

Ferment at 20° C (68° F) for 72 hours, 90-85% humidity.

Dry at 16-12° C (60-54° F), 85-80% humidity for 1-2 months. The sausage is dried until around 30-35% in weight is lost.

Store sausages at 10-15° C (50-59° F), <75% humidity.

Note: some fuets are covered with white mold, others not. Mold 600 culture is usually applied.

Fuet de Barcelona

Fuet is a Spanish pork sausage, dry cured, like salami. It is a smaller version of salchichón. Fuet sausage is frequently found in Catalonia, Spain, and most European countries Unlike the Butifarra, another in the family of Catalan sausages, fuet is dry cured. The name fuet means whip (látigo) in the Catalan language. Fuet de Barcelona is closely related to much smaller Secallona, Sumaya (Somalla) or Espatec. The main difference is that the fuet is covered with mold, and the small sausages mentioned above are not.

Lean pork	600 g	1.32 lb
Skinless pork belly	400 g	0.88 lb

Ingredients per 1 kg (2.2 lb) of meat

Salt	25 g	4 tsp
Cure #1	2.5 g	1/2 tsp
White pepper	3.0 g	1.5 tsp
Sugar	5.0 g	1 tsp

Grind lean pork and pork belly through 6 mm (1/4").
Mix all ingredients with meat.
Stuff into 34-36 mm pork casings making straight links.
Dry at 14-15° C (54-59° F), 75-80% humidity for 4 weeks.
Store sausages at 10-12° C (50-53° F), <75% humidity or refrigerate.

Notes
Fuet is covered with white mold.

Geräucherte Bratwurst
(Smoked Bratwurst)

This bratwurst fits into the fermented sausage category. Due to the lack of sugar, no significant fermentation can occur; however, the product is a kind of spreadable bratwurst-mettwurst sausage. *Geräucherte Bratwurst* is listed (2.211.17) in the German government publication Guide to Meats and Meat Products - *Leitsätze für Fleisch und Fleischerzeugnisse.*

Pork belly, lean	700 g	1.44 lb
Pork shoulder, lean	300 g	0.66 lb

Ingredients per 1 kg (2.2 lb) of material

Salt	22 g	3.5 tsp
Cure #1	2.5 g	1/2 tsp
White pepper	3.0 g	1.5 tsp
Caraway, ground	0.5 g	1/4 tsp
Mace	1.0 g	1/2 tsp
Coriander	1.0 g	1/2 tsp
Cardamom	0.5 g	1/4 tsp

Grind all meat with all ingredients through 6 mm (1/4") plate.
Mix with all ingredients.
Stuff into 32 mm pork casings forming 15-20 cm (6-8") links.
Hold for 12-24 hours in refrigerator at 75-80% humidity.
Cold smoke at <18° C (64° F) for 12 hours until gold-yellow.
Hold for 3 days at 18° C (64° F), 75% humidity.
Refrigerate.

Goan Sausage

Goa is a state in western India which was a Portuguese colony prior to 1961. In Goa, chouriço is made from a mixture of pork, vinegar and spices - a combination which is extremely hot, spicy, and flavorful.

Pork, lean	700 g	1.54 lb
Pork back fat or hard fat trimmings	300 g	0.66 lb

Ingredients per 1 kg (2.2 lb) of meat

Salt	30 g	6 tsp
Cure #1	2.5 g	1/2 tsp
Pepper	2.0 g	1 tsp
Red chilies, ground	2.0 g	1 tsp
Cumin	2.0 g	1 tsp
Turmeric	1.0 g	1/2 tsp
Cinnamon	1.0 g	1/2 tsp
Cloves, ground	0.5 g	1/4 tsp
Ginger	0.5 g	1/4 tsp
Garlic	7.0 g	2 cloves
Vinegar	90 ml	3 oz fl

Grind pork through 3/8" (10 mm) plate.
Grind fat through 3/8" (10 mm) plate.
Mix ground meat with salt and cure #1, vinegar and spices.
Stuff firmly into 32-36 mm hog casings. Make links 6" (15 cm) long.
Dry for 2 months at 15 →12° C (59 → 54° F), 85-75% humidity.
Store sausages at 10-15° C (50-59° F), 70% humidity.

Goin Chong - Dry

Going Chong is a Chinese dry sausage that includes pork liver.

Pork, lean	500 g	1.10 lb
Pork back fat	250 g	0.55 lb
Pork liver	250 g	0.55 lb

Ingredients per 1 kg (2.2 lb) of meat

Salt	25 g	4 tsp
Cure #1	3.0 g	3/4 tsp
Pepper	1.0 g	1/2 tsp
Sugar	30 g	2 Tbsp
Soy sauce	15 ml	1 Tbsp
Rice wine	15 ml	1 Tbsp
Cinnamon	1.0 g	1/2 tsp
Cloves, powdered	0.3 g	1/5 tsp
Ginger, powdered	0.3 g	1/5 tsp
Cardamom	0.3 g	1/5 tsp

Grind pork trimmings through 12 mm (1/2 in) plate and dice the chilled back fat into 6 mm (1/4") cubes). Grind liver through a 3 mm (1/8 in) plate.
Mix lean meat and liver with salt, sugar, soy sauce, wine, Cure #1 and spices. Add diced fat and mix all together.
Stuff into 26 -28 mm sheep casings. Make links 10 cm (4") long.
Dry sausages at 45-48° C (113-120° F) for 48 hours. This is a semi-dry sausage that must be refrigerated and cooked to at least 59° C (137° F) internal temperature before serving.

Notes
To make a dry sausage keep on drying/storing at 12° C (53° F) until the sausage loses 35% of its original weight. Dry sausage need not to be cooked.

Gornooryahovski Sudzhuk
(Горнооряховски суджук)

The emergence and popularity of Bulgarian Gornooryahovski Sudzhuk sausages were the results of the relatively constant climatic conditions, gentle air currents in the area of Gorna Oryahovitsa, and the propagation of a specific local combination of white molds *(Penicillium* and *Aspergillus).*

Beef 70/30 lean/fat)	1000 g	2.2 lb

Ingredients per 1 kg (2.2 lb) of meat

Salt	30 g	5 tsp
Cure #2	3.0 g	1/2 tsp
Sugar	5.0 g	1 tsp
Pepper	3.0 g	1.5 tsp
Cumin	2.0 g	1 tsp
Savory, rubbed	1 Tbsp	1 Tbsp
Starter culture, T-SPX	0.12 g	use
scale		

Grind meat through 6 mm (1/4") plate.
30 minutes before mixing dissolve starter culture in 1 tablespoon de-chlorinated water.
Mix ground meat with salt, sugar, Cure #2, culture and spices.
Stuff into 40 mm beef casings. Make links about 45 cm (18") long, tie the ends together making a loop.
Ferment at 20° C (68° F) for 72 hours, 90 → 85% humidity.
Dry at 18-15° C (64-59° F), 85→75% decreasing humidity for 20 days. The sausages are compacted once or twice with metal presses arranged on wooden boards. During the drying process, the surface of the sausage acquires an even coating of white mold which grows naturally in the room.
Store sausages at 10-15° C (50-59° F), <75% humidity.

Notes
Savory is a strong pepper flavored herb which can be found almost everywhere. It plays an important role in Bulgarian cuisine where it is known as chubritsa (chubritsa). You can substitute with thyme which is stronger. Or, combine thyme with a pinch of sage or mint.

Gornooryahovski Sudzhuk carries PGI, 2011 certification.

Goteborg

Swedish dry sausage.

Pork butt	400 g	0.88 lb
Beef chuck	400 g	0.88 lb
Pork cheeks (jowls) or pork belly	200 g	0.44 lb

Ingredients per 1 kg (2.2 lb) of meat

Salt	28 g	5 tsp
Cure #2	2.5 g	1/2 tsp
Dextrose (glucose)	2.0 g	1/2 tsp
Sugar	2.0 g	1/2 tsp
White pepper	3.0 g	1.5 tsp
Cardamom	2.0 g	1 tsp
Coriander	2.0 g	1 tsp
T-SPX culture	0.12 g	use
scale		

Grind pork and back fat through 3/16" plate (5 mm). Grind beef with 3 mm (1/8") plate.
Mix all ingredients with meat.
Stuff firmly into 60 mm beef middles or protein lined fibrous casings. Make 16" long links.
Ferment at 20° C (68° F) for 72 hours, 90-85% humidity.
Cold smoke at 20° C (68° C) or lower for 24 hours.
Dry at 16-12° C (60-54° F), 85-80% humidity, for 2-3 months. The sausage is dried until around 30-35% in weight is lost.
Store sausages at 10-15° C (50-59° F), <75% humidity.

Gothaer

German semi-dry sausage.

Lean pork	800 g	1.76 lb
Beef	200 g	0.44 lb

Ingredients per 1 kg (2.2 lb) of meat

Salt	23 g	4 tsp
Cure #1	2.5 g	1/2 tsp
Dextrose	10.0 g	2 tsp
Black pepper	3.0 g	1.5 tsp
Bactoferm® LHP	0.18 g	use
scale		

Grind pork through plate 5 mm (3/16") mm.
Grind beef through 3 mm (1/8") plate.
Mix all ingredients with meat.
Stuff into beef middles or fibrous casings 40-60 cm, (20") long.
Ferment at 24-30° C (75-86° F) for 24 hours, 90-85% humidity.
Introduce warm smoke (43° C, 110° F), 70% humidity, for 6 hours. Gradually increase smoke temperature until internal meat temperature of 140° F (60° C) is obtained.
For a drier sausage: dry for 3 days at 22 → 16° C (70 → 60° F), 65-75% humidity or until desired weight loss has occurred.
Store sausages at 10-15° C (50-59° F), <75% humidity.

Göttinger Feldkieker

This fermented sausage originates in the area of the German city of Göttingen. Göttinger Feldkieker is predominantly made from older animals. The proportion of pork used from older animals must be at least 65 %. This meat has a unique fat quality due to the specific diet the pigs were subjected to. The prime cuts of the pigs, i.e., shoulders, hams (legs), and bellies, are used to produce the sausage. The sausage will, therefore, not turn rancid either. Göttinger Feldkieker is dried until it loses at least 35% of its original weight, and the water content Aw is 0.88 or less.

Lean pork: shoulder, leg	700 g	1.54 lb
Pork belly	300 g	0.66 lb

Ingredients per 1 kg (2.2 lb) of meat

Salt	28 g	5 tsp
Cure #2	3.0 g	1/2 tsp
Pepper	2.0 g	1 tsp
Dextrose	3.0 g	1/2 tsp
Sugar	2.0 g	1/3 tsp
Coriander	1.0 g	1/2 tsp
Nutmeg	0.5 g	1/4 tsp
Garlic	3.5 g	1 clove
Rum	5 ml	1 tsp
T-SPX culture	0.12 g	use scale

Grind lean meat and belly meat through 6 mm (1/4") plate. Cut belly fat into 6 mm (1/4") cubes. Mix ground meat with salt and Cure #2. Add fat cubes, spices and the culture and mix all together. Stuff into 70-105 mm natural casings. Typically, it is filled into bladder-shaped natural casings, the bladder shape being either long-drawn-out or compressed. Ferment at 20° C (68° F) for 72 hours, 90-85% humidity. Dry for 45-90 days at 15→12° C (59→53° F), 80-75% humidity until the sausage looses 35% of its original weight. Store at 10-12° C (50-53° F), <75% humidity.

Notes: Göttinger Feldkieker differs from Göttinger Stracke by its shape, diameter and weight. The diameter of Göttinger Feldkieker varies over the length of the sausage so it has an elongated pear shape, whilst Göttinger Stracke is straight and uniform in diameter. This means that it matures in a different way and develops a different taste.

Göttinger Feldkieker carries PGI 2011 certification.

Göttinger Stracke

Göttinger Stracke is German dry sausage from the city of Göttingen. The manufacturing process, meat and spice selection is similar to that for Göttinger Feldkieker. Göttinger Feldkieker is dried down until it looses at least 35% of its original weight and the moisture content Aw is 0.88 or less. Göttinger Stracke is cylindrical in shape; intestines with calibres of 40-60 mm and of varying lengths are normally used.

| Lean pork-shoulder, leg | 700 g | 1.54 lb |
| Pork belly | 300 g | 0.66 lb |

Ingredients per 1 kg (2.2 lb) of meat

Salt	28 g	5 tsp
Cure #2	3.0 g	1/2 tsp
Pepper	2.0 g	1 tsp
Dextrose	3.0 g	1/2 tsp
Sugar	2.0 g	1/3 tsp
Coriander	1.0 g	1/2 tsp
Nutmeg	0.5 g	1/4 tsp
Garlic	3.5 g	1 clove
T-SPX culture	0.12 g	use scale

Grind lean meat and belly meat through 6 mm (1/4") plate.
Cut belly fat into 6 mm (1/4") cubes.
Dissolve culture in 1 tablespoon of de-chlorinated water 30 minutes before use.
Mix ground meat with salt and Cure #2. Add fat cubes, spices and the culture and mix all together. Stuff into 40-60 mm natural casings making straight links which can vary in length. Ferment at 20° C (68° F) for 72 hours, 90-85% humidity. Dry for 4-5 weeks at 15 → 12° C (59 → 53° F), 80-75% humidity until the sausage looses 35% of its original weight.
Store at 10-12° C (50-53° F), <75% humidity.

Notes
Göttinger Stracke can be distinguished from 'Göttinger Feldkieker' by means of the shape, diameter and weight of the sausage. Göttinger Stracke is straight and uniform in diameter, whereas the diameter of Göttinger Feldkieker' varies over the length of the sausage having an elongated pear-shape. This means that it matures in a different way and develops a different taste.
Göttinger Stracke carries PGI 2011 certification.

Grassland Sausage
(Kresowa)

In many Eastern countries, Mongolia included, there are vast grasslands that are known as prairies in the USA. In Polish, they are called "kresy," hence the name of the sausage. The following is the traditional Polish recipe.

Lean pork	600 g	1.32 lb
Lean beef or veal	200 g	0.44 lb
Pork back fat or		
hard fat trimmings	200 g	0.44 lb

Ingredients per 1 kg (2.2 lb) of meat

Salt	28 g	5 tsp
Cure #2	2.5 g	1/2 tsp
Allspice, ground	2.0 g	1 tsp
Marjoram	1.0 g	1/2 tsp
Cloves, ground	0.5 g	1/4 tsp
Bay leaf, crushed	1 leaf	1 leaf
Rum	60 ml	1/4 cup

Grind meats with 10 mm (3/8") plate. Cut fat into 20 mm (3/4") cubes.
Mix all ingredients with meat adding rum. Then add diced fat and mix everything together. Stuff firmly into 45 mm beef middles or fibrous casings.
Place sausages between two wooden boards, place weight on top and leave in a cool place 10-12° C (50-54° F), for 2 weeks.
Remove boards and hang sausage in a ventilated cool place for 3 days.
Cold smoke for 7 days.
Dry at 15→12° C (59→53° F), 80-75% humidity for 7 days.
Store in a cool, dry place.

Note: to make an easier hot smoked version of the sausage, replace Cure #2 with Cure #1, decrease salt to 18 g, mix all ingredients, then hot smoke and bake the sausage in the smokehouse. The sausage is shelf stable and can be stored at 10-12° C (50-53° F), <75% humidity.

Greußener Salami

Greußener Salami originates in the German town of Greußen in the Thuringia region of Germany. Greußener Salami is made from select beef, pork, and pork belly and is mildly flavored with pepper and other natural spices. The sausage is smoked with beech wood and matured in separate, air-drying chambers. The product is characterized by its attractive appearance when cut, its stable color retention, and its mild peppery flavor.

Pork	300 g	0.66 lb
Beef	300 g	0.66 lb
Pork belly	200 g	0.44 lb
Back fat	200 g	0.44 lb

Ingredients per 1 kg (2.2 lb) of material

Salt	28 g	5 tsp
Cure #2	2.5 g	1/2 tsp
Dextrose	3.0 g	1/2 tsp
Sugar	2.0 g	1/2 tsp
Pepper	4.0 g	2 tsp
Coriander	1.0 g	1 tsp
Nutmeg	0.5 g	1/4 tsp
Cumin	1.0 g	1/2 tsp
Ginger	0.3 g	1/8 tsp
Garlic	3.5 g	1 clove
T-SPX culture	0.12 g	use scale

Grind pork through 6 mm (1/4") plate.
Grind beef with 6 mm (1/4") plate.
Grind pork belly with 6 mm (1/4") plate.
Cut back fat into 6 mm (1/4") cubes.
Mix lean pork and beef with salt and Cure #2.
Add ground pork belly, spices, culture and mix.
Add fat cubes and mix all together.
Stuff into 40 mm natural or fibrous casings.
Ferment at 20° C (68° F) for 72 hours, 90-85% humidity. Apply a thin cold smoke (with intervals) at 18° C (64° F) for 4 days. Traditionally, the sausage was smoked with beech wood.
After smoking the sausages are stacked in two layers on the shelves in drying/ripening chambers and dried for 4-5 weeks at 12-15° C (54-59° F), 75-80% humidity until sausages loose 30-35% of its original weight.
Store at 10-12° C (50-53° F), 75% humidity.

Notes
Greußener Salami carries PGI 2008 certification. classification.

Güeña

Güeña is a Spanish small diameter sausage popular in La Nueva, which is the region of Castilla-La Mancha and Madrid.

Lean pork	300 g	0.66 lb
Pork belly	400 g	0.88 lb
Pork liver, lungs, heart	300 g	0.66 lb

Ingredients per 1 kg (2.2 lb) of meat

Salt	28 g	4.5 tsp
Cure #1	2.5 g	1/2 tsp
Black pepper	2.0 g	1 tsp
Pimentón, sweet	25 g	4 Tbsp
Pimentón, hot	2.0 g	1 tsp
Nutmeg	1.0 g	1/2 tsp
Cloves, ground	0.3 g	1/8 tsp
Garlic	3.5 g	1 clove

Cook lungs and heart in water for 30 minutes. Drain and cool.
Scald liver in hot water for 5 minutes. Drain and cool.
Grind all meats through 6 mm (1/4") plate.
Mix with all ingredients. Hold for 12 hours in refrigerator.
Stuff into 20-24 mm sheep casings forming 10-15 cm (4-6") links.
Dry at 12-15° C (53-59° F), 75-80% humidity for 14 days.

Notes
Fry in oil or grill and serve with eggs and potatoes, on sandwiches or in stews.

Gyulai Kolbasz

Gyulai sausage is a very famous Hungarian sausage named after the Hungarian town of Gyula. At the World Exhibition of Food in Brussels 1919 and 1935, the Gyulai kolbász was awarded a gold diploma. It has received many other rewards including PGI protection.

Pork (shoulder, leg, loin belly)	700 g	1.54 lb
Back fat	300 g	0.66 lb

Ingredients per 1 kg (2.2 lb) of meat

Salt	30 g	5 tsp
Cure #2	2.5 g	1/2 tsp
Pepper	2.0 g	1 tsp
Paprika, sweet	9.0 g	3 tsp
Paprika, hot	9.0 g	3 tsp
Caraway, crushed	3.0 g	1.5 tsp
Garlic, smashed	7.0 g	2 cloves

Grind meat through 6 mm (1/4") plate.
Grind fat through 6 mm (1/4") plate.
Mix with salt, Cure #2 and spices.
Stuff into 36 mm hog casings forming 20 cm (8") links.
Apply a thin cold smoke for 2-3 days at 20° C (66° F), 70-90% humidity. Original Gyulai kolbasz is smoked with beech wood.
Dry for 2 weeks at 18° → 16° C (64-60° F), 90-92% humidity, then gradually reduce humidity to 70 → 65%.
Store at 12° C (54° F), 65% humidity.

Note: You can make the entire process easier by introducing 0.12 g T-SPX starter culture. All other production steps remain the same.

Gyulai Kolbász carries PGI, 2010 classification.

Haussalami
(Home Salami)

Austrian salami. In Austria Italian style salami started to appear in 1800/1900.

Beef, regular quality	300 g	0.66 lb
Pork, lean	200 g	0.44 lb
Pork fat, hard	300 g	0.66 lb

Ingredients per 1 kg (2.2 lb) meat

Salt	25 g	4 tsp
Cure #2	2.5 g	1/2 tsp
Dextrose	2.0 g	1/2 tsp
Sugar	2.0 g	1/2 tsp
Pepper	2.0 g	1 tsp
Garlic, diced	3.5 g	1 clove
Red wine	15 ml	1 Tbsp
T-SPX culture	0.12 g	use scale

Grind pork and beef through 6 mm (1/4") plate. Grind partially frozen pork fat through 6 mm (1/4") plate.
Mix ground meat with all ingredients, including starter culture. Add ground fat last and mix again.
Stuff firmly into 60 mm beef middles or synthetic fibrous casings.
Ferment at 22° C (72° F), 90% humidity for 72 hours.
Dry at 22 → 14° C (72 → 58° F), 85 → 80% humidity for 5 days.
Dry at 14 → 12° C (57 → 53° F), 80 → 75% humidity for 5 weeks until the sausage loses about 32% of its original weight..
Store at 10-12° C, <70% humidity.

Hofer Rindfleischwurst

Hofer Rindfleischwurst is a spreadable sausage from the Hof region of Germany. Hofer Rindfleischwurst is made from 70% first grade beef low in fatty tissue and free of sinews like beef round (top rear leg) and 30% of pork back fat, preferably from older animals. Only freshly slaughtered meat is used in the production.

The Hofer Rindfleischwurst is elongated in shape and is packed into a synthetic casing from 40 mm to 55 mm in diameter. Depending on the size, individual Hofer Rindfleischwurst can measure up to 50 cm in length and weigh from 150 to 800 grams.

Beef, lean	700 g	1.54 lb
Pork back fat	300 g	0.66 lb

Ingredients per 1 kg (2.2 lb) of meat

Salt	25 g	4 tsp
Cure #1	2.5 g	1/2 tsp
Ascorbic acid (vitamin C) as reddening agent (optional)	0.5 g	1/4 tsp
Dextrose	1.0 g	1/4 tsp
Sugar	2.0 g	1/2 tsp
Pepper	3.0 g	1.5 tsp
Paprika, sweet	1.0 g	1/2 tsp
Nutmeg	0.5 g	1/4 tsp
Coriander	0.5 g	1/4 tsp

Grind beef through 3 mm (1/8") plate. Place in refrigerator to cool. Grind fat through 3 mm (1/8") plate. Place in freezer for 20-30 minutes. Grind beef second time through 3 mm (1/8") plate adding salt and all ingredients. Grind fat second time through 3 mm (1/8") plate.
Mix all together. Stuff into 40 mm cellulose casings.
Hold at 15° C (59° F), high humidity for 10 hours.
Cold smoke with beech wood at 18° C (64° F) for 8 hours.
Refrigerate. Serve as it is, the sausage is not cooked.

Notes

In 1950 in Hof, the butcher Hans Millitzer began producing the Rindfleischwurst (beef sausage) from lean beef. This tradition was continued by his former apprentice Gottfried Rädlein, who produced the Hofer Rindfleischwurst from 1962 to 1993 in his own firm in Hof and made it famous in surrounding areas. In January 1993, Gottfried Rädlein passed his butcher shop on to the renowned butcher's Albert Schiller in Hof, which today continues to specialize in producing the Hofer Rindfleischwurst in the same way as Gottfried Rädlein.

Hofer Rindfleischwurst carries PGI 2011 certification.

Holsteiner

German dry sausage.

| Beef (chuck) | 600 g | 1.32 lb |
| Pork butt | 400 g | 0.88 lb |

Ingredients per 1 kg (2.2 lb) of meat

Salt	28 g	5 tsp
Cure #2	2.5 g	1/2 tsp
Dextrose	2.0 g	1/2 tsp
Sugar	2.0 g	1/2 tsp
White pepper, ground	2.0 g	1 tsp
White pepper, cracked	2.0 g	1 tsp
T-SPX culture	0.12 g	use
scale		

Grind pork through 6 mm (1/4") plate. Grind beef with 3 mm (1/8") plate.
Mix all ingredients with meat.
Stuff firmly into 60 mm beef middles or protein lined fibrous casings. Make 16" long links.
Ferment at 20° C (68° F) for 72 hours, 90-85% humidity.
Cold smoke at 18° C (64° C) for 24 hours.
Dry at 15 → 12° C (59 → 53° F), 85-80% humidity, for 5 weeks. The sausage is dried until around 30-35% in weight is lost.
Store sausages at 10-12° C (50-53° F), <75% humidity.

Holsteiner-American

American version of German dry sausage.

Pork trimmings	500 g	1.10 lb
Beef trimmings	400 g	0.88 lb
Pork back fat or hard fat trimmings	100 g	0.22 lb

Ingredients per 1 kg (2.2 lb) of meat

Salt	28 g	5 tsp
Cure #2	2.5 g	½ tsp
Dextrose	2.0 g	⅓ tsp
Sugar	2.0 g	⅓ tsp
White pepper, ground	2.0 g	1 tsp
White pepper, cracked	2.0 g	1 tsp

Weigh a slab of skinless back fat and rub in 5% salt (50 g salt per 1 kg of back fat) on all sides. Place in refrigerator at 4° C (40° F) for 2 weeks. Rinse with cold water to remove any crystallized salt. Cut into 1/4" (6 mm) cubes.
Grind pork with 6 mm (1/4") plate.
Grind beef with 6 mm (1/4") plate.
Mix all meats and back fat with salt, Cure #2 and spices. Pack tightly in a container about 15 cm (6") deep and hold for 4 days in refrigerator at 4° C (40° F).
Stuff firmly into beef rounds.
Dry for 1 week at 10° C (50° F).
Apply cold smoke at 18° C (68° F) for 2 days. Use hickory, hard maple or oak sawdust.
Store sausages at 10-15° C (50-59° F), <75% humidity.

Hungarian Dry Sausage

Although this sausage carries the Hungarian name it has been always made in Poland and might as well be considered a local product.

Lean beef	300 g	0.66 lb
Pork back fat or		
hard fat trimmings	700 g	1.54 lb

Ingredients per 1 kg (2.2 lb) of meat

Salt	28 g	5 tsp
Cure #2	2.5 g	1/2 tsp
Dextrose	2 g	1/2 tsp
Pepper	2 g	1 tsp
Sweet paprika	3 g	1.5 tsp
T-SPX culture	0.12 g	use
scale		

Grind meat through 3 mm (1/8") plate. Refreeze and grind again. Cut back fat into 20 mm (3/4") pieces.

30 minutes before mixing dissolve starter culture in 1 tablespoon de-chlorinated water. Mix all ingredients with ground meat and diced back fat.

Stuff firmly into beef middles or 3" protein lined fibrous casings.

Ferment at 20° C (68° F) for 72 hours, 90-85% humidity.

Cold smoke for 4 days at 22° C (72° F) or lower. You can apply smoke during the second half of fermentation.

Dry at 16-12° C (60-54° F), 85-80% humidity for 2-3 months.

Store sausages at 10-15° C (50-59° F), 75% humidity.

Hungarian Smoked Sausage
(Kiełbasa węgierska wędzona)

This cold smoked sausage recipe comes from the official Polish Government archives.

Beef,	300 g	0.66 lb
Pork back fat or		
hard fat trimmings	700 g	1.54 lb

Ingredients per 1 kg (2.2 lb) of meat

Salt	21 g	3.5 tsp
Cure #1	2.5 g	1/2 tsp
Pepper	1.5 g	3/4 tsp
Sweet paprika	1.5 g	3/4 tsp

Curing: cut back fat into strips, rub in 2/3 (14 g) salt into fat strips and hold for 10 days in refrigerator. Back fat does not need Cure #1. Cut beef into 2.5-5 cm (1-2") pieces and mix with 1/3 (8 g) salt and all Cure #1. Pack tightly in container, cover and keep in refrigerator for 72 hours.

Grind beef through 3 mm (1/8") plate. Dice back fat into 15 mm (5/8") cubes. Mix back fat with paprika and then mix all together. Add fat cubes last.

Stuff firmly into 40 mm beef rounds or hog casings and form rings. Tie both ends with twine.

Hang for 1-2 days at 2-4° C (35-40° F), 85-90 % humidity.

Apply cold smoke at ≤ 20° C (68° C) for 2-3 days until sausages develop yellow color.

Dry at 15-12° C (59-54° F), 85-80% humidity for 30 days.

Store at 10-12° C (50-53° F), <70% humidity or refrigerate.

Imperial de Bolaños

Imperial de Bolaños is a type of finely ground salchichón. When salchichón is stuffed into casing smaller than than 40 mm, it may be called *longaniza imperial*. It originates in Bolaños de Calatrava, a city situated in the Ciudad Real province in the autonomous community of Castile-La Mancha, Spain.

Lean pork	750 g	1.55 lb
Back fat or		
hard fat trimmings	250 g	0.55 lb

Ingredients per 1 kg (2.2 lb) of meat

Salt	20 g	3 tsp
Cure #1	2.5 g	1/2 tsp
Pepper	4.0 g	2 tsp
Nutmeg	0.5 g	1/4 tsp
Oregano	1.0 g	1 tsp

Grind lean pork and fat through 3 mm (1/8") plate.
Mix ground meats with salt and spices. Hold for 24 hours in refrigerator.
Stuff the mixture into 38-40 mm natural casings forming straight links 30 cm (12") long.
Dry/ferment at 20-27° C (68-80° F), 90-85% humidity, for 30 hours.
Dry at 15-12° C (59-53° F), 85-75% humidity, for 15 days.
Store at 10-12° C (50-53° F), <70% humidity or refrigerate.

Notes
The sausage is ready to eat without cooking.

Imperial de Lorca

Imperial de Lorca is a well-known dry longaniza from Lorca. Lorca is a municipality and city in the autonomous community of Murcia in southeastern Spain, and this is where the sausage originates from. When salchichón is stuffed into casing smaller than than 40 mm, it may be called *longaniza imperial*.

Lean pork	700 g	1.54 lb
Pork belly	300 g	0.66 lb

Ingredients per 1 kg (2.2 lb) of meat

Salt	25 g	4 tsp
Cure #1	2.5 g	1/2 tsp
White pepper	3.0 g	1.5 tsp
Nutmeg	0.5 g	1/4 tsp

Grind lean pork and belly through 6 mm (1/4") plate.
Mix ground meats with salt and spices. Hold for 24 hours in refrigerator.
Stuff into 38-40 mm calf casings forming links 20 cm (8") long.
Dry at 15-12° C (59-53° F), 85-75% humidity for 15-20 days.
Store at 10-12° C (50-53° F), <70% humidity or refrigerate.

Notes
Consume raw.

Isterband
(Isterband korv)

Isterband is a traditional semi-dry fermented sausage. Its texture is soft due to pork belly and barley groats, but not soft enough to be considered a spreadable sausage. In the past, this sausage was and is often referred as "hanging sausage" as it was hung to dry in front of the fireplace. As barley contains a small amount of sugar, the naturally present in meat lactic acid-producing bacteria would trigger fermentation, and some lactic acid will be produced. This is the reason why the Isterband is characterized by a slightly sour flavor.

Pork shoulder	500 g	1.10 lb
Back fat, pork belly, fat trimmings	200 g	0.44 lb
Pearl barley groats, cooked	300 g	0.66 lb

Ingredients per 1 kg (2.2 lb) of material

Salt	24 g	4 tsp
Cure #1	2.0 g	1/3 tsp
Dextrose	4.0 g	1 tsp
White pepper	2.0 g	1 tsp
Allspice	1.0 g	1/2 tsp
Ginger	0.25 g	1/8 tsp
T-SPX culture * scale	0.12 g	use

Take 170 g (6 oz) of barley and soak in 330 ml (11 oz fl) of water overnight. Simmer the barley in this liquid 60 minutes, add more water if needed. Filter the barley.
Grind meats and fat through 6 mm (1/4" plate). Mix ground meats and fat with barley and all ingredients. Stuff the mixture into 36 mm hog casings, forming 25 cm (10") links.
Hold at 15° C (59° F), 85% humidity for 24 hours. Hold for 72 hours at around 18° C (64° F), 75-80% humidity. Apply cold smoke for 12 hours at 18° C (64° F). **Refrigerate.

Notes: * starter culture is optional, but recommended. This is a semi-dry sausage that must be cooked. The sausages can be pan-fried or oven-baked, and they are often served with pickled beets and potatoes doused in a creamy dill-based sauce.
** The sausage can be made shelf-stable by cooking in water at 80° C (176° F) until its internal temperature is maintained for 4 min at 63° C (145° F).

Jauntauler Salami
(Jauntaler Bauersalami)

Jauntaler Bauersalami has been made by farmers since Middle Ages in Jauntal region of Austria. The meat was from local pigs and this salami was cured, cold smoked over beech wood and matured.

Pork, lean	800 g	1.76 lb
Back fat	200 g	0.44 lb

Ingredients per 1 kg (2.2 lb) of material

Salt	27 g	4.5 tsp
Cure #2	2.5 g	1/2 tsp
Pepper	2.0 g	1 tsp
Dextrose	2.0 g	1/2 tsp
Sugar	2.0 g	1/2 tsp
Garlic, diced	3.5 g	1 clove

Grind meat through 6 mm (1/4") plate.
Manually cut partially frozen back fat into 6 mm (1/4") cubes.
Mix ground meat with all ingredients. Add fat cubes and mix again.
Stuff firmly into 60 mm natural casings making 50 cm (20") links.
Hold for 2-3 days in cool room at 1° C (34° F) and 95-100% humidity.
Cold smoke at 18° C (64° F) using beech wood for 12 hours. Wipe off any slime with clean wet cloth.
Ferment/dry at 9-12° C (48-53° F), 90-95% humidity. When mold appears wash it off by hand with pure water and then proceed to the drying stage.
Dry at 10° C (50° F), 75-80% humidity for about 8 weeks. During that time the sausage looses around 40% of its original weight.

Notes
Meat for Jauntaler salami: 80-85% pork, 15-20% pork back fat.

Jesus

This is a large sausage stuffed into pig's caecum (blind cap) casings. The sausage derives its name from its appearance, which resembles the newborn baby Jesus in swaddling cloth.

Lean pork	750 g	1.55 lb
Pork back fat	250 g	0.55 lb

Ingredients per 1 kg (2.2 lb) of meat

Salt	28 g	4.5 tsp
Cure #2	2.5 g	1/2 tsp
Sugar	5.0 g	1 tsp
Pepper	1.5 g	1 tsp
Pepper, whole	2.0 g	1 tsp
Garlic powder	2.0 g	1 tsp
Red wine	15 ml	1 Tbsp
T-SPX culture	0.12 g	use
scale		

Grind lean meat through 12 mm (1/2") plate.
Cut partially frozen fat into 5 mm (1/4") cubes.
Dilute starter culture in 15 ml (1 Tbsp) of distilled water to facilitate distribution.
Mix ground meat with salt and Cure #2, then add all spices, and lastly cubes of fat and starter culture.
Stuff firmly into pork caecum (blind caps), then prick casings with a needle at least dozen times to let any remaining air out.
Ferment at 22° C (70° F), 90 → 80% humidity for 72 hours.
Dry at 15° C (59 F) → 12° C (53° F) for about 12 weeks, until the sausage looses about 33% of its original weight.

Notes
This is a general recipe for Jesus. One of the best known is Jesus de Lyon which has the same composition as Rosette de Lyon, the only difference is that Rosette is stuffed into smaller pork bung ("rosette" in French).

Kaminwurz

Kaminwurz or kaminwurze – an air-dried and cold-smoked Austrian sausage made of beef, pork and back fat is also produced in the South Tyrol region of northern Italy.

Pork shoulder	300 g	0.66 lb
Pork back fat or hard fat trimmings	200 g	0.44 lb
Beef	500 g	1.10 lb

Ingredients per 1 kg (2.2 lb) of meat

Salt	28 g	5 tsp
Cure #2	2.5 g	1/2 tsp
Sugar	2.0 g	1/2 tsp
Pepper	2.0 g	1 tsp
Marjoram, dried, rubbed	1.0 g	1 tsp
Thyme, dried, rubbed	1.0 g	1 tsp
Cumin	2.0 g	1 tsp
Juniper berries, crushed		1/2 tsp
Garlic, finely diced	3.5 g	1 clove
Red wine	30 ml	2 Tbsp

Cut fat into 12 mm (1/2") cubes.
Grind pork through 6 mm (1/4") plate.
Grind beef through 6 mm (1/4") plate.
Mix beef with salt and Cure #2. Add pork and remix.
Mix spices with wine and add to the mixture. Finely, add cubed fat and mix all again.
Stuff firmly into beef middles or 40-42 mm hog casings. Form 20 cm (8") long links.
Hang for 1-2 days at 2-6° C (35-42° F) and 85-90% humidity.
Apply a thin cold smoke at 18° C (64° F) for 2 days. Dry at 12° C (53° F), 75-80% humidity for 3-4 weeks.
Store at 10° C (53° F) or lower.

Kantwurst

Kantwurst is an original Austrian dry sausage, unique in its characteristic square shape.

Lean pork	800 g	1.76 lb
Back fat or		
hard fat trimmings	200 g	0.44 lb

Ingredients per 1 kg (2.2 lb) of meat

Salt	28 g	5 tsp
Cure #2	2.5 g	1/2 tsp
Dextrose (glucose)	3.0 g	3/4 tsp
Pepper	3.0 g	1.5 tsp
Coriander	2.0 g	1 tsp
Caraway	2.0 g	1 tsp
Garlic powder	1.5 g	1/2 tsp
T-SPX culture	0.12 g	use scale

Grind pork and back fat through 5 mm (3/16"). 30 minutes before mixing dissolve starter culture in 1 tablespoon de-chlorinated water. Mix all ingredients with meat.

Stuff into 70 mm diameter fibrous casings. Place stuffed sausage between two boards with some weight on top to flatten the sausage. Then move to a fermentation room.

Ferment at 20° C (68° F) for 96 hours, 95-90% humidity.

Remove boards and wipe off any slime that might have accumulated between the boards. Hold at room temperature until casings are dry to the touch. Hang square shaped sausages on smokesticks.

Cold smoke at 20° C (68° F) for a few hours to prevent growth of mold.

Dry for 2 days at 20-18° C (68-64° F), 90-85% humidity. Apply smoke from time to time.

Dry at 16-12° C (60-54° F), 85 -80% humidity. In about 8 weeks a shrink of 30% should be achieved.

Store sausages at 10-15° C (50-59° F), <75% humidity.

Katenrauchwurst

Katenrauchwurst is listed (2.211.05) in the German government publication Guide to Meats and Meat Products - *Leitsätze für Fleisch und Fleischerzeugnisse.* The sausage derives its name from a smoking process (Katenrauch) that was common in the past. Meats and sausages were suspended for 6-8 weeks in the kitchen or living room of small cottages (Katen) where they acquired smoky flavor from wood fired kitchen stoves. Those were the home made salami type of products as they were dried with a very thin cold smoke.

Lean pork without fat or		
connective tissue	500 g	1.10 lb
Pork belly side	500 g	1.10 lb

Ingredients per 1 kg (2.2 lb) of material

Salt	28 g	4.5 tsp
Cure #2	2.5 g	1/2 tsp
Dextrose	2.0 g	1/2 tsp
Pepper	4.0 g	2 tsp
Rum with junipers*	5.0 g	1 tsp
T-SPX culture	0.12 g	use scale

Smoke raw belly at 18° C (64° F) for 6 hours. Grind lean pork through 6 mm (1/4") plate. Grind pork belly through 6 mm (1/4") plate. Mix meat, fat and all ingredients together. Stuff into 60 mm natural casings.

Ferment at 3 days at 20° C (68° F), 95 → 90% humidity.

Dry for 2 days at 18° C (64° F), 90 → 85% humidity.

Dry at 14→ 12° C (58 → 53° F), 85 → 75% humidity for 5 weeks until sausages loose 30% of their original weight.

Notes

Traditionally smoked sausages were dark due to uncontrolled smoking process and a variety of cooked foods. To approximate this the casings were often soaked for 6-8 hours in salted blood which painted them almost black.

* Rum/Juniper. Rum - 100 ml, crushed juniper berries - 14 g (1/2 oz). The solution is drained and only the liquid is added to sausage mix.

Kindziuk

Kindziuk is the Polish version of Lithuanian Skilandis, an almost legendary product famous for its long keeping properties.

Lean pork	850 g	1.87 lb
Lean beef	150 g	0.33 lb

Ingredients per 1kg (2.2 lb) of meat

Salt	33 g	5.5 tsp
Cure #2	5.0 g	1 tsp
Sugar	1.0 g	1/4 tsp
Pepper	2.0 g	1 tsp
Herbal pepper*	1.0 g	1/2 tsp
Garlic	3.5 g	1 clove

Cut meat into 5 cm (2") pieces. Rub in salt, Cure # 2 and sugar and pack tight in a container. Cover with a clean cloth and hold for 3-4 days at 3-4° C (37-40° F). Discard brine (if any).
Cut pork into 20-30 mm (3/4 - 1.25") by 10-15 mm (3/8-5/8") pieces.
Grind beef through 3 mm (1/8") plate.
Mix beef with all spices. Add pork and mix everything together.
Stuff firmly into pork stomach, bladder, 60 mm beef middles or 60 mm fibrous casings. Avoid creating air pockets. Reinforce with butcher's twine: two loops lengthwise and loops across the casings every 5 cm (2"). Form 10-12 cm (4-5") hanging loop on one end.
Dry for 2 months at 8° C (46° F) and 75% humidity. Apply cold smoke 18° C (64° F) for 8 hours. Dry in a cool, dry and ventilated area (12° C, 53° F) for 2 weeks.
Apply cold smoke again at 18-22° C (64-72° F) for 8 hours.
The sausage should lose about 35% of its original weight.
Store a cool, dry and ventilated area (12° C, 53° F).

Notes: * herbal pepper: white mustard seed, caraway, marjoram, chili, hot and sweet paprika, bay leaf.
Originally the ingredients were stuffed into pork stomach or bladder. The stomach was sewn and the bladder was tied off with butcher twine. Then the casing was placed between two wooden boards and pressed together. The boards were tied with twine and hung. Original Kindziuk was smoked with alder wood.

Kohlwurst
(Kale/Cabbage Sausage)

There is a number of German sausages with the word "kohl" (cabbage) in their name, however, they do not contain cabbage in their composition nor they are stuffed in cabbage leaves. They are usually fermented sausages (salami type) simply served with cabbage, peas and beans, kale and potatoes. Kohl in German stands for kale and for white cabbage (used for sauerkraut).

Beef, lean	200 g	0.44 lb
Pork, lean	400 g	1.10 lb
Back fat, hard fat pork trimmings	400 g	0.66 lb

Ingredients per 1 kg (2.2 lb) of meat

Salt	28 g	4.5 tsp
Cure #2	2.5 g	1/2 tsp
Sugar	3.0 g	1/2 tsp
Pepper	2.0 g	1 tsp
Allspice, ground	1.0 g	1/2 tsp
T-SPX culture	0.12 g	use
scale		

Grind beef through 3 mm (1/8") plate.
Grind pork through 3 mm (1/8") plate.
Grind fat through 6 mm (1/4") plate.
Mix beef with pork and spices. Add fat and culture and mix again.
Stuff into 36 mm hog casings.
Ferment at 20° C (68° F), 95-85% humidity for 3 days.
Apply cold smoke at 18° C (64° F) for 24 hours.
Dry at 14→12° C (58→54° F), 85-80% humidity for 4 weeks or until sausage looses 30% of its original weight.
Store at 10-12° C (50-53° F), <75% humidity.

Kohlwurst-Lippsche

Lippsche Kohlwurst is a cold smoked fermented German sausage from the German County of Lippe. Served with potatoes, cabbage ,or peas and beans. Fatty pork is essential, beef is often added for its excellent binding properties.

Beef	200 g	0.44 lb
Pork*..............................	500 g	1.10 lb
Pork trimmings rich in connective tissue, some skins** permitted ..	300 g	0.66 lb

Ingredients per 1 kg (2.2 lb) of meat

Salt	28 g	4.5 tsp
Cure #2	2.5 g	1/2 tsp
Sugar	3.0 g	1/2 tsp
Pepper	2.0 g	1 tsp
Allspice, ground	1.0 g	1/2 tsp
T-SPX culture	0.12 g	use scale

Grind beef through 3 mm (1/8") plate.
Cook skins** (if used) in water until soft, cool and grind through 3 mm (1/8") plate.
Grind pork through 3 mm (1/8") plate.
Mix beef with pork and spices. Add culture and mix again.
Stuff into 30 mm hog casings.
Ferment at 18° C (64° F), 80-90% humidity for 4 days.
Apply cold smoke at 18° C (64° F) for 24 hours.
Dry at 14→12° C (58→54° F), 85-80% humidity for 3 weeks or until sausage looses 30% of its original weight.
Store at 10-12° C (50-53° F), 65-70% humidity.

Notes
* butt and picnic quality (upper front leg), fat and connective tissue included.
** up to 10% (100 g) of skins are permitted.

Kümmelwurst-Roh
(Fermented Caraway Sausage)

Kümmelwurst is a German sausage made with whole caraway seeds. Caraway is added to rye bread, often to sauerkraut, it is the spice that people either hate or love. The spice is very popular in Polish, German and Jewish cuisine.

Lean beef	300 g	0.66 lb
Lean pork	200 g	0.44 lb
Fatty pork, hard fat trimmings	500 g	1.10 lb

Ingredients per 1 kg (2.2 lb) of meat

Salt	25 g	4 tsp
Cure #2	2.5 g	1/2 tsp
Sugar	3.0 g	1/2 tsp
White pepper	3.0 g	1/2 tsp
Caraway seeds, whole	1.0 g	1/2 tsp
Garlic	3.5 g	1 clove
T-SPX culture	0.12 g	use scale

Grind lean beef through 3 mm (1/8") plate.
Grind lean pork through 3 mm (1/8") plate.
Grind fatty pork and fat trimmings through 5 mm (3/16") plate.
Mix beef and pork with salt and Cure #2. Add fat, remaining spices, starter culture and mix all together.
Stuff into 45-50 mm natural or synthetic fibrous casings.
Ferment at 18° C (64° F), 80-90% humidity for 4 days.
Apply cold smoke at 18° C (64° F) for 24 hours.
Dry at 14→12° C (58→54° F), 85-80% humidity for 4 weeks or until sausage looses 30% of its original weight.

Lamb Sausage

(Баранья колбаса)

Russian dry sausage. Original sheep sausages were made with sheep tail fat not only in Russia, but in other countries as well, for example Turkish "sojouk."

Lean beef	150 g	0.33 lb
Lamb meat rich in connective tissue	750 g	1.65 lb
Sheep tail fat or other sheep fat	100 g	0.22 lb

Ingredients per 1 kg (2.2 lb) of meat

Salt	30 g	5 tsp
Cure #2	5 g	1 tsp
Sugar	2 g	1/2 tsp
Black pepper	1 g	1/2 tsp
Garlic	2 g	1/2 clove

Curing meat. Dice fat into 6 mm (1/4") cubes and mix with 3 g (1/2 tsp) salt only.
Cut meat into 25 mm (1") pieces. Place beef and sheep meat in separate food grade containers and add remaining salt, Cure #2 and sugar proportionally (estimate amounts). Pack tightly to eliminate air and cover with clean cloth. Hold for 72 hours in refrigerator.
Grind beef through 3 mm (1/8") plate. Grind sheep meat with 3 mm (1/8") plate. Mix beef and lamb with spices. Add fat and remix everything together. Don't add any water.
Stuff sausages firmly into 40-55 mm beef middles or fibrous casings.
Hang sausages for 5-7 days at 2-4° C (34-40° F).
Cold smoke for 2-3 days at 18-22° C (64-72° F).
Dry sausages for 5-7 days (depending on sausage diameter) at 11-15° C (53-59° F), 80-84% humidity.
Dry 20-23 days more at 10-12° C (50-54° F), 74-78% humidity.

Finished sausage should retain 60% of its original weight.

Landjager

Landjäger is a German sausage similar to Austrian Kantwurst as both sausages are flattened during fermentation, which gives them a rectangular shape.

Pork, regular	700 g	1.54 lb
Lean beef	300 g	0.66 lb

Ingredients per 1 kg (2.2 lb) of material

Salt	28 g	5 tsp
Cure #2	2.5 g	1/2 tsp
Dextrose	3.0 g	1/2 tsp
Pepper	3.0 g	1.5 tsp
Cumin	2.0 g	1 tsp
Nutmeg	1.0 g	1/2 tsp
T-SPX culture	0.12 g	use scale

Grind pork through 6 mm (1/4") plate. Grind beef through 3 mm (1/8") plate.
Mix all ingredients with meat.
Stuff loosely (80% capacity) into 32-36 mm hog casings. Make links 20 cm (8") long. Place stuffed sausage between two boards, with some weight on top, to flatten the sausage. Then move to a fermentation room.
Ferment at 20° C (68° F) for 72 hours, 95-90% humidity.
Remove boards and wipe off any slime that might have accumulated under boards.
Dry at room temperature until casings are dry to the touch. Hang square shaped sausages on smoke sticks.
Cold smoke at < 20° C (68° F) for a few hours to prevent growth of mold.
Dry at 14→12° C (58→54° F), 85-80% humidity for 3 weeks or until sausage looses 30% of its original weight.
Store at 10-12° C (50-53° F), <75% humidity.

Notes
To make a semi-dry version of the sausage, add total of 1% dextrose and ferment at 24° C (75° F) for 24 hours. Dry for 2 weeks.

Lap Cheong

Lap Cheong is a dried, hard sausage usually made from pork meat and has a high fat content. The Chinese name for sausages is "Lap Chong," which means the "winter stuffed intestine" or "waxed intestine" because "Chong" not only means "intestine" but also "sausage." This sausage is usually smoked, sweetened, and seasoned. It is used as an ingredient in many dishes in some parts of southern China, including Hong Kong and Southeast Asian countries. It is, for example, used in fried rice, noodles, and other dishes. Chinese sausage formulations are unique and based on a long tradition. Ingredients such as monosodium glutamate, soy sauce, and sugar are added to the sausages at very high levels. The addition of selected Chinese rice wines or even scotch or sherry is common for certain quality products.

Pork butt	1000 g	2.2 lb

Ingredients per 1 kg (2.2 lb) of meat

Salt	23 g	4 tsp
Cure #1	2.5 g	1/2 tsp
Dextrose	10 g	2 tsp
Sugar	20 g	4 tsp
Soy sauce	30 ml	2 Tbsp
Cinnamon	2.0 g	1 tsp
Chinese rice wine	15 ml	1 Tbsp
MSG	2.0 g	1/2 tsp
F-LC culture	0.25 g	use scale

Grind pork and back fat through 10 mm (3/8") plate. 30 minutes before mixing dissolve starter culture in 1 tablespoon de-chlorinated water. Mix all ingredients with meat. Add culture last. Stuff firmly into 18-26 mm (3/4-1") hog or sheep casings. Form 15 cm (5-6") long links. Ferment at 38° C (100° F) for 14 hours, 90-85% humidity.
Apply light smoke at 45° C (115° F), 70% humidity for 6 hours then gradually increase smoke temperature to 85° C (185° F) until meat reaches 154° F (68° C) temperature inside. Store sausages at 10-15° C (50-59° F), 75% humidity.

Chinese are fond of using MSG (monosodium glutamate), but it may be removed from the recipe.
(If using lean pork or lean pork trimmings add 30% of back fat).

Lebanon Bologna
(With starter culture)

An American semi-dry sausage.

Beef	1000 g	2.2 lb

Ingredients per 1 kg (2.2 lb) of meat

Salt	28 g	5 tsp
Cure #1	2.5 g	1/2 tsp
Dextrose	10 g	2 tsp
Sugar	30 g	2 Tbsp
Black pepper	3.0 g	1.5 tsp
Allspice, ground	1.5 g	3/4 tsp
Cinnamon	2.0 g	1 tsp
Cloves, ground	1.0 g	1/2 tsp
Ginger	1.0 g	1/2 tsp
F-LC culture	0.25 g	use scale

Grind beef through 3-5 mm (1/8 - 3/16") plate. Mix ground beef with all ingredients.
Stuff sausage mix into 40-120 mm casings. Natural beef middles, collagen or fibrous casings. The larger casings are tied and stockinetted or laced with butcher twine for support as this is a large and heavy sausage. Ferment at 24° C (75° F) for 72 hours, 90-85% humidity.
Cold smoke for 2 days at 22° C (72° F) or lower, 85% humidity.
For a drier sausage: dry at 16-12° C (60-54° F), 85-80% humidity.
Store sausages at 10-15° C (50-59° F), 75% humidity. Sausages will keep on drying out.

Lebanon Bologna-Traditional
(Traditional method)

This well-known American sausage has its roots in Lebanon, Pennsylvania, where German settlers made it. It is a semi-dry, fermented, heavily smoked, uncooked all-beef sausage. The traditional process (without starter cultures) calls for curing beef at 4-6° C (40-43° F) for 10 days.

Beef	1000 g	2.2 lb

Ingredients per 1 kg (2.2 lb) of meat

Salt	28 g	5 tsp
Cure #1	2.5 g	1/2 tsp
Dextrose	10 g	2 tsp
Sugar	30 g	2 Tbsp
Black pepper	3.0 g	1.5 tsp
Allspice, ground	1.5 g	3/4 tsp
Cinnamon	2.0 g	1 tsp
Cloves, ground	1.0 g	1/2 tsp
Ginger	1.0 g	1/2 tsp

Curing: cut or grind beef with a large plate 20 mm (3/4"), mix with salt, Cure #1 and sugar and keep for 10 days at 4-6° C (40-43° F). Grind cured beef through 3-5 mm (1/8 - 3/16") plate.
Mix ground meat with all ingredients.
Stuff sausage mix into 40-120 mm casings. Natural beef middles, collagen or fibrous casings. The larger casings are tied and stockinetted or laced with butcher twine for support as this is a large and heavy sausage.
Cold smoke for 7 days at 22° C (72° F) or lower, 85% humidity.
Refrigerate.

For a drier sausage: dry at 16-12° C (60-54° F), 85-80% humidity.
Store sausages at 10-15° C (50-59° F), 75% humidity. Sausages will keep on drying out.

Note: if no cold smoke is available, smoke with hot smoke for 6 hours. Start at 110° F (43° C), then gradually increase temperature and smoke at 120° F (49° C) for 3-4 hours.

Traditionally made Lebanon Bologna is not cooked. To comply with increasingly tougher government regulations for preventing the growth of E. coli O157:H7, most manufacturers subject this sausage to heat treatment.

Linguíça do Baixo Alentejo

Linguíça do Baixo Alentejo also known as Chouriço de carne do Baixo Alentejo, is a Portuguese sausage produced in the district of Faro from Alentejo pigs.

Lean pork - shoulder, leg loin, lean trimmings	700 g	1.54 lb
Fat pork - belly, back fat, fat trimmings	300 g	0.66 lb

Ingredients per 1 kg (2.2 lb) of meat

Salt	28 g	5 tsp
Cure #1	2.5 g	1/2 tsp
Pepper	2.0 g	1 tsp
Sugar	5.0 g	1 tsp
Red pepper paste*	30 g	2 Tbsp
Cloves, ground	0.5 g	1/4 tsp
Cumin	2.0 g	1 tsp
Garlic, minced	7.0 g	2 cloves
White wine	60 ml	2 oz fl
Water	60 ml	2 oz fl

* Pepper paste. Cut bell peppers lengthwise into halves. Discard stems and seeds. Get a suitable pan and sprinkle salt on the bottom. Place peppers on salt, then cover them with more salt. Repeat the procedure creating a multilayer combination with salt being the top layer. Hold for 8 days. Rinse with water, pat dry with paper towel and grind through 10 mm (3/8") plate or emulsify in food processor. Make marinade by mixing salt, cure #1, sugar and spices with wine and water. Chop meat and fat into 10 mm (3/8") pieces. Mix meat and fat with marinade and hold for 2 days at 10 °C (50° F) or lower (refrigerator). Drain marinade. Mix marinated meat and red pepper paste together. Stuff into 36 mm hog casings, tie the ends together making 30 cm (12") long loops. Using oak wood apply a thin smoke at 18° C (64° F) for 7 days. Smoking need not be continuous as long as the temperature inside of the smokehouse stays below 18° C. Think of the process as drying with smoke. Due to seasonal variations in temperature the sausage is smoked for 3-4 days in the summer and 5-6 days in the winter.
Dry at 12-15° C (54-59° F), 75-80% humidity for 10 days. Store at 12° C (54° F), 70% humidity.

* red pepper paste (in Portuguese "massa de pimentão") is an essential condiment in Portuguese cooking:

Home method for making red pepper paste (about 1 cup):

3 red bell peppers
24 g (4 tsp) salt
2 cloves of garlic
1 fl oz (30 ml=2 Tbsp) olive oil

Cut peppers into quarters. Remove the stems and seeds. Remove the white pulp from the inside of the peppers.

Place peppers in a jar and sprinkle them with salt. Shake the jar. Leave uncovered for 24 hours at room temperature. Rinse the peppers and pat them dry with a paper towel.

Spread peppers on a pan and bake them for 20 minutes until the skins are charred and dark. Remove the tray and let the peppers cool. Remove the skins from the peppers, they come off easily.

Using a mixer blend the peppers with 2 garlic cloves gradually adding olive oil. The mixture should reach the consistency of a fine creamy paste. Place the paste in a jar and store in refrigerator. Use it as a topping for hot dogs or any grilled sausage.

Linguíça do Baixo Alentejo carries PGI 1997 certification.

Linguiça de Portalegre

Linguiça de Portalegre is produced in the Portalegre region of Portugal.

Lean pork - shoulder, leg loin, lean trimmings	700 g	1.54 lb
Fat pork - belly, back fat, fat trimmings	300 g	0.66 lb

Ingredients per 1 kg (2.2 lb) of meat

Salt	28 g	5 tsp
Cure #1	2.5 g	1/2 tsp
Pepper	2.0 g	1 tsp
Sugar	5.0 g	1 tsp
Red pepper paste*	30 g	2 Tbsp
Nutmeg	0.5 g	1/4 tsp
Cumin	1.0 g	1/2 tsp
Garlic, minced	7.0 g	2 cloves
White wine	60 ml	2 oz fl
Water	60 ml	2 oz fl

* Pepper paste. Cut bell peppers lengthwise into halves. Discard stems and seeds. Get a suitable pan and sprinkle salt on the bottom. Place peppers on salt, then cover them with more salt. Repeat the procedure creating a multilayer combination with salt being the top layer. Hold for 8 days. Rinse with water, pat dry with a paper towel and grind through 3 mm (1/8") plate or emulsify in a food processor.

Make marinade by mixing salt, cure #1, sugar and spices with wine and water.
Chop meat and fat into 10 mm (3/8") pieces.
Mix meat and fat with marinade and hold for 3 days at 10° C (50° F) or lower or in refrigerator. Drain.
Mix marinated meat and red pepper paste together.
Stuff into 28 mm hog or sheep casings, tie the ends together making 50 cm (20") long loops.
Using oak wood apply a thin smoke at 18° C (64° F) for 7 days.
Dry at 12-15° C (54-59° F), 75-80% humidity for 10 days.
Store at 12° C (54° F), 70% humidity.

* red pepper paste (in Portuguese "massa de pimentão") is an essential condiment in Portuguese cooking.

Home method for making red pepper paste (about 1 cup):

3 red bell peppers
24 g (4 tsp) salt
2 cloves of garlic
1 fl oz (30 ml=2 Tbsp) olive oil

Cut peppers into quarters. Remove the stems and seeds. Remove the white pulp from inside of the peppers.
Place peppers in a jar and sprinkle them with salt. Shake the jar. Leave uncovered for 24 hours at room temperature. Rinse the peppers and pat them dry with a paper towel.
Spread peppers on a pan and bake them for 20 minutes until the skins are charred and dark. Remove the tray and let the peppers cool. Remove the skins from the peppers, they come off easily.
Using a mixer blend the peppers with 2 garlic cloves gradually adding olive oil. The mixture should reach the consistency of a fine creamy paste. Place the paste in a jar and store in refrigerator. Use it as topping for hot dogs or any grilled sausage.

Linguiça de Portalegre carries PGI 1997 certification.

Lithuanian Sausage

Lithuanian Dry Sausage

Pork butt	500 g	1.10 lb
Beef chuck	150 g	0.33 lb
Rabbit meat	200 g	0.44 lb
Pork back fat or hard fat trimmings	150 g	0.33 lb

Ingredients per 1 kg (2.2 lb) of meat

Salt	28 g	5 tsp
Cure #2	2.5 g	1/2 tsp
Pepper	2.0 g	1 tsp
Sugar	2.0 g	1/2 tsp
Marjoram	1.5 g	1 tsp
Allspice, ground	2.0 g	1 tsp
Cloves, ground	2.0 g	1 tsp
Rum	60 ml	1/4 cup

Grind all meats with 10 mm (3/8") plate. ut back fat into 3 mm x 3 mm x 20 mm (1/8 x 1/8 x 3/4") strips.
Mix everything together.
Stuff firmly into beef middles or fibrous casings.
Place sausages between two wodden boardsw, place weight on top and leave in a cool place ~ 10-12 C (50-54 F) for 2 weeks.
Remove boards and hang sausages in a ventilated cool place for 3 days.
Cold smoke at 18 C (64 F) for 7 days.
Store in a cool place at 12 C (54 F), 70% humidity.

Llangonisa Rotja - Alicantina

Llangonisa Rotja or Llonganissa Alacantina (in Valencian language which is a dialect of Catalan) is a longaniza sausage popular in País Valenciano region of Spain. This all pork dry sausage is stuffed into small diameter natural casing and dried for about 3 weeks. Then it is ready to eat, but may be fried or grilled.

Pork, semi-fat*	700 g	1.54 lb
Pork, lean	300 g	0.66 lb

Ingredients per 1 kg (2.2 lb) of meat

Salt	28 g	4.5 tsp
Cure #1	2.5 g	1/2 tsp
Pepper	4.0 g	2 tsp
Pimentón	10 g	5 tsp
Cloves, ground	0.3 g	1/8 tsp

Grind meats through 8-10 mm (3/8") plate.
Mix ground meat with salt and spices. Hold in refrigerator for 24 hours.
Stuff into 20-22 mm sheep or hog casings.
Form links about 35-40 cm (13-16") long.
Dry at 16-12° C (59-53° F), 75-85% humidity for 15-20 days.
Store at 10-12° C (50-53° F), <65% humidity or in refrigerator.

Notes
* pork shoulder (butt) is a good choice.
Consume raw, fried or grilled.

Lomo Embuchado

Spanish cured loin. The loin is marinated, stuffed into casing, and dried whole. It is consumed raw (cold), cut into thin slices, and served as a tapa, sometimes in a sandwich.

Whole loin	2-3 kg	4.4-6.6 lb

Multiply the ingredients below per weight of loin. Ingredients per 1 kg (2.2 lb) of meat.

Coarse salt for salting loin, *as needed.*

Cure #2	5.0 g	1 tsp
Pimentón, sweet	25 g	4 Tbsp
Pimentón, hot	5.0 g	1 tsp
Oregano, ground	2.0 g	1 tsp
Cumin, ground	1.0 g	1/2 tsp
Bay leaf, ground	0.25 g	1/8 tsp
Garlic, smashed	7.0 g	2 cloves
White wine or vinegar	30 ml	2 Tbsp
Olive oil	60 ml	2 oz fl

Trim off the skin and connective tissue from the loin. Rub forcefully a generous amount of coarse salt (as needed) all over loin. The loin should rest on a layer of salt and be well covered with salt all around leaving no exposed areas. Hold in refrigerator for 24 hours. Brush off the salt, wash briefly in running water and pat dry with paper towels. No more salt is needed. Mix all ingredients with wine and oil together to form the marinade paste. Apply the paste all around the loin. Hold in refrigerator for 48 hours. Stuff the loin into pork bungs that will tightly accommodate the piece. Ferment/dry at 22-24° C (72-75° F), 85-90% humidity, for 2 days. Dry at 15 → 12° C (59 → 53° F), 85 → 75% humidity for 2 months. The loin should lose about 35% of its original weight. Store at 10-12° C (°F), <75% humidity.

Notes: The size of the casing is chosen to fit the loin snugly. A little oil is applied to the surface of the loin to make the operation easier. One end of the loin is tied with butcher twine and the loin is pulled through the casing. Then, both ends are tied and a hanging loop is created. Pork bung *(tripa cular)* is a traditionally used casing for drying loins as its structure (surface holes) is perfect for extended drying. Artificial casings can also be used as long as they allow moisture and smoke to pass through. For artificial casings the drying cycle is shorter, so weigh the loin to verify that it lost 33% of its original weight. Consume cold.

Lomo Embuchado de Segovia

Lomo embuchado is a Spanish pork loin cured with salt, garlic, and paprika and stuffed into a natural or artificial permeable casing. Depending on its diameter, the loin is left to dry for 2-3 months. As its name suggests, this sausage originates in Segovia, a city in the Segovia province of the Castilla-León region of Spain.

Whole loin	2-3 kg	4.4-6.6 lb

Multiply the ingredients below per weight of loin. Ingredients per 1 kg (2.2 lb) of meat.

Coarse salt for salting loin, *as needed.*

Cure #2	5.0 g	1 tsp
Pimentón, sweet	30 g	5 Tbsp
Pimentón, hot	2.0 g	1 tsp
Oregano	3.0 g	3 tsp
Garlic	10 g	3 cloves
Olive oil	60 ml	2 oz fl

Trim off the skin and connective tissue from the loin. Forcefully rub in a generous amount of salt (as needed) all over loin. The loin should rest in a container on a layer of salt and be well covered with salt all around leaving no exposed areas. Hold in refrigerator for 24 hours. Brush off the salt, wash briefly in running water and pat dry with paper towels. Mix all ingredients with wine and oil together to form the marinade paste. Apply the paste all around the loin. Hold in refrigerator for 48 hours. Wipe off the paste and stuff the loin into 55-70 mm beef bungs *(tripa cular)*. The length of stuffed loin around 70-90 cm (28") or fibrous protein lined casings. Ferment/dry at 18-22° C (64-72° F), for 15 days. Dry at 12-14° C (53-57° F), 75-80% humidity for 6-8 weeks until the sausage loses 33% of its original weight.

Notes: the size of the casing is chosen to fit the loin snugly. A little oil is occasionally applied to the surface of the loin to make the operation easier. One end of the loin is tied with butcher twine and the loin is pulled through the casing. Then, both ends are tied and a hanging loop is created. Pork bung is a traditionally used casing for drying loins and its structure (surface holes) is perfect for extended drying. Artificial casings can also be used as long as they are permeable (allow moisture and smoke to go through), however, in most cases for artificial cases the drying cycle is shorter, so weigh the loin to verify that it lost 33% of its original weight.

Lomo Picado

Lomo picado is made of loin trimmings, which are big enough to form a loin. It is a similar product to molded ham; the difference is that the ham pieces are held together under pressure in mold and cooked in water, and loin pieces are stuffed tightly in a casing and fermented and dried. This, of course, results in a different texture and flavor. Loin pieces must be well trimmed off of any fat, silver screen (film), and connective tissue; otherwise, they will not stick well together. They must be cold and cut with a sharp knife to obtain a clean surface. The salt will do the rest; the cells will release proteins that will dissolve in the salt, and this solution, known as "exudate," will glue individual meat cuts together.

Pork loin pieces	1 kg	2.2 lb

Ingredients per 1 kg (2.2 lb) of meat

Salt	25 g	4 tsp
Cure #2	3.0 g	1/2 tsp
Dextrose	2 g	1/2 tsp
Sugar	3.0 g	1/2 tsp
Pimentón, sweet	25 g	4 Tbsp
Pimentón, hot	5.0 g	1 tsp
Oregano, ground	2.0 g	1 tsp
Thyme, ground	0.5 g	1/4 tsp
Rosemary	0.3 g	1/8 tsp
Garlic, diced	7.0 g	2 cloves

Trim off the skin and connective tissue from loin pieces which should be about 2-2.5 cm (3/4 - 1") in size.
Mix meat with all ingredients well together. Hold in refrigerator for 48 hours.
Stuff *tightly* into 50-80 mm pork bungs, synthetic permeable casings or blind cap (caecum).
Ferment at 20-22° C (68-72° F), 95→90% humidity, for 48 hours.
Dry at 15→12° C (59-53° F), 85→75% humidity for 2-3 months, depending on diameter. The loin should lose around 33% of its original weight.
Store at 10-12° C (°F), <75% humidity.

Notes

Using smaller diameter casings will result in a shorter drying time.

Longaniza

Longaniza is a Spanish long and slim sausage that can be fresh, dry or smoked and dried. The sausage composition and processing steps are similar to that of chorizo's, but longanizas are much longer, around 30-50 cm (12-30").

Pork, semi-fat	800 g	1.76 lb
Back fat	200 g	0.44 lb

Ingredients per 1 kg (2.2 lb) of meat

Salt	28 g	4.5 tsp
Cure #1	2.5 g	1/2 tsp
Pepper	4.0 g	2 tsp
Pimentón, sweet	20 g	3.5 Tbsp
Pimentón, hot	2.0 g	1 tsp
Oregano, ground	1.0 g	1/2 tsp
Nutmeg	0.5 g	1/4 tsp
Garlic	3.5 g	1 clove
Wine	15 ml	1 Tbsp
Water	60 ml	2 oz fl

Smash garlic and using mortar and pestle grind it with wine into the paste.

Grind meat and back fat through 10-12 mm (3/8-1/2") plate.

Mix meat, fat and all ingredients adding water as necessary to produce a firm paste. Hold the paste for 48 hours in refrigerator.

Stuff into 34-36 mm pork or beef casings forming 40-60 cm (16-24") sections.

Ferment/dry at 22-24° C (72-75° F) for 24 hours, 90-85% humidity.

Dry sausages for 16 days at 12-15° C (53-59° F), 75-80% humidity.

Store at 10° C (50° F) in a cool and ventilated area or refrigerate.

Longaniza Andaluza

Longaniza from Andalusia, the southern region of Spain.

Pork, semi-fat	1000 g	2.2 lb

Ingredients per 1 kg (2.2 lb) of meat

Salt	28 g	4.5 Tbsp
Cure #1	2.5 g	1/2 tsp
Pepper, black	2.0 g	1 tsp
Pimentón, sweet	25 g	4 Tbsp
Oregano, ground	1.0 g	1/2 tsp
Cinnamon	1.0 g	1/2 tsp
Garlic, smashed	3.5 g	1 clove
White wine	30 ml	1 oz fl
Water	60 ml	2 oz fl

Grind meat through 12 mm (1/2") plate.

Mix meat with all ingredients. Hold for 48 hours in refrigerator.

Stuff into 36 mm pork or beef casings, making sections 40-60 cm (16-24") long.

Apply a thin smoke at 22-24° C (72-75° F) (smoking step optional) or dry sausages at 22-24° C (72-75° F) for 24 hours.

Dry at 15-12° C (59-54° F), 75-80% humidity for 15 days.

Store sausages at 10-12° C (50-53° F), <70% humidity or refrigerate.

Notes

Shoulder butt is a good cut for this sausage.

Longaniza de Aragón

Longaniza de Aragón is a Spanish semi-dry sausage popular in the region of Aragón. The sausage is made with lean pork, pork belly, back fat, and aromatic spices such as cinnamon, cloves, nutmeg and anise. It includes typical chorizo spices like oregano and garlic, *but no pimentón*, just regular pepper. The color of longaniza differs from that of chorizo due to the lack of pimentón.

Pork, lean	750 g	1.65 lb
Pork belly	150 g	0.33 lb
Back fat	100 g	0.22 lb

Ingredients per 1 kg (2.2 lb) of meat

Salt	28 g	4.5 tsp
Cure #1	2.5 g	1/2 tsp
Sugar	3.0 g	1/2 tsp
Pepper	2.0 g	1 tsp
Nutmeg	0.5 g	1/4 tsp
Star anise, ground	0.3 g	1/8 tsp
Cloves	0.3 g	1/8 tsp
Cinnamon	1.0 g	1/2 tsp
Oregano, dry	2.0 g	2 tsp
Garlic	7.0 g	2 cloves
Water	30 ml	2 Tbsp

Grind meat and fat through 8 mm (3/8") plate. Mix ground meats with all ingredients. Hold the mixture for 24-36 hours in refrigerator.

Stuff into 22-32 mm pork or sheep casings, making horseshoe loops about 40 cm (16") long. Hold for 8-10 hours in refrigerator or at low temperature.

Hang the sausages for 3-4 days at 15-20° C (59-68° F), 60-70% humidity. At this point longaniza can be classified a semi-dry sausage which is served fried or cooked.

To make a dry sausage continue drying at 12-15° C (53-59° F), 75-90% for 1-2 weeks depending on diameter. The dry sausage can be consumed raw.

Longaniza de Mezcla

Depending on the region of Spain, this longaniza can be made from lean pork, semi-fat pork, including some offal meat (lungs, heart) or pork and beef.

Beef, lean	550 g	1.21 lb
Pork, semi-fat (shoulder)	350 g	0.77 lb
Pork back fat	100 g	0.22 lb

Ingredients per 1 kg (2.2 lb) of meat

Salt	28 g	4.5 tsp
Cure #1	2.5 g	1/2 tsp
Pepper	4.0 g	2 tsp
Pimentón, sweet	10 g	5 tsp
Pimentón, hot	10 g	5 tsp
Oregano, ground	1.0 g	1/2 tsp
Garlic	3.5 g	1 clove
Wine	15 ml	1 Tbsp
Water	60 ml	2 oz fl

Smash garlic and using mortar and pestle grind it with wine into the paste.

Grind meat and back fat through 12 mm (1/2") plate.

Mix meat, fat and all ingredients adding water as necessary to produce a firm paste.

Hold the paste for 48 hours in refrigerator.

Stuff into 25-35 mm veal casings forming 40-60 cm (16-24") sections. Prick air pockets with a needle.

Ferment at 24° C (75° F) for 12 hours, 90-85% humidity.

Dry sausages for 12-14 days at 12-15° C (53-59° F), 75-80% humidity.

Store at 10° C (53° F) in a cool and ventilated area or refrigerate.

Longaniza de Pascua

Longaniza de Pascua is a Valencian small-diameter dry sausage made at Easter time ("Pascua" means Easter in Spanish). This snack type sausage is made with pork and veal and the drying process is relatively short due to the small diameter of the sausage.

Pork, lean	300 g	0.66 lb
Veal	300 g	0.66 lb
Semi-fat pork	400 g	0.88 lb

Ingredients per 1 kg (2.2 lb) of meat

Salt	25 g	4 tsp
Cure #1	2.5 g	1/2 tsp
Black pepper	4.0 g	2 tsp
Anise, ground	1.0 g	1/2 tsp

Grind all meats through 8-10 mm (3/8") plate. Mix meat with salt and spices.

Stuff into 12 mm sheep casings forming 20-30 cm (8-12") long links.

Dry at 18→12° C (64→59° F) for 7-10 days. Store at 10-12° C (50-53° F) in a cool and ventilated area or refrigerate.

Longaniza de Payés

The name of this longaniza is derived from the Catalan word "pagès" which means "peasant." Longaniza de Payés is a narrow and long dry sausage covered with mold.

Lean pork, shoulder	800 g	1.76 lb
Pork belly	200 g	0.44 lb

Ingredients per 1 kg (2.2 lb) of meat

Salt		28 g	4.5 tsp
Cure #1		2.5 g	1/2 tsp
Black pepper		2.0 g	1 tsp
Dextrose	2.0 g		1/2 tsp
Sugar		2.0 g	1/2 tsp
Sweet sherry		15 ml	1 Tbsp

Grind meat and fat through 6 mm (1/4") plate. Mix meat, fat and all ingredients. Hold the paste for 48 hours in refrigerator.

Stuff into 55 mm pork middles. Prick air pockets with a needle.

Dry/ferment at 24° C (75° F) for 12 hours, 90-85% humidity.

Dry sausages for 30 days at 12-15° C (53-59° F), 75-80% humidity.

Store at 10° C (53° F) in a cool and ventilated area or refrigerate.

Longaniza Dominicana

Traditional Dominican longaniza is prepared with the juice of bitter oranges (*naranja de Sevilla*) or lime, garlic, oregano and salt.

Lean pork (shoulder)	700 g	1.54 lb
Back fat or		
hard fat trimmings	300 g	0.66 lb

Ingredients per 1 kg (2.2 lb) of meat

Salt	28 g	5 tsp
Cure #1	2.5 g	1/2 tsp
Sugar	5.0 g	1 tsp
Pepper	2.0 g	1 tsp
Paprika, sweet	6.0 g	3 tsp
Oregano, rubbed	6.0 g	6 tsp
Garlic, smashed	7.0 g	2 cloves
Juice of bitter oranges	60 ml	2 oz fl
OR		
Bitter orange oil*	3 ml	5 drops

Grind pork through 8 mm (5/16") mm plate.
Mix ground meat with salt and Cure #1 until sticky. Add all remaining ingredients and mix well together. Marinate for 12 hours in refrigerator.
Stuff firmly into 36 mm hog casings.
Dry at 25° C (77° F) for 2 days at 85-90% humidity.
Dry at 12-15° C (53-59° F), 75-80% humidity, for 14 days.
Store at 12° C (53° F), <70% humidity or keep refrigerated.

Notes
* food grade essential oils are available on the Internet.
You can use 10 ml (2 tsp) of Curaçao - a liqueur flavored with the dried peel of the bitter orange laraha, a citrus fruit grown on the Dutch island of Curaçao.

For a hotter version add 1 g (1/2 tsp) of cayenne pepper or 1 tablespoon of Tabasco source.

Traditionally, after stuffing the sausage was dried in the sun for 2 days what produced a fresh sausage that needed to be refrigerated and fully cooked before serving.

Longaniza Navarra

Longaniza Navarra is a Spanish semi-dry or Longaniza Navarra is a semi-dry or dry sausage originating in the Navarra region of Spain. There are different varieties of longaniza depending on whether it's made in Cataluña, Aragon, Navarra, Andalucia, or other Spanish regions. It is usually stuffed into 30-34 mm pork casings. Longaniza sausage is also made in Argentina, Chile, and the Caribbean. This leads to different recipes, each influenced by local conditions. For example, in the Dominican Republic, longaniza is flavored with bitter orange or lemon juice.

Pork belly	1000 g	2.2 lb

Ingredients per 1 kg (2.2 lb) of meat

Salt	25 g	4 tsp
Cure #1	2.5 g	1/2 tsp
Dextrose	2.0 g	1/2 tsp
Sugar	3.0 g	3/4 tsp
Pimentón	12 g	6 tsp
Garlic, smashed	7.0 g	2 cloves

Grind meat with 8 mm (5/16") plate.
Mix meat with all ingredients. Hold for 12 hours in refrigerator.
Stuff firmly into 30-34 mm hog casings forming long loops.
Dry/ferment at 24° C (75° F) for 12 hours, 90-85% humidity.
Dry at 15-12° C (59-54° F), 80% humidity for 8 days.
Store sausages at 10-12° C (50-53° F), <70% humidity or refrigerate.

Notes
The sausage is usually cooked or fried.

Longaniza-Traditional

Pork		300 g	0.66 lb
Beef		500 g	1.10 lb
Pork back fat or			
hard fat trimmings		200 g	0.44 lb

Ingredients per 1 kg (2.2 lb) of meat

Salt		28 g	5 tsp
Cure #2		2.5 g	1/2 tsp
Dextrose	2.0 g		1/2 tsp
Sugar		3.0 g	3/4 tsp
Pepper		4.0 g	2 tsp
Red pepper		2.0 g	1 tsp
Coriander		2.0 g	1 tsp
Garlic		2.0 g	1 clove
Fennel, whole seeds		2.0 g	1 tsp
Mace		1.0 g	1/2 tsp
Red wine	30 ml		2 Tbsp
T-SPX culture		0.12 g	use
scale			

Grind pork and back fat through 3/16" plate (5 mm). Grind beef with 1/8" plate.
Mix all ingredients with meat.
Stuff firmly into 40-45 mm beef middles or protein lined fibrous casings. Make 6" (15 cm) long links.
Ferment at 20° C (68° F) for 72 hours, 90-85% humidity.
Dry at 16-12° C (60-54° F), 85-80% humidity for about 2 months. The sausage is dried until around 30-35% in weight is lost.
Store sausages at 10-15° C (50-59° F), 75% humidity.

Loukaniko Pitsilias

Loukaniko Pitsilias is produced in the area of Pitsilia in Cyprus, *without the addition of any preservatives* (e.g. nitrates, nitrites, poly-phosphates), flavor enhancers or any other additives. Salting, marinating in wine, adding spices and smoking the meat are important stages of the preparation process.

Pork, lean	750 g	1.65 lb
Pork back fat	250 g	0.55 lb

Ingredients per 1 kg (2.2 lb) of meat

Salt	30 g	5 Tbsp
Black pepper	2.0 g	1 tsp
Coriander, crushed	3.5 g	2 tsp
Cumin	2.0 g	1 tsp
Red wine, dry	250 ml	1 cup

Grind meat through 6 mm (1/4") plate and mix with salt, spices and wine. The salted minced meat remains in the wine for at least 3 days, and it is mixed regularly to ensure that the wine's characteristic taste, aroma and color are consistent in the mixture. The wine should be red and dry, from vineyards growing vines of the local Mavro variety that is predominant in the area.
The mixture is stuffed into 36 mm hog casing forming 20 cm (8") links. The links are pricked with a needle to allow moisture to escape during processing.
Apply cold smoke at <25° C (77° F) for 3 - 5 days.
Dry at 12 - 15° C (53 - 60° F), 75-80% humidity for 2-3 weeks.

Notes

The sausage was awarded PGI certificate on 10/02/2021.
Water content: 40 %-60 %;
Sodium chloride: 1.5 %-3 %;
Maximum fat percentage: 35 %.
Diameter of individual sausage: 2-4 cm;
Length of individual sausage: 5-40 cm.

Lucanica di Picerno

Wild fennel (Foeniculum vulgare) is the spice that
accounts for the characteristic flavor of Lucanica;
other spices, such as black pepper and chili
(*Capsicum annum*), also contribute to the aroma,
albeit to a lesser degree. A spicy version of the
product is permitted, in which the perceived intensity
of the 'chili' aroma is greater, although the 'wild
fennel' aroma must still predominate. The way in
which 'Lucanica di Picerno' sausages are traditionally
hung on special racks when they are being matured
gives them their characteristic 'U' shape, which
distinguishes the product to this day.

Lean pork shoulder	400 g	0.88 lb
Lean pork leh (ham) 300 g	0.66 lb	
Pork belly, jowls, back fat	300 g	0.66 lb

Ingredients per 1 kg (2.2 lb) of meat

Salt	25 g	4 tsp
Cure #1	2.0 g	1/3 tsp
Sugar	3.0 g	1/2 tsp
Pepper	1.0 g	1/2 tsp
Chili pepper, hot	1.0 g	1/2 tsp
Fennel seeds	2.0 g	1 tsp
T-SPX culture	0.12 g	use scale

Grind meat and fat through 10-14 mm (3/8 –
1/2") grinder plate.
Mix ground meat with all ingredients, except
starter culture. Hold at 8° C (48° F) between
4 - 24 hours to allow good absorption of spice
flavors by the meat.
Add starter culture, re-mix the paste and stuff
into 40 - 44 mm natural casings.
Hold the sausages for 5 hours at max 22° C
(70° F) (90% humidity, then ferment/dry for
3 - 7 days, until they lose about 15% of the
original weight. The acidity level pH should fall
between 4.8 and 5.3.
Dry/ripe sausages for at least 18 days at 18 →
13° C (64 → 54° F), 85% → 75% humidity.

Notes: Lucanica di Picerno was awarded PGI
certificate of origin on October 29, 2018.
The 'Lucanica di Picerno' production area lies in
the territories of Picerno, Tito, Satriano di Lucania,
Savoia di Lucania. The area has hot, dry summers
followed by seasons with plentiful precipitation
and frequently snowy winter months. A recipe from
Picerno, originating from peasant household tradition,
involved the use of this seasoning at a ratio of around
a hundred seeds per kilo of meat mixture, thus
underlining the distinctive feature of this product. The
seeds of this ancient perennial aromatic plant were
present everywhere and were gathered and sold by
elderly people. At present the wild fennel is generally,
but not necessarily, taken from the identified
geographical area.

Luftgetrocknete Mettwurst
(Air Dried Mettwurst)

Luftgetrocknete Mettwurst is listed (2.211.11)
in the German government publication Guide to
Meats and Meat Products - *Leitsätze für Fleisch
und Fleischerzeugnisse.*

Lean pork	500 g	1.10 lb
Pork belly, medium fat	500 g	1.10 lb

Ingredients per 1 kg (2.2 lb) of material

Salt	28 g	4.5 tsp
Cure #2	2.5 g	1/2 tsp
Dextrose	2.0 g	1/2 tsp
Pepper	2.0 g	1 tsp
Caraway, smashed	0.5 g	1/4 tsp
Coriander	0.5 g	1/4 tsp
Garlic, smashed	3.0 g	1 clove
Red wine, Madeira,		
Marsala	5 ml	1 tsp
T-SPX culture	0.12 g	use
scale		

Grind 1/2 lean pork (250 g) through 3 mm
(1/8") plate.
Grind remaining lean pork and belly through
5 mm (3/16") plate.
Mix ground meats with all ingredients.
Stuff into 60 mm pork or beef middles or
permeable synthetic casings.
Ferment at 20° C (68° F), 95 → 90% humidity
for 3 days.
Dry at 18° C (64° F), 90 → 85% humidity for
3 days.
Dry at 15 → 12° C (59 → 12° F), 85 → 75%
humidity for 4-5 weeks or until the sausage
looses 30% of its original weight..
Store at 10-12° C (50-53° F),75% humidity or
refrigerate.

Notes
If strong mold is desired use Chr-Hansen
Bactoferm® Mold-600 culture.

Lukanka

Lukanka is a well known Bulgarian dry sausage. It is formed into a traditional flat shape and it has great keeping qualities.

Lean pork	500 g	1.10 lb
Pork back fat or		
hard fat trimmings	200 g	0.44 lb
Veal	300 g	0.66 lb

Ingredients per 1 kg (2.2 lb) of meat

Salt	28 g	5 tsp
Cure #2	2.5 g	1/2 tsp
Black pepper	2.0 g	1 tsp
Dextrose	2.0 g	1 tsp
Cumin	2.0 g	1 tsp
Nutmeg	1.0 g	1/2 tsp
Coriander	1.0 g	1/2 tsp
Garlic	10.0 g	3 cloves
T-SPX culture	0.12 g	use scale

Grind lean pork and fat through 6 mm (1/4") plate.
Mix all ingredients with meat.
Stuff firmly into 50 mm beef middles.
Ferment at 20° C (68° F) for 72 hours, 90-85% humidity. At the beginning of the fermentation process place weight on sausages to flatten them out.
Dry at 16-12° C (60-54° F), 85-80% humidity for about 1-2 months.
Store sausages at 10-15° C (50-59° F), 75% humidity.

Notes
Lukanka is consumed throughout the country, but the two most prominent varieties are known as *Karlovska lukanka* and *Lukanka panagyurska.*

Medwurst

The addition of potatoes characterizes Swedish sausages, and this semi-dry Medwurst is no exception.

Pork (butt, picnic)	400 g	0.88 lb
Back fat or		
hard fat trimmings	100 g	0.22 lb
Potatoes. boiled	500 g	1.10 lb

Ingredients per 1 kg (2.2 lb) of material

Salt	28 g	5 tsp
Cure #1	2.5 g	1/2 tsp
Dextrose	10 g	2 tsp
Sugar	5.0 g	1 tsp
White pepper	4.0 g	2 tsp
Granulated or		
powdered onion ...	5.0 g	3 tsp
Allspice, ground	2.0 g	1 tsp
T-SPX culture	0.12 g	use scale

Boil potatoes. Drain and smash them.
Grind all meats through 5 mm (3/16") plate.
Re-freeze and grind again through 3 mm (1/8")) plate.
Mix everything together, add 1 cup of water.
Stuff into 35-40 mm hog, beef middles or fibrous casings.
Ferment at 24° C (75° F), 80-85% humidity for 48 hours.
Apply cold smoke at ≤ 25° C (77° F) for 4 hours. Cook in water at 80° C (176° F) until the meat reaches 65° C (149° F) internal meat temperature.
OR
Bake in smokehouse (with or without smoke) at ≤ 85° C (185° F) until the meat reaches 65° C (149° F) internal meat temperature.

Note: potatoes contain about 2% carbohydrates (sugars).

Merguez

Merguez is a spicy, short North African sausage made with lamb or beef and flavored with spices. Spices such as paprika, cayenne, harissa, and a hot chili paste all make Merguez sausage red. Sold by street vendors in Paris, it can also be found in London, Belgium, and New York. Merguez, the French transliteration of the Arabic word mirqaz, is a spicy small sausage used in Tunisia and Algeria.

Merguez sausage recipes include coriander, oregano, fennel seeds (used in Italian sausages), and ground cinnamon. This is a spicy sausage, and in addition to the spices listed in the ingredients above, please feel free to add any spices you like. Merguez is often made into hamburger patties or meatballs. It is served by frying it in olive oil until well browned or grilled.

Fast-fermented semi-dry version of the sausage follows below:

Lamb	1000 g	2.2 lb

Ingredients per 1 kg (2.2 lb) of meat

Salt	23 g	4 tsp
Cure #1	2.5 g	1/2 tsp
Dextrose	10 g	2 tsp
Black pepper	5.0 g	2 tsp
Garlic	6.0 g	2 cloves
Cayenne pepper	4.0 g	2 t sp
Paprika	5.0 g	2 tsp
Cumin	2.5 g	1 tsp
Coriander	2.0 g	1 tsp
Olive oil	14 g	1 Tbsp
F-LC culture	0.12 g	use scale

Grind lamb through 5 mm (3/16") plate.
Mix all ingredients with ground meat.
Stuff firmly into sheep casings 18-26 mm and form 15 cm (5-6") long links or leave in one continuous rope.
Ferment at 24° C (75° F) for 48 hours, 90-85% humidity.
Dry at 16-12° C (60-54° F), 85-80% humidity for 18 days.
Store sausages at 10-15° C (50-59° F), 75% humidity.

Many recipes call for Harrisa Paste, which is nothing more than a combination of the spices already listed above as ingredients (garlic, cumin, olive oil, hot chili peppers, and coriander). Making Harrisa paste:

1. Place 4 oz of red hot chilies in a bowl and cover with hot water for two hours, then drain.
2. In a blender process ¼ cup garlic cloves, ¼ cup ground cumin, ½ cup ground coriander, ¼ cup salt, drained chillies and ½ cup olive oil. Add olive oil slowly until a thick paste is produced. For a finer consistency rub paste through a sieve.

You can make a smaller amount of paste: 1 garlic clove crushed and finely chopped, ½ Tbsp salt, 2 Tbsp olive oil, 1 tsp cayenne pepper, ½ tsp ground cumin, ¼ tsp ground coriander. Mix ingredients in a jar and shake well. Cover with a lid.

Metka
(Metka)

Metka is a cold-smoked spreadable sausage related to German Mettwurst. Because Metka sausages were not cooked, they were less popular in the summer months. With the advent of refrigeration, the storing problem has been eliminated. This cold-smoked spreadable sausage recipe comes from *the official Polish Government archives.*

Pork (butt, picnic)	600 g	1.32 lb
Beef	400 g	0.88 lb

Ingredients per 1 kg (2.2 lb.) of meat

Salt	21 g	3.5 tsp
Cure #1	2.5 g	1/2 tsp
Pepper	1.0 g	1/2 tsp
Paprika	1.0 g	1/2 tsp
Sugar	2.0 g	1/2 tsp

Curing: cut all meat into 5-6 cm (2") cubes, mix with salt and Cure #1. Keep pork and beef separate. Pack tightly in containers and cover with a clean cloth. Hold in cooler at 4-6° C (40-42° F) for 72 hours.
Grind all meats through 3 mm (1/8") plate. Re-freeze and grind again.
Mix meats until sticky. During mixing add remaining ingredients.
Stuff firmly into 36-40 mm beef rounds, cellulose or fibrous casings.
Hang for 1-2 days at 2-6° C (35-43° F) and 85-90% humidity.
Apply cold smoke at 18-22° C (64-72° F) for 1-2 days until casings develop brown reddish color.
Cool in air to 12° C (53° F) or lower. Store in refrigerator.

Metka Brunszwicka
(Metka brunszwicka)

This metka sausage originated in Brunswick, Germany. This cold smoked spreadable sausage recipe comes from *the official Polish Government archives.*

Pork (butt, picnic)	400 g	0.88 lb
Beef	400 g	0.88 lb
Jowls (or belly), skinless	200 g	0.44 lb

Ingredients per 1 kg (2.2 lb.) of meat

Salt	21 g	3.5 tsp
Cure #1	2.5 g	1/2 tsp
Pepper	2.0 g	1 tsp
Paprika	1.0 g	1/2 tsp
Nutmeg	0.5 g	1/4 tsp

Curing: cut meat into 5-6 cm (2") cubes, mix with salt and Cure #1. Keep pork and beef separate. Pack tightly in containers and cover with a clean cloth. Place in a cooler at 4-6° C (40-42° F) for 72 hours.
Grind all meats through 3 mm (1/8") plate, refreeze and grind again OR grind once and then emulsify in a food processor without adding water. Add spices when grinding or emulsifying.
Stuff firmly into 40 mm beef middles or fibrous casings. Form 20-25 cm (8-10") links.
Hang for 1-2 days at 2-6° C (35-43° F) and 85-90% humidity.
Apply a thin cold smoke at 18-22° C (64-72° F) for 1-2 days until casings develop brown color.
Cool in air to 12° C (53° F) or lower. Store in refrigerator.

Metka Pomorska
(Metka pomorska)

Metka Sausage has its origin in the Northern areas of Poland known as Pomerania (Pomorze). *This cold smoked spreadable sausage recipe comes from the official Polish Government archives.*

Beef	300 g	0.66 lb
Back fat or		
fat trimmings	700 g	1.84 lb

Ingredients per 1 kg (2.2 lb.) of meat

Salt	21 g	3.5 tsp
Cure #1	1.5 g	1/3 tsp
Pepper	2.0 g	1 tsp
Paprika	1.0 g	1/2 tsp
Sugar	2.0 g	1/2 tsp

Curing: cut meat into 2.5-5 cm (1-2") pieces and mix with salt and cure #1. Pack tightly in a container, cover with cloth and keep in refrigerator for 3 days.

Grind all meats through 3 mm (1/8") plate, refreeze and grind again *OR* grind once and then emulsify in a food processor without adding water. During emulsifying the temperature of the meat should not exceed 15° C (59° F).

Mix meat, fat and spices together *without* adding water.

Stuff into 50 mm synthetic cellulose or fibrous casings. Form straight 20-25 cm (8-10") long links.

Hang for 1-2 days at 10° C (50° F) and 85-90% humidity.

Apply a thin cold smoke at 18-22° C (64-72° F) for 1-2 days until casings develop light brown color.

Cool in air to 12° C (53° F) or lower.

Metka Salmon Style
(Metka łososiowa)

There is no salmon inside though the name may imply it. Certain Polish meat products that call for bacon or pork loin in a recipe have the "salmon" nickname added. For instance, Smoked Pork Loin-Salmon Style. The reason is that the loin resembles the shape of a salmon. Both pork loin and salmon are very popular in Poland and are considered delicacies. *This cold smoked spreadable sausage recipe comes from the official Polish Government archives.*

Beef	200 g	0.44 lb
Pork belly, skinless	800 g	1.76 lb

Ingredients per 1 kg (2.2 lb.) of meat

Salt	21 g	3.5 tsp
Cure #1	2.5 g	1/2 tsp
Pepper	2.0 g	1 tsp
Nutmeg	0.5 g	1/4 tsp
Paprika	1.0 g	1/2 tsp

Curing: cut meat into 5-6 cm (2") cubes, mix with salt and cure #1. Keep pork and beef separate. Pack tightly in containers and cover with a clean cloth. Place in a cooler (4-6° C, 40-42° F) for 72 hours.

Grind all meats through 3 mm (1/8") plate, refreeze and grind again *OR* grind once and then emulsify in a food processor without adding water. Add spices when grinding or emulsifying.

Stuff firmly into 40 mm beef middles or fibrous casings. Form 20-25 cm (8-10") links.

Hang for 12 hours at 10° C (50° F) and 85-90% humidity.

Apply a thin cold smoke at 18-22° C (64-72° F) for 10-12 hours until casings develop gold brown color.

Cool in air to 12° C (53° F) or lower. Store in a refrigerator.

Meetvursti

Meetvursti is a Finnish version of the Dutch Metworst fermented dry sausage. Both sausages are very similar, however, Meetvursti, in addition to pork meat, often included horse meat. Some meetvursti still include horse meat, however, most sausages are made with pork or pork and beef.

Beef	300 g	0.66 lb
Pork, lean	400 g	0.88 lb
Back fat	300 g	0.66 lb

Ingredients per 1 kg (2.2 lb) of meat

Salt	28 g	4.5 tsp
Cure #2	2.5 g	1/2 tsp
Black pepper	2.0 g	1 tsp
Dextrose	2.0 g	1/2 tsp
Sugar	2.0 g	1/2 tsp
Coriander	1.0 g	1/2 tsp
Mustard seed	2.0 g	1 tsp
Cumin	1.0 g	1/2 tsp
Nutmeg	0.5 g	1/4 tsp
Ginger	0.3 g	1/8 tsp
T-SPX culture*	0.12 g	use scale

Grind cold pork through 6 mm (1/4") plate.
Grind partially frozen back fat through 6 mm (1/4") plate.
Grind cold beef through 3 mm (1/8") plate.
Dilute culture in 1 Tbsp (15 ml) not-chlorinated water.
Mix ground meats with all ingredients.
Stuff into 60 mm pork or beef middles or fibrous synthetic casings.
Ferment at 20° C (68° F), 95 → 90% humidity for 72 hours.
Dry at 18° C (64° F), 90 → 85% humidity for 2 days.
Dry at 15 → 12° C (59 → 12° F), 85 → 75% humidity for 4 weeks or until sausage looses 30% of its original weight.
Store at 10-12° C (50-53° F), <75% humidity.

Notes
* adding starter culture is recommended.

Metworst

Metworst, also known as "droge worst" (dry sausage) is a traditional Dutch slow-fermented sausage made from pork. It is basically a Dutch type of a dry salami. The sausage was always popular with the farmers and field laborers as a food snack when working outside.

Pork, lean	800 g	1.76 lb
Pork back fat, or hard fat trimmings	200 g	0.44 lb

Ingredients per 1 kg (2.2 lb) of meat

Salt	30 g	5 tsp
Cure #2	2.5 g	1/2 tsp
Black pepper	2.0 g	1 tsp
Sugar	3.0 g	1/2 tsp
Coriander	1.0 g	1/2 tsp
Cumin	1.0 g	1/2 tsp
Nutmeg	0.5 g	1/4 tsp
Ginger	0.3 g	1/8 tsp
T-SPX culture*	0.12 g	use scale

Grind cold lean meat through 6 mm (1/4") plate.
Grind partially frozen fat through 6 mm (1/4") plate.
Dilute culture in 1 Tbsp (15 ml) not-chlorinated water.
Mix ground meat with all ingredients. Add cold ground fat and mix again.
Stuff into 40 mm hog casings forming 25 cm (10") rings.
Ferment at 20° C (68° F), 95 → 90% humidity for 72 hours.
Dry at 18° C (64° F), 90 → 85% humidity for 2 days.
Dry at 15 → 12° C (59 → 12° F), 85 → 75% humidity for 3 weeks or until sausage looses 30% of its original weight.
Store at 10-12° C (50-53° F), <75% humidity.

Notes
* adding starter culture is recommended.

Mettwurst-Braunschweiger-Schnittfeste
(Sliceable Mettwurst)

Braunschweiger Mettwurst is listed (2.211.05) in the German government publication Guide to Meats and Meat Products - *Leitsätze für Fleisch und Fleischerzeugnisse.*

Beef	300 g	0.66 lb
Pork butt	400 g	0.88 lb
Back fat	300 g	0.66 lb

Ingredients per 1 kg (2.2 lb) of meat

Salt	28 g	4.5 tsp
Cure #2	2.5 g	1/2 tsp
Dextrose	1.0 g	1/3 tsp
Sugar	2.0 g	1/2 tsp
Pepper	3.0 g	1.5 tsp
Paprika	1.0 g	1/2 tsp
Nutmeg	0.5 g	1/4 tsp
Cardamom	0.3 g	1/8 tsp
T-SPX culture	0.12 g	use
scale		

Grind pork through 5 mm (3/16") plate.
Grind back fat through 5 mm (3/16") plate.
Grind beef through 3 mm (1/8") plate.
Mix ground meats with all ingredients.
Stuff into 60 mm pork or beef middles or permeable synthetic casings.
Ferment at 20° C (68° F), 95 → 90% humidity for 72 hours.
Dry at 18° C (64° F), 90 → 85% humidity for 2 days.
Cold smoke at 18° C (64° F) for 24 hours.
Dry at 15 → 12° C (59 → 12° F), 85 → 75% humidity for 3 weeks or until sausage looses 30% of its original weight.
Store at 10-12° C (50-53° F), <75% humidity.

Notes
If strong mold is desired use Chr-Hansen Bactoferm® Mold-600 culture.

Mettwurst - Streichfähige
(Spreadable Mettwurst)

German spreadable sausage. Spreadable Mettwurst is listed (2.212.2) in the German government publication Guide to Meats and Meat Products - *Leitsätze für Fleisch und Fleischerzeugnisse.*

Lean beef	200 g	0.44 lb
Pork belly	500 g	1.10 lb
Soft fat: pork belly, soft fat trimmings	300 g	0.66 lb

Ingredients per 1 kg (2.2 lb) of material

Salt	21 g	3.5 tsp
Cure #1	2.0 g	1/3 tsp
Dextrose	2.0 g	1/2 tsp
Sugar	2.0 g	1/2 tsp
Pepper	2.0 g	1 tsp
Paprika	1.0 g	1/2 tsp
Coriander	0.5 g	1/4 tsp
Mace	0.5 g	1/4 tsp
Ginger	0.3 g	1/8 tsp
T-SPX culture	0.12 g	use
scale		

Grind all meats through 3 mm (1/8" plate). Re-freeze meats and grind again.
You may grind once and then emulsify in the food processor without adding water. Add all ingredients during this step.
Stuff firmly into 40-60 mm beef middles or fibrous casings. Make 40 cm (16") links.
Ferment for 48 hours at 18° C (64° F), 75-80% humidity.
Apply cold smoke for 12 hours at 18° C (64° F).
Hold for 2 days at 18° C (64° F), 75% humidity.
Store in a refrigerator.

Morcón Andaluz

Morcón is a type of short (8", 20 cm) wide diameter chorizo-like sausage stuffed into a pig blind cap (caecum, also known as cecum), an intestine called in Spanish "morcón," thus its name. The large diameter dry sausage is very popular in the regions of Andalusia and Extremadura and in the province of Salamanca in Castilla-León. Morcón sausage has dark red color and deep flavor and aroma. Sliced morcón displays a vivid red color due to large amount of pimentón used in its manufacture. Best morcón is produced from Iberian pigs that feed on oak acorns.

Pork butt (shoulder), neck meat or both, preferably from
iberian pig .... 1000 g 2.20 lb

Ingredients per 1 kg (2.2 lb) of meat

Salt	28 g	4.5 tsp
Cure #2	2.5 g	1/2 tsp
Pimentón, sweet	25 g	4 Tbsp
Pimentón, hot	5.0 g	1 Tbsp
Garlic, smashed	12 g	4 cloves
White wine	60 ml	2 oz fl

Manually cut pork meat with fat attached into 20-30 mm (3/4-1.5") cubes.
Mix all ingredients with meat together. Hold for 24 hours in refrigerator.
Stuff firmly into pork cap (caecum) large intestine, around 18-25 cm (8-10") long.
Reinforce lengthwise and across with twine.
Dry at 12-15° C (53-59° F), 75-80% humidity for 2-3 months. The total time depends on the diameter of the sausage and temperature/humidity. In natural chambers without control of temperature and humidity the drying time could be from 3-4 months or even longer.*
Store at 12° C (53° F), 65% humidity.

Notes
* It is hard to maintain steady temperature and humidity in natural chambers. Finished product exhibits strong red color and is about 12-15 cm (5-6") thick, and 25-30 cm (12-14") long. Net weight around 1 kg (2.2 lb).
In traditional production the temperature was maintained by burning oak wood when necessary. Cure #2 was not added either.
Store in a cool, dry and lightly ventilated dark place. Consume cold.

Morcón Gaditano

Morcón Gaditano comes from Cádiz, a city and port in southwestern Spain. It is the capital of the province of Cádiz in Andalusia. The word "gaditano" describes a native of Cádiz city.

Lean pork from butt (upper   shoulder), neck
meat or both ....   1000 g   2.20 lb

Ingredients per 1 kg (2.2 lb) of meat

Salt	28 g	4.5 tsp
Cure #2	2.5 g	1/2 tsp
Pepper	2.0 g	1 tsp
Pimentón, sweet	30 g	5 Tbsp
Garlic, diced	12 g	4 cloves

Cut meat into 25 mm (1") pieces.
Mix well meat with salt and spices.
Stuff into pork large intestine blind cap (caecum) casing. The casing is about 18-25 cm long. Reinforce lengthwise and across with twine. The stuffed morcón looks like an oval small rugby ball.
Hold at 10° C (50° F), 90% humidity, for 8-10 days.
Dry at 12-14° C (53-57° F), 80% humidity, for 2-3 months. The total time depends on the diameter of the sausage and temperature/humidity. In natural chambers without control of temperature and humidity, drying time could be 3-4 months or even longer.
Store at 12° C (53° F), 65% humidity.

Notes
In traditional production the temperature was maintained by burning oak wood when necessary. In traditional production the temperature in natural chambers was maintained by burning oak wood when necessary. Cure #2 was not added either. Consume raw.
Net weight when stuffed into blind cap is around 1 kg (2.2 lb) and more when packed into pork stomach or bladder.

Other popular morcon sausages:

Morcón Extremeño - made from iberian pigs and stuffed into pork blind cap (caecum) casing.

Morcón de Lorca - technically speaking not a dry sausage as it is made from pork head meat and dewlap, stuffed in pork stomach or bladder and than fully cooked.

Morrpølse

Morr sausage is a Norwegian salami which
Morr sausage is a Norwegian salami, which
is probably one of the oldest processed food
products in Norway. More sausage, like other
sausages, has probably been made in Norway
ever since the Viking era. Traditionally, more
sausage was made from tripe, usually from
sheep, and offal meat such as heart, lungs,
kidneys, tongue, stomach, esophagus, and
colon. These were chopped or ground together,
spiced, and stuffed into the animal gut. Then,
the sausages were often hung in a cool place
for several months. The chamber had to be
occasionally heated by burning wood, so the
sausages were cold-smoked as well.

Pork, sheep, goat, wild game,
70% lean/ 30% fat .... 1000 g   2.2 lb
If using wild game meat add some pork fat to it.

Ingredients per 1 kg (2.2 lb) of meat

Salt	28 g	5 tsp
Cure #2	3.0 g	1/2 tsp
Pepper	4.0 g	2 tsp
Caraway	1.0 g	1/2 tsp
Nutmeg	0.5 g	1/4 tsp
Juniper berries, dry and crushed	2	2
T-SPX culture	0.12 g	use scale

Grind lean meat through 6 mm (1/4") plate.
Dice fat into 6 mm (1/4") cubes.
30 minutes before mixing dissolve starter
culture in 1 tablespoon de-chlorinated water.
Mix lean pork with salt and Cure #2. Add spices
and culture. Mix. Add diced fat and mix all
together.
Stuff firmly into 40 mm natural casings making
8" (20 cm) links.
Ferment at 20° C (68° F) for 72 hours, 90-85%
humidity.
Apply a thin cold smoke at 18° C (64° F), 65-
75% humidity for 2 days.
Dry at 15→12° C (59→53° F), 65-75% humidity
for 30 days.
Store at 10-12° C (50°-55 F), 75% humidity.

Mortadella-Dry

Mortadella is made from pork only, pork and
beef, or pork fat and veal. If back fat is diced
into 1/4" (6 mm) cubes and whole pistachio
nuts are included, the resulting product will
have a traditional look. Mortadella is not smoked.

Pork (butt)	550 g	1.21 lb
Beef (chuck)	250 g	0.55 lb
Back fat or hard fat trimmings	200 g	0.44 lb

Ingredients per 1 kg (2.2 lb) of meat

Salt	28 g	5 tsp
Cure #2	2.5 g	1/2 tsp
Dextrose	2 g	1/2 tsp
Sugar	3 g	3/4 tsp
White pepper	5 g	2 tsp
Garlic	2 g	1/2 clove
Rum	15 ml	1 Tbsp
Pistachio nuts	5 g	2 tsp
T-SPX culture	0.12 g	use scale

Cut back fat into 6 mm (1/4") cubes.
Grind pork through 10 mm (3/8"). Refreeze and
grind again through 3 mm (1/8"). Do the same
with beef.
Mix all ingredients with meat and diced fat.
Stuff firmly into 100-120 mm (4-5") protein
lined fibrous casings, 12" long.
Ferment at 20° C (68° F) for 72 hours, 90-85%
humidity.
Preheat smokehouse (no smoke applied)
to 49° C (120° F) and hold sausages at this
temperature for 12 hours (to remove the
moisture from the sausage). Gradually increase
temperature until an internal temperature of
138° F (59° C) is obtained. *
Cool down sausages by hanging them at room
temperature.
Dry at 16-12° C (60-54° F), 85-80% humidity.
The sausage is dried until around 30-35% in
weight is lost.

Note: * you may make the sausage ready to
eat at any time by cooking to 70° C (158° F)
internal meat temperature.
At your discretion the following spices may be
added (around 2 g spice/1 kg of meat): anise
seed, cardamom, cinnamon, ground clove,
coriander, nutmeg, juniper berries. Aromatic
liquids such as curacao or rum are also often
added.

Moscow Dry Sausage
(Московская колбаса)

Russian dry sausage.

Lean beef	750 g	1.65 lb
Pork back fat	250 g	0.55 lb

Ingredients per 1 kg (2.2 lb) of meat

Salt	30 g	5 tsp
Cure #2	5 g	1 tsp
Sugar	2 g	1 tsp
Ground pepper	1.5 g	1.5 tsp
Cardamom or nutmeg	0.25 g	1/4 tsp

Curing: cut meat into 25 mm (1") pieces. Place beef and fat in a separate food grade container. Mix beef with 24 g (4 tsp) salt, Cure #2 and sugar. Mix pork fat with 11 g (2 tsp) salt. Pack tightly to eliminate air and cover with clean cloth. Place for 72 hours in refrigerator. Discard any liquid brine and submit meat to grinding. Grind beef through 3 mm (1/8") plate. Dice back fat into 6 mm (1/4") cubes.
Mix beef with spices. Add fat cubes and mix everything together. Don't add water.
Stuff sausages firmly into 45-55 mm beef middles or fibrous casings. Make 25-50 cm (10-20") links. Hang sausages for 5-7 days at 2-4° C, (35-40° F), 85-90% humidity.
Smoke sausages for 2-3 days with cold smoke at 18-22° C (64-72° F).
Dry sausages for 5-7 days (depending on sausage diameter) at 11-15° C (52-59° F), 80-84% humidity. Dry 20-23 days more at 10-12° C (50-53° F), 74-78% humidity.

Finished sausage should retain 57% of its original weight.

Moscow Semi-Dry Sausage
(Московская колбаса)

Russian semi-dry sausage.

Beef	750 g	1.65 lb
Pork back fat	250 g	0.55 lb

Ingredients per 1 kg (2.2 lb) of meat

Salt	23 g	4 tsp
Cure #1	2.5 g	1/2 tsp
Dextrose	10 g	2 tsp
Black pepper	3 g	1.5 tsp
Nutmeg	0.5 g	1/2 tsp
F-LC culture	0.25 g	use
scale		

Grind beef through 3 mm (1/8"). Grind back fat through 5 mm (3/16") plate.
Mix all ingredients with meat.
Stuff into 40-60 mm beef middles or fibrous casings.
Ferment at 38° C (100° F) for 24 hours, 90-85% humidity.
Introduce warm smoke (43° C, 110° F), 70% humidity, for 6 hours. Gradually increase smoke temperature until meat reaches 145° F (63° C) internal temperature.
For a drier sausage: dry for 5 days at 14-12° C (57-53° F), 80-75% humidity or until desired weight loss has occurred.
Store sausages at 10-12° C (50-53° F), 75% humidity.

Nduja

Nduja is a spreadable Italian salami-type sausage from the southern Calabria region. Its name most likely comes from the French word andouille, a sausage made with innards, tripe, lung, and liver, boiled with vegetables and spices. Nduja was made locally from meat trimmings that remained after pig slaughter in winter. The sausages were made initially in Spilinga, Vibo Valentia province, Calabria, *"from pure meats and for the poor"*; by poor meats meant the cuts like lungs, heart, spleen, and meat and fat trimmings that remained after making cured noble products like hams, butts, bacon or loins. Nduja remained not widely known for a long time; however, what started as the sausage for the poor has since 2016 become a famous spreadable salami sausage in Europe, the UK, and the USA. Nowadays. Nduja is made from quality pork meat, fat, salt, and hot pepperoncino peppers. This spice, added at 3% or more, gives the sausage a very intense red color and an unmistakable taste.

Pork back fat, belly, jowls (cheeks)	700 g	1.55 lb
Pork meat: shoulder, ham (leg)	300 g	0.66 lb

Ingredients per 1 kg (2.2 lb) of meat

Salt 3%	30 g	5 tsp
Cure #1 (optional)	1.5 g	1/4 tsp
Red peperoncino, hot, powdered, 5%	50 g	1.76 oz
Red peperoncino, sweet, powdered, 5%*	50 g	1.76 oz

Meat and Ingredients. Meat (70%): shoulder and ham trimmings, loin, lean pork belly. Fat (30%): back fat, pork belly, jowls. The fat must not contain any connective tissue or leftover skin. Hot pepperoncino peppers are added at 3% or more. Outside Italy peperoncino may be hard to obtain so use Spanish pimentó or Hungarian paprika.

Grinding. The meat and fat must be finely ground. Cut meat and fat into 12 mm (1/2") strips or cubes, then grind through 3 mm(1/8") plate.

Mixing/kneading. In the past in artisanal production nitrates were not added, however, they are recommended today for protection against pathogenic bacteria and to delay the onset of fat rancidity.

Ground meat, fat, salt, cure #1 and pepperoncino powder are mixed very well together. Kneading with clenched fists, squeezing paste between the fingers, it is more like kneading the dough. Of course, with a mechanical mixer the mixing can be accomplished within minutes.

Stuffing. Usually, pork intestines are used, such as regular hog casings, pork bungs, or blind caps (caecum). The sausages are firmly stuffed and pricked around with a needle to allow movement of smoke and moisture. Nduja contains a lot of fat, which may clog some of the casing's pores and inhibit drying. Large diameter casings (blind caps) are reinforced alongside and across with cotton twine. The classic form of Nduja stuffed in blind caps (caecum) is known as "orba."

Conditioning. The sausages are hung for 4-6 hours at room temperature until the casings feel fry.

Smoking/Drying. The sausages are smoked/dried at 20-25° C (68-77° F) for 5-7 days with smoke applied for 1 hour each day. Nduja was traditionally smoked with hard woods such as oak, beech or olive. Using soft resinous (like pine) or aromatic wood, would impregnate sausage with turpentine like aromas. Although application of smoke imparts some smoky its main benefit is prevention of mold which would normally start growing on the moist surface of the sausage.

Maturing. After smoking, the sausages enter the proper drying - maturing stage, often called ripening which is done usually in a separate room at 15→12° C (59→53° F), 65-75% humidity and some ventilation. In Calabria, hilly and mountainous areas provided perfect conditions. The sausage stored in the small intestine is ready for consumption (always raw) in 20 days after stuffing, the one preserved in the caecum needs up to 2 months and is usually consumed within the year.

Storing. Keep Nduja at 10-12° C (50°-55 F), 75% humidity.

Notes
Nduja is served raw by spreading it on a slice of bread or on a roll.

Neva Sausage
(Колбаса невская)

Russian dry sausage. The Neva river flows through the second largest Russian city, Saint Petersburg, on the Baltic sea.

Lean beef	100 g	0.22 lb
Lean pork		550 g	1.21 g
Pork back fat		350 g	0.77 lb

Ingredients per 1 kg (2.2 lb) of meat

Salt	30 g	5 tsp
Cure #2	5 g	1 tsp
Sugar	2 g	1/2 tsp
Black pepper	1 g	1/2 tsp
Cinnamon	1 g	1/2 tsp
Cognac	2.5 ml	1/2 tsp

Curing: cut meat into 25 mm (1") pieces. Place beef, pork and pork back fat in separate food grade containers. Mix pork back fat with 12 g (2 tsp) salt. Mix beef and pork meat with 18 g salt, cure #2 and sugar according to the recipe (estimate amounts). Pack tightly to eliminate air and cover with clean cloth. Place for 72 hours in refrigerator. Discard any liquid brine and submit meat to grinding.

Grind beef through 3 mm (1/8") plate. Grind pork through 3 mm (1/8") plate. Dice back fat into 6 mm (1/4") cubes.

Mix beef with salt, cure, sugar and spices. Add pork, cognac and mix. Add fat cubes and remix everything together. Don't add water.

Stuff sausages firmly into 45 mm beef rounds or hog casings. Links in ring shape, from 8-15 cm 3-6") inside diameter.

Hang sausages for 5-7 days at 2-4° C (35-40° F), 85-90% humidity.

Using dry wood smoke sausages for 2 days with cold smoke, 18-22° C (64-72° F).

Dry sausages for 5 days (depending on sausage diameter) at 11-15° C (52-59° F), 80-85% humidity. Dry 20 days more at 10-12° C (50-53° F), 75-80% humidity.

Store at 10-12° C (50-53° F), 70-75% humidity.

Finished sausage should retain 60% of its original weight.

Nham

Nham is an uncooked, fermented, semi-dry Thai sausage that is very popular in Asia. It is made from fresh lean pork, pork skins, cooked rice, fresh garlic, and eye bird chilies. The sausage is wrapped in banana leaves or synthetic casings and fermented for 3-5 days (depending on the season and if no culture added) at about 30° C (86° F) and 50% humidity.

Rice serves not only as a value-added filler but also as a source of carbohydrates for lactic acid production during fermentation. Many Asian products employ rice as a fermentation source, such as "saki" - rice wine. The fermentation is performed at high Thai ambient temperatures, and undesirable bacteria are likely to grow if no lactic acid is produced during the first stage of the process. For this reason, glucose (dextrose) is added to jump-start fermentation as cooked rice is metabolized very slowly. The pH of boiled rice is about 7.40. If stored at room temperatures 20-30° C (68-86° F), the sausage has a shelf life of less than a week, but its life can be extended by keeping it under refrigeration. Then, it is served as a dish or eaten raw.

It is essential to remember that natural fermentations are difficult to replicate in other settings. For example, the meat mixture for Nham is traditionally wrapped in small banana leaf packets. The leaves contribute to the surface flora of the sausage, which undoubtedly changes the fermentation pattern.

Traditional Nham is made with Bird's Eye Chili Peppers, tiny, hot chilies found in Malaysia, Brunei, Indonesia, the Philippines, and Thailand. Although small in size compared to other types of chili, they are very hot , at 50,000 to 100,000 on the Scoville pungency scale. Tabasco and cayenne peppers are rated slightly lower, at 30,000-50,000 Scoville units.

Lean pork	700 g	1.54 lb
Pork skins	300 g	0.66 lb

Different ratios of lean pork to skins may be used: 80/20, 70/30, 60/40, 50/50 or 40/60. Don't replace pork skins with fat. The texture and flavor of this sausage depends largely on pork skins.

Ingredients per 1 kg (2.2 lb) of meat

Salt	25 g	4 tsp
Cure #1	2.5 g	1/2 tsp
Pepper	1.0 g	1/2 tsp
Dextrose,	10 g	2 tsp
Cooked rice, 3%	30 g	1 oz
Bird Eye Chillies, cayenne		
or Tabasco peppers	20 g	0.7 oz
Garlic, 3%, minced	30 g	1.0 oz
(8 cloves)		
F-LC culture	0.25 g	use
scale		

Trim meat of all connective tissue and fat. Grind through a small plate 3-5 mm (1/8-3/16"). Trim pork skins of any visible fat and cook in water for about 1.5 hours. Cut de-fatted skin (rind) into 3 mm (1/8") thick and 20 mm (3/4") long strips. Cut Bird Eye Chillies 3-5 mm (1/8-3/16"). Mix meat, skins, rice and all other ingredients well together.

Stuff tightly into air-impermeable plastic casings, about 30 mm diameter and 15-20 cm (6-8") long.

Ferment at 30° C (86° F) for 48 hours, high humidity. Nham is not dried, the microbiological safety of the sausage is accomplished by fermentation until the acidity in meat increases to pH 4.6.

Refrigerate.

Notes

Cooked rice is commonly used between 2.5 and 4%.

Sausage contains a high amount of garlic (5%).

If made traditionally (without starter culture):

- Increase salt to 3%.
- Ferment for 3 days at 30° C (86° F) or for 5 days if temperature is lower (but equal to or higher than 24° C (75° F).
- Refrigerate.

Ossenworst
(Ox sausage)

Ossenworst is a smoked raw beef sausage that is said to originate in Amsterdam. It is widely available in the Netherlands, but while you can find factory-made versions in Dutch supermarkets, these bear little resemblance to the real thing as they are often neither smoked nor aged. This Amsterdam specialty originated in the seventeenth century when oxen were mainly imported from Denmark and Germany.

Beef	1000 g	2.2 lb

Ingredients per 1 kg (2.2 lb) of meat

Salt	25 g	4 tsp
Cure #1	2.5 g	1 tsp
Sugar	5.0 g	1 tsp
Pepper	3.0 g	1.5 tsp
Nutmeg	0.5 g	1/4 tsp
Mace	0.5 g	1/4 tsp
Cloves, ground	0.3 g	1/8 tsp

Cut beef into 5 cm (2") cubes. Mix with salt, Cure #1, sugar and pack tightly in a container covering the meat with a clean cloth to prevent discoloration of the top layer of the meat. Hold in a refrigerator for 10 days.

Grind the meat through 3 mm (2/8") plate. Mix the ground meat with all ingredients. Stuff into beef middles. Hold in the refrigerator for 24 hours.

Apply a thin cold smoke at 18° C (64° F) for 1 day. Oak or beech wood is used. Refrigerate.

Notes

This is a nearly raw sausage and it must be consumed within a few days. Like steak tartare it is soft and tender and goes well with beer, bread, mustard and pickled gherkin or pearl onion.

Paio de Beja

Paio de Beja is a thick smoked Portuguese sausage produced in the Beja region. Paio sausages can be found throughout the country.

| Lean pork-butt, loin, legs | 750 g | 1.65 lb |
| Back fat, fat trimmings | 250 g | 0.55 lb |

Ingredients per 1 kg (2.2 lb) of meat

Salt	28 g	5 tsp
Cure #1	2.5 g	1/2 tsp
Pepper	2.0 g	1 tsp
Paprika, sweet	4.0 g	2 tsp
Red pepper paste*	30 g	1 oz
Cumin or caraway	1.0 g	1/2 tsp
Garlic, dehydrated	2.0 g	1 tsp
Water	60 ml	2 oz fl

* Pepper paste. Cut bell peppers lengthwise into halves. Discard stems and seeds. Get a suitable pan and sprinkle salt on the bottom. Place peppers on salt, then cover them with more salt. Repeat the procedure creating a multilayer combination with salt being the top layer. Hold for 8 days. Rinse with water, pat dry with paper towel and grind through 3 mm (1/8") plate or emulsify in a food processor.

Make marinade by mixing salt, cure #1, spices and 60 ml of water.

Chop meat and fat into 10 mm (3/8") pieces.

Mix meat and fat with marinade and hold for 2 days at 10° C (50° F) or lower (refrigerator). Drain.

Mix marinated meat and red pepper paste * together.

Stuff into a large hog casings like pork bungs. This is a large sausage which has a straight cylindrical section, measuring between 12-20 cm (5-8") in length and between 60-150 mm (2.3-6") in diameter.

Using oak wood apply thin smoke at 18° C (64° F) for 7 days. Smoking need not be continuous, as long as the temperature inside of the smokehouse stays below 18° C. Think of the process as drying with smoke. Due to seasonal variations in temperature, the sausage is smoked for 3-4 days in the summer and 5-6 days in the winter.

Dry/store at 5-15° C (41-59° F).

Notes

* red pepper paste (in Portuguese "massa de pimentão") is an essential condiment in Portuguese cooking.

Home method for making red pepper paste (about 1 cup):

3 red bell peppers
24 g (4 tsp) salt
2 cloves of garlic
1 fl oz (30 ml=2 Tbsp) olive oil

Cut peppers into quarters. Remove the stems and seeds. Remove the white pulp from the inside of the peppers.

Place peppers in a jar and sprinkle them with salt. Shake the jar. Leave uncovered for 24 hours at room temperature. Rinse the peppers and pat them dry with a paper towel.

Spread peppers on a pan and bake them for 20 minutes until the skins are charred and dark. Remove the tray and let the peppers cool. Remove the skins from the peppers, they come off easily.

Using a mixer blend the peppers with 2 garlic cloves gradually adding olive oil. The mixture should reach the consistency of a fine creamy paste. Place the paste in a jar and store in refrigerator. Use it as a topping for hot dogs or any grilled sausage.

Paio de Beja is produced from Alentejana breed of pig.

Paio de Beja carries PGI 2007 certification.

Painho de Portalegre

Painho de Portalegre is a smoked sausage produced in Portalegre's district.

Lean pork-shoulder,		
loin, legs	700 g	1.54 lb
Back fat, ft trimmings	300 g	0.66 lb

Ingredients per 1 kg (2.2 lb) of meat

Salt	24 g	4 tsp
Cure #2	2.5 g	1/2 tsp
Paprika, sweet	4.0 g	2 tsp
Garlic, dehydrated	1.0 g	1 tsp
Red pepper paste*	30 g	1 oz
White wine	30 ml	1 oz fl

Make marinade by mixing salt, cure #1, spices and wine.
Chop meat and fat into 20 mm (3/4") pieces.
Mix meat and fat with marinade and hold for 2 days in a refrigerator.
Mix marinated meat and red pepper paste * together.
Stuff into 36-40 mm hog casings forming 30 cm (12") links.
Using oak wood apply a thin smoke at 18° C (64° F) for 7 days. Smoking need not be continuous as long as the temperature inside of the smokehouse stays below 18° C. Think of the process as drying with smoke. Due to seasonal variations in temperature the sausage is smoked for 3-4 days in the summer and 5-6 days in the winter.
Dry/store at 12° C (53° F) 70% humidity or hold in refrigerator.

Given that the sausage has a small diameter it can be easily further dried becoming a dry sausage.

Note: * red pepper paste (in Portuguese "massa de pimentão") is an essential condiment in Portuguese cooking.

* Pepper paste. Cut bell peppers lengthwise into halves. Discard stems and seeds. Get a suitable pan and sprinkle salt on the bottom. Place peppers on salt then cover them with more salt. Repeat the procedure creating a multilayer combination with salt being the top layer. Hold for 8 days. Rinse with water, pat dry with a paper towel and grind through 1/8" (3 mm) plate or emulsify in a food processor. Store in refrigerator.

Home method for making red pepper paste (about 1 cup):

3 red bell peppers
24 g (4 tsp) salt
2 cloves of garlic
1 fl oz (30 ml=2 Tbsp) olive oil

Cut peppers into quarters. Remove the stems and seeds. Remove the white pulp from the inside of the peppers.
Place peppers in a jar and sprinkle them with salt. Shake the jar. Leave uncovered for 24 hours at room temperature. Rinse the peppers and pat them dry with a paper towel.
Spread peppers on a pan and bake them for 20 minutes until the skins are charred and dark. Remove the tray and let the peppers cool. Remove the skins from the peppers, they come off easily.
Using a mixer blend the peppers with 2 garlic cloves gradually adding olive oil. The mixture should reach the consistency of a fine creamy paste. Place the paste in a jar and store in a refrigerator. Use it as a topping for hot dogs or any grilled sausage.

Painho de Portalegre is made from Alentejo breed of pig.

Painho de Portalegre carries PGI 1997 certification.

Pafitiko Loukaniko

Pafitiko Loukaniko also known as Paphos sausage, is produced in the Paphos province in Cyprus.

Semi-fat pork	1000 g	2.2 lb

Ingredients per 1 kg (2.2 lb) of meat

Salt, coarse	28 g	4.5 tsp
Black pepper	2.0 g	1 tsp
Coriander	1.0 g	1/2 tsp
Cumin	1.0 g	1/2 tsp
Nutmeg	1.0 g	1/2 tsp
Cinnamon	0.5 g	1/4 tsp
Cloves, ground	0.3 g	1/8 tsp
Ginger	0.5 g	1/4 tsp
Dry red wine from local Mavro grapes	120 ml	1/2 cup

Grind pork through 6 mm (1/4") plate.
Marinate ground pork with salt and local red wine for 4 days.
Drain any excess of wine, add spices and mix all together.
Stuff into 32 mm hog casings and form 3-7, six inch long links in each consecutive section.
Dry sausages at 12 -15° C (53-59° F), low humidity for 30 days.

Note: the sausages can be eaten at any time by frying or grilling them. They are often eaten with bread, cucumber and tomatoes.
Traditionally made sausages were sun-dried.

Pafitiko Loukaniko carries PGI, 2015 certification.

Patatera Extremeña

La Extremadura is the western Spanish province that borders Portugal. The main ingredient in the sausage is potatoes ("patata" means "potato" in Spanish).

Lean pork	100 g	0.22 lb
Back fat or hard fat trimmings	400 g	0.88 lb
Boiled potatoes	500 g	1.10 lb

Ingredients per 1 kg (2.2 lb) of material

Salt	28 g	5 tsp
Cure #2	1.2 g	1/4 tsp
Dextrose	3.0 g	1/2 tsp
Pimentón sweet	10 g	3 tsp
Garlic, minced	10 g	3 cloves
T-SPX culture	0.12 g	use scale

Grind pork through 6 mm (1/4") plate.
Grind fat through 6 mm (1/4") plate.
Peel potatoes and boil them until soft. Drain potatoes and smash them. Set mashed potatoes on a flat surface and allow them to release steam and moisture.
Except starter culture, mix meat, fat, and potatoes with other ingredients.
30 minutes before mixing add starter culture to 1 tablespoon de-chlorinated water.
Mix meat, fat, potatoes and all other ingredients together.
Stuff firmly into 36 mm hog casings. Make 12" 30 cm (12") loops.
Ferment at 20° C (68° F) for 72 hours, 90-85% humidity.
Dry at 16-12° C (60-54° F), 85-80% humidity for 30 days. The sausage is dried until around 30% in weight is lost.
Store sausages at 10-15° C (50-59° F), <75% humidity.

Pepperoni - Dry

Traditional pepperoni is an Italian dry sausage, smoked, air-dried, and sometimes cooked. Pepperoni can be made from beef or pork or in combination with 30% beef and 70% pork. Pepperoni is a lean sausage with a fat content of < 30%. Cheaper, fast-fermented (semi-dry), and cooked types are toppings to pizzas worldwide to give flavor. Traditionally made Italian pepperoni was not smoked.

Pork	700 g	1.54 lb
Beef	300 g	0.66 lb

Ingredients per 1 kg (2.2 lb) of meat

Salt	28 g	5 tsp
Cure #2	2.5 g	1/2 tsp
Dextrose (glucose)	2.0 g	1/3 tsp
Sugar	3.0 g	1/3 tsp
Black pepper	3.0 g	1.5 tsp
Paprika	6.0 g	3 tsp
Anise seeds, cracked, or fennel seeds	2.5 g	2 tsp
Cayenne pepper	2.0 g	1 tsp
T-SPX culture	0.12 g	use scale

Grind pork and beef through 5 mm (3/16") plate.
Mix all ingredients with meat.
Stuff firmly into 60 mm beef middles or fibrous casings.
Ferment at 20° C (68° F) for 72 hours, 90-85% humidity.
Optional step: cold smoke for 8 hours (< 22° C, 72° F).
Dry at 16 -12° C (60-54° F), 85-80% humidity. In about 6-8 weeks a shrink of 30% should be achieved.
Store sausages at 10-15° C (50-59° F), < 75% humidity.

Note: original Italian pepperoni was5 not smoked.

Pepperoni-Semi-Dry

Italian sausage. Fast fermented, semi-dry pepperoni.

Pork	700 g	1.54 lb
Beef	300 g	0.66 lb

Ingredients per 1 kg (2.2 lb) of meat

Salt	24 g	4 tsp
Cure #1	2.5 g	1/2 tsp
Dextrose (glucose) 10.0 g	2 tsp	
Sugar	10.0 g	2 tsp
Black pepper	3.0 g	1½ tsp
Paprika	6.0 g	3 tsp
Anise seeds, cracked or fennel seeds	2.5 g	2 tsp
Cayenne pepper	2.0 g	1 tsp
F-LC culture	0.24 g	use scale

Grind pork and beef through 5 mm (3/16") plate. Mix all ingredients with meat.
Stuff into 60 mm beef middles or fibrous casings.
Ferment at 38° C (100° F) for 24 hours, 90-85% humidity.
Optional step: introduce warm smoke at 43° C (110° F), 70% humidity, for 6 hours.
Gradually increase smoke temperature until meat reaches a temperature of 63° C (145° F) inside.
For a drier sausage: dry for 2 days at 22-16° C (60-70° F), 65-75% humidity or until desired weight loss has occurred.
Store sausages at 10-15° C (50-59° F), < 75% humidity.

Note: original Italian pepperoni was5 not smoked.

Petrohan

Petrohan is a traditional Bulgarian dry fermented sausage made with beef and pork.

Beef	600 g	1.32 lb
Pork, lean	300 g	0.66 lb
Pork back fat	100 g	0.22 lb

Ingredients per 1 kg (2.2 lb) of material

Salt	28 g	4.5 tsp
Cure #2	2.5 g	1/2 tsp
Black pepper	2.0 g	1 tsp
Sugar	3.0 g	1/2 tsp
Cumin	1.0 g	1/2 tsp
Paprika, sweet	1.0 g	1/2 tsp
Savory	0.5 g	1/4 tsp
T-SPX culture	0.12 g	use
scale		

Grind cold pork through 6 mm (1/4") plate.
Grind partially frozen fat through 6 mm (1/4") plate.
Grind cold beef through 3 mm plate (1/8").
Dilute starter culture in 15 ml (1 Tablespoon) of non-chlorinated water.
Mix ground meats with all ingredients together. Add cold ground fat and mix again.
Stuff into 32 mm hog casings.
Ferment at 20° C (68° F), 90 → 85% humidity for 72 hours.
Smoke at 18° C (64° F) for 24 hours.
Dry at 14 → 12° C (57 → 53° F), 80 → 75% humidity for 4 weeks or until sausage looses 33% of its original weight.
Store at 10-12° C (50-53° F), <75% humidity.

Plockwurst

Plockwurst is a type of German salami. The sausage is listed (2.211.13) in the official guide of German meat products "Guidelines For Meat and Meat Products" (*Leitsätze für Fleisch und Fleischerzeugnisse, 25.11.2015*).

Beef, lean, some connective tissue	500 g	1.10 lb
Pork, semi-fat	250 g	0.33 lb
Back fat, hard fat trimmings	250 g	0.33 lb

Ingredients per 1 kg (2.2 lb) of material

Salt	25 g	4 tsp
Cure #2	2.5 g	1/2 tsp
Dextrose	2.0 g	1/2 tsp
Sugar	2.0 g	1/2 tsp
Pepper	2.0 g	1 tsp
Paprika	0.5 g	1/4 tsp
Coriander	0.5 g	1/4 tsp
T-SPX culture	0.12 g	use scale

Grind pork through 10 mm (3/8") plate.
Grind fat through 6 mm (1/4") plate.
Grind beef through 6 mm plate (1/4"), then grind again with 3 mm (1/8") plate.
Mix meats with all ingredients together. Add ground fat and mix again.
Stuff into 60 mm beef middles.
Ferment at 20° C (68° F), 90 → 85% humidity for 72 hours.
Smoke at 18° C (64° F) for 24 hours.
Dry at 14 → 12° C (57 → 53° F), 80 → 75% humidity for 5 weeks or until sausage looses 33% of its original weight.
Store at 10-12° C (50-53° F), <75% humidity.

Polish Dry Sausage - Russian Style
(Польская колбаса)

Russian version of Polish cold smoked sausage. Polish smoked sausage is usually made from pork alone, most Russian sausages are made with beef and pork. Polish version always includes garlic.

Lean beef	400 g	0.88 lb
Lean pork	300 g	0.66 lb
Pork back fat	300 g	0.66 lb

Ingredients per 1 kg (2.2 lb) of meat

Salt	30 g	5 tsp
Cure #2	5 g	1 tsp
Sugar	2 g	1/2 tsp
Pepper	1 g	1/2 tsp
Allspice	0.5 g	1/4 tsp
Cardamom or nutmeg............	0.3 g	1/2 tsp
Madeira wine	2.5 ml	1 tsp

Curing: cut meat into 25 mm (1") pieces. Place beef, pork and fat in separate food grade containers and mix beef and pork with salt, Cure #2 and sugar according to the recipe (estimate amounts). Fat needs salt only. Pack tightly to eliminate air and cover with clean cloth. Place for 72 hours in refrigerator. Discard any liquid brine and submit meat to grinding. Grind beef through 3 mm (1/8") plate. Grind pork through 3 mm (1/8") plate. Dice partially frozen pork fat into 6 mm (1/4") cubes. Mix beef with spices. Add pork and wine and mix. Add fat cubes and remix everything together. Don't add any water.
Stuff sausages firmly into 35-45 mm beef rounds or hog casings. Sausage in ring shape, inside diameter (8-15 cm) (3-6"). Both ends tied together.
Hang sausages for 5-7 days at 2-4° C, 85-90% humidity.
Smoke sausages for 2-3 days with cold smoke, 18-22° C (64-72 F).
Dry sausages for 5-7 days (depending on sausage diameter) at 11-15° C (53-59° F), 80-84 humidity. Dry 20-23 days more at 10-12° C (50-54° F), 74-78% humidity.
Finished sausage should retain 60% of its original weight.
Store at 10-12° C (50-53° F) <75% humidity.

Polish Sausage-Cold Smoked
(Polska kiełbasa wędzona)

This is the predecessor of the Polish Smoked Sausage as it came to be known all over the world. When it was originally made, food preservation was of the utmost importance, and that is why it was cold-smoked. The process of making Polish cold-smoked sausage resembles making traditional Italian salami, Spanish chorizo, or Hungarian salami. It makes little difference whether the sausage is dried in cool air or with cold smoke; in both instances, it is dried to remove moisture. Today, the hot-smoked version of Polish Smoked Sausage is popular as it is faster and cheaper to make. In addition, the texture and the flavor of cold smoked sausages are less popular with modern consumers. Nevertheless, the materials and ingredients used for making Cold Smoked or Hot Smoked Polish sausage are the same; what is different is the manufacturing process. The following is the original recipe and instructions for making Polish Cold Smoked Sausage made by Polish meat plants in the 1950-1990's.

Lean pork, (ham, lean butt)	400 g	0.88 lb
Pork trimmings (butt)	600 g	1.32 lb

Ingredients per 1 kg (2.2 lb) of meat

Salt	28 g	5 tsp
Cure #2	2.5 g	1/2 tsp
Sugar	2.0 g	1/2 tsp
Pepper	2.0 g	1 tsp
Marjoram	1.0 g	2/3 tsp
Garlic	3.5 g	1 clove

Curing: cut meat into 5-6 cm (2") cubes, mix with salt, sugar and cure #2. Pack tightly in a container and cover with a clean cloth. Place in a cooler 4-6° C (40-42° F) for 72-96 hours. Grind meats through 10 mm (3/8") plate. Add remaining ingredients and mix until sticky. Do not add water. Stuff firmly into 32-36 mm hog casings. Form 12" 30-35 cm (12") long links but leave them in a continuous coil. Hang for 1-2 days at 2-6° C (35-42° F) and 85-90% humidity. Apply cold smoke at 22° C (72° F) for 1-1.5 days until the casings develop yellow-light brown color. Dry at 10-12° C (50-53° F), 75-80% humidity, until sausages lose 15% of its original weight. Divide into pairs.
Store at 10° C (53° F) or lower.

Rheinische Mettwurst

A spreadable mettwurst sausage, originally from Rheine, the town in the district of Steinfurt in Westphalia, Germany.

Pork, lean (shoulder)	600 g	1.32 lb
Pork belly (50% fat)	400 g	0.88 lb

Ingredients per 1 kg (2.2 lb) of material

Salt	22 g	3.5 tsp
Cure #1	2.5 g	1/2 tsp
Pepper	3.0 g	1.5 tsp
Dextrose	2.0 g	1/2 tsp
Sugar	2.0 g	1/2 tsp
Mace	1.0 g	1/2 tsp
Allspice	1.0 g	1/2 tsp
Cardamom	0.5 g	1/4 tsp
Ginger	0.3 g	1/8 tsp

Grind lean pork and belly through 5 mm (3/16") plate.
Mix the sausage mass with all ingredients.
Stuff into 36 mm pork casings forming 36 cm (15") links.
Ferment for 24 hours at 18° C (64° F), 75-80% humidity.
Cold smoke at 18° C (64° F) for 12 hours.
Hold at 18° C (64° F), 75% humidity for 2 days.
Refrigerate.

Rosette de Lyon

Rosette de Lyon, a French dry sausage, is the most famous of Lyon's sausages. This traditionally dried sausage is made from lean pork, hard fat, garlic, wine, and spices. In general, Rosette sausages derive their name from the casing they are stuffed in: the pig's last part of the digestive tract is called "rosette" in French (pork bung in English).

Lean pork (shoulder)	700 g	1.54 lb
Pork back fat	300 g	0.66 lb

Ingredients per 1 kg (2.2 lb) of meat

Salt	28 g	5 tsp
Cure #2	5.0 g	1 tsp
Dextrose	3.0 g	1/2 tsp
Sugar	2.0 g	1/2 tsp
Pepper	2.0 g	1 tsp
Garlic, minced	10 g	3 cloves
Nutmeg	1.0 g	1/2 tsp
Ginger	0.5 g	1/4 tsp
Cloves, ground	0.3 g	1/8 tsp
Red wine	15 ml	1 Tbsp
T-SPX culture	0.12 g	use scale

Grind meat through 8 mm (5/16") plate.
Using a sharp knife cut partially frozen back fat into 8 mm (5/16") cubes.
Dilute culture in 1 tablespoon of de-chlorinated water 30 minutes before mixing.
Mix ground lean meat with salt and Cure #2 until sticky.
Add fat cubes, culture and spices and mix all together.
Stuff firmly into 50 mm pork bung.
Ferment at 20° C (68° F) for 72 hours, 90-85% humidity.
Dry at 15 → 12° C (59 → 53° F), 85 → 80% humidity for 45 days. The sausage is dried until around 30% in weight is lost. The sausage should develop a white mold which is expected and desired.
Store sausages at 10-12° C (50-53° F), <75% humidity.

Notes
Rosette de Lyon must be stuffed into natural casings.

Russian Dry Sausage

Russian cold smoked sausage.

Lean pork	500 g	1.10 lb
Pork back fat or		
hard fat trimmings	300 g	0.66 lb
Beef	200 g	0.44 lb

Ingredients per 1 kg (2.2 lb) of meat

Salt	28 g	4.5 tsp
Cure #2	5.0 g	1 tsp
Pepper	2.0 g	1 tsp
Sugar	2.0 g	1/2 tsp
Cardamom	2.0 g	1 tsp
Allspice	2.0 g	1 tsp
Madeira wine or brandy	60 ml	1/4 cup

Curing: cut meat and fat into 5-6 cm (2")
pieces, mix with salt, sugar and Cure # 2 and
place in a cool area for 4 - 5 days. Keep beef
and pork separate.
Grind pork with 10 mm (3/8") plate.
Grind beef with 3 mm (1/8") plate.
Cut partially frozen back fat into 6 mm (1/4")
cubes.
Mix all ingredients with meat adding wine. Mix
until all wine is absorbed by the mixture. Then
add diced fat and mix everything together.
Stuff into 40-60 mm beef middles or synthetic
fibrous casings and form 30 cm (12") long
links.
Hang for 2 days in a cool place.
Cold smoke at 18-22° C (64-72° F) for 6 days.
Dry for 25-30 days in a cool, dry and drafty
area.
Store at 10-12° C (50-53° F) <75% humidity

Sabadiego or Sabadeña

Sabadiego also known as *Sabadeña* or *Chorizo
Sabadiego* is a popular sausage in Noreña, a
municipality in the Asturias region of Spain.
The name means "Saturday Sausage" (*Sabado*
means Saturday). In Spain and in other
European Christian countries, the consumption
of any meat was strictly forbidden on Friday,
with noble meats on Saturday as well. This was
rigidly observed during Lent, a 40 day period of
fasting preceding Easter.

It has been accepted that in the eighteenth
century, Alonso Marcos de Llanes Argüelles,
bishop of Segovia and archbishop of Seville,
Christianized this sausage with the approval
of King Carlos III and also authorized
the consumption of a certain type of meat
exclusively on Saturdays.

This meat was called "Saturday meat" and
generally used to be a wild game or an injured
animal. Offal meats (heart, liver, lungs, kidneys,
blood, skin, stomach, tripe) were considered
inferior meats and were also permitted. Thus,
Sabadiego (Saturday) sausage was invented,
and as long as it was made with strict adherence
to church requirements (made from less noble
meats), there was no conflict.

The pigs were slaughtered during
Christmas or soon after, so the meat supply
was short-lived, and Sabadiego sausage
was available for only a few months. Today,
Sabadiego can be produced at any time.

Offal meat: heart,		
lungs, liver, stomach	600 g	1.32 lb
Back fat, belly fat,		
fat trimmings	250 g	0.55 lb
Beef	150 g	0.33 lb

Ingredients per 1 kg (2.2 lb) of meat

Salt	30 g	5 tsp
Cure #2	2.5 g	1/2 tsp
Pimentón, sweet	25 g	4 Tbsp
Pimentón, hot	5.0 g	1 tsp
Oregano, ground	1.0 g	1/2 tsp
Nutmeg	1.0 g	1/2 tsp
Garlic	7.0 g	2 cloves
Wine	60 ml	2 oz fl

Cook heart, lungs, stomach in water (below boiling point) until soft. Scald liver in hot water for 5 minutes.
Grind beef and fat through 10 mm (3/8") plate.
Grind offal meats through 3 mm (1/8") plate.
Mix meats, fat and all ingredients together.
Hold for 12 hours in refrigerator.
Stuff into 40-50 mm pork or beef middles.
Ferment/dry at 25° C (77° F), 90% humidity for 48 hours.
Dry at 14-15° C (57-59° F), 70% humidity for 30 days.
Store at 10-12° C (50-52° F), 60-65% humidity or refrigerate.

Sächsische Mettwurst
(Saxonian Mettwurst)

Sächsische Mettwurst is listed (2.212.3) in the German government publication Guide to Meats and Meat Products - *Leitsätze für Fleisch und Fleischerzeugnisse.* Saxony *(Sächsische)* is the German part of the Elbe Sandstone Mountains known as Saxon Switzerland.

Lean pork	650 g	1.43 lb
Pork belly	350 g	0.77 lb

Ingredients per 1 kg (2.2 lb) of material

Salt	22 g	3.5 tsp
Cure #1	2.5 g	1/2 tsp
Dextrose	1.0 g	1/4 tsp
Sugar	2.0 g	1/2 tsp
Pepper	3.0 g	1.5 tsp
Caraway, ground	1.0 g	1/2 tsp
Cardamom	0.3 g	1/8 tsp
Mace	0.5 g	1/4 tsp

Grind lean pork and belly through 5 mm (3/16") plate.
Mix with all ingredients.
Stuff into 42 mm pork or beef casings forming 50 cm (20") rings.
Ferment for 24 hours at 18° C (64° F), 75-80% humidity.
Cold smoke at 18° C (64° F) for 12 hours.
Hold at 18° C (64° F), 75% humidity for 2 days.
Refrigerate.

Sai Krok Isan

Sai Krok Isan is a salty, fermented sausage from the Isan region of Thailand with a hint of sourness. It is made with ground pork meat and fat, garlic, sticky rice, salt, and pepper in a natural casing.

Pork shoulder, pork trimmings	800 g	1.76 lb
Cooked sticky rice	200 g	0.44 lb

Ingredients per 1 kg (2.2 lb) of material

Salt	25 g	4 tsp
Cure #2*	2.0 g	1/3 tsp
Sugar	4.0 g	1 tsp
Black pepper	4.0 g	2 tsp
Coriander	2.0 g	1 tsp
Garlic, minced	15 g	5 cloves
Galangal***, grated	10 g	1 Tbsp
F-LC culture **	0.25 g	use scale

Steam the rice.
Dilute culture in 30 ml (2 tsp) of distilled water.
Grind pork through 6 mm (1/4") plate.
Mix ground pork, sticky rice and all ingredients together. Stuff into 36 mm pork casings. Tie off into links 5 cm (2") long or shape into little balls like a rosary type continuous coil in Colombian Butifarra Soledeña. Ferment at 28° C (82° F) for 48 hours, 90-85% humidity. Dry for 1 day at 18° C (63° F), 85% humidity. Dry for 3 weeks at 16→12° C (60→54° F), 85-75% humidity. Store sausages at 10-15° C (50-59° F), 75% humidity.

Notes: originally Sai Krok Isan was fermented and dried in the sun, like Belutak from Brunei.
* recommended for safety reasons.
** recommended for a better fermentation process.
*** galangal *(Kaempferia galangal)* is aromatic wild ginger.
Thai sticky rice, a variety of sweet rice is enjoyed throughout Thailand and Laos.

Making sticky rice:
Cover rinsed rice with 5 cm (2") of water and let it stand for 6 hours. Drain the rice, place it in a cheesecloth, wrap it up and place it inside a rice steamer. Make sure that the rice is steamed and does not touch the boiling water. Cover with a lid and steam the rice for 15 minutes. The sausage is served for breakfast or locals buy them from local street carts as snacks that are grilled on a stick and consumed on the go.

Salama da Sugo

Salama da sugo is produced in the territory of the province of Ferrara, except in the municipalities of Goro, Codigoro, Lagosanto, and Comacchio. Salama da sugo is made from a blend of seasoned pork meats encased in a natural pig's bladder. It is sold as an uncooked edible product after being dried and matured or as a cooked edible product following subsequent heat treatment. A 'Salama da sugo' typically weighs between 700 g (1.5 lb) and 1,400 g (3 lbs) following maturing. It is round and tied with string to form six or eight segments, with a constricting horizontal band around the middle. The outer surface is uneven and may feature traces of mold formed naturally during maturing.

Pork shoulder	200 g	0.44 lb
Pork butt (neck part)	250 g	0.55 lb
Pork belly	250 g	0.55 lb
Pork back fat	250 g	0.55 lb
Pork tongue	25 g	1.0 oz
Pork liver	25 g	1.0 oz

Ingredients per 1 kg (2.2 lb) of meat

Sea salt	28 g	5 tsp
Cure #2	2.5 g	1/2 tsp
Black pepper, ground	1.0 g	1/2 tsp
Black peppercorns	2.0 g	1 tsp
Cinnamon	1.0 g	1/2 tsp
Nutmeg	1.0 g	1/2 tsp
Cloves, ground	0.3 g	1/8 tsp
Red wine (Merlot, Lambrusco)	5 ml	1 tsp
T-SPX culture	0.12 g	use scale

1. Chop the tongue into 6 mm (1/4") cubes and marinate in red wine for at least 2 hours.
2. Cut the liver into 3 mm (1/8") slices.
3. Dice back fat into 6 mm (1/4") cubes.
4. Grind other meats through 6 mm (1/4") plate.
5. 30 minutes before mixing dissolve starter culture in 1 tablespoon de-chlorinated water.
6. Mix everything well together.
7. Stuff firmly into pork bladder.
8. Ferment at 20° C (68° F) for 72 hours, 90-85% humidity.
9. Dry at 9-13° C (48-56° F) for 6 months.
10. Store at 10-12° C (50-55° F), 75% humidity.

Cooked Salama da Sugo:

1. Chop the tongue into 6 mm (1/4") cubes and marinate in red wine for at least 2 hours.
2. Cut the liver into 3 mm (1/8") slices.
3. Dice back fat into 6 mm (1/4") cubes.
4. Grind other meats through 6 mm (1/4") plate.
5. 30 minutes before mixing dissolve starter culture in 1 tablespoon de-chlorinated water.
6. Mix everything well together.
7. Stuff firmly into pork bladder.
8. Ferment at 20° C (68° F) for 72 hours, 90-85% humidity.

9. Dry at 9-13° C (48-56° F) for 4 months.
10. Scald the bladder in hot water at 35-45° C (95-113° F) to remove the mold.
11. Cook in water at 85° C (185° F) for 2 hours.

Note: Salama da Sugo carries PGI, 2014 classification.

Salam de Sibiu

Sibiu is a well-known Romanian salami with over a hundred years of tradition. The production area of the Sibiu sausages includes regions of Bacau, Brasov county, city Bucharest, Covasna County, Calarasi, Ilfov County, Prahova and Sibiu.

Lean pork	700 g	1.54 lb
Back fat	300 g	0.66 lb

Ingredients per 1 kg (2.2 lb) of meat

Salt	30 g	5 tsp
Cure #2	5.0 g	1 tsp
Dextrose	2.0 g	1/2 tsp
Sugar	2.0 g	1/2 tsp
Pepper	4.0 g	2 tsp
Garlic powder	1.0 g	1/2 tsp
Red wine	15 ml	1 Tbsp
T-SPX culture	0.12 g	weigh
Mold 600 *(Penicillium nalgiovense)*		

Grind lean meat through 3 mm (1/8") plate. Cut fat into 3 mm (1/8") cubes or grind through 3 mm (1/8") plate. 30 minutes before mixing dissolve starter culture in 2 tablespoons de-chlorinated water. Mix lean pork with salt and Cure #2. Add spices, culture and diced fat and mix all together. Stuff firmly into 60-90 mm horse or collagen or fibrous casings making 20-30 cm (8-12") straight links, clipped or tied at both ends. Dry sausages for 24 hours at 10-15° C (50-59° F) with moderate air circulation. Apply cold smoke at 10-24° C (50-75° F) for 3 to maximum 10 days with relative humidity of 85 to 92% using oak, beech or a mixture of both woods. Smoking does not have to be continuous as long as low temperature is maintained. Fermentation takes place during the smoking step. When no more smoke is applied the sausages are sprayed with *Penicillium nalgiovense* mold growing culture (Mold-600). The temperature is maintained at 10-24° C (50-75° F), 85% humidity for about 10-12 days. When the sausages are completely covered with white, grey, or white yellow mold, they are manually brushed what creates a better look and facilitates drying. Then the sausages are dried/matured at 10-15° C (50-59° F) for about 60 days. As the drying continues the humidity is lowered.

Note: store at 10-12° C (50°-55 F), 60-70% humidity.

Salam de Sibiu carries PGI 2016 certification.

Salame Brianza

Salame Brianza is produced in the Lombardy region of Italy in the provinces of Lecco, Como, and Milan. The sausage has ruby-red color, and the flavor is very mild and subtle and never sour.

Lean pork (shoulder)	700 g	1.54 lb
Back fat	300 g	0.66 lb

Ingredients per 1 kg (2.2 lb) of meat

Salt	28 g	5 tsp
Cure #2	3.0 g	1/2 tsp
White pepper	2.0 g	1 tsp
Black peppercorns	4.0 g	2 tsp
Dextrose	3.0 g	1/2 tsp
Garlic powder	3.0 g	1/2 tsp
White wine	15 ml	1 Tbsp
T-SPX culture scale	0.12 g	use

Grind lean pork through 6 mm (1/4") plate.
Dice fat into 6 mm (1/4") cubes.
30 minutes before mixing dissolve starter culture in 1 tablespoon de-chlorinated water.
Mix lean pork with salt and Cure #2. Add spices, wine and culture. Add diced fat and mix all together.
Stuff firmly into 40 mm hog casings.
Ferment at 20° C (68° F) for 72 hours, 90-85% humidity.
Dry at 9-13° C (48-56° F) for 3 weeks.
Store at 10-12° C (50-55° F), 75% humidity.

Note: Salami Brianze is produced in different size casings and that will affect drying times:

40 mm - 3 weeks
41-50 mm - 4 weeks
51-60 mm - 5 weeks
61-70 mm - 6 weeks
71-80 mm - 8 weeks
81-90 mm - 10 weeks
91 mm or bigger - 15 weeks

Salame Brianza carry PDO 1996 certification.

Salame Cremona

The area where Salame Cremona is manufactured comprises the regions of Lombardy, Emilia, Romagna, Piedmont, and Veneto.

Lean pork (shoulder)	700 g	1.54 lb
Back fat	300 g	0.66 lb

Ingredients per 1 kg (2.2 lb) of meat

Salt	28 g	5 tsp
Cure #2	2.5 g	1/2 tsp
Pepper	2.0 g	1 tsp
Black peppercorns	2.0 g	1 tsp
Dextrose	3.0 g	1/2 tsp
Sugar	3.0 g	1/2 tsp
Garlic, smashed	7.0 g	2 cloves
Red wine	5 ml	1 tsp
T-SPX culture scale	0.12 g	use

Grind lean pork through 6 mm (1/4") plate.
Dice fat into 6 mm (1/4") cubes.
30 minutes before mixing dissolve starter culture in 1 tablespoon de-chlorinated water.
Mix lean pork with salt and Cure #2. Add spices, wine and culture. Mix. Add diced fat and mix all together.
Stuff firmly into 65 mm natural casings.
Ferment at 20° C (68° F) for 72 hours, 90-85% humidity.
Dry at 15→12° C (59→53° F), 65-75% humidity for 6 weeks.
Store at 10-12° C (50°-55 F), 75% humidity.

Note: Salame Cremona carries PGI 2007 certification.

Salame di Fabriano

Salami Fabriano comes from Le Marche, an eastern region of Italy that sits between the Apennine Mountains and the Adriatic Sea. Salami production was already known in Fabriano, Montefeltro, and Ascoli areas in 1600 -1700, and the sausage was made from pork meat only, but now the mixture of pork meat, pork fat, and beef is quite common. Meats are ground finely, but the fat is diced into 10 mm (1/2") cubes to act as a showpiece when the sausage is cut. The salt is added at 4%, so to offset the harshness of salt, the sausage is consumed with locally produced non-salted bread.

Lean pork, well trimmed	750 g	1.65 lb
Back fat, diced	250 g	0.55 lb

Ingredients per 1 kg (2.2 lb) of meat

Salt	40 g	7 tsp
Pepper, whole	1.5 g	1 tsp
Pepper, ground	0.5 g	1/4 tsp
White wine	5 ml	1 tsp

Grind lean meat with 5 mm (3/16") plate. Cut partially frozen fat into 10 mm (3/8") cubes or grind through 10 mm (3/8") grinder plate. Mix meat, fat and all ingredients together. Stuff into pork bungs making 30-35 cm (12-12") links. Reinforce with butcher twine, making a lengthwise loop and few a few steps across. The sausage can also be stuffed into beef middles.
The stuffed sausage is conditioned for 1 day at 18° C (64° F), 90% humidity and some air flow. Then for about 6 days the sausage is dried from 17° C (63° F) → 14° C (56° F), 88% → 75% humidity, both parameters gradually being lowered every day. The air flow can be decreased, too.
Then the sausage enters maturing stage at 12-14° C (53 – 56° F), 65-75% humidity that continues for 2 months or longer depending on the diameter of its casing. The final product is covered in white mold.

Salame di Varzi

Salame di Varzi is Italian sausage that is produced in the mountain community of Montana Oltrepò Pavese, adjoining the municipality of Varzi. Salame di Varzi das a dark red color with visible particles of white fat. The flavor has subtle and sweet, the pleasant aroma is the result of a long maturing process.

Lean pork, shoulder, leg (ham), loin	700 g	1.54 lb
Back fat, jowls, pork belly	300 g	0.66 lb

Ingredients per 1 kg (2.2 lb) of meat

Salt	28 g	5 tsp
Cure #2	2.5 g	1/2 tsp
Sugar	3.0 g	1/2 tsp
Pepper	1.0 g	1/2 tsp
Peppercorns, whole	2.0 g	1 tsp
Nutmeg	0.5 g	1/4 tsp
Garlic, minced	7.0 g	2 cloves
Red wine	15 ml	1 Tbsp
Dextrose	3.0 g	1/2 tsp
T-SPX culture scale	0.12 g	use

Grind lean pork through 6 mm (1/4") plate. Dice fat into 6 mm (1/4") cubes.
Soak minced garlic in red wine.
30 minutes before mixing dissolve starter culture in 1 tablespoon de-chlorinated water.
Mix lean pork with salt and Cure #2. Add spices, wine and culture. Mix. Add diced fat and mix all together.
Stuff firmly into 65 mm natural casings.
Ferment at 20° C (68° F) for 72 hours, 90-85% humidity.
Dry at 15→12° C (59→53° F), 65-75% humidity for 6 weeks.
Store at 10-12° C (50°-55 F), 75% humidity.

Notes
Salame di Varzi carries PDO 1996 certification. The first records about Salame di Varzi sausage go back to the 12th century, but today the sausage is manufactured in a wide geographical area.

Salame Piacentino

Salame Piacentino is produced in the province of Piacenza. The area, which provides raw meat material, is also known for the development of livestock farming, which in turn is linked to the widespread cultivation of cereal crops and the well-functioning and highly specialized dairy sector, which has encouraged pig farming locally. Salame Piacentino is produced using lean pork meat with added pork fat at between 10% and 30%. The finished product is cylindrical in shape; its slices are bright red in color, with visible chunks of pinkish-white fat. It has a particular, very intense, rather sweet flavor with a characteristic aroma of sausage meat.

Lean pork	700 g	1.54 lb
Back fat, pork belly	300 g	0.66 lb

Ingredients per 1 kg (2.2 lb) of meat

Salt	28 g	5 tsp
Cure #2	2.5 g	1/2 tsp
Pepper	1.0 g	1/2 tsp
Peppercorns, whole	1.0 g	1/2 tsp
Dextrose	3.0 g	1/2 tsp
Sugar	2.0 g	1/3 tsp
Nutmeg	0.5 g	1/4 tsp
Garlic	7.0 g	2 cloves
White or red wine	5 ml	1 tsp
Starter culture, T-SPX scale	0.12 g	use

Grind meat through 10 mm (3/8") plate.
Cut fat into 6 mm (1/4") cubes.
Dissolve starter culture in 1 tablespoon de-chlorinated water 30 minutes before mixing step.
Mix ground meat with salt and Cure #2.
Add fat, spices, wine and culture to the mixture and re-mix.
Stuff into 40 mm hog casings.
Ferment at 20° C (68° F) for 72 hours, 90 → 85% humidity.
Dry at 15→12° C (59→54° F), 85→75% decreasing humidity for 45 days. The sausage is dried until around 30-35% in weight is lost.
Store sausages at 10-15° C (50-59° F), <75% humidity.

Note: Salame Piacentino carries PDO, 1996 certification.

Salame S. Angelo

The production area of Salame S. Angelo comprises the territory of the municipality of Sant'Angelo di Brolo, Messina, Sicily. The sausage is stuffed into a variety of pork casings and is distinguished by its irregular, cylindrical shape covered with white mold. Its slices are red in color with white particles of fat, and they have a delicate and distinctive aroma and slightly spicy and fragrant taste.

Lean pork - shoulder, loin, ham, trimmed belly	1000 g	2.2 lb

Fat content must stay below 20%.

Ingredients per 1 kg (2.2 lb) of meat

Sea salt	28 g	5 tsp
Cure #2	3.0 g	1/2 tsp
Pepper	1.0 g	1/2 tsp
Dextrose	3.0 g	1/2 tsp
Sugar	2.0 g	1/3 tsp
Starter culture, T-SPX scale	0.12 g	use

Cut meat into 10 mm (3/8") cubes.
Mix meat with all ingredients.
Stuff into large 40-60 mm hog casings.
Ferment at 20° C (68° F) for 72 hours, 90 → 85% humidity.
Dry at 15-12° C (59-54° F), 85→75% decreasing humidity for 30-45 days. The sausage is dried until around 30-35% in weight is lost.
Store sausages at 10-15° C (50-59° F), <75% humidity.

Note: a white mold is expected on the sausage. Salame S. Angelo carries PGI, 2008 classification.

Proof of Salame S. Angelo's reputation and sales may be found in the sales invoices for Salame S. Angelo dating back to 10 January 1982. The master's dissertation entitled 'Salame S. Angelo: Prodotto di Nicchia' (Salame S. Angelo: a niche product) shows that, for many years, there has existed a district in the production area set out in the product specification well-known and reputed not only for the quality and organoleptic characteristics of the product but also for the expertise of local inhabitants who have carefully passed down from generation to generation the techniques of producing Salame S. Angelo.

Salametti

Salametti sausage is listed (2.211.05) in the German government publication Guide to Meats and Meat Products - *Leitsätze für Fleisch und Fleischerzeugnisse.* Salametti is a salami type dry sausage, but shorter and packed in smaller diameter casings.

Lean beef	300 g	0.66 lb
Lean pork	400 g	0.88 lb
Back fat	300 g	0.66 lb

Ingredients per 1 kg (2.2 lb) of material

Salt	28 g	4.5 tsp
Cure #2	2.5 g	1/2 tsp
Dextrose	2.0 g	1/2 tsp
Pepper	4.0 g	2 tsp
Red sweet wine (Madeira or Marsala)	5 ml	1 tsp
T-SPX culture	0.12 g	use
scale		

Grind beef and pork with connective tissue through 3 mm (1/8") plate.
Grind lean pork through 6 mm (1/4") plate.
Grind partially frozen back fat through 3 mm (1/8") plate.
Mix meats, and all ingredients together. Add fat and mix again.
Stuff into 28 mm pork casings linking every 20 cm (8").
Ferment at 20° C (68° F), 95 → 90% humidity for 3 days.
Dry at 18° C (64° F), 90 → 80% humidity for 2 days.
Dry at 15 → 12° C (59 → 53° F), 80 → 75% humidity for 3 weeks.
Store at 10-12° C (50-53° F), <75% humidity.

Salami-All Beef

American salami.

Beef, lean	900 g	1.88 lb
Beef kidney fat or fat beef trimmings	100 g	0.22 lb

Ingredients per 1 kg (2.2 lb) of meat

Salt		28 g	1 oz
Cure #2		5.0 g	1 tsp
Dextrose	3.0 g	1/2 tsp	
Garlic powder		1.0 g	1/4 tsp
Nutmeg		1.0 g	1/2 tsp
T-SPX culture		0.12 g	use
scale			

Grind beef through 6 mm (1/4").
30 minutes before mixing dissolve starter culture in 1 tablespoon de-chlorinated water.
Mix all ingredients with ground meat.
Stuff into 60 mm beef middles or fibrous casings.
Ferment at 20° C (68° F) for 72 hours, 90-85% humidity.
Apply cold smoke at 18-22° C (64-72° F) for 12 hours.
Dry for 6-8 weeks at 15-12° C (59-54° F), 85-80% humidity.
Store sausages at 10-12° C (50-53° F), < 75% humidity.

Salami Calabrese

The Calabria is a region in Southern Italy known for spicy foods. This coarsely ground pork salami is mildly hot due to a generous addition of red pepper flakes and paprika. These ingredients create chorizo-like red color.

Pork shoulder, lean	700 g	1.54 lb
Fat, preferably hard	300 g	0.66 lb

Ingredients per 1 kg (2.2 lb) of meat

Salt	28 g	5 tsp
Cure #2	2.5 g	1/2 tsp
Dextrose	2.0 g	1/2 tsp
Sugar	2.0 g	1.2 tsp
Pepper	2.0 g	1 tsp
Red pepper flakes	4.0 g	2 tsp
Paprika	2.0 g	1 tsp
Wild fennel seeds	2.0 g	1 tsp
Sweet vermouth or red wine	60 ml	2 oz fl
Starter culture, T-SPX scale	0.12 g	use

Grind lean pork through 10 mm (3/8").
Grind fat through 10 mm (3/8") plate.
30 minutes before mixing dissolve starter culture in 1 tablespoon de-chlorinated water.
Mix lean pork with salt and Cure #2.
Grind spices in a spice mill.
Add spices, wine and culture to the mixture and re-mix. Finally, add fat and mix again.
Stuff into 40-42 mm hog casings forming 60 cm (24") links.
Ferment at 20° C (68° F) for 72 hours, 90 → 85% humidity.
Dry at 15-12° C (59-54° F), 85 → 75% decreasing humidity for 1 month. The sausage is dried until around 30-35% in weight is lost. Store sausages at 10-15° C (50-59° F), <75% humidity.

Notes
You can use less fragrant regular fennel seeds or even anise seeds.
A fine white mold will grow on the surface of salami which is desirable as it contributes to a better more mellow flavor. If the mold is objectionable you can wipe it off with a cloth moistened with vinegar.

Salami de Arles

French salami. This recipe does not include spices. The flavor of this salami depends entirely on the quality of raw materials and good manufacturing practices. Make sure that beef is well-trimmed without sinews, gristles, or fat. The same applies to regular pork trimmings. Some fat is acceptable, but no sinews or poor-quality trimmings.

Pork trimmings (butt)	400 g	0.88 lb
Beef (chuck)	300 g	0.66 lb
Lean pork (butt, ham)	300 g	0.66 lb

Ingredients per 1 kg (2.2 lb) of meat

Salt	28 g	5 tsp
Cure #2	2.5 g	1/2 tsp
Dextrose	2.0 g	1/2 tsp
Sugar	2.0 g	1/2 tsp
T-SPX culture scale	0.12 g	use

Grind pork and back fat through 10 mm (3/8") plate.
Grind beef with 10 mm (3/8") plate, refreeze and grind again with 3 mm (1/8") plate.
Mix all ingredients with meat.
Stuff firmly into 60-70 mm beef middles or protein lined fibrous casings. Make 12" long links.
Ferment at 20° C (68° F) for 72 hours, 90-85% humidity.
Dry at 16-12° C (60-54° F), 85-80% humidity for 2-3 months until the sausage loses around 30-35% in weight.
Store sausages at 10-15° C (50-59° F), 75% humidity.

Note: if mold is desired spray with Mold 600 culture after stuffing.

Salami de Verona

This Italian sausage originates in the province of Verona.

Beef	300 g	0.66 lb
Pork	350 g	0.77 lb
Pork back fat	350 g	0.77 lb

Ingredients per 1 kg (2.2 lb) of meat

Salt	28 g	5 tsp
Cure #2	2.5 g	1/2 tsp
Pepper	2.0 g	1 tsp
Dextrose	3.0 g	1/2 tsp
Sugar	2.0 g	1/3 tsp
Garlic, minced	7.0 g	2 cloves
Nutmeg	0.5 g	1/2 tsp
Cumin	0.5 g	1/2 tsp
Cognac or red wine	10 ml	2 tsp
Starter culture, T-SPX scale	0.12 g	use

Grind pork through 6 mm (1/4") plate.
Grind beef through 6 mm (1/4") plate.
Cut back fat into 6 mm (1/4") cubes.
Soak nutmeg and minced garlic in red wine.
30 minutes before mixing dissolve starter culture in 1 tablespoon de-chlorinated water.
Mix meat and fat with all ingredients.
Stuff into 40 mm hog casings.
Ferment at 20° C (68° F) for 72 hours, 90 → 85% humidity.
Dry at 15-12° C (59-54° F), 85→75% decreasing humidity for 30 days. The sausage is dried until around 30-35% in weight is lost.
Store sausages at 10-15° C (50-59° F), <75% humidity.

Note: the fat content of this salami is rather high, it can reach 40-50%.

Salami Felino

Salame di Felino is a pure pork salame from Felino, a small town located in the green Baganza valley, the food-rich region around Parma. This dry-aged sausage is recognized by its uneven shape, one end being smaller than the other. The salami is aged for three months in the same climactic conditions that create the world famous Prosciutto di Parma.

Lean pork (shoulder)	600 g	1.32 lb
Pork belly	200 g	0.44 lb
Pork back fat	200 g	0.44 lb

Ingredients per 1 kg (2.2 lb) of meat

Salt	28 g	5 tsp
Cure #2	4.0 g	3/4 tsp
Pepper	1.0 g	1/2 tsp
Peppercorns, whole	2.0 g	1 tsp
Dextrose	3.0 g	1/2 tsp
Sugar	2.0 g	1/3 tsp
Pepper	2.0 g	1 tsp
Garlic	3.5 g	1 clove
White wine	5 ml	1 tsp
Starter culture, T-SPX scale	0.12 g	use

Separately grind lean pork and fat through 6 mm (1/4") plate.
30 minutes before mixing dissolve starter culture in 1 tablespoon de-chlorinated water.
Mix ground meat with salt and Cure #2.
Add fat, spices, wine and culture to the mixture and re-mix.
Stuff into large pork casings and make 45 cm (18") sections.
Ferment at 20° C (68° F) for 72 hours, 90 → 85% humidity.
Dry for 30 days at 15-12° C (59-54° F), 85→75% decreasing humidity.
The sausage is dried until around 30-35% in weight is lost.
Store sausages at 10-15° C (50-59° F), <75% humidity.

Note: A fine white mold will grow on the surface of salami which is desirable as it contributes to a better more mellow flavor. If the mold is objectionable you can wipe it off with a cloth moistened with vinegar.
Salame Felino is packed exclusively in natural casings (i.e. never synthetic ones).
Salami Felino carries PGI 2013 certification.

Salami Finocchiona

The Italian name for fennel is "finocchio," so it comes as no surprise that Finocchiona salami is characterized by the aroma of the fennel, which is typical of the regional cuisine and which grows in the production area. There is a story about a thief stealing a fresh salami at a fair near the Italian town of Prato and hiding it in a wild fennel field. When he picked it up a few days later, he discovered that the sausage developed a wonderful aroma.

Lean pork trimmings	400 g	0.88 lb
Beef (chuck)	400 g	0.88 lb
Pork back fat or		
hard fat trimmings	200 g	0.44 lb

Ingredients per 1 kg (2.2 lb) of meat

Salt	28 g	5 tsp
Cure #2	2.5 g	1/2 tsp
Dextrose	2.0 g	1/2 tsp
Sugar	2.0 g	1/2 tsp
White pepper	2.0 g	1 tsp
Black peppercorns	4.0 g	1 tsp
Whole fennel seeds	3.0 g	2 tsp
Garlic	3.0 g	1 clove
Red wine (Chianti)	25 ml	2 Tbsp
T-SPX culture	0.12 g	use
scale		

Grind meat and fat through 5 mm (3/16"). 30 minutes before mixing dissolve starter culture in 1 tablespoon de-chlorinated water. Mix all ingredients with ground meat. Stuff firmly into beef middles or 46-60 mm protein lined fibrous casings. Ferment at 20° C (68° F) for 72 hours, 90-85% humidity. Dry at 16-12° C (60-54° F), 85-80% humidity for about 30 days until the sausage loses around 30-35% in weight. Store sausages at 10-15° C (50-59° F), 75% humidity.

Note: the following spice and herb combination can be found in some recipes:

spices: 4 parts coriander, 3 parts mace, 2 parts allspice, 1 part fennel.

herbs: 3 parts marjoram, 1 part thyme, 1 part basil.

Finocchiona carries PGI 2015 certification.

Salami Genoa

Italian salami. Salami Genoa and Salami Milano but incorporate different proportions of raw materials. Some typical combinations: 50/30/20, 40/40/20 (this recipe) or 40/30/30. Salami Genoa is also known as Salami di Alessandra. Salami Milano is chopped somewhat finer than Salami Genoa.

Lean pork trimmings		
(ham, butt)	400 g	0.88 lb
Beef (chuck)	400 g	0.88 lb
Pork back fat or		
hard fat trimmings	200 g	0.44 lb

Ingredients per 1 kg (2.2 lb) of meat

Salt	28 g	5 tsp
Cure #2	2.5 g	1/2 tsp
Dextrose	2.0 g	1/2 tsp
Sugar	3.0 g	3/4 tsp
White pepper	3.0 g	1.5 tsp
Garlic powder	1.0 g	1/2 tsp
OR fresh garlic	3.5 g	1 clove
T-SPX culture	0.12 g	use
scale		

Grind pork and back fat through 3/8" plate (10 mm). Grind beef with 1/8" (3 mm) plate. 30 minutes before mixing dissolve starter culture in 1 tablespoon de-chlorinated water. Mix all ingredients with ground meat. Stuff firmly into beef middles or 46-60 mm protein lined fibrous casings. Make links 16-20" long. Ferment at 20° C (68° F) for 72 hours, 90-85% humidity. Dry at 16-12° C (60-54° F), 85-80% humidity for 2-3 months until the sausage loses around 30-35% in weight. Store sausages at 10-15° C (50-59° F), 75% humidity.

Note: if mold is desired spray with Bactoferm® Mold 600 culture after stuffing.

The following spice and herb combination can be found in some recipes:

spices: 4 parts coriander, 3 parts mace, 2 parts allspice, 1 part fennel.

herbs: 3 parts marjoram, 1 part thyme, 1 part basil.

Some recipes ask for the addition of red wine and you may add around 30 ml (3 oz fl).

Salami - German

Salami sausage is listed (2.211.05) in the German governmen publication Guide to Meats and Meat Products - *Leitsätze für Fleisch und Fleischerzeugnisse.*

Beef	300 g	0.66 lb
Lean pork (shoulder)	200 g	0.44 lb
Lean pork, little fat, some connective tissue (shoulder)	200 g	0.44 lb
Back fat	300 g	0.66 lb

Ingredients per 1 kg (2.2 lb) of material

Salt	28 g	4.5 tsp
Cure #2	2.5 g	1/2 tsp
Dextrose	2.0 g	1/2 tsp
Sugar	2.0 g	1/2 tsp
Pepper	4.0 g	2 tsp
Coriander	0.5 g	1/4 tsp
Garlic, smashed	3.0 g	1 clove
T-SPX culture	0.12 g	use scale

Grind beef and pork with connective tissue through 3 mm (1/8") plate.
Grind lean pork through 5 mm (1/4") plate.
Grind partially frozen back fat through 3 mm (1/8") plate.
Mix meats, and all ingredients together. Add fat and mix again.
Stuff into 70 mm synthetic protein lined fibrous casings.
Ferment for 3 days at 20° C (68° F), 95 → 90% humidity.
Dry for 2 days at 18° C (64° F), 90 → 80% humidity.
Smoke at 18° C (64° F) for 24 hours.
Dry at 15 → 12° C (59 → 53° F), 85 → 75% humidity for 6 weeks or until sausage looses 30% of its original weight.

Salami-Hungarian

Hungarian salami is a unique smoked sausage with a white mold. In the traditional process, starter cultures and sugars are not allowed, and the sausage should not exhibit any acidity. The recipe below contains very little dextrose (sugar) just to provide a margin of safety during the first stage of fermentation.

Lean pork	800 g	1.76 lb
Back fat or		
hard fat trimmings	200 g	0.44 lb

Ingredients per 1 kg (2.2 lb) of meat

Salt	28 g	5 tsp
Cure #2	2.5 g	1/2 tsp
Dextrose	2.0 g	1/2 tsp
White pepper	3.0 g	1.5 tsp
Paprika	6.0 g	3 tsp
Garlic powder	2.0 g	1 tsp
OR fresh garlic	7.0 g	2 cloves
Tokay wine (Hungarian sweet wine)	15 ml	1 Tbsp
T-SPX culture	0.12 g	use scale

Grind pork and back fat through 3/16" plate (5 mm).
30 minutes before mixing dissolve starter culture in 1 tablespoon de-chlorinated water.
Mix all ingredients with ground meat.
Stuff firmly into beef middles or 3" protein lined fibrous casings.
Ferment at 20° C (68° F) for 72 hours, 90-85% humidity.
Cold smoke for 4 days (<22° C, 72° F). You can apply smoke during the 2nd stage of fermentation.
Dry at 16-12° C (60-54° F), 85-80% humidity for 2-3 months.
Store sausages at 10-12° C (50-53° F), <75% humidity.

Salami -Hungarian-Traditional
(Salami węgierskie)

Although this salami carries a Hungarian name, it has alwaysbeen made in Poland and might as well be considered a local product. The following is the official Polish Government recipe for making traditional salami, which comes from 1956 archives.

Pork	800 g	1.76 lb
Pork back fat	200 g	0.44 lb

Ingredients per 1 kg (2.2 lb) of meat

Salt	28 g	5 tsp
Cure #2	5.0 g	1 tsp
Pepper	4.0 g	2 tsp
Paprika	2.0 g	1 tsp
Sugar	2.0 g	1/2 tsp
Garlic	3.5 g	1 clove

Curing: cut meat into 3-4" (10 cm) pieces and place in a slightly raised container with holes in the bottom to allow for draining of liquid. Leave for 24 hours at 1-2° C (33-35° F), then grind with 3/4" plate and leave for an additional 2-3 days. During that period turn meat around 1-2 times. Leave sheets of unsalted back fat for 2-3 days at -2° C (28° F) to -4° C (24° F) and then dice into 1/8" (3 mm) cubes.
Mix meat, back fat, salt, nitrite and spices together. Grind through 1/8" (3 mm) plate.
Leave the sausage mass for 36-48 hours at 2-4° C (35-40° F).
Stuff firmly into 55-60 mm beef middles. Make links 16-18" long. Lace up with twine: once lengthwise and every 4-5 cm (1.5-2") across. The ends tied with twine, 10-12 cm (4-5") hanging loop on one end.
Hang for 2-4 days at 2-4° C (35-40° F), 85-90% humidity.
Apply a thin cold smoke 16-18° C (60-64° F) for 5-7 days until a dark red color is obtained.
Dry in a dark, lightly drafty area at 10-12° C (50-53° F), humidity 90%, for 2 weeks until salami develops white dry mold on outside. If green mold appears wipe it off and move the sausage for 4-5 hours to a drier place. Then it can go back to the original room for drying. Place sausage covered with white mold in a dark and lightly drafty area for 2-3 months at 12-15° C (54-59° F), 75-85% humidity, until 63% yield is obtained.

Salami-Kosher

American sausage.

Beef chuck	750 g	1.65 lb
Brisket fat	250 g	0.55 lb

Ingredients per 1 kg (2.2 lb) of meat

Salt	28 g	5 tsp
Cure #2	2.5 g	1/2 tsp
White pepper	4.0 g	2 tsp
Dextrose	2.0 g	1/2 tsp
Paprika	2.0 g	1 tsp
Manischewitz sweet wine	15 ml	1 Tbsp
T-SPX culture	0.12 g	use
scale		

Grind meats through 3/16" plate (5 mm).
30 minutes before mixing dissolve starter culture in 1 tablespoon de-chlorinated water. Mix all ingredients with ground meat.
Stuff firmly into beef middles or 3" protein lined fibrous casings.
Ferment at 20° C (68° F) for 72 hours, 90-85% humidity.
Cold smoke for 4 days at 22° C, (72° F) or lower.
Dry at 16-12° C (60-54° F), 85-80% humidity for 2-3 months.
Store sausages at 10-15° C (50-59° F), <75% humidity.

Salami Lombardia

Italian salami.

Lean pork (butt, ham)	450 g	0.99 lb
Beef (chuck)	200 g	0.44 lb
Pork trimmings	350 g	0.77 lb

Ingredients per 1 kg (2.2 lb) of meat

Salt	28 g	5 tsp
Cure #2	2.5 g	1/2 tsp
Dextrose	3.0 g	1/2 tsp
Whole white pepper	4.0 g	1 tsp
Garlic	3.0 g	1 clove
T-SPX culture	0.12 g	use
scale		

Grind pork and back fat through 3/16" plate (5 mm). Grind beef with 1/8" (3 mm) plate.
30 minutes before mixing dissolve starter culture in 1 tablespoon de-chlorinated water.
Mix all ingredients with ground meat.
Stuff firmly into large hog casings or 40-60 mm protein lined fibrous casings. Make 12-16" long links.
Ferment at 20° C (68° F) for 72 hours, 90-85% humidity.
Dry at 16-12° C (60-54° F), 85-80% humidity for 1-2 months until the sausage loses around 30-35% in weight.
Store sausages at 10-15° C (50-59° F), <75% humidity.

Note: Although smoking is not mentioned in the instructions, this salami is sometimes given a very light cool smoke after fermentation.

Salami - Mailänder

(Salami Milano-German Style)

This is a German version of Salami Milano, one of the best-known Italian dry sausages. The meat and fat pieces stand out, the latter being the size of rice grains. The duration of maturation depends on the weight of the sausages. Traditionally, it takes place in well-ventilated, dry rooms for three to six months.

Lean pork	400 g	0.88 lb
Lean beef	300 g	0.66 lb
Pork back fat	300 g	0.66 lb

Ingredients per 1 kg (2.2 lb) of material

Salt	28 g	5 tsp
Cure #2	2.5 g	1/2 tsp
Pepper	4.0 g	2 tsp
Dextrose	2.0 g	1/2 tsp
Sugar	3.0 g	1/2 tsp
Coriander	0.5 g	1/4 tsp
Allspice	0.5 g	1/4 tsp
Red wine	5.0 g	1 tsp
T-SPX culture	0.12 g	use
scale		

Grind pork through 5 mm (3/16") plate.
Grind partially frozen back fat through 5 mm (3/16") plate.
Grind beef with 3 mm (1/8") plate.
Mix all ingredients with ground meat adding fat last.
Stuff firmly into 60 mm protein lined fibrous casings. Make 25" long links.
Ferment at 20° C (68° F) for 72 hours, 90→85% humidity.
Dry at 14→12° C (57-54° F), 85→75% humidity for 5 weeks. The sausage is dried until around 30-35% in weight is lost.
Store sausages at 10-12° C (50-53° F), <75% humidity.

Note

If mold is desired spray with Bactoferm® Mold-600 culture after stuffing.

Salami Milano

Salami Milano and Salami Genoa are very similar; however, they incorporate different proportions of raw materials. Some typical combinations are 50/30/20 (this recipe), 40/40/20, or 40/30/30. Salami Genoa is also known as Salami di Alessandra. Salami Milano is chopped somewhat finer than Salami Genoa.

Lean pork trimmings (ham, butt)	500 g	1.10 lb
Beef (chuck)	300 g	0.66 lb
Pork back fat or hard fat trimmings	200 g	0.44 lb

Ingredients per 1 kg (2.2 lb) of meat

Salt	28 g	5 tsp
Cure #2	2.5 g	1/2 tsp
Dextrose	2.0 g	1/2 tsp
Sugar	3.0 g	1/3 tsp
White pepper	3.0 g	1.5 tsp
Garlic powder	1.0 g	1/2 tsp
OR fresh garlic	3.5 g	1 clove
T-SPX culture	0.12 g	use
scale		

Grind pork and back fat through 3/16" plate (5 mm). Grind beef with 1/8" (3 mm) plate.
30 minutes before mixing dissolve starter culture in 1 tablespoon de-chlorinated water.
Mix all ingredients with ground meat.
Stuff firmly into 80 mm protein lined fibrous casings. Make 25" long links.
Ferment at 20° C (68° F) for 72 hours, 90-85% humidity.
Dry at 16-12° C (60-54° F), 85-80% humidity for 2-3 months until the sausage loses around 30-35% in weight.
Store sausages at 10-15° C (50-59° F), 75% humidity.

Note: if mold is desired spray with Mold 600 culture after stuffing.

The following spice and herb combination can be found in some recipes:

spices: 4 parts coriander, 3 parts mace, 2 parts allspice, 1 part fennel.
herbs: 3 parts marjoram, 1 part thyme, 1 part basil.

Some recipes ask for the addition of red wine and you may add around 30 ml (1 oz fl).

Salamini Italiani alla Cacciatora

A very popular small sausage also known as Hunter's sausage. Hunter's sausage can also be found in other countries, for example German Jadgwurst or Polish Myśliwska sausage. The sausage owes its name to the tradition that once it was the meal of hunters who used to carry it their bags during hunting.

Lean pork, shoulder, leg (ham), loin	700 g	1.54 lb
Back fat, jowls, pork belly	300 g	0.66 lb

Ingredients per 1 kg (2.2 lb) of meat

Salt	28 g	5 tsp
Cure #2	2.5 g	1/2 tsp
Pepper	1.0 g	1/2 tsp
Garlic, minced	7.0 g	2 cloves
Dextrose	3.0 g	1/2 tsp
Sugar	3.0 g	1/2 tsp
Red wine	15 ml	1 Tbsp
T-SPX culture	0.12 g	use
scale		

Grind lean pork through 1/4" (6 mm) plate.
Dice fat into 1/4" (6 mm) cubes.
Soak minced garlic in red wine.
30 minutes before mixing dissolve starter culture in 1 tablespoon de-chlorinated water.
Mix lean pork with salt and cure #2. Add spices, wine and culture. Mix. Add diced fat and mix all together.
Stuff firmly into 65 mm natural casings making 6" (15 cm) links.
Ferment at 20° C (68° F) for 72 hours, 90-85% humidity.
Dry at 18-25° C (64-77° F), 65-75% humidity for 1 week.
Dry at 15→12° C (59→53° F), 65-75% humidity for 3-4 weeks.
Store at 10-12° C (50°-55 F), 75% humidity.

Note: Salamini italiani alla cacciatora carries PDO, 2001 classification.

Salami Nola

This salami is lightly smoked, which is why it differs from other Italian salamis. It is also more coarsely ground and formed into shorter links.

Lean pork (butt, ham)	500 g	1.1 lb
Pork trimmings (butt)	500 g	1.1 lb

Ingredients per 1 kg (2.2 lb) of meat

Salt	28 g	5 tsp
Cure #2	2.5 g	1/2 tsp
Dextrose	2.0 g	1/2 tsp
Sugar	2.0 g	1/2 tsp
Cracked black pepper	4.0 g	1 tsp
Ground red pepper	2.0 g	1 tsp
Allspice	2.0 g	1 tsp
T-SPX culture	0.12 g	use
scale		

Grind pork through 3/8" plate (10 mm).
30 minutes before mixing dissolve starter culture in 1 tablespoon de-chlorinated water.
Mix all ingredients with ground pork.
Stuff firmly into 60 mm beef middles or protein lined fibrous casings. Make 8" (20 cm) long links.
Ferment at 20° C (68° F) for 72 hours, 90-85% humidity.
Apply thin cold smoke at 20° C (68° F) for a few hours.
Dry at 16-12° C (60-54° F), 85-80% humidity for 1 month. The sausage is dried until around 30-35% in weight is lost.
Store sausages at 10-15° C (50-59° F), 75% humidity.

Salami Piemonte

"Salame Piemonte" is produced in the Piedmont region of Italy.

Lean pork - shoulder, rear leg (ham)	700 g	1.54 lb
Jowls, pork belly	300 g	0.66 lb

Ingredients per 1 kg (2.2 lb) of meat

Salt	28 g	5 tsp
Cure #2	3.0 g	1/2 tsp
Pepper, ground	1.0 g	1/2 tsp
Pepper, crushed	1.0 g	1 tsp
Dextrose	3.0 g	1/2 tsp
Sugar	2.0 g	1/3 tsp
Garlic, minced	7.0 g	2 cloves
Nutmeg	1.0 g	1/2 tsp
Red wine	10 ml	2 tsp
Starter culture, T-SPX	0.12 g	use
scale		

Grind lean pork through 3/8" (10 mm) cubes.
Cut fat into 1/4" (6 mm) cubes.
Soak nutmeg and minced garlic in red wine.
30 minutes before mixing dissolve starter culture in 1 tablespoon de-chlorinated water.
Mix meat and fat with all ingredients.
Stuff into large 40 mm hog casings.
Ferment at 20° C (68° F) for 72 hours, 90 → 85% humidity.
Dry at 15-12° C (59-54° F), 85→75% decreasing humidity for 30 days. The sausage is dried until around 30-35% in weight is lost.
Store sausages at 10-15° C (50-59° F), <75% humidity.

Note: Salami Piemonte is stuffed in natural casings from 40 to 90 mm in diameter. The drying time will vary accordingly from 30 to 80 days.

Salami Piemonte carries PGI, 2015 classification.

Salami-Polish
(With Culture)

Most countries make their version of salamis, and Poland does, too. The following is the famous traditional recipe made with starter culture.

Lean pork	400 g	0.88 lb
Lean beef	300 g	0.66 lb
Back fat	300 g	0.66 lb

Ingredients per 1 kg (2.2 lb) of meat

Salt	28 g	5 tsp
Cure #2	2.5 g	1/2 tsp
Dextrose	3.0 g	1/2 tsp
Pepper	3.0 g	1 tsp
Cardamom	0.5 g	1/4 tsp
T-SPX culture scale	0.12 g	use

Grind pork and back fat through 3/16" plate (5 mm). Grind beef with 1/8" (3 mm) plate.
30 minutes before mixing dissolve starter culture in 1 tablespoon de-chlorinated water.
Mix all ingredients with ground meat.
Stuff firmly into beef middles or 3" protein lined fibrous casings.
Ferment at 20° C (68° F) for 72 hours, 90-85% humidity.
Cold smoke for 12 hours at 18° C (64° F).
Dry at 16-12° C (60-54° F), 85-80% humidity. In about 6-8 weeks a shrink of 30% should be achieved.
Store sausages at 10-15° C (50-59° F), <75% humidity.

Salami-Polish-Traditional
(Traditional)

The following is the official Polish Government recipe from the 1956 archives. It makes a great reading. This sausage was made and sold in Poland to the consumers.

Lean pork cuts	800 g	1.76 lb
Pork back fat or hard fat trimmings	200 g	0.44 lb

Ingredients per 1 kg (2.2 lb) of meat

Salt	28 g	5 tsp
Cure #2	2.5 g	1/2 tsp
Sugar	1.5 g	1/2 tsp
Pepper	2.0 g	1 tsp
Paprika	1.5 g	3/4 tsp
Garlic powder	1.0 g	1/2 tsp
OR fresh garlic	3.5 g	1 clove

Cut meat into 10 cm (3-4") pieces and place in a slightly raised container with holes in the bottom to allow for draining of curing liquid. Leave for 24 hours at 1-2° C (33-35°F), then grind with 3/4" (20 mm) plate and leave for an additional 2-3 days following the above procedure. During that period turn meat around 1-2 times. Leave sheets of unsalted back fat for 2-3 days at -2° C (28° F) to -4° C (24° F) and then cut into 1/8" (3 mm) pieces.
Mix meat, back fat, salt, nitrate and spices together. Grind through 1/8" (3 mm) plate.
Leave the sausage mass for 36-48 hours at 2-4° C (35-40° F).
Stuff casings firmly. Do not add water. Prick any visible air pockets with a needle.
Hang for 2-4 days at 2-4° C (35-40° F), 85-90% humidity.
Apply thin cold smoke at 16-18° C (60-64° F) for 5-7 days, until a dark red color is obtained.
Hang in a dark, lightly drafty area at 10-12° C (50-53° F), humidity 90% for 2 weeks until salami develops white dry mold on outside. If green and moist mold appears on the surface it must be washed with warm salty water and wiped off dry with a cloth. Hang for 4-5 hours in a drier place then move back to the original room and continue drying.
Place salamis covered with white mold for 2-3 months in a dark and lightly drafty area at 12-16° C (54-60° F), 75-85% humidity, until desired yield (~ 63%) is obtained.

Salami-Russian
(Салями особенная)

A popular Russian dry sausage.

Lean beef	400 g	0.88 lb
Lean pork	100 g	0.22 lb
Pork belly	500 g	1.10 lb

Ingredients per 1 kg (2.2 lb) of meat

Salt	28 g	5 tsp
Cure #1	3.5 g	3/4 tsp
Sugar	2.0 g	1/2 tsp
Black pepper	1.0 g	1/2 tsp
Allspice	0.5 g	1/4 tsp
Cardamom or nutmeg	0.3 g	1/4 tsp
Madera wine or cognac	5 ml	1 tsp

Curing: cut meat into 1 inch (25 mm) pieces. Place beef, pork and pork belly in separate food grade containers and mix with salt, Cure #1 and sugar according to the recipe (estimate amounts). Pack tightly to eliminate air and cover with clean cloth. Place for 72 hours in refrigerator. Discard any liquid brine and submit meat to grinding.

Grind beef through 1/8" (2 mm) plate. Grind pork through 1/8" (2 mm) plate. Slice pork belly into strips,1/2" x 1/4" x 1/4" (12 mm x 5 mm x 5 mm).

Mix beef with spices. Add pork and mix. Add bacon strips and remix everything together. Don't add any water.

Stuff sausages firmly into 45-55 mm beef middles or fibrous casings. Make links up to 20" (50 cm) long.

Hang sausages for 5-7 days at 2-4° C, 85-90% humidity.

Apply cold smoke at 18-22° C (64-72° F) for 2-3 days.

Dry sausages for 5-7 days (depending on sausage diameter) at 11-15° C (53-59° F), 80-84% humidity. Dry 21 days more at 10-12° C (50-54° F), 74-78% humidity.

Store sausages at 10-15° C (50-59° F), <75% humidity.

Finished sausage should retain 65% of its original weight.

Salami Sorrento

Italian Salami.

Lean pork (butt, ham)	600 g	1.32 lb
Beef (chuck)	200 g	0.44 lb
Pork trimmings	200 g	0.44 lb

Ingredients per 1 kg (2.2 lb) of meat

Salt	28 g	5 tsp
Cure #2	2.5 g	1/2 tsp
Dextrose	3.0 g	1/2 tsp
White pepper, ground	3.0 g	1.5 tsp
White pepper, whole	4.0 g	1.5 tsp
Garlic	3.0 g	1 clove
T-SPX culture scale	0.12 g	use

Grind pork and back fat through 3/16" plate (5 mm). Grind beef with 1/8" (3 mm) plate.

30 minutes before mixing dissolve starter culture in 1 tablespoon de-chlorinated water.

Mix all ingredients with ground meat.

Stuff firmly into 40-60 mm protein lined fibrous casings. Make 12" long links.

Ferment at 20° C (68° F) for 72 hours, 90-85% humidity.

Dry at 16-12° C (60-54° F), 85-80% humidity for 1 month. The sausage is dried until around 30-35% in weight is lost.

Store sausages at 10-15° C (50-59° F), 75% humidity.

Salami Spanish *(Salami Español)*

It traditionally made dry salami using modern starter culture technology. The salami will develop an intense color and a typical cheesy flavor in usually produced products.

Lean pork	700 g	1.54 lb
Back fat	300 g	0.66 lb

Ingredients per 1 kg (2.2 lb) of meat

Salt	28 g	4.5 tsp
Cure #2	2.5 g	1/2 tsp
Dextrose	2.0 g	1/2 tsp
Sugar	3.0 g	1/2 tsp
Pepper	2.0 g	1 tsp
Oregano, ground	2.0 g	1 tsp
Garlic powder	1.0 g	1/2 tsp
T-SPX, starter culture	0.12 g	use
scale		

Trim meat from all gristle, sinews, tendons, and silver film.
Grind meat through 6 mm (1/4") plate.
Dice partially frozen fat into 6 mm (1/4") cubes.
Dilute starter culture in 15 ml (1 tablespoon) of distilled or spring water. Mix lean meat with salt, Cure #1, spices and starter culture. Add fat and mix again.
Stuff firmly into 50-60 mm hog middles forming sections 40 cm (16") long.
Ferment at 20° C (68° F) for 72 hours, 90-85% humidity.
Dry at 16 → 12° C (60-54° F), 85 → 80% humidity for 45 days (or longer depending on a diameter of the casing). The sausage is dried until around 30% in weight is lost.
Store sausages at 10-12° C (50-53° F), <75% humidity.

Notes
Sausage can be made without the culture, *the traditional way:*

Mix lean meat with salt, Cure #1, spices and fat. Hold for 48 hours in refrigerator.
Stuff firmly into 50-60 mm hog middles forming sections 40 cm (16") long.
Ferment/dry at 20-25° C (68-77° F) for 48 hours, 90-85% humidity.
Dry at 16 → 12° C (60-54° F), 85 → 80% humidity for 45 days (or longer depending on a diameter of the casing). The sausage is dried until around 30% in weight is lost.
Store sausages at 10-12° C (50-53° F), <75% humidity or refrigerate.

Salchicha de Zaratán

Salchicha de Zaratán is a small semi-cured sausage made of lean pork and pork belly and a hefty dose of pimentón, responsible for the sausage's brilliantly red color. As its name implies, the Salchicha de Zaratán originates in the city of Zaratán in the Valladolid province of the Castilla-León region of Spain.

Lean pork	700 g	1.32 lb
Pork belly	300 g	0.66 lb

Ingredients per 1 kg (2.2 lb) of meat

Salt	21 g	3.5 tsp
Cure #1	2.5 g	1/2 tsp
Pimentón, sweet	20 g	3 Tbsp
Pimentón, hot	5 g	1 Tbsp
Oregano, dry	1.0 g	1 tsp
Garlic, smashed	3.5 g	1 clove

Grind meats through 10 mm (3/8") plate.
Mix meats with salt and spices and hold for 30 hours in refrigerator.
Stuff into 18-20 mm sheep casings forming 15-20 cm (6-8") links.
Dry at 15-12° C (59-53° F) for 40 hours. Refrigerate.

Notes
Cook before serving by: frying in fat, boiling in white or rose wine or grilling. The sausage is often cooked in apple cider. It is also added to stews, paella dishes or fried with eggs and peppers.

Salchichón

Spanish "salchichón" can be dried, dried/ smoked, and even cooked. Typical meat is pork, but recipes with other meats, such as ox, veal, or horse meat, can be found in Spanish books. Quite often, pork liver is added. A traditional method of making these sausages at home was adding salt, nitrate, and spices to the meat and then hanging the sausage for 4-5 days in the kitchen or in the open air. Then the sausage was transferred to a dry and drafty area where it remained for 2-3 months. After that time, it was ready for consumption. Most traditional Spanish recipes don't include sugar, which produces a product with little acidity. Due to low temperatures, fermentation is slow, and the pH drop is low. The sausage was not fermented but just air-dried like American beef jerky. We do not advocate this kind of manufacture at home and recommend using a starter culture to make the process safer and more predictable.

| Lean pork | 700 g | 1.54 lb |
| Pork back fat | 300 g | 0.66 lb |

Ingredients per 1 kg (2.2 lb) of meat

Salt	28 g	5 tsp
Cure #2	2.5 g	1/2 tsp
Dextrose	2 g	1/2 tsp
Non-fat dry milk	16 g	3 tsp
Black pepper	3 g	1.5 tsp
Cinnamon	0.5 g	1/2 tsp
Cloves, ground	0.3 g	1/4 tsp
Nutmeg	0.5 g	1/2 tsp
Garlic	7.5 g	2 cloves
T-SPX culture	0.12 g	use
scale		

Grind meat and fat through 3/8" plate (10 mm). 30 minutes before mixing dissolve starter culture in 1 tablespoon de-chlorinated water. Mix all ingredients with ground meat. Stuff firmly into beef middles or 46-60 mm protein lined fibrous casings. Ferment at 20° C (68° F) for 72 hours, 90-85% humidity. Cold smoke (optional) at 20° C (68° F) for 8 hours. Dry at 16-12° C (60-54° F), 85-80% humidity for 1-2 months. The sausage is dried until around 30-35% in weight is lost. Store sausages at 10-15° C (50-59° F), <75% humidity.

Salchichón de Vic/Llonganissa de Vic

Salchichón de Vic, also known as Llonganissa de Vic, is made in the province of Barcelona. The first references written about the sausage date back to 1456. In the past, this product was produced in farms located in the Plana de Vic as a method of preserving meats, taking advantage of the area's suitable climate conditions.

Lean pork (shoulder, leg)	850 g	1.87 lb
Pork belly	150 g	0.22 lb
Back fat	50 g	0.11 lb

Ingredients per 1 kg (2.2 lb) of meat

Salt	25 g	4 tsp
Cure #2	2.5 g	1/2 tsp
Dextrose	3.0 g	1/2 tsp
White pepper	3.0 g	1.5 tsp
Black pepper, whole	1.0 g	1 tsp

Dice back fat into 6 mm (1/4") cubes. Grind meats through 8 mm (3/8") plate. Mix ground meats with all ingredients. Hold for 24-48 hours at 4-6° C (40-43° F) or in refrigerator. Stuff firmly into pork bungs, 50-60 cm (20-24") long. Ferment/dry at 20° C (68° F) for 48 hours, 90-95% humidity. Dry at 15 → 12° C (59-54° F), 80 → 75% humidity for 45 days (or longer depending on a diameter of the casing). The sausage is dried until around 30% in weight is lost. The sausage should develop a white mold which is expected and desired. Store sausages at 10-12° C (50-53° F), <70% humidity.

Notes

Salchichón de Vic carries PGI, 2001 classification.

In traditional production the fermentation step was often skipped and the stuffed sausage was only dried for 5-11 months at room temperatures, depending on the diameter of the casing.

Salchichón Gallego

Salchichón is a Spanish dry sausage made usually from pork. Salchichón de Lugo is Galician version that is made from pork and beef. Because Lugo is a province in Galicia, the sausage might as well be called Salchichón Gallego. Salchichón de Lugo is made with white and black pepper; the sausage is dried but not smoked.

Pork, lean (shoulder)	650 g	1.43 lb
Beef	100 g	0.22 lb
Back fat or		
hard fat trimmings	250 g	0.55 lb

Ingredients per 1 kg (2.2 lb) of meat

Salt	25 g	4 tsp
Cure #2	2.5 g	½ tsp
Sugar	3.0 g	1/2 tsp
White pepper, ground	1.0 g	1/2 tsp
Black pepper, ground	1.0 g	1/2 tsp
Black pepper, crushed	2.0 g	1 tsp

Grind meats and fat through 3-5 mm (1/8-1/4") plate.
Mix with salt, cure #2 and pepper and hold in refrigerator for 24 hours.
Stuff into large diameter (55-60 mm) pork casings.
Dry at 15 -12° C, (59-53° F), 75-85% humidity for 2 months.
Store at 12° C (53° F), <70% humidity.

Notes
Oregano, garlic and nutmeg are often added.

Salmon Sausage
(Kiełbasa łososiowa)

There is no salmon in this recipe. In Poland certain high quality products carried the name "salmon" to imply that the product was of high quality. *This cold smoked sausage recipe comes from the official Polish Government archives.*

Lean pork	800 g	1.76 lb
Beef	200 g	0.44 lb

Ingredients for 1 kg (2.2 lb) of meat

Salt	25 g	4 tsp
Cure #1	2.5 g	1/2 tsp
Sugar	1.0 g	1/4 tsp
Pepper	2.0 g	1 tsp
Sweet paprika	1.0 g	1/2 tsp
Nutmeg	1.0 g	1/2 tsp
Garlic	1.5 g	1/2
clove		

Curing: cut meat into 2.5-5 cm (1-2") pieces and mix with salt and Cure # 1. Pack tightly in a container, cover with cloth and keep in refrigerator for 3 days.
Cut pork into 20 mm (3/4") pieces, grind beef through 3 mm (1/8") plate.
Mix ground meats with spices.
Stuff into 36 mm hog casings.
Hang at 2-4° C (35-40° F) 85-90% humidity for 4-6 days, then at 10-12° C (50-53° F), 75-80% humidity for 3-4 days.
Cold smoke at 18-22° C (64-72° F) for 3-4 days until dark red color is obtained.
Cool in air and dry at 10-12° C (50-53° F) for about 6-8 days.
Store sausages at 10-15° C (50-59° F), <75% humidity.

Salpicão de Vinhais

Salpicão de Vinhais is produced in the region of Vinhais, Portugal.

Pork loin, tenderloin	1000 g	2.2 lb

Ingredients per 1 kg (2.2 lb) of meat

Salt	30 g	5 tsp
Cure #2	3.0 g	1/2 tsp
Pimentón, sweet	2.0 g	1 tsp
Pimentón, hot	2.0 g	1 tsp
Bay leaf, crushed	1	1
Garlic, dehydrated	2.0 g	1 tsp
Wine, red or white	15 ml	1 Tbsp
Water	15 ml	1 Tbsp

Cut the meat into 2" (5 cm cubes.

Mix salt, cure #2, crushed bay leaf, spices, wine and water. Add meat and mix all together. Hold in refrigerator for 4 days.

Stuff into 50-80 mm hog middles or bungs.

Apply a thin smoke at 18° C (64° F) for 10 days. Smoking need not be continuous, as long as the temperature inside of the smokehouse stays below 18° C. Think of the process as drying with smoke. Oak, chestnut or both are used for smoking.

Dry at 15 →12° C (59 →-53° F), 80→70% humidity for 30 days. Total smoking and drying time at least 40 days.

Store at 10-12° C (50-53° F).

Note: Salpicão de Vinhais is produced from Bisaro breed of pig.

Salpicão de Vinhais carries PGI, 1998 classification.

Salsiccia di Calabria

A typical Calabrian matured sausage is distinguished by its typical U or chain shape. This shape and the composition of its mixture determine the product. The traditional production area for 'Salsiccia di Calabria' is the Calabria Region in Italy.

Pork shoulder	500 g	1.10 lb
Pork loin, fat included	400 g	0.88 lb
Back fat	100 g	0.22 lb

Ingredients per 1 kg (2.2 lb) of meat

Salt	28 g	5 tsp
Cure #2	3.0 g	1/2 tsp
Dextrose	3.0 g	1/2 tsp
Sugar	2.0 g	1/3 tsp
Pepper	1.0 g	1/2 tsp
Red pepper	2.0 g	1 tsp
Paprika, sweet	2.0 g	1 tsp
Fennel seeds, whole	1.0 g	1 tsp
Red wine	10 ml	2 tsp
Starter culture, T-SPX	0.12 g	use scale

Grind lean pork through 3/8" (10 mm) plate.

Cut fat into 1/4" (6 mm) cubes.

30 minutes before mixing dissolve starter culture in 1 tablespoon de-chlorinated water.

Mix meat and fat with all ingredients.

Stuff into large 36-40 mm hog casings. Twist into links 16" (40 cm) long or make individual horse-shoe shape loops.

Ferment at 20° C (68° F) for 72 hours, 90 → 85% humidity.

Dry at 15-12° C (59-54° F), 85→75% decreasing humidity for 30 days. The sausage is dried until around 30-35% in weight is lost.

Store sausages at 10-15° C (50-59° F), <75% humidity.

Note: Salsiccia di Calabria carries PDO, 1998 classification.

Salsiccia Sarda

Salsiccia Sarda has been produced in Sardinia for centuries. In Sardinia the sausage is also known as Saltrizza or Saltizza. As Sardinia is the island off the coast of Italy, for practical reasons and pure necessity the locally raised pigs were the source of the meat. In the past Salsiccia Sarda was produced to satisfy the needs of local population or used as an instrument of barter trade, however, in time the sausage has gained popularity and now can be available all over Europe.

Lean pork	850 g	1.76 lb
Pork back fat, jowls	150 g	0.33 lb

Ingredients per 1 kg (2.2 lb) of meat

Salt	28 g	4.5 tsp
Cure #1	2.5 g	1/2 tsp
Pepper	1.0 g	1/2 tsp
Nutmeg	0.5 g	1/4 tsp
Cinnamon	0.5 g	1/4 tsp
Garlic	1.0 g	1/3 clove
Vinegar	5 ml	1 tsp

Separately grind lean pork and fat through 6 mm (1/4") plate. Mix lean pork with all ingredients. Add fat and mix again. Stuff meat paste firmly into 38-40 mm hog casings forming individual U-shaped loops. Tie the ends together. Hold in a cold room for 3 hours to dry out the casings.
Apply a thin cold smoke at <18° C 64° F) for 4 hours. Dry the sausages at 15 C → 12° C (60 → 53° F), 80 – 85% humidity for two weeks. Mature/dry the sausages at 12 → 10° C (53 → 50° F), 70 – 75% humidity for 1 more week.*
Store at 10-12° C (50 – 53° F), 60% humidity.

Notes: Sardinia is surrounded by water so the right humidity is always present.
* The drying/maturing time depends on the diameter of the casings. For sausages over 40 mm in diameter, bovine casings will be selected which are thicker than pork casings. That would affect drying and the sausage will need at least 30 days total time to be finished.
General considerations: lean pork 10-15%, pork hard fat 10-15%; ingredients: salt, pepper, wild fennel, aniseed, nutmeg, cinnamon, garlic, parsley, vinegar or white wine, sodium nitrite. The sausage is stuffed into natural casings, pork or beef. The sausage is briefly cold smoked, then dried and matured.

Saucisson au Camembert
(Sausage with Camembert Cheese)

Dry sausages made with cheese are very popular in France. Saucisson au Camembert, Saucisson au Roquefort, Saucisson au Beaufort, and Saucisson au Fromage de Chèvre (goat cheese) are everywhere. In the USA, hard cheese such as Cheddar, Pepperjack, or Calbot will be a good choice. Dry Camembert sausage is a popular item in France. It was first made in the late 18th century at Camembert, Normandy, in northern France.

Lean pork	750 g	1.65 lb
Back fat	150 g	0.33 lb
Cheese (Camembert)	100 g	0.22 lb

Ingredients per 1 kg (2.2 lb) of material

Salt	28 g	4.5 tsp
Cure #2	2.5 g	1/2 tsp
Dextrose	2.0 g	1/2 tsp
Sugar	3.0 g	3/4 tsp
Pepper	2.0 g	1 tsp
Nutmeg	1.0 g	1/2 tsp
Cumin	1.0 g	1/2 tsp
Garlic powder	1.0 g	1/2 tsp
T-SPX culture	0.12 g	use scale

Grind lean meat into 8 mm (5/16") particles. Cut partially frozen back fat into 6 mm (1/4") cubes.
Dissolve starter culture in 1 tablespoon de-chlorinated water.
Mix ground meats with salt and Cure #2 until sticky. Add spices, culture, chopped fat and mix again. Finely add cheese and mix all together.
Stuff firmly into 60 mm pork bungs forming sections 20-30 cm (8-12") long.
Ferment at 20° C (68° F) for 72 hours, 90-85% humidity.
Dry at 16 → 12° C (60-54° F), 85 → 80% humidity for 30 days. The sausage is dried until around 30% in weight is lost.
Store sausages at 10-15° C (50-59° F), <75% humidity.

Saucisson aux Noisettes
(Sausage with Hazelnuts)

Because of their wonderful flavor, hazelnuts are used to produce such famous products as Nutella™ spread or Ferrero Rocher™ chocolates. When mixed with meat hazelnuts release their aroma during drying period creating a wonderful dry sausage. Hazelnuts have strong antioxidant properties and are excellent for health.

Lean pork, no connective tissue	750 g	1.65 lb
Back fat or hard fat trimmings	100 g	0.22 lb
Hazelnuts	150 g	0.33 lb

Ingredients per 1 kg (2.2 lb) of material

Salt	28 g	4.5 tsp
Cure #2	2.5 g	1/2 tsp
Dextrose	2.0 g	1/2 tsp
Sugar	3.0 g	3/4 tsp
Pepper	2.0 g	1 tsp
Nutmeg	1.0 g	1/2 tsp
Cinnamon	0.5 g	1/4 tsp
Cloves	0.25 g	1/8 tsp
T-SPX culture	0.12 g	use
scale		

Grind lean meat into 8 mm (5/16") particles. Cut partially frozen back fat into 6 mm (1/4") cubes.
Dissolve starter culture in 1 tablespoon dechlorinated water.
Mix ground meats with salt and Cure #2 until sticky. Add spices, culture, whole hazelnuts, chopped fat and mix again.
Stuff firmly into 60 mm pork bungs forming sections 20-30 cm (8-12") long.
Ferment at 20° C (68° F) for 72 hours, 90-85% humidity.
Dry at 16 → 12° C (60-54° F), 85 → 80% humidity for 30 days. The sausage is dried until around 30% in weight is lost.
Store sausages at 10-15° C (50-59° F), <75% humidity.

Saucisson aux Noix
(Sausage with Walnuts)

French dry walnut sausage has a unique taste and flavor. Use lean shoulder meat without connective tissue. For the best particle definition, process cold meat and partially frozen fat.

Lean pork, no connective tissue	750 g	1.65 lb
Back fat or hard fat trimmings	100 g	0.22 lb
Walnuts, halved	150 g	0.33 lb

Ingredients per 1 kg (2.2 lb) of material

Salt	28 g	4.5 tsp
Cure #2	2.5 g	1/2 tsp
Dextrose	2.0 g	1/2 tsp
Sugar	3.0 g	3/4 tsp
Pepper	2.0 g	1 tsp
Nutmeg	1.0 g	1/2 tsp
Garlic powder	1.0 g	1/2 tsp
T-SPX culture	0.12 g	use
scale		

Grind lean meat into 8 mm (5/16") particles. Cut partially frozen back fat into 6 mm (1/4") cubes.
Dissolve starter culture in 1 tablespoon dechlorinated water.
Mix ground meats with salt and Cure #2 until sticky. Add spices, culture, halved walnuts, chopped fat and mix again.
Stuff firmly into 60 mm pork bungs forming sections 20-30 cm (8-12") long.
Ferment at 20° C (68° F) for 72 hours, 90-85% humidity.
Dry at 16 → 12° C (60-54° F), 85 → 80% humidity for 30 days. The sausage is dried until around 30% in weight is lost.
Store sausages at 10-15° C (50-59° F), <75% humidity.

Saucisson d'Alsace

French dry sausage.

Lean pork	800 g	8.8 lb
Back fat	200 g	2.2 lb

Ingredients per 1 kg (2.2 lb) of meat

Salt	28 g	5 tsp
Cure #2	2.5 g	1/2 tsp
Dextrose	2.0 g	1/2 tsp
Non-fat dry milk	20 g	3 tsp
White pepper	3.0 g	1.5 tsp
Garlic	2.0 g	1/2 clove
Nutmeg	0.5 g	1/2 tsp
Cloves, ground	0.3 g	1/4 tsp
Cinnamon	0.5 g	1/2 tsp
Dark rum	15 ml	1 Tbsp
T-SPX culture	0.12 g	use scale

Grind pork and back fat through 5 mm (3/16")
plate.
30 minutes before mixing dissolve starter
culture in 1 tablespoon de-chlorinated water.
Mix all ingredients with ground meat.
Stuff firmly into beef middles or 3" protein
lined fibrous casings.
Ferment at 20° C (68° F) for 60 hours, 90-85%
humidity.
Cold smoke at 18-22° C (64-72° F) 12 hours.
Dry at 16-12° C (60-54° F), 85-80% humidity
for 1-2 months.
Store sausages at 10-15° C (50-59° F), <75%
humidity.

Saucisson d'Ardenne / Collier d'Ardenne / Pipe d'Ardenne

The Ardennes, also known as Ardennes Forest,
is a region of extensive forests, rough terrain,
rolling hills, and ridges. Most of the Ardenne is
located in southeastern Wallonia, the southern
part of Belgium.

Pork shoulder	700 g	1.54 lb
Back fat, pork belly	300 g	0.66 lb

Ingredients per 1 kg (2.2 lb) of meat

Salt	28 g	5 tsp
Cure #2	2.5 g	1/2 tsp
Dextrose	3.0 g	3/4 tsp
Sugar	2.0 g	1/2 tsp
Cumin	1.0 g	1/2 tsp
Nutmeg	0.5 g	1/4 tsp
Garlic	3.5 g	1 clove
Juniper berries, crushed	1.0 g	1 tsp
T-SPX culture	0.12 g	use scale

Grind pork shoulder through 6 mm (1/4") plate.
Grind fat through 6 mm (1/4") plate.
30 minutes before mixing dissolve starter
culture in 1 tablespoon de-chlorinated water.
Mix pork shoulder with salt and cure #2. Add
spices and culture. Mix. Add ground fat and
mix all together.
Stuff firmly into 40 mm hog casings.
Ferment at 20° C (68° F) for 72 hours, 90-85%
humidity.
Apply a thin cold smoke at 18° C (64° F) for 2
days. Smoking does not have to be continuous
as long as 18° C temperature is maintained. Oak
wood or beech wood is used. Juniper berries
(not wood or twigs) may be added to fire as
well.
Dry at 15→12° C (59→53° F), 65-75%
humidity for 3 weeks until the sausage loses at
least 20% of its original weight (after stuffing).
Store at 10-12° C (50°-55 F), <75% humidity.

Note: The raw material consists of either pork
or pork and beef. The beef can be added at 40%
maximum of the total wet weight of the raw
material. The sausage comes in three forms:
Long-30 and 90 mm dia., max length of 60 cm
The collar (ring)- 20-40 mm dia.
Short-30 mm dia., 6" (15 cm) long.

Saucisson d'Ardenne carries PGI 2015
certification.

Saucisson de Lacaune

Lacaune is a French city located in the province of Tarn, in the region Languedoc-Roussillon, Midi-Pyrenees.

Pork, lean	700 g	1.54 lb
Back fat	300 g	0.66 lb

Ingredients per 1 kg (2.2 lb) of meat

Salt	28 g	5 tsp
Cure #2	2.5 g	1/2 tsp
Pepper	4.0 g	2 tsp
Nutmeg	1.0 g	1/2 tsp
Dextrose	3.0 g	1/2 tsp
Sugar	2.0 g	1/2 tsp
T-SPX culture	0.12 g	use scale

Cut with a knife or grind lean meat through 5/16" (8 mm) plate.

Using a sharp knife cut partially frozen back fat into 5/16" (8 mm) cubes. Dilute culture in 1 tablespoon of de-chlorinated water around 30 minutes before mixing.

Mix ground lean meat with salt and cure #2 until sticky.

Add fat cubes, culture, spices and mix all together.

Stuff firmly into 36 mm hog casings.

Ferment at 20° C (68° F) for 72 hours, 90-85% humidity.

Dry at 16 → 12° C (60-54° F), 85 → 80% humidity for 21 days. The sausage is dried until around 30% in weight is lost. The sausage should develop a white mold which is expected and desired.

Store sausages at 10-15° C (50-59° F), <75% humidity.

Note: the sausage can be formed into a loop or a straight stick weighing from 200-500 g (7.0-17.0 oz)

Saucisson de L'Ardéche

The sausage Ardèche is a specialty of the mountainous areas of the Ardèche. It first appeared on the market in the 17th century. Markets expanded between 1900 and 1939, and, according to Guy Dürrenmatt, helped make 'saucisson de l'Ardéche' well known.

Lean pork from shoulder or ham	700 g	1.54 lb
Pork belly	200 g	0.44 lb
Back fat	100 g	0.22 lb

Ingredients per 1 kg (2.2 lb) of meat

Salt	28 g	5 tsp
Black pepper	2.0 g	1 tsp
Whole peppercorns	2.0 g	1 tsp
Cure #2	5.0 g	1 tsp
Dextrose	3.0 g	1/2 tsp
Sugar	3.0 g	1/2 tsp
Garlic	10 g	3 cloves
Cumin	1.0 g	1/2 tsp
Nutmeg	1.0 g	1/2 tsp
Cloves, ground	0.3 g	1/8 tsp
Ginger	0.5 g	1/4 tsp
T-SPX culture	0.12 g	use scale

Chop meat into 1/4" (6 mm) particles. Chop belly and fat into 1/4" (6 mm) particles. 30 minutes before mixing dissolve starter culture in 1 tablespoon de-chlorinated water. Mix ground meats with salt and cure #2 until sticky. Add spices, culture and chopped fat and mix again. Stuff firmly into 36 mm hog casings. Ferment at 20° C (68° F) for 72 hours, 90-85% humidity.

Dry at 16 → 12° C (60-54° F), 85 → 80% humidity for 21 days (or longer when larger casing are used). The sausage is dried until around 30% in weight is lost. The sausage should develop a white mold. Store sausages at 10-15° C (50-59° F), <75% humidity.

Note: saucisson de l'Ardèche comes in different shapes, weights and diameters, depending on the natural casing used. Particle size varies from 6-8 mm. Casings from 30-90 mm, or even larger (caecum, anal canal). The size of casings will influence the drying time which varies from 17-63 days.

Saucisson de l'Ardeche carries PGI 2011 classification.

Saucisson sec au Beaufort

This is a French dry sausage made with Beaufort cheese. Beaufort is a firm that produces raw cow's milk cheese in Beaufort, which is located in the Savoie region of the French Alps.

Pork, lean	700 g	1.54 lb
Pork back fat	200 g	0.44 lb
Beaufort cheese	100 g	3.5 oz

Ingredients per 1 kg (2.2 lb) of material

Salt	28 g	5 tsp
Cure #2	2.5 g	1/2 tsp
White pepper	4.0 g	2 tsp
Dextrose	3.0 g	1/2 tsp
Sugar	3.0 g	1/2 tsp
Garlic	10 g	3 cloves
Nutmeg	1.0 g	1/2 tsp
White wine	15 ml	1 Tbsp
T-SPX culture scale	0.12 g	use

Grind lean meat through 1/4" (6 mm) plate.
Using a sharp knife cut partially fried back fat into 1/4 (6 mm) cubes.
Cut cheese into 3/8" (10 mm) chunks.
30 minutes before mixing dissolve the starter culture in 1 tablespoon de-chlorinated water.
Mix ground meats with salt and cure #2 until sticky. Add spices, culture, wine and chopped fat and mix again.
Stuff firmly into 50 mm hog or beef casings making 6" (15 cm) straight links.
Ferment at 20° C (68° F) for 72 hours, 90-85% humidity.
Dry at 16 → 12° C (60-54° F), 85 → 80% humidity for 45 days. The sausage is dried until around 30% in weight is lost. The sausage should develop a white mold which is expected and desired.
Store sausages at 10-15° C (50-59° F), < 75% humidity.

Saucisson sec d'Auvergne/Saucisse sèche d'Auvergne

Saucisson sec d'Auvergne/Saucisse sèche d'Auvergne is a French dry pork sausage awarded a PGI certificate of origin (20.09.2016). The certificate lists two names; however, it is the same sausage. The difference is in the size: the diameter of Saucisson sec d'Auvergne is larger than the diameter of Saucisse sèche d'Auvergne. The selection of materials and spices, as well as the manufacturing process, are the same for both sausages. However, drying times will be longer for Saucisson sec d'Auvergne as it is packed in a bigger casing.

The only pieces of meat allowed in the production of 'Saucisson sec d'Auvergne'/'Saucisse sèche d'Auvergne' are the loin, shoulder, shank, belly, and back fat. During the fattening stage, pigs are fed a diet that contains at least 60% cereals, oilseeds, and derived products. All animals are identified and traced. The sausage is made from mature heavy pigs, which accounts for its dark red color. It is rather a lean, dry sausage with only about 20% of fat, which is hardly visible in the finished product. The sausage contains garlic at a dose two to ten times higher than that found typically in dry sausage. Therefore 'Saucisson sec d'Auvergne'/'Saucisse sèche d'Auvergne' has a characteristic garlicky flavor and taste.

Saucisson sec d'Auvergne – diameter from 4 to 12 cm, drying time from ≥21 to ≥42 days.
Form: straight and more or less even.
Casing: bound with twine with the shape of the casing reinforced or not by tying or with a clipped net bag. Bound with twine or a clip.
Saucisse sèche d'Auvergne – diameter from 2.5 to 5 cm, drying time from ≥18 to ≥28 days.
Form: horseshoe piece, U-shaped or straight, coil.
Casing: bound with twine or a clip.

Lean pork (shoulder, loin)	800 g	1.76 lb
Back fat	200 g	0.44 lb

Ingredients per 1 kg (2.2 lb) of meat

Salt	28 g	5 tsp
Cure #2	2.5 g	1/2 tsp
Dextrose	3.0 g	3/4 tsp
Sugar	2.0 g	1/2 tsp
Pepper	2.0 g	1 tsp
Garlic	25 g	7 cloves
Nutmeg	1.0 g	1/2 tsp
Cumin	1.0 g	1/2 tsp
T-SPX culture	0.12 g	use
scale		

Grind lean meat into 8 mm (5/16") particles. Cut partially frozen back fat into 6 mm (1/4") cubes.

Dissolve starter culture in 1 tablespoon de-chlorinated water.

Mix ground meats with salt and Cure #2 until sticky. Add spices, culture and chopped fat and mix again. Stuff firmly into 60 - 90 mm pork bungs forming sections 20-50 cm (8-20") long.

Ferment at 20° C (68° F) for 72 hours, 90-85% humidity.

Dry at 16 → 12° C (60-54° F), 85 → 80% humidity for 30 days. The sausage is dried until around 30% in weight is lost.

Store sausages at 10-15° C (50-59° F), <75% humidity.

Notes

Auvergne is a historical region in central France. The primarily rural, mountainous area is famous for hiking and skiing, with vast forests and dormant volcanoes such as Puy de Dôme. The area lies at an average altitude of around 1000 m (3,300 ft), and prevailing winds contribute to drying meats and sausages.

Saucisson sec d'Auvergne/Saucisse sèche d'Auvergne has been awarded PGI certificate of origin (20.09.2016).

Schlackwurst

Schlackwurst is a German dry fermented sausage that is similar to Zervelatwurst. The sausage is finely ground and is classified as sliceable raw sausage. This requires a firm texture obtained using hard fat and sufficient drying time. The sausage derives its name from the casings it was traditionally filled in; the end part of the intestine was called the "slag gut," also known as Schlackdarm. The Schlackwurst is especially popular in the eastern part of Germany. Schlackwurst is listed (2.211.06) in the German government publication Guide to Meats and Meat Products - Leitsätze für Fleisch und Fleischerzeugnisse.

Beef, lean	250 g	0.55 lb
Pork, lean	500 g	1.10 lb
Pork back fat	250 g	0.55 lb

Ingredients per 1 kg (2.2 lb) of material

Salt	28 g	4.5 tsp
Cure #2	2.5 g	1/2 tsp
Dextrose	1.0 g	1/4 tsp
Honey	3.0 g	1/2 tsp
Pepper	2.0 g	1 tsp
Nutmeg	0.5 g	1/4 tsp
Coriander	0.5 g	1/4 tsp
Cardamom	0.3 g	1/8 tsp
Ginger	0.3 g	1/8 tsp
T-SPX culture	0.12 g	use
scale		

Grind beef and pork through 3 mm (1/8") plate. Grind partially frozen back fat through 3 mm (1/8") plate.

Mix meats, and all ingredients together. Add fat and mix again.

Stuff into 80-90 mm pork bungs.

Ferment for 3 days at 20° C (68° F), 95 → 90% humidity.

Ferment/dry for 2 days at 18° C (64° F), 90 → 80% humidity.

Smoke at 18° C (64° F) for 24 hours.

Dry at 15 → 12° C (59 → 53° F), 85 → 75% humidity for 8 weeks.

Store at 12° C (53° F), <75% humidity.

Schmierwurst
(Schmierwurst - Fatty Mettwurst)

Schmierwurst is a fatty spreadable metwurst sausage. Schnierwurst is listed (2.212.04) in the German government publication Guide to Meats and Meat Products - *Leitsätze für Fleisch und Fleischerzeugnisse.*

Pork butt, little connective tissue	200 g	0.44 lb
Pork belly, pork jowls	700 g	1.54 lb
Beef with little fat and connective tissue	100 g	0.22 lb

Ingredients per 1 kg (2.2 lb) of material

Salt	22 g	3.5 tsp
Cure #1	2.0 g	1/3 tsp
Dextrose	1.0 g	1/4 tsp
Sugar	2.0 g	1/2 tsp
Pepper	2.0 g	1 tsp
Paprika	1.0 g	1/2 tsp
Nutmeg	0.5 g	1/4 tsp
Ginger	0.3 g	1/8 tsp

Grind pork belly through 3 mm (1/8") plate.
Grind beef through 3 mm (1/8") plate.
Grind pork butt through 3 mm (1/8") plate.
Partially freeze all ground material then grind again through 3 mm (1/8") plate. Mix meat and fat with all ingredients.
Stuff into 45 mm artificial permeable casings forming 40 cm (16") links.
Ferment at 18° C (64° F), 75% humidity for 24-48 hours.
Cold smoke at 18° C (64° F) for 12 hours.
Hold at 18° C (64° F), 75% humidity for 2 days.
Refrigerate.

Šebreljski Želodec
(Stuffed pork stomach)

Sebreljski želodec is produced in a small area in western Slovenia, located less than 60 kilometers west of the capital city of Ljubljana.

Lean pork - shoulder, leg	750 g	1.65 lb
Pork back fat	250 g	0.55 lb

Ingredients per 1 kg (2.2 lb) of meat

Sea salt	30 g	5 tsp
Sugar	5.0 g	1 tsp
Pepper	3.0 g	1.5 tsp
Garlic	10 g	3 cloves

Grind lean pork through 3/8" (10 mm) plate.
Cut pork belly into 5/16" (8 mm) cubes.
Mix meat and spices together.
Stuff into pork stomach, bladder or permeable artificial casings.
Hold for 10 days in a cool room (4° C/40° F) between two wooden planks. Place weight on top board.
Apply a thin cold smoke at 18° C (64° F) for 2 days.
Dry between 10-15° C (50-59° F), 60-80% humidity for 3-5 months.

Note: Šebreljski želodec carries PGI, 2011 classification.

This is a specialized product that requires practical experience and in order to carry PGI mark it must be made without nitrite or nitrate. It can, however, be made at home using modern fermenting technology what will greatly increase the safety and will contribute to the success of the finished sausage:

Include 3.0 g of cure #2.
Include T-SPX culture (0.12 g - use scale).
Follow the above instructions (1, 2, 3), but skip step #4 (no holding required).
5. Ferment at 20° C (68° F), 85-90% humidity for 2 days.
6. Apply a thin cold smoke at 18° C (64° F) for 2 days.
7. Dry between 10-15° C (50-59° F), 60-80% humidity for 3-5 months.
You can flatten the product for 2-3 days using boards during the drying step.

Secallona-Somalla-Petador-Espetec

Secallona, Somalla, Petador, Espetec - although those names sound mysterious and exotic, the truth is that they all are dry sausages, and they all can be called fuet or longaniza. The manufacturing process is basically the same; what separates them is the size. Longaniza is packed into a large diameter, fuet into a medium, and secallona into a small diameter casing. Secallona is very dry and wrinkled, and somalla is more moist. Secallona or somalla are U-shaped and usually not covered with mold, unlike fuet, which always carries white mold. Petador is the name that is common for those sausages in the Catalonian city of Sabadell, 20 km north of Barcelona. Espetec or fuet is basically the same Catalonian sausage.

Lean pork	800 g	1.76 lb
Back fat	200 g	0.44 lb

Ingredients per 1 kg (2.2 lb) of meat

Salt	22 g	3.5 tsp
Cure #1	2.5 g	1/2 tsp
Dextrose	2.0 g	1/2 tsp
Sugar	3.0 g	3/4 tsp
White pepper	3.0 g	1.5 tsp

Grind lean pork and pork belly through 6-8 mm (1/4-5/16") plate.

Mix all ingredients with meat. Hold in refrigerator for 24 hours.

Stuff into 32-34 mm pork casings making straight links.

Dry at 14-15° C (54-59° F), 75-80% humidity for 12 days.

Store sausages at 10-12° C (50-53° F), <75% humidity or refrigerate.

Servolatka
(Serwolatka miękka)

This cold smoked spreadable sausage recipe comes from the official Polish Government archives.

Lean beef	650 g	1.43 lb
Pork belly, skinless	350 g	0.77 lb

Ingredients per 1 kg (2.2 lb) of meat

Salt	21 g	3-1/2 tsp
Cure #1	2.5 g	1/2 tsp
Pepper	1.5 g	3/4 tsp
Coriander	0.5 g	1/4 tsp
Paprika	1.0 g	1/2 tsp

Curing: cut beef into 1-2" (2.5-5 cm) pieces and mix with 12 g salt and 2.0 g cure # 1. Cut belly into 1-2" (2.5-5 cm) pieces and mix with 9 g salt and 0.5 g cure # 1. Pack tightly separately in a container, cover with cloth and keep in refrigerator for 3 days.

Grind beef through 3 mm (1/8") plate. Partially freeze and grind again. Grind pork belly through 5 mm (3/16") plate.

Mix all meats with spices until sticky.

Stuff firmly into 65 mm synthetic fibrous casings forming 10" (25 cm) links.

Hang for 1-2 days at 2-4° C (35-40° F), 85-90% humidity.

Cold smoke at 18° C (64° F) for 1-2 days until casings are brown. Keep refrigerated.

Skilandis

Skilandis (in Lithuanian) also known as Kindziuk (in Polish) is an almost legendary product, famous for its long keeping properties.

Lean pork (ham)	800 g	1.76 lb
Fresh belly	200 g	0.44 lb

Ingredients per 1 kg (2.2 lb) of meat

Salt	33 g	6.5 tsp
Cure #2	5.0 g	1 tsp
Sugar	2.0 g	1/2 tsp
Pepper	4.0 g	2 tsp
Smashed garlic	3.5 g	1 clove

Pure alcohol, 95%, (American *EverClear* 190 proof), 50 ml.

Cut meat and belly into 1.5" (30 mm) pieces and mix with pepper and smashed garlic.
Fry salt briefly on a hot pan (removes moisture) stirring often. Rub salt thoroughly into the meat. Add sugar, cure #2 and alcohol. Pure alcohol evaporates rapidly removing moisture at the same time.
Mix everything well together. Stuff firmly into pork stomach, bladder or 60 mm fibrous casing. Avoid creating air pockets. Reinforce with butcher's twine: two loops lengthwise and loops across the casings every 2" (5 cm). Form 10-12 cm (4-5") hanging loop on one end.
Hang for at least 10 days in a cool, dry and ventilated area. This is when curing, drying and fermenting are taking place.
Cold smoke (below 18° C, 64° F) for 3 weeks, applying smoke 3-4 hours daily. On the last day of smoking add juniper berries or juniper twigs into the fire.
Dry for 2 months at 8° C (46° F) and 75% humidity. The sausage should lose about 35% of its original weight.
Store in a dark, cool and dry place.

Note:

Originally the ingredients were stuffed into pork stomach or bladder. The stomach was sewn and the bladder was tied off with butcher twine. Then the casing was placed between two wooden boards and pressed together. The boards were tied with twine and hung. Original Skilandis was smoked with alder wood.

Slavonski Kulen

Slavonski kulen is produced in the Croatian region of Slavonia. It is a preserved sausage made from a mixture of the highest-quality pork cuts, back fat, salt, and spices stuffed into the caecum of a pig. It is a large sausage; when placed on the market, it must weigh at least 900 g (2 lbs).

Lean pork (legs, loin)	700 g	1.76 lb
Pork butt	200 g	0.44 lb
Back fat	100 g	0.22 lb

Ingredients per 1 kg (2.2 lb) of meat

Salt	30 g	5 tsp
Cure #2	5.0 g	1 tsp
Dextrose	2.0 g	1/2 tsp
Sugar	2.0 g	1/2 tsp
Paprika, sweet	8.0 g	4 tsp
Garlic, dehydrated	2.0 g	1 tsp
Red wine	15 ml	1 oz fl
T-SPX culture	0.12 g	use scale

Grind meat through 10 mm (3/8") plate.
30 minutes before mixing dissolve starter culture in 1 tablespoon de-chlorinated water. Mix lean pork with salt and cure #2. Add spices and wine. Lastly, add culture and mix all together.
Stuff tightly into pork caecum, bung or bladder. Ferment at 20° C (68° F) for 72 hours, 90-85% humidity.
Apply a thin cold smoke at 18° C (64° F) for 4 weeks using oak, beech or mixture of both woods. Maintain high humidity. Smoking does not have to be continuous as long as a low temperature is maintained. Fermentation takes place during the smoking step.
Dry at 15→12° C (59→53° F), 80-75% humidity for 6 weeks.
Dry at 10-12° C (50-55° F), 75% humidity for 10 weeks.
Store at 10-12° C (50-53° F), <75% humidity.

Note: Slavonski Kulen has pending application (published in 2015) for PGI classification.

Snijworst
(Dutch Cervelat)

Dutch semi-dry sausage.

Lean beef	200 g	0.44 lb
Pork	400 g	0.88 lb
Pork belly	300 g	0.66 lb
Back fat or		
hard fat trimmings	100 g	0.22 lb

Ingredients per 1 kg (2.2 lb) of meat

Salt	23 g	4 tsp
Cure #1	2.5 g	1/2 tsp
Dextrose	5.0 g	1 tsp
Black pepper	3.0 g	1.5 tsp
Coriander	2.0 g	1 tsp
Nutmeg	1.0 g	1/2 tsp
Mace	1.0 g	1/2 tsp
F-LC culture	0.25 g	use
scale		

Grind all meats through 3/16" plate (5 mm).
Mix all ingredients with ground meat.
Stuff into beef middles or 90-100 mm fibrous casings.
Ferment at 24° C (75° F) for 48 hours, 90-85% humidity.
Dry for 2 months at 16→12° C (60→54° F), 85-75% humidity.
Store sausages at 10-15° C (50-59° F), 75% humidity.

Sobrasada

Spanish Sobrasada has a characteristic reddish-orange color, that is the result of mixing ground lean pork and pork fat with paprika, salt and spices. In the islands sobrasada is made from the locally grown black pig which is related to Iberico pig from the mainland known for producing famous Iberico hams.

Lean pork	700 g	1.54 lb
Back fat or		
hard fat trimmings	300 g	0.66 lb

Ingredients per 1 kg (2.2 lb) of meat

Salt	30 g	5 tsp
Cure #2	2.5 g	1 tsp
Dextrose (glucose)	2.0 g	1/3 tsp
Sugar	2.0 g	1/3 tsp
Pimentón paprika, sweet	30 g	1 oz
Pimentón paprika, hot	30 g	1 oz
Cilantro	2.0 g	1 tsp
Garlic	7.0 g	2 cloves
T-SPX culture	0.12 g	use
scale		

Grind pork through 3/8" (10 mm) plate. Grind fat through 1/4" (6 mm) plate.
30 minutes before mixing dissolve starter culture in 1 tablespoon de-chlorinated water.
Mix meat, fat, salt, cure and spices together
Stuff into 38-40 mm hog casings.
Ferment at 20° C (68° F) for 72 hours, 90-85% humidity.
Dry for 1 month at 16→12° C (60→54° F), 85-80% humidity.
Store sausages at 10-15° C (50-59° F), <75% humidity.

Note: exact drying time will be determined by the type and the size of the casings used. Different casings are used including bladder and stomach. You can use 90 mm fibrous protein lined synthetic casings. Increase drying time to 2 months.

Sobrasada de Mallorca

As the name implies, this sausage originated on the island of Majorca. Sobrasada includes a lot of pimentón; when made with sweet pimentón only, it is known as sweet sobrasada ("dulce"), and when hot pimentón is added, it becomes hot sobrasada ("picante"). The sausage must meet the following requirements: lean pork (30-60%), back fat (40-70%), pimentón (4-7%), salt (1.8-2.8%), spices: pepper, rosemary, thyme, oregano. Neither garlic nor sugar is added to Sobrasada de Mallorca. Sobrasada is a very popular sausage in the Balearic Islands.

Pork, lean	380 g	0.83 lb
Pork belly	270 g	0.59 lb
Back fat, fat trimmings	350 g	0.77 lb

Ingredients per 1 kg (2.2 lb) of meat

Salt	24 g	4 tsp
White pepper	2.0 g	1 tsp
Pimentón, sweet	48 g	7 Tbsp
Thyme, ground	2.0 g	2 tsp
Oregano, ground	2.0 g	2 tsp

Grind meat and fat through 5 mm (3/16").
Mix ground meat and fat with salt and spices.
Hold in refrigerator for 24 hours.
Stuff into 40-100 mm pork casings.
Dry at 15-18° C (59-64° F), 75-80% humidity for 30-45 days depending on the diameter of the sausage.
Store at 10-12° C (50-53° F), 60-65% humidity or refrigerate.

Notes
Although Pimentón de La Vera is the highest quality pimentón it is, however, made from smoked peppers and *must not be added* to Sobrasada de Mallorca in order not to introduce the smoky flavor.
Majorcan Sobrasada is traditionally served on bread and topped with variety of spreads such as honey, sugar or apricot jam.
For hot version add 6 g (1 Tbsp) of hot pimentón.
Sobrasada de Mallorca carries PGI 1996 certification.

Sobrasada de Mallorca de Cerdo Negro

Sobrasada de Mallorca de Cerdo Negro must be made from meat that comes exclusively from black pig (*cerdo negro*) that grows in the island of Majorca.

Pork, lean	380 g	0.83 lb
Pork belly	270 g	0.59 lb
Back fat, fat trimmings	350 g	0.77 lb

Ingredients per 1 kg (2.2 lb) of meat

Salt	24 g	4 tsp
White pepper	2.0 g	1 tsp
Pimentón, sweet	48 g	7 Tbsp
Thyme, ground	2.0 g	2 tsp
Oregano, ground	2.0 g	2 tsp

Grind meat and fat through 5 mm (3/16").
Mix ground meat and fat with salt and spices.
Hold in refrigerator for 24 hours.
Stuff into 40-100 mm pork casings.
Dry at 15-18° C (59-64° F) for 30-45 days depending on the diameter of the sausage.
Store at 10-12° C (50-53° F), 60-65% humidity or refrigerate.

Notes
Although Pimentón de La Vera is the highest quality pimentón it is, however, made from smoked peppers and *must not be added* to Sobrasada de Mallorca in order not to introduce the smoky flavor.
Neither *garlic* nor *sugar* is added to Sobrasada de Mallorca de Cerdo Negro.
Majorcan sobrasada is traditionally served on bread and topped with variety of spreads such as honey, sugar or apricot jam.
The sausage carries PGI 1996 certification.

Sobrasada Picante Casera

Sobrasada sausage has a characteristic reddish-orange color, that is the result of mixing ground lean pork and pork fat with paprika, salt and spices. In Balearic islands sobrasada is made from the locally grown pigs.

Lean pork (<20% fat)	600 g	1.32 lb
Back fat or fat pork trimmings ,,,,,,,,,,,,	400 g	0.88 lb

Ingredients per 1 kg (2.2 lb) of meat

Salt	25 g	4 tsp
Cure #1	2.0 g	1/2 tsp
Pimentón, sweet	30 g	5 Tbsp
Pimentón, hot	10 g	5 tsp
Garlic, diced	7.0 g	2 cloves

Grind pork and fat through 5 mm (3/16") plate. Mix meat, fat, salt, cure and spices together. Hold for 12 hours in refrigerator.
Stuff into large hog casings. Different casings are used including bladder and stomach. You can used fibrous synthetic casings.
Dry for 2 months at 16-12° C (60-54° F), 85-80% humidity.
Store sausages at 10-12° C (50-53° F), <70% humidity.

Notes
Exact drying time will be determined by the type and the size of the casings used.

Sobrasada Valenciana

Sobrasada sausage from the municipality of Alicante, País Valenciano region of Spain.

Lean pork	300 g	0.66 lb
Back fat	300 g	0.66 lb
Pork belly	400 g	0.88 lb

Ingredients per 1 kg (2.2 lb) of meat

Salt	25 g	4 tsp
Cure #2	2.5 g	1/2 tsp
Pepper	4.0 g	2 tsp
Pimentón, sweet	36 g	6 Tbsp
Pimentón, hot	4.0 g	2 tsp
Cloves, ground	0.5 g	1/4 tsp

Grind meat and fat through 3 mm (1/8") plate. Mix ground materials with all ingredients. Hold for 12 hours in refrigerator.
Stuff into 60-80 mm pork bungs forming 30 cm (1 foot) straight sections or 30-40 mm pork casings forming 30 cm (1 foot) rings.
Dry at 15-12° C (59-53° F), 65-70% humidity for 2-3 months depending on the diameter of the sausage.
Store at 10-12° C (50-53° F), <70% humidity.

Notes
Consume raw.
In Valencia, the sausage is often sliced and served on bread with honey.

Soppressata

Soppressata is made with natural flavors such as cumin, black pepper, red pepper, and chili peppers, which are added to the meat and are then aged. Depending on the product type, the aging process may last from a minimum of thirty to a maximum of one hundred days.

Pork butt	800 g	1.76 lb
Back fat or hard fat trimmings	200 g	0.44 lb

Ingredients per 1 kg (2.2 lb) of meat

Salt	28 g	5 tsp
Cure #2	2.5 g	1/2 tsp
Dextrose	10 g	2 tsp
Black pepper	2.0 g	1 tsp
Red pepper flakes	1.0 g	1/2 tsp
Whole peppercorns	2.0 g	1 tsp
Chili powder	1.0 g	1/2 tsp
Garlic powder	1.5 g	1/2 tsp

Grind meat and fat through 1/2" (12 mm) plate.
Mix ground meat and fat with all ingredients.
Pack tightly in a container, cover with cloth and hold in refrigerator for 48 hours.
Grind through 10 mm (3/8") plate.
Stuff into 60 mm hog middles. Make links 8-10" long.
Hang sausage at 20° C (68° F), 80-90% humidity for 2 days.
If smoky flavor is desired, apply cold smoke at 20° C (68° F).
Hold sausage at around 14° C (56° F), 80% humidity for about 2 months until it loses about 30% of its original weight.
If mold appears wipe it off with a cloth moistened with vinegar. You can cold smoke sausage again for a few hours which prevents the formation of mold.

Soppressata di Calabria

Sopressata di Calabria is produced in the Calabria region of Italy from locally grown and slaughtered pigs.

Lean pork - thigh (ham), shoulder loin	850 g	1.87 lb
Back fat, fat from the front of the loin	150 g	0.33 lb

Ingredients per 1 kg (2.2 lb) of meat

Salt	28 g	5 tsp
Cure #2	2.5 g	1/2 tsp
Pepper	1.0 g	1/2 tsp
Peppercorns, whole	2.0 g	1 tsp
Dextrose	1.0 g	1/5 tsp
Sugar	1.0 g	1/5 tsp
Cinnamon	0.5 g	1/4 tsp
Red peppers, ground	1.0 g	1/2 tsp
Cloves	0.3 g	1/8 tsp
Garlic	3.0 g	1 clove
Red wine	10 ml	2 tsp
Starter culture, T-SPX	0.12 g	use scale

Grind lean meat through 5/16" (8 mm) plate.
Cut fat into 1/4" (6 mm) cubes.
30 minutes before mixing dissolve starter culture in 1 tablespoon de-chlorinated water.
Mix lean meat with all ingredients. Add fat cubes and mix again.
Stuff into large 40-80 mm hog casings, middles or bungs. Make links 16-24" (40-60 cm) long.
Ferment at 20° C (68° F) for 72 hours, 90 → 85% humidity.
Dry at 15-12° C (59-54° F), 85→75% decreasing humidity for 40-80 days, depending on diameter. The sausage is dried until around 30-35% in weight is lost.
Store sausages at 10-15° C (50-59° F), <75% humidity.

Note: Sopressata di Calabria carries PDO, 1998 classification.
The sausage possesses the following characteristics: length between 10 - 18 cm (4 – 7") and diameter between 4 - 8 cm (1.6 – 3"); when cut it is firm to soft, with a natural red or bright red color depending on the ingredients used in the mixture.

Soprèssa Vicentina

The production area of Soprèssa Vicentina comprises the whole province of Vicenza.

Lean pork - shoulder, loin, ham	700 g	1.54 lb
Back fat, pork belly	300 g	0.66 lb

Ingredients per 1 kg (2.2 lb) of meat

Salt	28 g	5 tsp
Cure #2	2.5 g	1/2 tsp
Pepper	3.0 g	1.5 tsp
Dextrose	1.0 g	1/5 tsp
Sugar	2.0 g	1/2 tsp
Cinnamon	0.5 g	1/4 tsp
Cloves	0.3 g	1/8 tsp
Rosemary, ground	0.3 g	1/8 tsp
Garlic	3.0 g	1 clove
Starter culture, T-SPX scale	0.12 g	use

Grind lean meat through 5/16" (8 mm) plate. Cut fat into 1/4" (6 mm) cubes.
30 minutes before mixing dissolve starter culture in 1 tablespoon de-chlorinated water. Mix lean meat with all ingredients. Add fat cubes and mix again.
Stuff into large 80 mm hog casings - pork middles or bungs.
Ferment at 20° C (68° F) for 72 hours, 90 → 85% humidity.
Dry at 15-12° C (59 -54° F), 85→75% decreasing humidity for 80 days. The sausage is dried until around 30-35% in weight is lost.
Store sausages at 10-15° C (50-59° F), <75% humidity.

Note: Soprèssa Vicentina carries PDO, 2003 classification.

Soviet Sausage

Russian dry sausage.

Lean pork	500 g	1.10 lb
Pork fat	300 g	0.66 lb
Beef	200 g	0.44 lb

Ingredients per 1 kg (2.2 lb) of meat

Salt	28 g	5 tsp
Cure #2	2.5 g	1/2 tsp
Dextrose	3.0 g	1/2 tsp
White pepper	3.0 g	1.5 tsp
Cardamom	2.0 g	1 tsp
Allspice	1.5 g	3/4 tsp
Madeira wine or brandy	30 ml	1 oz fl
T-SPX culture scale	0.12 g	use

Grind pork and back fat through 3/16" plate (5 mm). Grind beef with 1/8" (3 mm) plate.
30 minutes before mixing dissolve starter culture in 1 tablespoon de-chlorinated water. Mix all ingredients with meat.
Stuff firmly into beef middles or 3" protein lined fibrous casings.
Ferment at 20° C (68° F) for 72 hours, 90-85% humidity.
Cold smoke at 18-20° C (64-68° F) for 24 hours.
Dry at 15 →12° C (59 →54° F), 85-80% humidity. In about 6-8 weeks a shrink of 30% should be achieved.
Store sausages at 10-15° C (50-59° F), <75% humidity.

Stolichnaya

Stolichnaya means the sausage originated in the capital (Moscow). Everybody is familiar with Stolichnaya Vodka, but there are also many stolichnaya type sausages.

Lean beef	350 g	0.77 lb
Lean pork	350 g	0.77 lb
Back fat or		
hard fat trimmings	300 g	0.66 lb

Ingredients per 1 kg (2.2 lb) of meat

Salt	30 g	5 tsp
Cure #1	5 g	1 tsp
Sugar	2 g	1/2 tsp
Pepper	1.5 g	1 tsp
Allspice	0.5 g	1/4 tsp
Cardamom or nutmeg	0.5 g	1/4 tsp
Cognac	5 ml	1 tsp

Curing: cut meat into 1 inch (25 mm) pieces. Place beef, pork and pork fat in separate food grade containers. Mix back fat with 10 g (2 tsp) of salt. Mix beef and pork with salt, Cure #1 and sugar according to the recipe (estimate amounts). Pack tightly to eliminate air and cover with clean cloth. Place for 72 hours in refrigerator. Discard any liquid brine and submit meat to grinding.
Grind beef through 1/8" (3 mm) plate. Grind pork through 1/8" (3 mm) plate. Dice back fat into 1/8" (3 mm) cubes.
Mix beef with spices. Add pork and mix. Add fat cubes and remix everything together. Don't add any water.
Stuff sausages firmly into 45-55 mm beef middles or fibrous casings. Make links up to 20" (50 cm) long.
Hang sausages for 5-7 days at 2-4° C (34-40° F). Apply cold smoke at 18-22° C (64-72° F) for 2-3 days.
Dry sausages for 5-7 days (depending on sausage diameter) at 11-15° C (53-59° F), 80-84% humidity. Dry 20-23 days more at 10-12° C (50-54° F), 74-78% humidity.

Note: finished sausage should retain 65% of its original weight.

Sucuk
(Fast-fermented - heat treated)

Following American trends, some Turkish sucuk manufacturers start to pre-cook sucuks after a very short fermentation. Primary reasons are: shorter production time, elimination of pathogens during cooking (safer product) and lower costs of production.

Lean beef	600 g	1.32 lb
Lean lamb/mutton	250 g	0.55 lb
Beef tallow or		
sheep tail fat	150 g	0.33 lb

Ingredients per 1 kg (2.2 lb) of meat

Salt	24 g	4 tsp
Cure #1	2.5 g	1/2 tsp
Dextrose	10 g	2 tsp
Black pepper	5.0 g	2 tsp
Red pepper	5.0 g	2 tsp
Cumin	10 g	2.5 tsp
Garlic	10 g	3 cloves
Allspice	2.0 g	1.0 tsp
Cinnamon	1.0 g	1/2 tsp
Cloves	0.5 g	1/4 tsp
F-LC culture scale	0.24 g	use

Grind beef, lamb and lamb fat through 3/16" plate (5 mm).
30 minutes before mixing dissolve starter culture in 1 tablespoon de-chlorinated water.
Mix all ingredients with meat.
Stuff firmly into 38 mm collagen or fibrous casings.
Ferment at 24° C (75° F) for 72 hours, 95-90% humidity.
Dry for 3 days at 22° C (71.6° C), 80-85% humidity.
Bake at 80° C (176° F) *OR* until sausage reaches 63° C (145° F) temperature inside.
Store in refrigerator.

Sucuk-Traditional
(Slow-fermented-traditional)

The Turkish Sucuk (Soudjouk) is the most popular dry fermented meat product in Turkey and other Middle Eastern Countries. As most of those countries practice Muslim it comes as no surprise that pork is not included in the recipe and the sausage is made from beef and lamb.

Lean beef	700 g	1.54 lb
Lean lamb/mutton	300 g	0.66 lb

Ingredients per 1 kg (2.2 lb) of meat

Salt	28 g	5 tsp
Cure #2	2.5 g	1/2 tsp
Dextrose	3.0 g	1/2 tsp
Black pepper	5.0 g	2.5 tsp
Red pepper	5.0 g	2.5 tsp
Cumin	10 g	2.5 tsp
Garlic	10 g	3 cloves
Allspice	2.0 g	1 tsp
Olive oil	5 ml	1 tsp
T-SPX culture	0.12 g	use scale

Grind beef and lamb through 5 mm (3/16") plate.
30 minutes before mixing dissolve starter culture in 1 tablespoon de-chlorinated water.
Mix all ingredients with meat.
Stuff firmly into 38 mm beef casings.
Ferment at 20° C (68° F) for 72 hours, 90-85% humidity.
Dry at 16→12° C (60→54° F), 85-80% humidity for 1 month.
Store sausages at 10-15° C (50-59° F), <75% humidity.

Note: cinnamon and cloves are often added. Original sucuks are made with sheep tail fat (40% beef, 40% lamb, 20% sheep tail fat). Sucuk is a very lean sausage.
Up to 5% of olive oil (50 g per 1 kg of meat) can be added as a replacement for beef fat which has poor sensory qualities.

Summer Sausage

Summer sausage is an American semi-dry fermented sausage made of pork and beef, although sausages made from beef alone are common. The sausage was made in the winter, and after drying and storing it, it was consumed in the summer when working in the field. Summer sausage displays a long shelf life without refrigeration and is often used as a component of food for gift baskets, along with different cheeses and jams. The diameter of the casings varies from 40-120 mm, and so does the length of the sausage.

Pork	700 g	1.54 lb
Beef	300 g	0.66 lb

Ingredients per 1 kg (2.2 lb) of meat

Salt	23 g	4 tsp
Cure #1	2.5 g	½ tsp
Dextrose	10.0 g	2 tsp
Sugar	5.0 g	1 tsp
Black pepper	3.0 g	1½ tsp
Coriander	2.0 g	1 tsp
Whole mustard seeds	4.0 g	1½ tsp
Allspice	2.0 g	1 tsp
Garlic	3.5 g	1 clove
F-LC culture	0.24 g	use scale

Grind pork and beef through 5 mm (3/16") plate.
Mix all ingredients with ground meat.
Stuff into 60 mm beef middles or fibrous casings.
Ferment at 30° C (86° F) for 48 hours, 90-85% humidity.
Introduce warm smoke at 43° C (110° F), 70% humidity for 6 hours. Gradually increase the temperature until meat reaches 63° C (145° F) inside.

Note: some sausages may contain around 10% diced cheddar cheese.

Szegedi Szalámi

Hungarian Szegedi szalámi or Szegedi téliszalámi has been produced for over 140 years in Szeged, where even today existing manufacturer uses the same local methods as in the past. The nearby river Tisza creates a microclimate ensuring the production of a salami with different characteristics to similar products.

Pork meat - leg shoulder, loin	700 g	1.54 lb
Back fat, jowl or hard fat trimmings	300 g	0.66 lb

Ingredients per 1 kg (2.2 lb) of meat

Salt	30 g	5 tsp
Cure # 2	5.0 g	1 tsp
White pepper	2.0 g	1 tsp
Sweet paprika	10 g	3 tsp
Allspice, ground	2.0 g	1 tsp
Nutmeg	1.0 g	1/2 tsp

Meat is manually boned which enables the thorough removal of sinews, gristle and connective tissue.
Cut the meat into 1/8" (3 mm) pieces.
Cut fat into 1/8" (3 mm) pieces.
Mix lean meat with all ingredients. Add fat and remix.
Stuff into 65 mm fibrous casings forming 6-22" (15-54 cm) long links.
Apply a thin cold smoke at 12° C (54° F) for 12-14 days using beech wood. Cold smoking is not a continuous process, it can be interrupted often, however, the temperature of 12° C should be maintained. You are drying the meat with smoke.
Place sausages in a fermenting/drying room at 16° C (60° F), 86-90% humidity to permit the growth of mold. The drying process continues for 2-3 months depending on the diameter (not the length) of the sausage at 60-90% humidity. The total production time from filling the sausages is at least 90 days.

Note: the sausage should be evenly covered with white noble mold. For a better particle definition commercial producers cut meat and fat with bowl cutters. In home production using a grinder is acceptable.
Szegedi Salami carries PDO, 2007 classification.

Tambov

Russian dry sausage.

Pork	200 g	0.44 lb
Pork bellies	400 g	0.88 lb
Beef	400 g	0.88 lb

Ingredients per 1 kg (2.2 lb) of meat

Salt	28 g	5 tsp
Cure #2	2.5 g	1/2 tsp
Dextrose	3.0 g	1/2 tsp
Pepper	3.0 g	1.5 tsp
Nutmeg	0.5 g	1/2 tsp
T-SPX culture	0.12 g	use scale

Grind pork and beef through 3/16" plate (6 mm). Dice pork belly into 1/4" (6 mm) cubes or grind through 3/8" (10 mm) plate.
30 minutes before mixing dissolve starter culture in 1 tablespoon de-chlorinated water.
Mix all ingredients with meat.
Stuff firmly into beef middles or 3" protein lined fibrous casings.
Ferment at 20° C (68° F) for 72 hours, 90-85% humidity.
Cold smoke for 24 hours at 22° C (72° F) or lower.
Dry at 16→12° C (60-54° F), 85-80% humidity. In about 6-8 weeks a shrink of 30% should be achieved.
Store sausages at 10-12° C (50-53° F), <75% humidity.

Teewurst

Teewurst is a German spreadable raw (fermented) sausage. Teewurst is listed (2.212.1) in the German government publication Guide to Meats and Meat Products - *Leitsätze für Fleisch und Fleischerzeugnisse.* Teewurst was invented in Pomerania, probably in the small Baltic town of Rügenwalde (now Darłowo, Poland), in the middle of the 19th century. In German "tee" means tea and the sausage got its Teewurst name from the habit of serving it in sandwiches at teatime.

Beef	200 g	0.44 lb
Lean pork	300 g	0.66 lb
Pork belly side...............	250 g	0.55 lb
Pork belly (soft bottom part)	250 g	0.55 lb

Ingredients per 1 kg (2.2 lb) of material

Salt	24 g	4 tsp
Cure #1	2.0 g	1/3 tsp
Dextrose	1.0 g	1/4 tsp
Sugar	1.0 g	1/4 tsp
White pepper	3.0 g	1.5 tsp
Allspice	1.0 g	1.5 tsp
Dark rum	3 ml	1/2 tsp

Grind all meats through 3 mm (1/8") plate. Re-freeze and grind again. You may grind once and then emulsify in the food processor without adding water.
Mix meats with all ingredients together.
Stuff firmly into 45 mm beef middles or fibrous casings. Form 40 cm (16") links or shorter.
Ferment for 48 hours at 18° C (64° F), 75-80% humidity.
Apply cold smoke for 12 hours at 18° C (64° F).
Hold at 18° C (64° F), 75% humidity for 2 days.
Refrigerate.

Teewurst Rugenwalder Art
(Teewurst Rugenwalder Style)

Teewurst Rugenwalder is a German spreadable raw sausage. Teewurst Rugenwalder Art is listed (2.212.1) in the German government publication Guide to Meats and Meat Products - *Leitsätze für Fleisch und Fleischerzeugnisse.*

Quote from Wikipedia: Up to 1945, the sausage industry in Rügenwalde was well established, and Teewurst was its best-known product. In 1927, the term Rügenwalder Teewurst was declared a Protected Designation of Origin. After World War II, sausage makers from Rügenwalde fled or were expelled to the Federal Republic of Germany, where they established new companies and resumed the production of Teewurst. They established an association of former Rügenwald sausage makers, which registered the trademark Rügenwalder Teewurst in 1957. Today, only companies that once had their headquarters in Rügenwalde are allowed to use the term Rügenwalder Teewurst. All others use the terms Teewurst or Rügenwalde-style Teewurst.

Pork butt (upper shoulder)	300 g	0.66 lb
Pork belly or back fat	400 g	0.88 lb
Lean beef	300 g	0.66 lb

Ingredients per 1 kg (2.2 lb) of material

Salt	22 g	3.5 tsp
Cure #1	2.5 g	1/2 tsp
Pepper	3.0 g	1.5 tsp
Paprika, sweet	1.0 g	1/2 tsp
Cardamom	0.3 g	1/8 tsp
Ginger	0.5 g	1/4 tsp
Rum	5 ml	1 tsp

Cold smoke pork belly or back fat at 18° C (64° F) for 8 hours, then cool well in refrigerator.
Grind all meats and smoked fat through 3 mm (1/8") plate. Cool in refrigerator and grind again *OR* emulsify in food processor adding all ingredients.
Mix ground meats with all ingredients (if not done previously).
Stuff into 40 mm natural or artificial permeable casings.
Hold at 18° C (64° F), 75% humidity for 24-48 hours. Cold smoke at 18° C (64° F) for 12 hours.
Hold at 18° C (64° F), 75% humidity for 3 days. Refrigerate.

Thuringer

Thüringer semi-dry fermented and partially cooked beef and pork sausage.

Lean pork	350 g	0.77 lb
Lean beef	350 g	0.77 lb
Pork back fat	300 g	0.66 lb

Ingredients per 1 kg (2.2 lb) of material

Salt	23 g	4 tsp
Cure #1	2.5 g	1/2 tsp
Dextrose	10 g	2 tsp
Coriander	2.0 g	1 tsp
Whole mustard seeds	2.0 g	1.5 tsp
Allspice	2.0 g	1 tsp
Bactoferm® LHP culture scale	0.18 g	use

Grind pork and beef through 6 mm (1/4") plate. Grind partially frozen back fat through 6 mm (1/4") plate.

Mix pork, beef and all ingredients together.

Stuff into beef middles or fibrous casings 40-120 mm.

Ferment at 30° C (86° F) for 24 hours, 90-85% humidity.

Introduce warm smoke at 43° C (110° F), 70% humidity for 5 hours. Gradually increase smoke temperature until meat reaches 63° C (145° F) internal temperature.

For a drier sausage: dry 2 days at 15-12° C (59-53° F), 75% humidity or until desired weight loss has occurred.

Store sausages at 10-12° C (50-53° F), <75% humidity.

Touristenwurst
(Tourist Sausage)

Touristenwurst is listed (2.211.15) in the German government publication *Guide to Meats and Meat Products - Leitsätze für Fleisch und Fleischerzeugnisse.* Touristenwurst is fermented dry sausage.

Lean pork	500 g	1.10 lb
Pork back fat	300 g	0.66 lb
Lean beef	200 g	0.44 lb

Ingredients per 1 kg (2.2 lb) of materials

Salt	28 g	4.5 tsp
Cure #2	2.5 g	1/2 tsp
Dextrose	2.0 g	1/2 tsp
Pepper	2.0 g	1 tsp
Garlic, smashed	3.0 g	1 clove
Madeira wine	5.0 g	1 tsp
T-SPX culture scale	0.12 g	use

Grind lean beef through 3 mm (1/8") plate.

Grind lean pork through 5 mm (1/4") plate.

Grind back fat through 5 mm (1/4") plate.

Mix beef and pork with all ingredients. Add fat and mix all together.

Stuff into 60 mm pork or beef middles or synthetic fibrous casings. Form 50 cm (20") sections.

Ferment at 20° C (68° F), 95-85% humidity for 3 days.

Ferment/dry at 18° C (64° F), 85-80% humidity for 2 days.

Cold smoke at 18° C (64° F) for 24 hours.

Dry at 15 → 12° C (59 → 54° F), 80-75% humidity for 4 weeks or until sausage looses 30% of its original weight.

Store at 10-12° C (50-53° F), <75% humidity.

Tourist Sausage Russian-Dry

Russian dry sausage. Small sizes made these sausages a convenient item to carry when travelling, hence the name tourist.

Pork	200 g	2.2 lb
Pork bellies	400 g	4.4 lb
Lean beef	400 g	4.4 lb

Ingredients per 1 kg (2.2 lb) of meat

Salt	28 g	4.5 tsp
Cure #2	2.5 g	1/2 tsp
Dextrose	3.0 g	3/4 tsp
Pepper	3.0 g	1.5 tsp
Caraway	2.5 g	1 tsp
Garlic	3.5 g	1 clove
T-SPX culture	0.12 g	use
scale		

Grind pork and beef through 6 mm (1/4"). Dice bacon into 6 mm (1/4") cubes or grind through 10 mm (3/8") plate.
30 minutes before mixing dissolve starter culture in 1 tablespoon de-chlorinated water. Mix all ingredients with meat.
Stuff into 32-36 mm hog casings and form 20 cm (8") long links.
Ferment at 20° C (68° F) for 72 hours, 90-85% humidity.
Cold smoke for 12 hours at 22° C (72° F) or lower.
Dry at 16→12° C (60-54° F), 85-80% humidity. In about 6-8 weeks a shrink of 30% should be achieved.
Store sausages at 10-15° C (50-59° F), <75% humidity.

Urutan
(Balinese Fermented Sausage)

Urutan is a traditional Balinese dry fermented sausage whose technology differs from that of European sausages. No nitrite/nitrate is used in the process, and the sausage owes its yellowish-brown color to turmeric (the main ingredient of curry powder). Laos powder (Galanga pinata) and aromatic ginger (Kaempferia galangal) contribute greatly to its Eastern flavor. The climate in Bali is hot, and the sausage is fermented at 25° C (77° F) at night and at 50° C (122° F) during the day. Such warm temperatures permit fast fermentation, which is accomplished within 5 days. Urutan is not smoked.

Lean pork	700 g	1.54 lb
Back fat or		
fatty pork trimmings	300 g	0.66 lb

Ingredients per 1 kg (2.2 lb) of meat

Salt	28 g	5 tsp
Cure #1	2.5 g	1/2 tsp
Dextrose	5.0 g	1 tsp
Black pepper	5.0 g	2.5 tsp
Red chili pepper	10.0 g	5 tsp
Ginger	5.0 g	2 tsp.
Garlic, 2%	20.0 g	6 cloves
Turmeric	10.0 g	5 tsp
Laos powder*	15.0 g	7 tsp
T-SPX culture	0.12 g	weigh

Grind meat and fat through 3/16" plate (6 mm). Mix all ingredients with ground meat.
Stuff into 24-26 mm collagen or sheep casings and form 5" (12 cm) long links. Ferment at 24° C (75° F) for 72 hours, 90-85% humidity.
Dry for two weeks at 16→12° C (60-54° F), 85-80% humidity. Store sausages at 10-15° C (50-59° F), <75% humidity.

Note: Cure #1 and T-SPX culture has been added to the recipe to provide additional safety. Traditional recipe calls for 5% garlic (similar to Thai Nham sausage) which stimulates fermentation and provides safety.
* Laos powder *(Galanga pinata)* - the aromatic, peppery, ginger-like spice is indigenous to Southeast Asia. Its pungent cardamom-like eucalyptus flavor enhances the overall flavor profiles of Thai and Indonesian cuisines. Used in pungent Thai curry pastes, meat marinades and stir-fries. Added to Indonesian spice pastes that are rubbed on duck and fish.

Venison Salami

Venison salami.

| Lean venison | 700 g | 1.54 lb |
| Pork back fat | 300 g | 0.66 lb |

Ingredients per 1 kg (2.2 lb) of meat

Salt	30 g	5 tsp
Cure #2	2.5 g	1/2 tsp
Dextrose	5.0 g	1 tsp
Whole white pepper	4.0 g	1 tsp
Garlic	3.0 g	1 clove
Juniper berries, crushed	6	6
Madeira wine	5 ml	1 Tbsp
Bactoferm® LHP culture scale	0.18 g	use

Grind pork and back fat through 10 mm (3/8"), keep separate.
Add starter culture to 30 ml (2 Tbsp) of chlorine free water to facilitate distribution in meat.
Mix all ingredients with ground meat, adding fat last.
Stuff firmly into large hog casings, beef middles or 40-60 mm protein lined fibrous casings.
Make 12-16" long links.
Ferment at 25° C (77° F) for 48 hours, 90-85% humidity.
Optional step: Cold smoke at 18° C (64° F) for 12 hours.
Dry at 15-12° C (59-54° F), 85-80% humidity for 1-2 months until the sausage loses around 30-35% in weight.
Store sausages at 10-15° C (50-59° F), <75% humidity.

Notes
It is recommended to use LHP or T-SPX culture.
If mold appears wipe it off with a cloth moistened with vinegar.

Westfälische Mettwurst
(Westphalian Mettwurst)

Westfälische grobe Mettwurst is listed (2.212.3) in the German government publication Guide to Meats and Meat Products - *Leitsätze für Fleisch und Fleischerzeugnisse.* Spreadable Mettwurst sausage from Westphalia.

| Pork, lean | 700 g | 1.54 lb |
| Pork belly | 300 g | 0.66 lb |

Ingredients per 1 kg (2.2 lb) of material

Salt	22 g	3.5 tsp
Cure #1	2.5 g	1/2 tsp
Pepper	2.0 g	1 tsp
Allspice	0.5 g	1/2 tsp

Grind all meats through 6 mm (1/4") plate.
Mix ground meats with all ingredients.
Stuff into 42 mm artificial permeable casings forming 45 cm (18") loops.
Hold at 18° C (64° F), 75-80% humidity for 24 hours.
Cold smoke at 18° C (64° F) for 12 hours.
Refrigerate.

Zervelatwurst

Zervelatwurst also known as Cervelatwurst is listed (2.211.08) in the German government publication - *Leitsätze für Fleisch und Fleischerzeugnisse.* Cervelatwurst or Zervelatwurst is a fine grind salami type smoked sausage made from pork and beef.

Lean pork	400 g	0.88 lb
Beef, little fat and		
some connective tissue	300 g	0.66 lb
Back fat/neck fat	300 g	0.66 lb
T-SPX culture	0.12 g	use
scale		

Ingredients per 1 kg (2.2 lb) of material

Salt	28 g	4.5 tsp
Cure #2	2.5 g	1/2 tsp
Dextrose	2.0 g	1/2 tsp
Honey	4.0 g	1 tsp
Pepper	3.0 g	1.5 tsp
Nutmeg	0.5 g	1/2 tsp
Ginger	0.3 g	1/8 tsp

Grind all meats through 3 mm (1/8") plate. Cool and grind again.
Grind partially frozen back fat through 3 mm (1/8") plate.
Mix meats, and all ingredients together. Add fat and mix again.
Stuff into 60 mm beef middles or synthetic protein lined fibrous casings.
Ferment at 3 days at 20° C (68° F), 95 → 90% humidity.
Ferment/dry for 2 days at 18° C (64° F), 90 → 80% humidity.
Smoke at 18° C (64° F) for 24 hours.
Dry at 14 →12° C (57→53° F), 80-75% humidity for 5 weeks or until sausage looses 33% of its original weight.
Store at 12° C (53° F),<75% humidity.

Zgornjesavinjski želodec

Zgornjesavinjski želodec is produced in the Upper Savinja valley in Slovenia.

Lean pork-shoulder, leg	800 g	1.76 lb
Back fat	200 g	0.44 lb

Ingredients per 1 kg (2.2 lb) of meat

Salt	30 g	5 tsp
Sugar	5.0 g	1 tsp
Pepper	3.0 g	1.5 tsp
Garlic	15 g	5 cloves

Grind lean pork through 10 mm (3/8") plate.
Cut back fat into 8 mm (5/16") cubes.
Mix meat and spices together.
Stuff into pork stomach, bladder or artificial casing.
Hold for 10 days in a cool room 4° C (40° F) between two wooden planks. Place some weight on top board.
Dry between 12-18° C (53-64° F), 60-80% humidity for 3-5 months. The sausage should lose at least 36% of its original weight. It should be covered with a greyish mold.
Store at 8° C (48° F) or lower.

Note: Zgornjesavinjski želodec carries PGI 2011 certification.

The shape of the sausages that are available in supermarkets is usually straight (hot dogs, frankfurters, liverwurst, American salami) or ring-shaped (Polish sausage). European-type classical fermented sausages are stuffed into various natural casings, especially the ones that carry European Certificates of Origin.

Photo 15. 1 Lomo embuchado, pork loin stuffed in pork bung.

Photo 15. 2 Morcón, stuffed in pork caecum. Also in bladders or stomachs.

Photo 15. 3 Botelo, stuffed in pork blind cap (caecum). Also in bladders or stomachs.

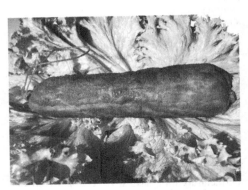

Photo 15. 4 Androlla, stuffed in pork bung.

Photo 15. 5 Salami and fuet, natural pork casings.

Photo 15. 6 Salchichón or salami, large diameter pork casing.

Index

stuffing tube 129
sugar 67, 71, 149, 206
  discovery 103
  sucrose (saccharose) 69
  table of sweetness 70
summer sausage 96

T

talc 160
temperature control 83
toxins 38
Trichinea 97
troubleshooting problems , 197
types of fermentation 42

U

US degree-temperature tables 89
  constant temperature fermentation 90
  variable temperature fermentation 90
US standards and regulations 88

V

vacuum 131
  vacuum-packed products 37
venison 194
vinegar 72

W

water 17
  bound 17
  free 17
wood for smoking 136
  hardwood 136
  wet wood 136

Y

yeasts 37, 52
  Debaryomyces hansenii 52

Made in the USA
Monee, IL
09 February 2025

11706862R00201